Ashes of Glory

Ashes of Glory

RICHMOND AT WAR

~~~~~~

ERNEST B.
FURGURSON

ALFRED A. KNOPF   NEW YORK   1996

Library of Congress Cataloging-in-Publication Data
Furgurson, Ernest B.
Ashes of glory: Richmond at war / by Ernest B. Furgurson. —1st ed.
p.   cm.
Includes bibliographical references and index.
ISBN 0-679-42232-3 (hc)
1. Richmond (Va.)—History—Civil War, 1861–1865.   I. Title.
F234.R557F87   1996
975.5'451043—dc20   95-49591   CIP

Manufactured in the United States of America
First Edition

for Cassie

Contents

16 pages of illustrations will be found following page 174

Preface

By the last spring of the American Civil War, *New York World* correspondent George Alfred Townsend had reported the conflict from the Virginia Peninsula, Cedar Mountain, the Shenandoah Valley, and the lines around Petersburg, and had considered it from Europe, an ocean away. Outside Richmond with U. S. Grant's army, Townsend put into words what hundreds of thousands of Union soldiers were thinking—that "this town *is* the Rebellion," the "sheet-anchor . . . roof-tree . . . abiding hope" of the Confederacy, which has withstood "longer, more frequent and more persistent sieges than any in Christendom. . . .

"Its history is the epitome of the whole contest," he wrote—"and to us, shivering our thunderbolts against it for more than four years, Richmond is still a mystery."

From April 1861 to April 1865, some 2,154 military events large and small took place in Virginia. They included major battles like Manassas, Malvern Hill, Chancellorsville, Cold Harbor, and Petersburg, plus cavalry skirmishes, raids, sieges, expeditions, bridge-burnings, occupations, and diversions. Until the final days, all of them—indeed, directly or indirectly, most of the campaigns in the Civil War—were fought for the ultimate prize of Richmond.

From the moment Virginia's capital became the capital of the Confederacy, "On to Richmond!" became the battle cry of the Union army in the East. The city was more than the political capital and military headquarters of the South; it was also the chief manufacturing, hospital, prison, and rail center. Above all, as the war went on, it was recognized on both sides and abroad as the very symbol of Southern independence. That is why the Union spent so many thousands of lives to reach it, and why the Confederates clung to it through despair and near-starvation.

Federal commanders drove at Richmond from every direction—by sending gunboats up the James River, by inching up the Peninsula, by surprise in the night, finally by depending on siege and attrition. For four years, Richmond stood and the Confederacy fought on while Norfolk, New Orleans, Vicksburg, Chattanooga, Atlanta, and all the other major cities of the South were captured. But once Richmond fell, the war was over within days.

More than 130 years later, it is hardly correct to say, as Townsend did, that Richmond remains a mystery. Books have been written about the Confederate government and all its principals, about the campaigns on the city's outskirts, about Confederate knights in gray and their ladies, and about the city's fiery downfall. A handful of historians, over the decades, have brought those elements together. But few have tried, as this book does, to reach beyond the lives of the celebrated, to the preachers, slave dealers, refugees, spies, nurses, political prisoners, editors, prostitutes, and black and white underclass that kept the city going. Even fewer have considered Richmond's wartime trials and gallantry against the background of conservative Virginia's long struggle against secession, and given full attention to the stubborn resistance of the city's Union loyalists from before Sumter to the day the Yankees marched in.

To the researcher it sometimes seems that a memoir was published by every Confederate politician and his wife, every Yankee prisoner, and every soldier on both sides who witnessed the capital's last hours. As for most periods of the past, there is the least material about the least literate makers of history, the laboring thousands. This is particularly true of black Richmonders, slave and free. But I have found unused manuscripts, official records, and contemporary accounts that add life and passion to what has gone before.

Many of these materials reflect the prejudices of the time, and this would not be a true account if all derogatory racial and religious language were edited out—though far more has been omitted than retained. The personal accounts also reflect the education of the time; rather than clutter the pages with hundreds of "[sic]" notices, I now advise that all spelling and grammatical eccentricities found within quotation marks are those of the original.

I am especially grateful for the interest and help of Frances Pollard, Nelson Lankford, Joseph Robertson, Howson Cole, the late Waverly Winfree, and their colleagues at the Virginia Historical Society, and for an Andrew W. Mellon research fellowship made available by the society. In addition, I wish to thank Gregg Kimball and Teresa Roane at the Valentine Museum; Guy Swanson and Corinne P. Hudgins at the Museum of the Confederacy; Louis H. Manarin, formerly chief state archivist, Brent Tarter, and their associates at the Library of Virginia; Richard W. Sommers and his colleagues at the U.S. Army Military History Institute at Carlisle Barracks; the Civil War Library and Museum in Philadelphia, as well as the staffs of the manuscript divisions of the Library of Congress and the New York Public Library; the National Archives; the Perkins Library at Duke University; the Southern Historical Collection at the University of North Carolina; the Maryland Historical Society in Baltimore; and the institutions mentioned in the source notes following the text.

For their close reading of the manuscript, which saved me from many embarrassments, I am indebted to Robert E. L. Krick, historian at the Richmond National Battlefield Park; John Coski, historian at the Museum of the Confederacy; and Robert W. Waitt, Jr., formerly executive secretary of the Richmond Civil War Centennial Committee. Whatever errors remain are my own.

I greatly enjoyed the hospitality of Bertie and Bill Selvey during my many working visits to Richmond. In this as in other projects, I have been sustained by the generous advice and encouragement of my friends Nathan Miller and Thomas N. Bethell. I am also grateful for the high professionalism of my editor, Ashbel Green, and his associates Jennifer Bernstein, Anthea Lingeman, and Melvin Rosenthal, as well as my literary agent, David Black.

Most of all, I am thankful for the patience and support of Cassie Furgurson.

E.B.F.

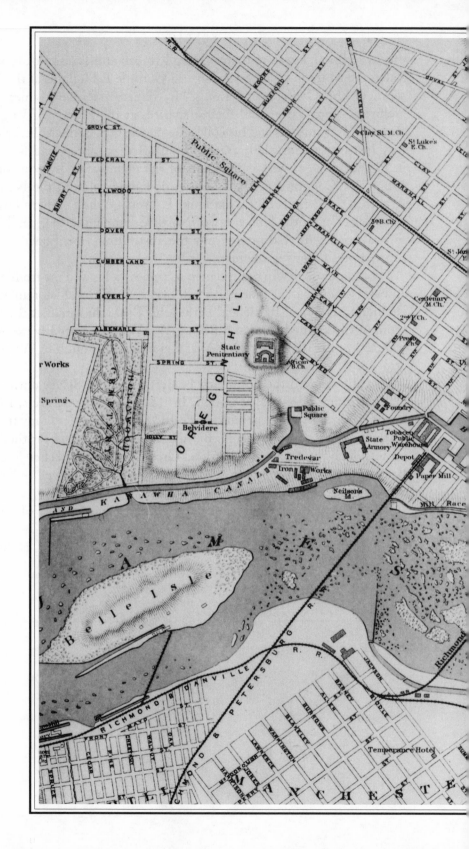

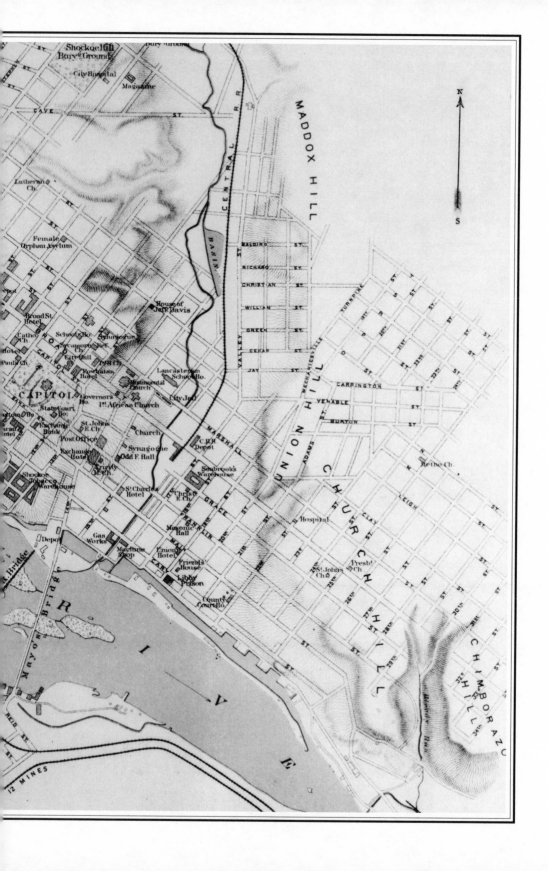

Ashes of Glory

CHAPTER ONE

WHO ARE NOT FOR US
ARE AGAINST US

RIOT AT HARPER'S FERRY
Military Called Out

Baltimore, Oct. 17—The following despatch has been received from Frederick, Md., but as it seems very improbable, it should be received with great caution until confirmed.

Frederick, Oct. 17, A.M.—An insurrection has broken out at Harper's Ferry. A band of armed abolitionists have full possession of the U.S. Arsenal. . . . The band is composed of about 250 whites, followed by a band of negroes who are fighting with them.

LATER—Baltimore, Oct. 17, 10 A.M.—Despatches received at the Railroad Office say that the affair is greatly exaggerated, and that it has its foundation in a difficulty at the United States Armory; that the negroes have nothing to do with it.

Halfpast 12 p.m.—It is apprehended that the affair at Harper's Ferry is more serious than people here are willing to believe. The Telegraph wires have been cut. . . . It is reported that there has been a general stampede of negroes from Maryland. . . . Many wild rumors are afloat, but we have nothing authentic. . . .

*I*n the footloose way of a 12-year-old, John Sergeant Wise ambled out of the governor's mansion into the sunny warmth of an Indian summer afternoon. The leaves of the twin row of lindens that led west were nearing their golden peak of color. To John's left, the pillars of the Virginia Capitol inspired by Thomas Jefferson loomed over the square and the city. The boy strolled between the building and the towering statue of George Washington, who pointed from his horse across the James River, toward the Deep South. Downhill rose the brick guard tower whose bell summoned Richmond's militiamen in times of trouble. Drifting down out of Capitol Square, along the tobacco-stained walk in front of the American Hotel, John had no idea that the alarm would ring again so soon.

As the pampered son of the governor of Virginia, he considered this heart of Richmond his personal domain. From the playground and stable at the governor's mansion, for nearly four years he had ranged gradually farther, in and out of Main Street shops and Franklin Street gardens, Pizzini's confectionery and Van Lew & Taylor's hardware store, along dusty avenues and through alleyways where servants curried horses and plucked chickens. A few blocks from home, he had heard an auctioneer assure bidders that for every dollar spent they would get "a full dollar's worth of real genuine nigger, healthy, well-raised, well-mannered, respectful, obedient and willing"—and from the roof of the Capitol, John had looked east to St. John's Church, where Patrick Henry had challenged George III to "give me liberty or give me death." The other way, he could see up the James to Hollywood Cemetery, "the most beautiful Necropolis anywhere to be found," where couples strolled at twilight and President James Monroe had been reburied amid great ceremony the year before.[1]

Nearly 38,000 Richmonders, white and black, went about their daily lives that October afternoon, with no suspicion that a wild-eyed fanatic from far away was about to throw Virginia into crisis. Their Richmond was a river town, originally a fort, sited at the falls more than two centuries earlier to protect the Jamestown colony downstream against Indians. After it became the capital of Virginia in 1780, as it grew into a city, homes and businesses had spread from the river outward across seven hills and more, causing municipal boosters to liken the place to Rome.

Now, in 1859, the most important industrial complex in the South was busy along the Richmond waterfront. Coastal and oceangoing vessels steamed up the James to Rocketts wharf. The Tredegar Iron Works spewed black smoke beside the James River & Kanawha Canal, down which mule-drawn packet boats brought coal and ore, tobacco and wheat, from the Piedmont and the Shenandoah Valley. Blacksmiths, boatyards, cooperages, and livery stables were scattered among seven major flour mills, the Crenshaw Woolen Mills, Franklin Paper Mill, and fifty tobacco factories.

On the next streets above the industrial riverside, proprietors lived upstairs from their shops, among the banks and newspapers. Here were some of the hotels and taverns that welcomed distinguished foreigners like Charles Dickens, Anthony Trollope, and the Prince of Wales, visitors whose American tour could not be complete without seeing "the capitol of the Mother of States and Statesmen."[2]

Richmond was not the largest city in the South; slightly smaller than Charleston, it had less than a quarter of New Orleans's population. But political transients and seasonal society made it bigger and more worldly than official figures suggested. Though more than a third of its people were black, nearly as many were foreign-born—mainly Irish and Germans who had fled famine and revolution across the sea. Census takers in 1860 would record a surprising number of Bridgets, the wives and daughters of Irish immigrants who had helped build the canal and flocked on Sundays to St. Peter's Cathedral. The hardworking Germans, who had listed their homelands as Bavaria, Prussia, or other separate states on arrival in America, were brought together by their language at church, at the city's two synagogues, and in choral clubs and lager saloons.

But away from clanging foundries, sweltering tobacco factories, and babbling tenements, aside from the political rhetoric that scathed the Capitol, the tone of the city was as genteel as the accents of its crino-lined dowagers. On and near the crest of the hills stood the homes of the gentry, redbrick townhouses with high ceilings, where dignified domestics served fine Madeira in heavy crystal and James River oysters on old silver. They lived in the afterglow of Virginia's golden age, where conversation left the impression that breeding and etiquette counted more than vulgar commerce, and that Governor Jefferson or Chief Justice Marshall might drop in for dinner that very evening.

*   *   *

Young John Wise acknowledged friendly waves from grandees and servants alike as he rambled along Main Street, past the banks and the telegraph office, toward Richmond's newspaper row. There, Obadiah Jennings Wise, his adored older brother, wrote passionate editorials for the *Enquirer.* Outside one of the newspaper offices, an angry crowd milled around the bulletin board where the latest news was posted. John ran to see what was stirring such excitement.

No one in the crowd knew yet that the captain of the insurrection at Harpers Ferry was John Brown, an angry, perhaps mad abolitionist originally from New England. In "bleeding Kansas," where the fight over slavery had already exploded into violence, Brown had led a band that murdered five pro-slavery settlers. Soon his very name would be an

epithet in the South; for the moment, his raid into Virginia left Richmonders cursing in the streets. John Wise pushed his way through them
and ran up Eleventh Street, back across Capitol Square toward home.

His father, Governor Henry Alexander Wise, had just been roused
from an afternoon nap. He was in his library, scanning a handful of
telegrams. John gasped out the news, but his father already knew. The
governor pulled down a volume of the Virginia Code, found the reference he needed to make his next step official, and began dictating orders
for militia units to head for Harpers Ferry, 150 miles away on the Potomac River border with Maryland. Then he sent John scooting to tell
civil and military officers.

A cross section of white Richmond came alert—not only scions of famous old families but also immigrants like the Polish Jew Philip Whitlock, of the Richmond Grays, and Irish John Dooley, who reveled in the
vivid green, gold-trimmed uniform of the Montgomery Guards. John
Wise finally found the First Virginia Regiment's adjutant, unaware of
trouble, playing dominoes as he enjoyed another beaker of lager at a
German tavern. With him the boy hurried back to the governor, who
ordered the regiment to report armed and equipped at the Richmond,
Fredericksburg & Potomac Railway depot at eight o'clock that evening.

John was mascot of a junior drill company called Guard of the Metropolis. He put on his brass-buttoned jacket and Navy cap, picked up
an old squirrel rifle and powder horn, and raced to fall in with the full-
fledged militia. The gaudily uniformed troops knew him, and joked as
he marched with them to the station. On the way, they passed one of the
governor's maids, who asked John where he was going, and the boy
made the mistake of sticking out his chest and shouting, "To Harpers
Ferry!"

At the depot at Broad and Eighth streets, he boarded the cars with
his uniformed friends. But before the train moved, he heard the familiar voice of the governor's butler, Jim, as he searched through the train.
John hid under a seat with his long rifle until an outburst of laughing
gave him away and the butler marched him home.[3]

*   *   *

John Wise was not the only young man who felt left out of the excitement.

Across Broad Street from the depot, at the colonnaded Marshall
Theatre, a 21-year-old actor who styled himself "J. B. Wilkes" was conspicuous in the cast supporting the "fascinating, bewitching, attractive,
incomparable, brilliant" Maggie Mitchell, star of *Beauty and the Beast*.
His real name was John Wilkes Booth—the junior member of Amer-

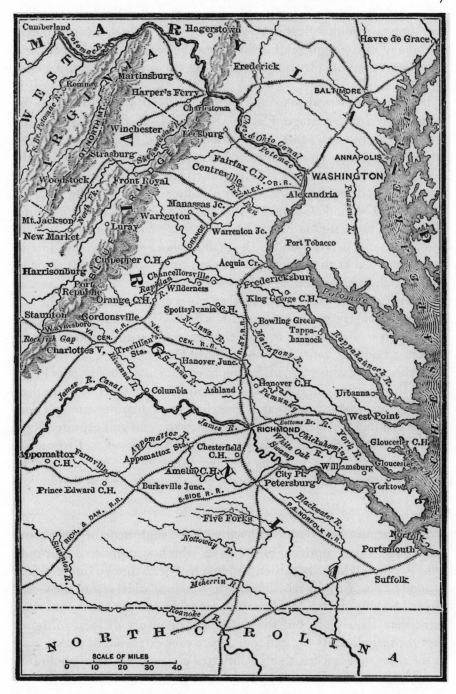

EASTERN VIRGINIA

ica's most famous stage family. His father, the great English tragedian and drunkard Junius Brutus Booth, had made his American debut in Richmond thirty-eight years earlier. Now the dashing "J. B. Wilkes" was a $20-a-week utility player at the Marshall, backing up the touring stars who topped the bill.[4]

If Booth's theatrical roles did not always feed his inherited ego, he found sustenance offstage. His dark eyes and swagger weakened the knees of Richmond belles, who mobbed shops for his pictures and crowded the stage door to beg for his autograph.[5] Among these girls, Booth's main competition came from the young militiamen who strutted at balls and parades in the uniforms of the Richmond Light Infantry Blues, the Grays, F Company, the Montgomery Guard, the Young Guard, and the Virginia Rifles. Booth was so envious that the summer before, at home in Maryland, he had talked about joining them. Now, as they assembled at the depot across Broad Street and the girls came to wave goodbye, he wished he had done just that.

Jennings Wise, John's older brother, got a tender send-off as he left for Harpers Ferry with the Blues. His father the governor had gone ahead with F Company to oversee the action. They rode north by train to Aquia Landing, on the Potomac above Fredericksburg, and by boat from there to Washington, intending to entrain again to Harpers Ferry, where the Shenandoah River joins the Potomac. But when they reached Washington, word came that a detachment of marines under Lieutenant Colonel Robert E. Lee had quashed the raid and captured John Brown. Most of the disappointed militiamen returned to Richmond, but Governor Wise kept going, to take charge of the hectic scene, to question Brown—and to make sure the public knew he was there.

*   *   *

For generations the South had lived with the nightmare of "servile insurrection," a mass uprising of the slaves who now numbered four million. Twenty-eight years earlier, Virginia had been thrown into political turmoil by Nat Turner's rebellion, in the flat farmlands west of the Great Dismal Swamp. In truth, there were far more alarming speeches than there were slave plots, but the occasional discovery of local intrigues kept the fear alive. As the national debate over extension of slavery rose in the 1850s, red-hot Southern politicians accused Northern abolitionists of inspiring murder and pillage.

For Henry Wise, the John Brown raid was a perfectly timed political opportunity. A tall, hatchet-faced, tobacco-chewing Eastern Shoreman from Accomack County, Wise was legally unable to succeed himself as governor. But, as a Virginia contemporary wrote, he was driven by "unbounded ambition. . . . His unbounded assurance & affrontery . . . leave nothing untried that can push on his claims to popular favor."[6] He had spent twelve years as a combative congressman, four as U.S. minister to Brazil, and four as governor, during which he unsuccessfully campaigned for a statewide public school system. Now he wanted the badly split Democratic Party's 1860 nomination for president of the United States. His brilliant son Jennings, editor of the *Enquirer* when he was not soldiering with the Blues, was point man in his father's efforts.

John Wise wrote later that Jennings had a disposition "so amiable that in all his life he never had a boyish quarrel with any one." Perhaps so, but in the two years of his editorship, Jennings fought eight duels, mostly in defense of his father's reputation. Almost fondly, John recalled that in the Virginia of those days, "fighting was as easily obtainable as blackberries in June." The governor had set a family example by wounding his defeated opponent in a duel after his first election to Congress in 1832.

In the antebellum South, the code duello lived on, the outgrowth of an exaggerated sense of honor that would soon send hundreds of thousands of men to death. In peacetime, it demanded that perceived insults be met by a challenge if they came from a man of social standing, while lesser offenders could merely be caned or horsewhipped. John heard that a cabal of his father's political rivals had decided that since Jennings was their most effective editorial enemy, he should be provoked into duel after duel until he was out of the way. But Jennings was lucky. A notoriously poor shot, he wounded only one opponent, in his last duel, and never got pinked himself.[7]

When the governor came back from Harpers Ferry, F Company, a brass band, and "a large concourse of citizens" escorted him from the depot along the five blocks to the mansion. To the cheering crowd, Wise said that he would have given his arm up to the shoulder if state soldiers instead of U.S. Marines had captured Brown. Virginia troops must "become perfect in military tactics," he warned, because they might be called on to defend their homes, their rights, and their state.[8]

No one, North or South, was happier about the nationwide uproar over Harpers Ferry than a long-haired old Virginia radical who saw in John Brown a mirror image of himself. Edmund Ruffin had first made his reputation as an agricultural scientist, publishing a magazine that taught Southern farmers to use fertilizer to bring their played-out fields back into production. But his overriding obsession was the preservation of slavery. In 1855 he abandoned agronomy and started campaigning across the South for secession from the Union. By 1859 he had become depressed by his crusade's slow movement through courts, conventions, and Congress.

Then John Brown struck, and the 65-year-old Ruffin was rejuvenated, especially by proof that the raid had been planned and financed by Northern abolitionists. "Such a practical exercise of abolition principles is needed to stir the sluggish blood of the South," he said. As officials put the wounded Brown through trial preliminaries at Charles Town, Ruffin rode into Richmond from his nearby plantation, Marlbourne, circulating urgent petitions for secession.[9]

The governor had a chance to temper the rising furor over Brown when some of the prisoner's Northern friends sent affidavits that he was mentally ill. Wise could have avoided a sensational trial by having Brown certified and locked away in an asylum for life. Instead, he let the trial for murder and treason proceed, and the old raider was sentenced to the gallows. Thus Brown as martyr became a greater hero to his admirers than he had ever been as guerrilla warrior.

The hanging was scheduled for December 2. When rumors swept the state that abolitionists were plotting a raid to rescue Brown, Wise took them seriously. He, Ruffin, and the newspapers worked Richmond into a state of high tension.

But not everyone was alarmed.

From a grand mansion on Church Hill, a little, birdlike spinster named Elizabeth Van Lew watched the excitement with more scorn than anger. "There were rumors that the whole North was coming, thousands of men marching in battle array to overwhelm us," she recalled. ". . . No time was given the people for a sane breath, and a perception of the truth. . . . Our people required blood, the blood of all who were of the Brown party. They thirsted for it; they cried for it. It was not enough that one old man should die. No plea of feeble intellect, or misguided youth, would be listened to. . . ."[10]

Van Lew had never been afraid to speak her mind, and she was not about to change. In the months ahead she would do more than speak against what she considered the madness around her. What she saw as madness, however, was principled patriotism for those who let brass bands speak for them. Red-hot politicians farther south offered Governor Wise their militia to help protect Virginia against any incursion. Wise declined their aid, but on the weekend of November 19–20, he ordered the First Virginia Regiment to Charles Town.[11]

John Wilkes Booth was on his way to play another minor role at the theater when Richmond's militia responded once again to the alarm bell sounding in Capitol Square. He could no longer stand by and watch while other boys tasted the goodbye kisses of Richmond's fairest. Although Maryland-born, Booth was as vocal as any Deep South fire-eater against the Northern abolitionists, and just as irate about the outrage at Harpers Ferry. As the uniformed troops streamed toward the depot, he fell in among them.

One of the Grays, George W. Libby, described how he and Louis Bossieux were on guard inside the company's baggage car when Booth poked his head in. He wanted to go, too. They told him nobody was allowed on the train except men in uniform. Wilkes asked if he could buy one. The two guards talked it over, then pulled him aboard. According to Libby, each removed part of his uniform, and from these Booth put together his own.[12]

At about the time the Richmond troops were arriving at Charles Town, rumors of a rescue attempt stirred suggestions that Brown be moved to a safer prison, away from the state's northern border. On that late-November Sunday, Richmonders milled about the depot on Broad Street, hoping to hear news from their boys. When the afternoon train arrived from the North, one car was detached to a siding. The crowd rushed that way, "under a panic notion that it contained Ossawottamie Brown & Co." One curious citizen peeked inside the darkened car and reported that he recognized Brown by his beard. Shortly thereafter the car was opened, and out came the goats, dogs, and trained monkeys of Donetti's Star Excelsior Company, a vaudeville troupe arriving for its limited local appearance.[13]

Chuckles over John Brown's rumored appearance in Richmond did not last long. The newspapers reported that some firms had fired men who left their jobs to go with the militia. Jennings Wise's *Enquirer* promised to publish the names of the unpatriotic employers. "In our endeavors to put down and punish traitors, thieves and villains," it proclaimed, "let us well bear in mind that the men or party who are not for us are against us, and the sooner people discover them the better it will be."

In the same issue, the paper noted arrests for "tampering with negroes," and reported that "a few others, including some storekeepers in Richmond, are suspiciously looked after on charges of having offered talk not henceforth orthodox in the Old Dominion. Let none, however, be condemned without full and satisfactory proof." Wesley Simmons, an "Armory soldier," already had been fined $20 and given thirty days in jail for "using seditious language."[14]

* * *

In camp at Charles Town, the Grays were in a holiday mood, aided by delicacies from home. such as those sent by Gottfried Lange, who ran a German beer hall. Some of these youths were Lange's loyal customers, and the rest were prime prospects. He dispatched four quarter-barrels of lager, thirty pounds of Swiss cheese, twenty-four cans of sardines, twenty-two loaves of black bread and five hundred cigars, "all of which was greatly appreciated."[15]

Night after night, some nervous soldier on picket would fire his musket, rousing the Grays, who would rush to form a protective square around the jail where Brown was kept. In off-hours, Booth jollied his comrades around the campfire with Shakespearean histrionics, making himself popular with the troops he had envied.

Among them was Philip Whitlock, a 21-year-old tailor who had been in America for only five years and had just become a U.S. citizen. Though uneducated, he realized that he had been cast in a historic drama; years later, he would remember its details. Twelve days after he and the Grays arrived at Charles Town, they fell in beside other troops around the gallows. Nearby were Virginia Military Institute cadets, their artillery detachment commanded by an eccentric major named Thomas J. Jackson.

As militiamen scanned the cadet ranks, their eyes halted at a figure far more unlikely in uniform than the accomplished actor Booth. It was the bent and grizzled Edmund Ruffin, veteran of the War of 1812, who had spent a week speechifying among the militia and civilians who crowded Charles Town. Told that only the military guard could witness the hanging, Ruffin had wheedled his way into temporary status as a VMI student. Donning a uniform, he fell in with the cadet color guard, ignoring the smiles of the spic-and-span boys beside him.[16]

Whitlock recalled that Richmond's Grays were only about thirty feet from the gallows, and that "Booth being about the same hight as I was, he was right next to me in rank." They watched as Brown was brought out on a baggage wagon, sitting atop his own coffin, then climbed the stairs to face the hangman. Whitlock wrote that "When the drop fell, I noticed that [Booth] got very pale in the face, and I called his attention to it and he said he felt very faint and would give anything for a good drink of whiskey."[17]

When Brown's body was shipped north, a Pennsylvania newspaper printed a rumor that Southern medical students in Philadelphia planned to snatch the body for their dissecting room. In a scuffle at the Philadelphia railroad depot, some Southern students were hurt, some were arrested, and all were insulted by their treatment by police. Hunter Holmes McGuire, a Virginia surgeon teaching at Jefferson Medical

College, organized a mass resignation of indignant Southerners from three Philadelphia schools. Governor Wise sent a special train, flying the Virginia flag, to bring them home.

Of more than 300 students withdrawing, 140 transferred to the Medical College of Virginia, thus tripling the Richmond school's enrollment. They were welcomed in Richmond by one of the city's ever-ready brass bands playing "Carry Me Back to Old Virginny," and a speech from the governor at Capitol Square. The students later bragged that they had been "the first secessionists."[18]

From Charles Town, Booth returned to Richmond more swashbuckling than ever, more fervent than ever in the political debate that raged after Brown's death. George Libby, who had shared his uniform with Booth, returned to junior partnership in Libby & Son, commission merchants and ship chandlers, whose canal-front warehouse would become notorious in a different capacity. Philip Whitlock returned to his brother's tailor shop, more eager to catch every Shakespearean play from the 25-cent gallery at the Marshall than he was to march off to war. Edmund Ruffin returned as a collector of the iron-pointed pikes made by Yankee blacksmiths and captured from Brown's men; he sent one to each Southern governor as "a sample of the favors designed for us by our Northern Brethren."[19] Jennings Wise returned to the *Enquirer* to do battle against Northern editors and politicians inflamed by Brown's hanging. And Henry Wise came back to turn the ensuing crisis to his own purpose, in the final weeks of his governorship. In the storm foreshadowed by John Brown's raid, these six witnesses to his hanging would represent the spectrum of Southern manhood, from prudent self-preservation to deluded martyrdom. Only three would survive.

* * *

The day after Governor Wise welcomed the Richmond troops home with yet another fanfare at the mansion, he delivered his farewell message to the General Assembly. The state faced serious danger, he said, "and the way to avert it in all cases is to march up to it and meet it front to front." He considered the Brown raid a test—if the South backed down, Northern aggression would become "more and more insolent," but if the South stood firm, the North would either desist or go to war. The sooner a decision, the better.[20]

Not surprisingly, Henry Wise's rhetoric had the ring of his son's editorials, and vice versa. But Jennings was always ready to push things another step. In the *Enquirer,* he said, "Let us prepare for disunion; not precipitate it." Then he gave it a vigorous shove.

Before the next presidential inauguration day, he urged, Virginia should pass retaliatory trade laws, increase commerce with Europe, tax Northern goods, and spy on Northern visitors and their Virginia friends. "Thus we shall give [the North] a foretaste of abolition and disunion; pinch her food and clothing, injure her commerce and manufacture, turn her laborers out of employment, render her capital unprofitable, and depopulate her cities." Having prescribed a course to war, the editorial suggested that "we keep open the door of reconciliation, and leave room and opportunity for a pacific solution. . . ."[21]

Henry Wise's speeches and his son's editorials keynoted the months of political struggle ahead—but theirs was not the most urgent summons heard in Richmond. As editors outdid one another, politicians tried to keep up, and every exchange raised the temperature another degree.

To the outsider, all the public noise from the Wises, Ruffins, and their inflammatory brethren might have suggested that Virginia was of a kind with the angry cotton states of the Deep South. In that political mood, the John Brown raid could have been sufficient offense to say goodbye to the old Union. But the extremists did not speak for most Virginians, or most Richmonders.

True, only the likes of Elizabeth Van Lew openly cheered John Minor Botts, a bulldoglike former Whig congressman who so hated the Democrats that he suggested that Henry Wise had secretly plotted the Brown affair just to inflame the citizenry. When a group of state legislators asked Botts's opinion of the developing crisis, he was allowed some 15,000 words to answer in the columns of the Richmond *Whig*. Botts wrote that policymakers had "lionized, heroized, martyrized and canonized" Brown. Reading this, Jennings Wise editorially accused Botts of "slanders, abolitionism, falsehood and treason"—trying, unsuccessfully, to provoke the much older Botts to a duel. Afterward, Botts still maintained that the Brown raid was "aided and helped on by the scarcely less crazy fanatic who then exercised the function of chief magistrate of this state."[22]

But Virginia traditionalists disdained the impetuosity of South Carolina's Charleston fire-eaters as much as they did the crude materialism of the new rich in New Orleans and the Southwest. Non-slaveholders in western Virginia balanced the political weight of the planters in the Piedmont and Tidewater. The founding fathers of whom the state was so proud were masters of compromise, and the majority of Virginians still believed, or hoped, that some compromise could preserve the Union.

Young John Wise would grow up to note, at the turn of the century, that "the present generation finds it difficult to realize the position in the Union occupied by Virginia" before the Civil War. He remembered that there was "a certain romantic tenderness for Virginia felt towards no other state." Virginia was the second-biggest state, her boundaries the Atlantic and the Ohio; she was wealthy; her sons held commanding political positions in Washington and abroad, and "in every national assemblage her voice was hearkened to as that of a potent and conservative and reliable guide."[23]

The truest word was "conservative." Virginians—white Virginians—were conservative, Richmonders most of all. Many understood the flaws in their society but preferred what they had to anything else proposed. If they were not as emotional as John Minor Botts, they were closer to him on the ultimate question of secession than they were to those who spoke so easily of breaking up the Union. They were not eager to abandon what their grandfathers had done, the nation they had conceived. Rich and poor, they were proud of it—none of them more so than steady, stubborn John Letcher, who arrived on the last day of 1859 to succeed Henry Wise as governor of Virginia.

CHAPTER TWO

SAVE VIRGINIA, AND WE
SAVE THE UNION

*L*ike Patrick Henry and Thomas Jefferson, John Letcher had won the governorship of Virginia with the chance and the unavoidable duty to lead the state through mortal crisis. That New Year's Eve, at what should have been the high point of his life, he came to Richmond amid a driving snowstorm.

Letcher was an optimist by nature, but instead of looking forward to his inauguration with joy, he arrived from Lexington gloomier than the gray outside. His 10-year-old son had just died, and he himself was recovering from painful erysipelas. Shortly before leaving the Shenandoah Valley he had written to his fellow Virginia Democrat, Senator Robert Mercer Taliaferro Hunter, that "it really looks to me as if the days of the Republic were numbered." Only a sudden shift of course by Northern radicals could prevent disunion, he said. "If I am to have a stormy administration, so be it, I am prepared for it. . . . I know what my friends expect of me, and they shall not be disappointed."

Letcher's political metamorphosis, before and during the campaign, had been at least as tortuous as Virginia's. As a Lexington editor, he had been a Jacksonian Democrat in staunchly Whig Rockbridge County. But in 1847 he had signed a pamphlet published by his neighbor, the Reverend Henry Ruffner, president of little Washington College, calling for an end to "the consuming plague of slavery" in the counties of western Virginia.

"In the free states are seen all the tokens of prosperity," Ruffner had written. "In the older parts of the slave states . . . too evident signs of

stagnation or of positive decay—a sparse population—a slovenly culti-
vation spread over vast fields that are wearing out . . . instead of the stir
and bustle of industry, a dull and dreamy stillness, broken, if broken at
all, by the wordy brawl of politics."

Not many Virginians had the courage to undersign such heresy;
Letcher's dwindled as his ambition grew. He was a fourth-term congressman when the gubernatorial election approached, and he felt the
need to explain. In 1847, he wrote, he had regarded slavery as a social and
political evil, but not a moral one; he was, after all, a slave owner. Since
then, he had announced that he was wrong about the social and political evils of slavery, too. His ambivalence, his soul-searching, reflected
the strains that racked the state—between northwest and Piedmont,
Democrats and Whigs, radicals and conservatives, and within Virginians themselves.[1]

The election that made Letcher governor was the latest round in a
struggle between Henry Wise and R. M. T. Hunter—both of whom had
presidential ambitions—for domination of the state's Democratic Party.
Jennings Wise's *Enquirer*, known Southwide as "the Democratic Bible,"
assailed Letcher for his brief, now-repented flirtation with abolitionism.
But, with minimal backing from Hunter, Letcher took the nomination
and prevailed in the May election. His narrow victory as a Democrat
only made the outgoing governor and his journalist son more bitter.[2]

The party label was one of the few things that Henry Wise and
Letcher had in common. When Wise was in Congress his faithful opponent, ex-president John Quincy Adams, had described the tightly
wound, teetotaling Virginian in his diary: "Loud, vociferous, declama-
tory, furibund, he raved about the hell-hound of abolition. . . ."[3]

Letcher, who enjoyed his bourbon, was calm, gentlemanly, and determined not to be bullied by demagogues. Rather than rush Wise and his
family out of the governor's mansion, he checked into the Exchange
Hotel, three blocks from the Capitol. There friends welcomed him beneath the brass gas lamps of the expansive lobby, and he was sworn in by
Judge Richard Parker, who had presided over the trial of John Brown.[4]

*   *   *

From the Exchange, Letcher could walk uphill to his office in the Capitol, the classic temple conceived by the author of the Declaration of Independence. Closer, a few steps around the corner, was Odd Fellows'
Hall, where a dozen slave dealers did business, and a few steps beyond
that was Lumpkin's Alley, with its "negro jails" and auction blocks. If the
new governor found time between greeting well-wishers and preparing
his inaugural address, he could reflect on these two views of what John

Sergeant Wise would call "the centre of a society unsurpassed in all America for wealth, refinement, and culture."[5]

Only Letcher knew whether he had acted from the heart when he endorsed Ruffner's petition against "the consuming plague of slavery," and whether heart or ambition had made him recant. In his native valley and the mountain counties to the west, there were far fewer slaves than in the Tidewater and Piedmont counties. In Richmond, on the fall line between Tidewater and Piedmont, the 1860 census showed 11,699 slaves and 2,576 free blacks, together 37.6 percent of the city's total population.

At New Year's, Richmond residents and businesses traditionally contracted slave help for the months ahead. Some skilled slaves negotiated their own terms with employers, living out in the city while sending an agreed amount of pay to their owners, free to earn more for themselves by overtime or odd jobs. Hundreds of others were owned outright by the city government and by industries like the Tredegar works, which provided them housing and a hospital. More were hired through agents like Lucien Lewis, who promised: "Persons sending Negroes to me may expect to have good prices and homes obtained for them, with proper attention in cases of sickness, and prompt returns made quarterly."[6] The Carbon Hill Mines advertised for "sixty able Negro men, for service . . . on the Surface at the mines, on the Railroad, in the Canal boats, and at the Coal yards in this city. The above mines are entirely free from inflammable gas, and no accident from any cause, involving life or limb, has occurred therein, for the past seven years. . . ."[7]

The slave trade had existed in Richmond for almost 200 years, since soon after young William Byrd brought the first black laborers to his frontier outpost where Shockoe Creek flows into the James.[8] In 1733 his son, William Byrd II, an adventurous explorer, philanderer, and diarist, "laid the foundation of two large cities, one at Shacco's, to be called Richmond, and the other at the falls of Appomattox river, to be named Petersburg."[9]

By 1736 William Byrd II looked at the growing thousands of slaves in Virginia and saw that if some leader should incite "a Servile War," he "might be dreadfully mischievous before any opposition could be formed against him, and tinge our Rivers wide as they are with blood." Through the years, uprisings near and far kept those fears alive.[10]

As the Revolutionary War closed in, Virginia shifted its capital in 1780 from Williamsburg to the seeming safety of Richmond. But less than a year later, British troops under the turncoat Benedict Arnold came up the James and burned much of the nearly unprotected town. With Governor Jefferson looking on helplessly from across the river, Richmond—for the first but not the last time—went up in the flames of war.

Though the American Revolution did nothing about slavery, another revolution soon after spoke directly to it. In the 1790s news came of Toussaint L'Ouverture's bloody black uprising against the French in Santo Domingo. Rumors of slave plots swept Virginia. Richmond, wrote one historian, "seemed to be quaking with apprehension."[11] And there a 24-year-old slave named Gabriel Prosser came within hours of setting off insurrection on the grandest scale ever attempted by black Americans.

Just north of the capital, on Thomas Prosser's Brookfield plantation, the trusted Gabriel and his brothers planned to do in Virginia what Toussaint had done in the Caribbean. Hundreds, perhaps thousands, of slaves were ready to spring at midnight on August 30, 1800. Their watchword, proclaimed by Gabriel, was "Death or liberty." But some of Gabriel's fellows betrayed the plot, and what was left of his insurrection was washed out in a rainstorm. He and his collaborators were hunted down and hanged.

Thirty-one years later, Nat Turner led his slave rebellion in Southampton County, sixty-five miles below Richmond. Turner and his followers killed fifty-five whites before militia and freelance avengers rounded them up for execution. In the political row that followed, Virginia politicians seriously debated the gradual abolition of slavery. But the result instead was a new wave of laws to keep blacks in line.

By the late 1850s, Richmond's "black code" decreed that "No Negro shall smoke tobacco . . . on any public street or public place"—or carry a cane at night unless old and infirm, or block a sidewalk, or speak insolently to a white person, or ride in a licensed hack or carriage without written permission of his owner, or merely be present on the grounds of the Capitol, City Hall, city spring, or Atheneum unless attending a white person. Except in church, no gathering of five or more blacks was permitted. The area around black churches must be cleared within half an hour after services—which must be conducted by white pastors. Any black abroad at night required a pass, or risked thirty-nine "stripes."[12]

Most blacks in Richmond were leading lives independent of hour-by-hour surveillance. Compared with their plantation kinsmen, the city's domestic servants and artisans were urban sophisticates, often fashionably dressed on Sundays, en route to a church of their own. Slave and free blacksmiths, barbers, cooks, draymen, and tobacco-factory hands were hired out by the thousand, earning wages and socializing among themselves, almost as if they were not black at all. The repressive laws were passed to stifle conspiracy before it started; in daily practice, they served to put blacks in their place lest they behave too "uppity."

* * *

As slavery dominated the national debate over westward expansion, *Uncle Tom's Cabin* and other tales of slaveholder cruelty—some imagined, some true—fueled the Northern abolition movement. Virginia law forbade the education of blacks, lest they read dangerous ideas in abolitionist tracts; but many were literate, having been privately taught by their owners.

Charles Dickens had only hardened Richmond's defensive mind-set when he came in 1842, cut his stay short, and in his *American Notes* wrote of the "decay and gloom" that he felt brooding over the city. Dickens liked Richmond as a landscape, "delightfully situated on eight hills, overhanging James River; a sparkling stream, studded here and there with bright islands, or brawling over broken rocks." But he could not bear to look into the faces of the city's blacks. He departed "with a grateful heart that I was not doomed to live where slavery was, and had never had my senses blunted to its wrongs and horrors in a slave-rocked cradle."[13]

The rising debate drove those on each side far to the extremes. Slavery's most zealous defenders cited the Bible to prove it a positive good, especially for the slaves themselves. To most Richmonders on the sidelines, what Dickens saw was neither horrible nor a blessing; it was simply the way things had always been in their memory, and so should be.

Tobacco processing still employed more Richmonders than any other industry, most of them slaves and free blacks. But tobacco depleted the land, and thousands of Virginia acres were being left to grow up in broom sedge and scrub pine—while the labor force that had hoed those fields continued to grow, and could not be absorbed by the city's tobacco and iron factories.

Planters whose fathers had grown rich in tobacco now grew land-poor, rich only in one commodity—for which there was insistent demand from the cotton states of the Deep South. Before they let go the land, Virginia planters, often reluctantly, would let go what the census recorded as "personal property." In the 1850s, Richmond's biggest business by dollar volume was not tobacco, flour, or iron, but slaves.[14]

Slave auctions became a tourist attraction. Travelers described them for the world, telling of broken families, of humans treated less with cruelty than like so many head of valuable livestock. Strong black field hands and mulatto house servants were sold to Deep South buyers by Ben Davis, Dickenson & Hill, Pulliam & Betts, Browning & Moore, Silas Omohundro, McDaniel & Blackburn, Robert Lumpkin, and others. More than twenty traders did business in the neighborhood just east of the Capitol. Auction houses at Alexandria, Petersburg, Norfolk, and

Lynchburg were busy, too, but only faraway New Orleans exceeded the slave trade at Richmond. By 1859–60, sales in Richmond were running at more than $4 million a year. And as sales increased, the threat of being "sold south" boosted traffic in the other direction, on the Underground Railroad.[15]

Many slaves escaped Richmond by hiding aboard steamboats bound down the James and up the Chesapeake Bay. Others were smuggled up the road to Port Royal on the Rappahannock, and onward to the North. Once there, some were passed along by William Still, a former slave who ran Philadelphia's General Vigilance Committee. "No one Southern city furnished a larger number of brave, wide-awake and likely-looking Underground Rail Road passengers than the city of Richmond," Still wrote.[16]

Among them was the "refined and gentlemanly" James Hambleton Christian, who had been a butler in President John Tyler's White House before being inherited by Tyler's nephew by marriage, a Richmond merchant. Asked in Philadelphia how he had liked Tyler, he said, "I didn't like Mr. Tyler much, because Mr. Tyler was a poor man. I never did like poor people. I didn't like his marrying into our family. . . ." The light-skinned fugitive was the son of his original master on a Charles City County plantation.[17]

James Mercer and William Henry Gilliam stowed away in the hot boiler room of the steamer *Pennsylvania*. They had been owned by a widow, Louisa White, who hired them out to businesses in Richmond. She was, by their own testimony, a kindhearted woman—but she had once owned thirty slaves, and now only these two and a young boy were left. The men could see what was coming, so they fled.

The agent who had handled their hiring ran an advertisement in the *Dispatch* offering a reward for their return. That notice provoked an indignant editorial. "The question now is to find out how they got off," the paper said. "They must undoubtedly have had white men in the secret. Have we then a nest of Abolition scoundrels among us?"[18]

The *Dispatch* was wrong about these escapees, who had gotten away with the help of the steamer's black steward. But it was right in its suspicion; the Underground Railroad could not have worked as it did without the collusion of white captains and conductors, North and South—and there was more than a "nest" of abolitionists in Richmond. The 1860 Federal census found fourteen prisoners in the Richmond penitentiary who were there for aiding the Underground Railroad. Eleven of them were white. Sailors, captains, carpenters, blacksmiths, cooks, shoemakers, stonemasons and laborers, they were charged with "carrying off slave," "Negro stealing," and the like.[19]

Without such help, John Henry Hill and hundreds of others would not have made their way to freedom. Hill broke away as his master was taking him into an auction house to be sold. He hid for nine months before being told that a "State Room" awaited him on the steamer *City of Richmond.* He sneaked aboard at Rocketts landing. The "conductor" who hid him was nervous, but Hill felt composed, he said, "for I had started that morning from my Den for Liberty or for Death providing myself with a brace of pistels."[20]

"For Liberty or for Death"—words not meant for Hill and his kind still called to him, eighty years after Patrick Henry had inspired the thought at a church less than a mile away. Four blocks from the slave pen where Hill had broken to freedom, politicians still debated slavery in the Capitol conceived by one of their forefathers, who had declared in 1776 that "all men are created equal."

Now the inevitable showdown over what that meant was approaching. Nowhere did the contradiction between rhetoric and reality cut more painfully than in Richmond, where so many of the words of the American creed were first uttered.

* * *

On Tuesday, January 3, 1860, John Letcher moved into the governor's mansion to perfect his inaugural address to the General Assembly. Much had happened since his election the previous May. Events that he, the state, and the nation had seen then as distant possibilities now seemed imminent.

Letcher told the legislature that the good life promised by the U.S. Constitution had been "interrupted only by the interference of citizens of northern states with the rights and institutions of the Southern." This had stirred a crisis and "brought the Union of the States to the verge of destruction." The only way to head that off was to call a convention of the states to seek some settlement—or to work out a peaceful separation.

Then he looked beyond the borders of Virginia. "The 'irrepressible conflict' doctrine, announced and advocated by the ablest and most distinguished leader of the Republican party [the potential presidential candidate, Senator William H. Seward of New York], is an open declaration of war against the institution of African slavery, wherever it exists," Letcher wrote. "I would be disloyal to the United States and the South if I did not declare that the election of such a man, entertaining such sentiments, ought to be resisted by the slaveholding states."

Such warnings were appearing every day in journals like the *Enquirer,* and in legislators' conversations in the bars of the American, Powhatan,

Exchange, and Ballard House hotels. But when Letcher went on, in words that would have been pro forma insincerity for a Democratic firebrand, those who knew him understood that he meant what he said: "I am now, and have ever been, a friend to the Union of the States. I appreciate its value, ardently desire its preservation, and would not rashly hazard its existence. . . . A wise, prudent and considerate course may yet save the Union, in the hour of its peril. To this end, I am prepared to do all that honor, duty and patriotism enjoins me to do."

Nevertheless, he urged the legislators to order munitions, form a brigade of minutemen, expand the Virginia Military Institute, and otherwise prepare the state "at all times, and upon the shortest notice, to protect her honor, defend her rights, and maintain her institutions against all assaults of her enemies." The General Assembly rejected his call for a national convention to head off war, but it approved half a million dollars to buy arms. That seemed a lot at the time.[21]

The week after Letcher's speech, South Carolina's Christopher Memminger came to Richmond hoping to persuade Virginia to join a Southern-states convention clearly aimed toward secession. Letcher was gracious but noncommittal, as he was to a Mississippi delegation that followed. In early March, the General Assembly turned down those invitations. When the last defendants in the John Brown affair were hanged at Charles Town that month, Letcher pointedly stayed away. He was determined to remain, in his words, "calm and conservative."

Virginia Democrats, looking ahead to their party's national convention in Charleston, South Carolina, in April, met in county after county to choose between favorite sons Henry Wise and R. M. T. Hunter as candidates for president. By outdoing even Wise's ardent Southern-rights stand, Hunter managed to take the lead. But the Charleston convention, split by Deep South extremism, broke up without nominating anyone. When it reconvened in Baltimore in June, Northern Democrats chose Senator Stephen A. Douglas of Illinois, while Southerners walked out and held their own session, picking the incumbent vice president, Kentucky's John C. Breckinridge. In yet another rump convention, erstwhile Whigs and Know-Nothings formed the Constitutional Union Party, putting up Tennessee's former senator, John Bell. Meanwhile the Republicans, meeting in Chicago in May, had bypassed the early favorite, Senator Seward, in favor of a former congressman from Illinois, Abraham Lincoln.

*   *   *

In Virginia and the South, for at least three decades, race and politics had increasingly dominated public and intellectual life. Now in crisis little else was heard, in streets, taverns, drawing rooms, legislative halls and particularly in the press. North and South, radicals outshouted moderates. Yet there were those who sought accommodation—among them most citizens of Virginia, including the conservative former Whigs of Richmond.

John Letcher was still a national Democrat, so in August he defied the breakaway Southern wing of the party and endorsed Stephen Douglas, who urged the compromise of letting new states decide for themselves whether to allow slavery. While Letcher's approval did Douglas little good in Virginia, it probably made enough difference to defeat Breckinridge there: In November the Southern-rights Democrat lost the state by a mere 358 votes to the neo-Whig, the less provocative Constitutional Unionist, John Bell. Lincoln got only 1,929 votes statewide. Thus, while his election forced the hand of Deep South radicals, Virginia declared again its reluctance to sunder the Union of its fathers.

But pressure was rising. South Carolina had not been bluffing; it seceded from the Union on December 20. Henry Wise, the *Enquirer*, and the *Examiner* insisted that Virginia join the cotton states that were following South Carolina's lead. Richmond's *Southern Literary Messenger* said: "Let there be no plastering over of the great political cancer, but let us cut it off; for the time has fully come for us to do so."[22] Letcher asked Secretary of War John B. Floyd, a former Virginia governor, for early delivery of the state's 1861 quota of weapons from Federal armories, and Floyd granted the request. The governor moved the legislature's scheduled opening date forward a week, to January 7, 1861.

As the assemblymen gathered, one wrote: "Times are wild and revolutionary here beyond description."[23] Desperately trying to hold an even course, Letcher said that Virginia must mediate between "passion and recklessness." He affirmed the right of secession but criticized South Carolina for splitting away independently. He balked at calls for a state convention to consider the issue. Believing the emergency national conference he had urged a year earlier might have headed off this crisis, he asked again for such a gathering. This time, with Deep South states seceding one after another, the legislature agreed—but despite the governor's opposition, it also ordered the election of delegates to a state convention. That election and the national peace conference were both set for February 4.[24]

The three-week campaign for state convention seats saw "such a deluge of stump speeches as would have been impossible in any other state or country in the civilized world," wrote George Cary Eggleston. "When it became evident that the people of Virginia were not duly impressed with the wrong done them in the election of Mr. Lincoln," some country politicians, doubling as militia officers, assembled crowds for their speeches by simply mustering their local troops. The only question among many candidates was "whether the ordinance of secession should be adopted *before* or *after* breakfast on the first day of the convention's existence."[25] Statewide, opinion was that any such action should come after breakfast, if at all. Virginians chose Unionist delegates by a margin of 2 to 1—and by more than that, they ruled that whatever the convention decided, it must be approved by a popular referendum.

As Virginians were voting, delegates to the national "peace conference" checked in at Willard's Hotel in Washington. The futility of that meeting was clear on the first roll call: Only eleven states were present, and eventually all the Deep South states and seven from the West stayed away. Seventy-one-year-old former president John Tyler of Virginia presided over six former cabinet members, nineteen former governors, fourteen former U.S. senators, fifty former congressmen, and others voicing every shade of opinion. In two weeks of oratory and parliamentary wrangling, they produced a compromise report that was rejected by both Northern radicals and Southern fire-eaters in Congress.[26]

While what Horace Greeley called "the old gentlemen's convention" was going on in Washington, the seven states that had seceded—South Carolina, Georgia, Florida, Alabama, Mississippi, Louisiana, and Texas—met in Montgomery to form the Confederate States of America. To head their provisional government they chose former secretary of war and senator Jefferson Davis of Mississippi, with former congressman Alexander H. Stephens of Georgia as vice president.

All eyes now shifted to the Virginia convention. With more people, more industry, and more historic prestige than any other slave state, Virginia was essential to the newly formed Confederacy. Her course would influence other uncommitted states like North Carolina, Kentucky, Tennessee, Arkansas, and Missouri. Stephen Douglas wrote that there was still hope of preserving the Union, but that "all depends on the action of Virginia and the Border states. . . . Save Virginia, and we will save the Union."[27]

The convention election had realigned the state's party politics. It split former Whigs, Democrats, Know-Nothings, and Republicans into two clear camps, Unionist and secessionist. At the outset, two-thirds of the state's convention delegates opposed secession. They included almost all of those from beyond the Alleghenies in western Virginia, as well as most ex-Whigs and some non-slaveholders in the East. (Of the 152 delegates, 118, or 77.8 percent, owned slaves. Of these, half owned fewer than ten. Twenty-three percent of the total owned twenty or more and were therefore classed as "planters.")[28]

While Richmonders had refused to elect the stubborn Unionist John Minor Botts, they reflected the division of opinion in state and city by picking two less provocative Unionists, Marmaduke Johnson and William H. MacFarland. Their third delegate was the secessionist George Wythe Randolph. In Virginia, however, the Union label did not mean what it meant up north; many who wore it wanted to stay in the Union, but only if Southern rights—i.e., slavery—were protected. Secessionists quickly dubbed those who would stay in at all costs "submissionists."

Social Richmond crowded the galleries as the convention met in the House chamber of the Capitol, or at Mechanics Hall at Franklin and Ninth streets when the state legislature was in session. John Tyler took his seat as a delegate, maintaining that if Virginia seceded, the Federal government would see that coercion was useless and agree on a way to peace. Henry Wise was there, as were Randolph of Richmond and Patrick Henry Aylett of King William County, grandsons of Thomas Jefferson and the state's first governor.

The gathering marked time, awaiting the results of the peace convention at Washington, and then Lincoln's inaugural remarks. Politicians from South Carolina, Georgia, and Mississippi—envoys from the new Confederacy—were given floor privileges, and their appeals roused hectic applause in the galleries. Amid one furious exchange at Mechanics Hall, the presiding officer ordered the building cleared of spectators. Afterward crowds hissed "submissionists" in the streets and burned them in effigy, then cheered secessionists while a band serenaded them at their hotels.[29]

Both delegates and spectators were goaded by what was happening beyond the debate on the floor. Four hundred miles away, South Carolina's guns had defied Federal intentions since early January to resupply a U.S. fort in Charleston Harbor. And from Franklin Street just off Richmond's Capitol Square, a new voice slashed through the clamor over Fort Sumter, the incoming Federal president, and the cautious Virginia convention.

*   *   *

John Moncure Daniel returned to the editorship of the Richmond *Examiner* shortly before Abraham Lincoln became president of the United States. His arrival was "like turning an electric eel into a fish-pond."[30]

On March 4, 1861, Daniel welcomed Lincoln to office as "a creature whom no one can hear with patience or look on without disgust . . . the delightful combination of a western country lawyer with a Yankee bar-keeper. No American of any section has read the oratory with which he has strewn his devious road to Washington, condensed lumps of imbecility, buffoonery, and vulgar malignity, without a blush of shame." Lincoln, Daniel wrote, "is inaugurated to-day as John Brown was hung, under the mouths of cannon leveled at the citizens whom he swears to protect. . . . What can come of all this but civil war and public ruin?"[31]

Daniel, a country doctor's son from near Fredericksburg, had become editor of the *Examiner* in 1847, at the age of 22. Within a year he was a force in state politics, a frank spokesman to and for the educated planter class, disdainful of urban opinion. He came close to bringing Edgar Allan Poe's fleeting career to an even earlier end. Daniel had somehow offended Poe in discussing contributions to the *Examiner,* so Poe challenged him; arriving at the newspaper office in a wobbly state, Poe found Daniel ready to negotiate from strength, sitting at a table behind two giant pistols. When the editor offered to settle their differences on the spot, Poe decided the whole thing was just a misunderstanding.

Daniel "always had his war paint on," and was a true believer in the code duello. In 1852, when he and Edward Johnston of the *Whig* disagreed over sculptor Hiram Powers's decorous nude *Greek Slave,* they concluded their printed debate with pistols. Both combatants missed, so the merits of *Greek Slave* went unresolved in Richmond.[32]

By the rules of that day, it seems miraculous that Daniel's scathing editorials did not drag him into a gunfight a week. But his vigorous support of Democrat Franklin Pierce in the 1852 election won him appointment as U.S. chargé d'affaires to Sardinia, and there he remained for nearly eight years, until Lincoln's election and crisis brought him home.[33]

Only briefly after returning was he hesitant about secession. Then that "ugly and ferocious old Orang-Outang from the wilds of Illinois" was sworn in as president. Though Lincoln said that he had no intention of interfering with slavery where it already existed, he also declared that no state had the legal right to leave the Union. Daniel flailed not only at Lincoln but at those Virginians whose outrage fell short of his own. On March 19, the *Examiner* lampooned the state-convention delegates as a menagerie of jackasses, hyenas, and poodles, which understandably upset most of them.

Marmaduke Johnson, a portly lawyer, recognized himself as "a dark, sleek, fat Pony, from Richmond, supposed to be much affected with the Botts," who "lifted up his voice and neighed submission; one master would do as well for him as another; what he went in for was good feed-

ing, and he believed that he could get that from Old Abe as well as anybody else. . . ."*

After Johnson suggested that Virginia should be proud to mediate
between North and South, the *Examiner* asserted: "Those who have
heard Mr. Marmaduke Johnson need not be told that he belongs to the
'vox et preterea nihil' [sound without substance] school of orators, and
when, therefore, the state pays for reporting one of his speeches, it pays
for nothing but a bushel of very light chaff . . . soap bubbles. . . ."

Daniel clearly was daring Johnson to respond—and Johnson did.
That day, in a chance encounter on Franklin Street, he opened fire on
Daniel with a pistol. Daniel shot back, but both missed. The next day in
court, Mayor Joseph Carrington Mayo put them under a peace bond.[35]

* * *

Other convention delegates, less elaborately insulted than Johnson,
were less easily provoked. As the storm of outside criticism rose, inside
the hall a rough-cut hill-country Whig lawyer and West Point graduate
named Jubal Anderson Early ignored Daniel's description of him as "the
Terrapin from Franklin [county]." He stood with Johnson against secessionists trying to stampede the convention in reaction to Lincoln's inaugural address.

"I think that there was never a body assembled on the face of the
earth having before it so important a duty to perform as this Convention," said Early. It could decide "the existence and the preservation of
the fairest fabric of government that was ever erected. . . . we ought not
to act in hot haste, but rather coolly deliberate in view of the grave consequences which our action involves."

If the Deep South states had not already withdrawn from the Union,
Early suggested, Lincoln's inaugural promise to execute the laws in all
the states would have been "hailed throughout the country as a guarantee that he would perform his duty. . . . I ask why it is that we are placed
in this perilous condition? and if it is not solely from the action of these
States that have seceded from the Union without having consulted our
views."[36]

Lincoln's statement that he would not interfere with slavery in states
where it existed, but that he recognized no right of secession, heightened the uproar from radicals inside and outside the convention. That
uproar ground away at Unionist strength. But as late as April 4, the ap-

---

*Although Daniel took credit and blame for everything in the *Examiner,* he did not orig-
inate this satire, titled "The Parliament of the Beasts." He would not tell friends who
wrote it, but a later source says it was thought up by a civil engineer named Edmund Lor-
raine and then elaborated and versified by Daniel himself.[34]

proximate 2-to-1 majority still held when the convention voted 88 to 45 against a pro-secession motion.

As the elected convention balked, Henry Wise and fellow secessionists sent letters inviting known "friends of Southern Rights" from all over Virginia to a "Spontaneous People's Convention" in Richmond on April 16. "If the people were ready I am ready to-day to go out of this house of bondage with the North," Wise wrote. "But it is folly to tender naked Secession to Virginia and risk final defeat forever. We must train the popular head and heart." The rump convention would organize a "Resistance party . . . ready to concert action for any emergency, mild, middle and extreme."[37]

According to John Minor Botts, if the elected convention had adjourned after its anti-secession vote on April 4, the ensuing national tragedy might have been avoided. Lincoln had secretly invited the Virginia Unionist George W. Summers to Washington "on business of the first importance." Summers sent instead his colleague John B. Baldwin, who arrived in Washington a week later. Lincoln promised Baldwin confidentially that if the Virginia convention adjourned without deciding to secede, he would stop the Federal resupply mission that was about to sail to Charleston, and evacuate Fort Sumter. "If you will guarantee to me the State of Virginia I shall remove the troops," Lincoln said. "A State for a fort is no bad business." But Baldwin could not make that promise.[38]

Botts wrote that he heard about this not from Baldwin but from Lincoln, when he called on the president two days later. "I am no war man," said Lincoln. "I want peace more than any man in this country, and will make greater sacrifices to preserve it. . . ." But when Botts asked the president whether he could carry the same proposition to Richmond, Lincoln said it was too late, the expedition was on its way.

As Botts wrote after the war, this is history not generally known. "I have often wondered why Mr. Lincoln had not himself, in his own justification, made it known to the country," he said. Others will wonder the same thing, if indeed it happened the way Botts related.[39] Whether it did or not, the Federal ships did sail for Charleston, and Virginia moved with the nation toward the precipice of war.

The day after Botts's meeting with Lincoln, the Richmond convention named a three-man committee to call on the president, seeking some last-minute compromise. But bad weather delayed travel, and the committeemen did not reach Washington until April 12. When they met Lincoln, they did not realize that Confederate guns had already opened fire on Fort Sumter. The president informed them of this, adding that he meant to hold the fort, to meet force with force. But the

Virginia convention still held out against secession, and fire-eaters saw that only some outside shock could turn it around.

As the crisis over Sumter mounted, Roger A. Pryor, a militant Petersburg editor and congressman, was one of many who welcomed it as the lever that would force Virginia into the Confederacy. The Old Dominion held back in the crisis, but Pryor understood that if the crisis turned into a fight, that would be different. Traveling to Charleston, he told a cheering crowd that South Carolina must "strike a blow"—for if she did, Virginia would be at her side "in less than an hour by Shrewsbury clock."[40]

Inspired by Pryor's challenge, the South Carolinians offered him the chance to start the bombardment of Fort Sumter. But though he had urged it, he could not will himself to do it. The honor passed to old Edmund Ruffin, who had personally seceded from Virginia and volunteered for South Carolina's Palmetto Guards. At 4.30 a.m. on Friday, April 12, 1861, the elated Ruffin fired the first shell from Fort Morris against Sumter.

CHAPTER THREE

BLOOD BEFORE NIGHT

News by Telegraph
Official Dispatches

THE WAR COMMENCED!

BOMBARDMENT OF FORT SUMTER!!

*T*he streets of Richmond were noisy with newsboys hawking extras that morning when John Beauchamp Jones arrived from the North. A Baltimore-born author of Wild West novels, Jones had been in Philadelphia publishing a lonely pro-slavery journal called *The Southern Monitor.* Outside Polecat Station, below Fredericksburg, he had seen his first Confederate flag.

As soon as Jones checked into the Exchange Hotel he sought out Henry Wise in his suite. They were joined by ex-president John Tyler, for whose benefit Jones had edited a party newspaper two decades earlier. As they jollied one another with talk about secession, the ailing Wise rose from his couch. He reached for a musket that stood in a corner with fixed bayonet. Smiling, he waved it over his head and declared that even with old-fashioned flintlocks, brave Southerners would make "the popinjays of the Northern cities" break and run.[1]

His son's *Enquirer* was just as defiant: "Attention, Volunteers! Nothing is more probable than that President Davis will soon march an army through North Carolina and Virginia to Washington. Those of our volunteers who desire to join the Southern army as it shall pass through our borders had better organize at once for the purpose, and keep their arms, accoutrements, uniforms, ammunition and knapsacks in constant readiness."[2]

Virginia's Ordnance Department advertised for sealed bids by May 10 for converting 5,000 flintlock muskets to percussion, for 5,000 best rifle muskets, 2,000 best revolvers, 1,000 cavalry carbines, 1,000 light cavalry sabers, 1,000 artillery sabers, eight twelve-pounder howitzers, eight twenty-four-pounders, plus gun carriages, caissons, traveling forges, shot, tents, spades, axes, canteens, and other tools of war.[3]

For Virginia there was no war yet, and those numbers made it clear that no one imagined the scale of what was coming. In the convention and the governor's office, saddened loyalists still resisted the rush of events. But the cannoneers at Charleston were taking Virginia's decision on war or peace away from the popularly chosen convention. "If anything will precipitate the true men of Virginia into revolution, it will be the miserable shuffling of our State Convention," said the *Enquirer*.

Thirty-four hours after the first shot was fired at Sumter, the Union garrison there surrendered. The bulletin reached Richmond late on Saturday, April 13.

Crowds poured into the streets. Businesses shut down. Smith's Armory Band came running, buglers and snare drummers struggling into their fancy uniforms. Somebody rushed out with the seven-starred, three-striped flag of the Confederate States of America, sewn by hand to wave at this moment. Behind the flag, the band struck up the snappy minstrel tune "Dixie," and led a growing throng of Virginians through the streets of Richmond.

By the time the band reached the Tredegar Iron Works, beside the river and canal, a good 3,000 were cheering along behind. Workers inside ran up another huge Confederate flag, above the biggest iron mills in the South. The band paid tribute with "The Marseillaise," and the thousands roared. A cannon—cast at Tredegar for the Confederate government at Montgomery—thundered a salute.

Joseph R. Anderson, proprietor of the ironworks and soon to be a Confederate brigadier, shouted his welcome to the news. More speakers followed, each outdoing the other. J. Randolph Tucker, attorney general of Virginia, announced that the walls of Sumter had been breached by shells fired from columbiads made at Tredegar. Another roar went up.

From waterside, the demonstration flowed to the *Enquirer* office and called for the editor, Jennings Wise—now Captain Wise, of the Richmond Light Infantry Blues. Wise stepped onto the iron balcony and delivered a "soul-stirring" speech. Some of the growing crowd detoured to the armory, rolled out the guns of the Fayette Artillery, and dragged them to the south front of the Capitol.

Nothing less than a hundred-gun salute would do; for more than an hour the cannon boomed, while clusters of celebrants sang one song here, another there, and listened to impromptu speeches. Then a brass band and a wagon draped with banners led a parade to the governor's mansion at the northeast corner of Capitol Square.[4]

As the band played "Dixie," the crowd chanted "Letcher! Letcher!" Reluctantly, Virginia's governor came out to speak. He was not as exultant as they were.

Inside the mansion, while Letcher had awaited every bulletin from Sumter, his wife was entertaining Mrs. Roger Pryor as house guest. Like many social situations of the time, this one was delicate: Letcher was doing all he could to stave off secession, while Pryor was in Charleston, egging the South Carolinians on.

Amid all this, their ladies sat together and "sewed little gowns and pinafores, indulged in reminiscences" and pretended to ignore what was happening outside. "Mrs. Letcher thought the political storm must pass," wrote Sara Pryor. "It was hard to bear; the governor was nervous and sleeping badly, but quiet would surely come, and when it did—why, then, we would all go down to Old Point Comfort for June, bathe in the sea, and get strong and well. As for fighting—it would never come to that."[5]

But it had come to that, and John Letcher had to face the crowd. As he stepped out onto the porch of the mansion, his bald dome shone in the torchlight and his eyes were stern behind his little wire-rimmed spectacles.

"Thank you for this compliment," he told them, "but I must be permitted to say that I see no occasion for this demonstration." Pointedly, he said he did not "recognize" the flags they were flaunting, that they had no right to take the artillery from the armory and they should take it right back. Virginia, after all, was still a state of the Union.

"I have done all that my duty requires," Letcher said. "I can only assure you that come what may, I will be true to my duty to Virginia, without regard to the consequences that may affect me personally." Then he suggested that they all go home. With that, he bowed and turned back inside.[6]

The crowd hissed in disgust. A loud voice said the cannon should have been loaded with shot and aimed at the governor's mansion. Flag-bearers surged into the Capitol and out onto the portico,* exciting more cheers. "To the roof!" someone yelled. Thousands of voices joined in. "Raise the flag! Run it up!" Men and boys raced up the inside stairway. Within minutes the Rebel banner floated in the breeze atop the Capitol's highest flagpole. The applause, said the *Enquirer,* "fairly rent the sky."

Somebody called for speakers—a wholly unnecessary request, for no secessionist with ambition would have willingly missed this chance. One after another, they pushed forward on the Capitol's high portico to tell the crowd what it wanted to hear. Groans arose at every mention of the Virginia convention that had been resisting secession for two months. The final speaker offered a resolution "that we rejoice with high, exultant, heartfelt joy at the triumph of the Southern Confederacy over the accursed government at Washington in the capture of Fort Sumter." This met with "entire unanimity and enthusiastic applause."[8]

By then the hour was late. The crowd gradually split up into torch-light parades, winding into different neighborhoods, bands and banners leading the way. Hundreds of townhouses were lit from cellar to attic. Rebel flags flew from doorways, and inside women were stitching more of them to fly tomorrow. Tar barrels still burned at street corners when the noise died down near midnight. The celebrators dwindled home-ward, sure that at last Fort Sumter had forced the decision and Virginia could hold back no longer.

But many a house in Richmond had been dark and quiet all that Saturday evening. In some of them, Virginians were weeping. In the gloom of the governor's mansion, John Letcher ordered the Capitol guard to take down the Confederate flag during the night. The next morning, another was up in its place—not the colors of the United States but the deep-blue flag of Virginia, with its seal and motto: "Sic Semper Tyrannis."

* * *

Roger Pryor had been a shade too optimistic. After Sumter it took more than "an hour by Shrewsbury clock" for Virginia to join the Confederacy—but not much more.

---

*At that time there were no stairs to the Ionic portico on the Capitol's south front; a Northern visitor before the war thought it "as inaccessible from the exterior as if it had been intended to fortify the edifice from all ingress other than by scaling ladders." The building's main entrance was at the west end, closest to the sixty-foot outdoor monument to Washington. The wings at each end and the broad steps to the portico were added in 1904–05.[7]

Richmond spent that Sunday in a thrill of suspense. After church, crowds debated in Capitol Square and elbowed close to read the headlines posted outside newspaper offices. Some were eager and others dreaded to know how the state would respond to the cannon fire at Charleston. In Henry Wise's rooms at the Exchange Hotel, the ex-governor and friends plotted how to use the fall of Sumter to turn the convention around. Earlier, they had planned a street demonstration for Monday night, to excite the public before their Spontaneous People's Convention met on Tuesday. They postponed it without knowing that the president of the United States would provide all the excitement they needed.

On Monday morning the *Examiner* trumpeted: "Lincoln declares war on the South, and his Secretary demands from Virginia a quota of cut-throats to desolate Southern firesides."[9]

Lincoln had called for 75,000 militia to put down rebellion in the South. Though the newspapers sounded outrage, privately editors like John Daniel and Jennings Wise exulted at the news. Bulletins sped through the streets as the elected convention met at the Capitol. Onlookers jammed the galleries and harangued arriving Unionist delegates.

Despite this clamor, the conservatives still held back. Distrusting the Richmond papers, hoping the news was either rumor or forgery, Jubal Early and his fellow Unionists pleaded for the convention not to react without official confirmation. Governor Letcher would not respond until he got word directly from Washington.

It came late that night.

John Minor Botts, the most vocal of those who remained pro-Union, called Lincoln's mobilization proclamation "in many respects the most unfortunate state paper that ever issued from any executive since the establishment of the government."[10] With it, the long struggle to keep Virginia and the upper South in the Union was lost.

On Tuesday, April 16, as the elected convention met in a secret session at the Capitol, the Spontaneous People's Convention opened at Metropolitan Hall, on Franklin Street a block and a half away. There a door-keeper stood with drawn sword as fire-eaters like Jennings Wise insisted on action without waiting for the elected convention. This gathering adjourned for one more day to give the delegates at the Capitol a final chance to move.[11]

When a message came from Lincoln's secretary of war, Simon Cameron, formally asking the state for three regiments as its share of the 75,000 troops, John Letcher's reply made clear the turnabout in the minds of thousands of Virginians.

"Your object is to subjugate the Southern States, and the requisition made upon me for such an object . . . will not be complied with," the governor told Cameron. "You have chosen to inaugurate civil war, and having done so we will meet you, in a spirit as determined as the Administration has exhibited towards the South."[12] Delegate W. T. Sutherlin, from Danville in Pittsylvania County, said, "I have a Union constituency which elected me by a majority of one thousand, and I believe now that there are not ten Union men in that county to-day."[13]

But "Honest John" Letcher, asserting that Lincoln had acted illegally, meant to be sure that history could not accuse him of the same thing. He rejected demands by Henry Wise and the radicals that Virginia grab Federal bases in the state before the convention approved secession. Furious, Wise and friends met secretly at radical headquarters at the Exchange, and the ex-governor took the law into his own hands, ordering the Virginia militia to seize the Harpers Ferry arsenal and the Gosport navy yard opposite Norfolk. The next day Letcher could do nothing but endorse the fait accompli.

As the closed convention's climactic vote on secession neared on Wednesday, April 17, Henry Wise took the floor. Flourishing an enormous horse pistol, he placed it on the desk before him. To wild applause, he announced the secret moves against the Federal installations. "Blood will be flowing at Harpers Ferry before night!" he declared. Then, with all the anger that had accumulated inside him for months, he lashed those who still clung to the Union. He was "supernaturally excited," said one delegate. "His hair stood off his head, as if charged with electricity. . . . It was the most powerful display of the sort I ever witnessed."[14]

Within minutes after Wise's speech, the Virginia convention voted by 88 to 55 to secede from the Union; most of those who still held back were from west of the Shenandoah Valley. But convention leaders tried to keep the decision secret until the Norfolk and Harpers Ferry bases were in state hands. That a popular referendum was scheduled to ratify the decision a month later was hardly noted in the passion of the moment.

Botts maintained that if Lincoln had not called for the militia, Wise and the radicals intended to mount a coup against Letcher—at which the governor might have asked Washington for military help to put down rebellion within the state. Had that happened, said Botts, nothing could then have forced Virginia and the upper South into the Cotton States Confederacy.[15]

That night shaky ex-president Tyler stood before the People's Spontaneous Convention and with what seemed "supernatural strength" told the delegates that they acted in a direct line of struggles for freedom, from the Magna Carta through the Revolution. Henry Wise, still soaring, "electrified the assembly by a burst of eloquence, perhaps never surpassed by mortal orator."

Quite likely, Wise said, the Northern oppressors had seized his son and namesake, a minister in Philadelphia, but "if they suppose hostages of my own heart's blood will stay my hand in a contest for the maintenance of sacred rights, they are mistaken." He said Virginia forces should have occupied Washington before "the Republican hordes" took it over. And then John Letcher appeared, to endorse the secession vote and be cheered "by the very men who, two days before, would gladly have witnessed his execution."[16]

Even after this torrent of rhetoric, both conventions tried to withhold the news of secession. But no walls could contain the elation and despair of men who realized the enormity of what they had done. Word leaked out in a hundred ways, and the next day Richmond was awash with emotion. Secession banners broke out all over town. Elizabeth Van Lew maintained that the first, a South Carolina palmetto flag, "was flung to the breeze by Brown & Peasley, fishmongers, near the market on 7th street, with money furnished by negro traders."*[17] Slave dealers were indeed credited, or blamed, for quietly financing many of the street demonstrations that led to secession.

"Oh! joyful and ever to be remembered day, Virginia has seceded from the abolition government," wrote a midtown girl in her diary. At 12:30 her little brother had interrupted her drawing class, bringing a scrap of wood with gilt lettering from the sign on the U.S. Courthouse. He said the Confederate flag was flying over the Capitol, and "of course we were very much excited, and we all ran out to see it, and there it was sure enough waving in the breeze; we stayed there in the rain jumping and clapping our hands untill we were obliged to go in and then we couldn't draw our hands shook so much."[19]

On April 19, Federal troops shed the first blood of the war after Sumter—in Baltimore, where firing broke out when a street crowd

---

*On March 16, Lewis D. Crenshaw, Jr., wrote in his diary that he had hand-made a Confederate flag—a copy of the original Stars and Bars adapted by the Congress at Montgomery on March 4. That design was patterned on the U.S. flag, with a circle of seven stars in the blue field and only three broad horizontal stripes, two red and one white. Young Crenshaw raised his flag on March 19, and claimed that it was the first to fly in Richmond.

The familiar red Confederate "battle flag" with white stars on a blue St. Andrew's cross came into use after Southern soldiers in the smoke of battle at Manassas mistook the Stars and Bars for the U.S. flag. A new Confederate national standard, with this battle flag in the upper corner of a field of white, became official on May 1, 1863. But some felt that this version, when hanging limp around the staff, looked too much like a flag of truce, so a broad red vertical stripe was added across its end on March 4, 1865.[18]

stoned the Sixth Massachusetts Regiment en route to Washington. In Richmond, that news electrified a grand celebration parade. As bands played, torches lit the streets, and banners billowed in illuminated windows, cheers for Baltimore ran along the columns. Speakers imagined great things: "I am neither a prophet, nor the son of a prophet," said one, "yet I predict that in less than sixty days the flag of the Confederacy will be waving over the White House." From the crowd someone shouted, "Yes—in less than thirty days!"

Sallie Ann Brock Putnam, a young society matron, wrote: "A stranger suddenly transported to the city, without a knowledge of preceding facts, would have imagined the people in a state of intoxication or insanity. . . . All love for the Union appeared exhausted."[20]

But not quite. At the Powhatan Hotel a dozen or more resentful convention delegates from western Virginia, where there were few slaves, met quietly to consider what to do. Their constituents were not celebrating back home. Surrounded by the din in Richmond's streets, these men secretly started planning West Virginia's breakaway as a separate state of the Union.[21]

A few realists, even some of those who were pleased by what had happened, had reservations about the merrymaking. "Guns are fired on Capitol Hill in commemoration of secession, and the Confederate flag now floats unmolested from the summit of the capitol," John B. Jones wrote in his diary. "I think they had better save the powder. At night . . . a gay illumination. This too is wrong. We had better save the candles."[22]

On Church Hill, Elizabeth Van Lew read the news from Baltimore through "bitter, blinding tears," and moaned to herself, "My country! Oh, my country!" At the foot of her garden she watched the parade. "Such a sight! The transparencies with their painted . . . wicked and blasphemous mottoes . . . carriages with ladies . . . women on foot—the multitude—the mob—the whooping—the tin-pan music and the fierceness of a surging, swelling revolution. I thought of France, and as the procession passed I fell upon my knees under the angry heavens, clasped my hands and prayed, 'Father, forgive them, for they know not what they do.'"[23]

Others also thought of France, for "The Marseillaise" was heard as often as "Dixie" in those early wartime parades. "Secession," Jones mused, "by any other name would smell as sweet. For my part, I like the name of Revolution, or even Rebellion, better, for they are sanctified by the example of Washington and his compeers."[24]

* * *

George Washington's example was much on the mind of a courtly Virginian who went to Christ Church in Alexandria that Sunday morning, April 21, his first day as a civilian after thirty-six years in uniform.

Robert E. Lee, recently appointed colonel of the First U.S. Cavalry, had resigned his commission when he learned of Virginia's decision. After agonizing through the secession crisis he had concluded that "With all my devotion to the Union and the feeling of loyalty and duty of an American citizen, I have not been able to make up my mind to raise my hand against my relatives, my children, my home." Thus he left the army, saying, "Save in defense of my native state, I never desire again to draw my sword."[25]

Now, at services in the church where his father's friend and commanding officer Washington had worshipped, Lee could hear jubilation in the streets of Alexandria. But in him there was none.

Already the Alexandria *Gazette* had nominated him as the Washington of the new revolution. It said: "There is no man more worthy to head our forces and lead our army. There is no man who would command more of the confidence of the people of Virginia. . . . His reputation, his acknowledged ability, his chivalric character, his probity, honor, and—may we add, to his eternal praise—his Christian life and conduct—make his very name a 'tower of strength.' It is a name surrounded by revolutionary and patriotic associations and reminiscences."

And so, that evening at the Arlington mansion overlooking the nation's capital, Lee was little surprised when a messenger brought Governor Letcher's request that he come to Richmond "for conference with the chief executive."[26]

* * *

In Episcopal churches, the scripture for that Sunday was from the second chapter of Joel: "Then will the Lord be jealous for his land, and pity his people. Yea, the Lord will answer, and say unto his people, Behold, I will send you corn, and wine, and oil, and ye shall be satisfied therewith; and I will no more make you a reproach among the heathen. But I will remove far off from you the Northern Army, and will drive him into a land barren and desolate, with his face toward the east sea, and his hinder part toward the utmost sea. . . ."[27] Many in the congregations of Virginia took this as a prophecy.

About the time Lee and those at Christ Church filed out into the churchyard in Alexandria, Dr. Charles Frederic Ernest Minnigerode was closing his service at St. Paul's in Richmond. Suddenly, just across Ninth Street on the edge of Capitol Square, the alarm bell rang in its tower—two loud strokes, a pause, then a third. At St. Paul's, St. John's, and St. James's Episcopal churches, at St. Peter's Cathedral, First Baptist, Second Presbyterian and Centenary Methodist, at churches all over Richmond, worshippers rushed out into the April sunshine, wondering what had happened.

Again and again the alarm bell rang. Guards at the tower told why: The governor had word that the Union sloop of war *Pawnee* had passed City Point on the James and was headed for defenseless Richmond, intending to shell and burn the city to the ground!

Militiamen of the Blues, the Grays, F Company, the Howitzers, and the Fayette Artillery hurried to their drill rooms for accoutrements and then to the square. Tearful women hugged them, sending them off as to faraway battle. Unorganized volunteers, eager to defend their hearths and loved ones, resurrected whatever weapons they could find: "fowling-pieces mortally oxidized; immemorial duck-guns, of prodigious bore; ancient falchions that had flashed in the eyes of Cornwallis at Yorktown; pistols of every conceivable calibre, and of all possible shades of inutility; and, in one instance, at least, a veritable blunderbuss, so encompassed with verdigris that it passed for a cucumber of precocious growth. . . ."

George W. Bagby, who so described the armaments, told how a few men realized that something heavier would be needed for riverine warfare. They rushed to the armory and dragged out a pair of magnificent bronze cannon, a long-ago present to Virginia from the French government. Hoisted onto a wagon, these monsters were pulled by horses, mules, and men until one got away, rolled downhill toward the Custom House, leaped into the gutter, and lay there mute for many weeks.

The militia marched to Rocketts wharf, ready with bayonets and small arms to repel the enemy's landing force. The roof of the Capitol, as well as every high point in town, was thick with spectators, waiting. "Like a serpentine silver band the river lay stretched before them," wrote Bagby, "miles and miles away, without a cloud to dim its tranquil argent sheen. Far or near, none could descry the *Pawnee*. The sun sank low and at length set in the peaceful heavens, still no *Pawnee*." The troops bivouacked overnight in fields near the river, still ready. But the *Pawnee* never came.

Later, when real war came, Richmonders recalled "Pawnee Sunday" and laughed at themselves. Bagby said correctly that "The foolhardiest midshipman in Uncle Sam's service, even when crazed with sweet champagne extracted from the pippins of the Jerseys and medicated in the cellars of the Five Points, never dreamed of so insane a project" as the city had feared. Couriers had panicked some suburban ladies with a rumor that "the Pawnee Indians had come down the Central Railroad, taken possession of the city, and were scalping and tomahawking the citizens at a frightful rate." All this time, the USS *Pawnee* herself had been toiling up the Chesapeake between Norfolk and Washington.[28]

The embarrassment of "the Pawnee war" helped Richmond realize how ill-prepared it was for real war. By its own lights, Virginia was now a sovereign state, independent of both Union and Confederacy. Strictly speaking, that would last until the plebiscite scheduled for May 23, but both sides took its outcome for granted. Real war was coming, and Virginia had to prepare for it. First, someone must command its defenses.

*   *   *

When Robert E. Lee arrived on April 22, Richmond was still aflutter over the *Pawnee*. Wearing a high silk hat and a civilian suit, Lee did not look his age. He had turned fifty-four in January and his hair was beginning to gray, but he was beardless and his full mustache was still nearly black. When he stepped down at the Virginia Central depot at Union (Sixteenth) and Broad streets, a crowd was there to escort him to the Spotswood Hotel. He could not know yet that wherever the flow of battle led, the protection of this city would become the great mission of his life.

As he checked in at the new and elegant Spotswood, Lee heard that Confederate Vice President Alexander Stephens had just been welcomed to Richmond. Stephens had been sent from Montgomery to wrap sovereign Virginia as closely as possible into the Confederacy. That evening, celebrators serenaded him and his cause at the Exchange Hotel. Militarily, the alliance Stephens sought was essential. But achieving it was politics, which was not a soldier's business. Without unpacking, Lee headed to see John Letcher at the Capitol.

There the governor offered him the rank of major general and command of all Virginia's military and naval forces. Lee accepted without hesitation. The convention approved his appointment that same evening. The next morning he went up to the Capitol for his formal induction.

Waiting in the rotunda outside the House of Delegates chamber, Lee stood in contemplation beside the superb Houdon statue of his idol, Washington. In these halls his father, "Light Horse Harry" Lee, Washington's favorite cavalryman, had served as governor. After that, he became the congressman who eulogized Washington as "first in war, first in peace, first in the hearts of his countrymen."

Now Light Horse Harry's son entered the hall escorted by the erstwhile Unionist Marmaduke Johnson. On the platform were three other reluctant secessionists—Stephens, Letcher, and John Janney, president of the convention. There also was Matthew Fontaine Maury, the great ocean scientist who had just quit Federal service to join Virginia. In the convention, standing in welcome, were Henry Wise, Jubal Early, and at least four others who would become Confederate generals.[29]

Janney fully appreciated the historic moment. The disputes of past months were over, he declared. Now Virginia stood "animated by one impulse, governed by one desire and one determination, and that is that *she shall be defended;* and that no spot of her soil shall be polluted by the foot of an invader."

When Virginia was threatened, the convention turned to Lee because it knew his antecedents and his record, Janney told him. No small share of the glory of the Mexican war "was due to your valor and your military genius." The convention had confirmed Lee's appointment unanimously, believing that he was already "first in war." And now, "We pray God most fervently that you may so conduct the operations committed to your charge, that it will soon be said of you, that you are 'first in peace,' and when that time comes you will have earned the still prouder distinction of being 'first in the hearts of your countrymen.' "[30]

Surprised by Janney's outpouring, Lee replied that he was "profoundly impressed with the solemnity of the occasion, for which I must say I was not prepared. I accept the position assigned me by your partiality. I would have much preferred had the choice fallen upon an abler man. Trusting in Almighty God, an approving conscience, and the aid of my fellow-citizens, I devote myself to the service of my native State, in whose behalf alone will I ever again draw my sword."[31]

That was all. In a season of stormy, long-winded rhetoric, it was Lee's only speech, and Jubal Early said that those present would never forget it. No doubt Lee's conduct that day strengthened the devotion that Early would show him in the months ahead.

But Lee did not tell the convention all that was grinding inside him. "The war may last ten years," he wrote to his wife soon after arriving. He asked the Reverend Cornelius Walker to pray for guidance from "Him who alone can save us, and who has permitted the dire calamity of this fratricidal war . . . the calamity our sins have produced." Asked privately by Episcopal Bishop Richard Hooker Wilmer whether he thought the war would perpetuate slavery, Lee said, "The future is in the hands of Providence. If the slaves of the South were mine, I would surrender them all without a struggle to avert the war."[32]

The convention's other honored guest, Vice President Stephens, had much more to say. Urging Virginia's alliance with the Confederacy, he shrewdly suggested something that had already occurred to Richmond's fervid editorialists. "The enemy is now on your border—almost at your door," said Stephens. "He must be met. This can best be done by having your military operations under the common head at Montgomery—or it may be at Richmond."

While he could promise no such thing, Stephens said it was quite probable that if Virginia joined, within a few weeks the Confederate government "would be moved to this place . . . and should Virginia become, as it probably will, the theatre of the war, the whole may be transferred here. . . ."[33]

Stephens understood Virginia's sense of itself, and how to appeal to it. There was no doubt that the convention was ready to link the Old Dominion to the Confederacy, but if a clincher were needed, his suggestion of Richmond as capital was designed to make it so.

That evening Stephens invited Lee to his hotel. There might yet be a problem, he said: Lee, commanding Virginia's army, was a major general, but so far the highest rank in Confederate service was brigadier. If the two forces were to work together, that could create complications— it might even cause the Virginia convention to balk at alliance. Lee quickly promised that he would be no obstruction, that he wanted nothing to interfere with full cooperation.

And so the next day, April 24, Stephens and a convention committee headed by John Tyler signed the treaty by which Virginia adopted the Confederate constitution and placed its military resources under Confederate control—all subject to the May referendum. A day later, the convention ratified the agreement. Referendum or no, Virginia had joined the Confederacy.

The lonely voice of John Minor Botts protested that the whole process was illegal, carried out by a convention authorized only to recommend a course for the people's approval. Nobody paid attention except the quiet minority that was already convinced. Still objecting, Botts withdrew to his home, Elba Park—perhaps consciously named for a place of exile—near Broad and Belvidere streets on the city's western outskirts. He had Northern friends who realized the dangers in his stubbornness. One in Wisconsin wrote to Letcher: "Let John Minor Botts be injured and we will hang [Henry] Wise upon the same gallows where was executed John Brown and we will not be surprised that your body may dangle from the same gibbet. . . ." Letcher filed but did not answer it, and other letters like it; whether he forgot them is much less certain.[34]

* * *

Overnight, Virginia had become the North-South military frontier. Already President Jefferson Davis had ordered regiments there. Militia companies and unorganized volunteers poured into Richmond from every reach of Virginia. Some arrived with no training, no weapons, and no prior notice; some then were angry at being sent home until summoned to active duty. Meanwhile, the first of those on hand settled in at newly named Camp Lee, out West Broad Street at the fairgrounds. There 185 cadets in the uniform of the Virginia Military Institute, young enough to be sons of many volunteers, began to teach them close-order drill and the manual of arms.

On the same day that Lee and Stephens arrived, the battalion of cadets had come from Lexington in the Shenandoah Valley. Leading them was the dark-bearded major, awkward but all business, whose name was Tom Jackson.

With his students busy as drillmasters, Jackson called on Lee. Governor Letcher had known him in Lexington, and now nominated him as colonel. Other Lexingtonians, who thought Jackson more peculiar than promising, objected. Letcher not only insisted but ordered Lee to put Jackson in command at Harpers Ferry. Lee, too, knew and admired Jackson, for they had served together in Mexico. As he sent the newly promoted colonel away to the Potomac outpost, neither man had any inkling of how their names would soon be coupled in military history.

Harpers Ferry is at the mouth of the Shenandoah Valley. Though the valley angles southwest away from Richmond, for an invader it was a protected avenue into the heart of Virginia, flanked on the east by the Blue Ridge. Because of that, in addition to the arms and crucial machinery left unburned in its arsenal, Harpers Ferry was one of Lee's most urgent defensive problems. The port of Norfolk, with the Gosport shipyard at Portsmouth and hundreds of naval guns, was the other. Lee dispatched more troops in both directions. But he soon realized that with no navy, the state was most vulnerable along the deep tidal rivers reaching inland. He sent a veteran engineer officer to pick coast artillery sites on the Rappahannock and York rivers, at Jamestown Island, near the mouth of the James River, and at Aquia Creek, terminus of the rail line from Richmond to the Potomac.

As Lee proceeded with the methodical planning of real war, around him thousands of those unacquainted with the subject went on celebrating. Martial music rang in the streets, martial boasts filled saloons and newspapers; one of the more modest claims was that any Southerner could lick at least five Yankees. Girls applauded troops passing in their bright peacetime uniforms.

On the evening of April 24, crowds greeted the proud First South Carolina Regiment as it arrived with Milledge Luke Bonham, the very picture of a brigadier general, leading the way. The *Enquirer*'s reporter was "struck with their bold and manly appearance. Every man of them looked a hero, dark and sunburnt from exposure, their fine countenances lighted up with martial ardor, their fine physique, their perfect equipment, all denoted an invincible and heroic race of men."

Soon the papers would have to recycle their adjectives; these Gamecocks were the vanguard of thousands of Deep South soldiers sent by Jefferson Davis to Virginia, the field of imminent battle.[35]

In all the excitement, Richmond entrepreneurs were bullish about the future. Clothiers, saddlers, gunsmiths, hardware merchants, could not keep up with demand. Yet another slave trader set up in the building long used for that purpose by the firm of Betts & Gregory, on Franklin Street below Wall.

Obviously heartened at prospects now that Virginia's course was clear, the trader E. H. Stokes pledged his best effort "to promote the interest of his patrons, and flatters himself that from his long experience in the trade, he will be enabled to obtain the highest market prices." Amid the Sumter crisis, one of Stokes's Southside suppliers, Thomas A. Fowlkes, wrote apologizing for sending him damaged goods. Fowlkes said his agent "ought to have mentioned the burn—It does not hurt her in the least as I have had her working at the hoe several days at a time & no complaint," and added, "I have more for sale but wish to know the market."[36]

Other businessmen grabbed the opportunity to improve their balance sheets: Clarkson, Anderson & Co. advertised: "We the undersigned obligate ourselves not to pay, for the present, any debt to any citizens of any state that furnishes men or money on the call of Abraham Lincoln, to coerce or subjugate the Southern States."[37]

Each train from the North brought Southerners who had lived or visited there, heading home for safety. The Reverend Henry A. Wise, Jr., the ex-governor's son, was not held hostage as his father had feared, but a Yankee barber had refused to give him a shave; he reported that his Philadelphia rectory would have been sacked if a quick-thinking youth had not hung out a U.S. flag to protect it. Ex-president Tyler's son Robert also had fled after a mob threatened his Philadelphia home.[38]

But not everyone was welcome in this surge of refugees, first wave of a flood that would inundate Richmond in the months ahead. To feverish Virginians some of these transients, like some Richmonders who dared to differ with the prevailing euphoria, were suspicious characters.

John Daniel's *Examiner* called attention to "the fact that Richmond contains at present a large number of secret enemies of the South, in petticoats as well as pantaloons." Unless they are watched closely, it said, they may send "private information" to the Lincoln government.[39] The City Council promptly passed "An Ordinance Concerning Suspicious Persons."

The new law said that if "any person believes or suspects any one in the City of entertaining or of having expressed sentiments that render such person suspicious or unsafe to remain in the City, it shall be their duty to inform the Mayor of it." The mayor would then have that person tried, "and, if found guilty, or there is good reason to believe such person does entertain such opinions, such person shall be dealt with as a vagrant or person of evil fame." But it added that the mayor should also "suppress and put down committees of vigilance or safety or other collection of men, who without authority arrest or threaten any person who may be suspected as aforesaid."[40]

* * *

Letcher, Lee, and others officially responsible for preparing for war went about their serious business without bombast. But angry men like Daniel of the *Examiner* were not satisfied, even with secession and the alliance they had demanded.

To Daniel, Alexander Stephens's suggestion that the government might come to Richmond was much too cautious. At least for momentary propaganda, his paper touted Washington, not Richmond, as the seat of the Confederacy. "With that city as our capital," it said, "we should be looked upon by foreign nations as the victorious party—the real United States. Its name and prestige are worth much. . . ." Most Washingtonians were Southerners, either Virginians or Marylanders, so "Washington must be a Southern City—or a city of ruins. . . .

"Were it possible for the North to retain Washington, its capital could not be there, unless it succeeded in conquering Maryland and Virginia. To place the capital of one country within the territory of another is an absurdity too gross to be practiced by any sensible people. Washington has but one hope left, and that is to side with the South."[41]

Daniel, like many of those who had prodded Virginia into war, spoke as if Washington were there for the taking. Soon he would try himself out in uniform, but in the week after secession, he understood little of either Lincoln's determination or Northern military potential.

By the time he wrote about Washington as Confederate capital, both Richmond and Montgomery were busy with appeals for commander in chief Jefferson Davis, hero of Monterrey and Buena Vista in the Mexican War, to come to Virginia to lead Southern forces in the field. After all, when the Confederacy was formed, Davis had hoped to be named general in chief rather than president. Already Montgomery and its hotels were overcrowded by the infant government. On April 27, the Virginia convention formally invited the Confederacy to make Richmond—or anyplace else in Virginia—its capital.

For nearly a month the Congress in Montgomery debated the move. It was easy for cotton-states politicians, far from the North-South border, to speechify and clamor for blood. But Virginia was totally exposed. Richmond, the South's most important industrial center, with its only large-scale ironworks, was barely a hundred miles south of Washington. Virginia, the South's most important state, was about to become the battleground of the war. If the Confederacy committed itself wholly to her defense, the other border states should be confident that if they seceded, they would be protected, too.

In early May, Confederate Secretary of War Leroy Pope Walker sent D. G. Duncan from Montgomery to report on conditions in Richmond. Duncan found Letcher going steadily about preparations for war but balking at demands from Confederate officials; though Virginia had just sent five delegates to the provisional Confederate Congress, it had had no role in forming the executive branch. Lee's effort to organize arriving Confederate regiments and Virginia soldiers, troops with wildly varied weapons, uniforms, and levels of training, seemed at a peak of confusion. Unionists were still dominant in isolated northwest Virginia, which was closer to Pennsylvania and Ohio than to Richmond.

Duncan and other Davis informants apparently talked only with red-hots still resentful of Governor Letcher and impatient with Lee. Duncan telegraphed to Montgomery: "Intelligent and distinguished men believe Virginia on the very brink of being carried back; and say no man but President Davis can save her. The people will rally around him; they universally call for his presence."[42]

In truth, there was no remote chance of Virginia's reversing course. But if Davis came it might light a fire under the calm, deliberate Letcher. And with Davis's coming the rest of the Confederate government would seem superfluous and out of touch if it stayed so far from its president and the war. Furthermore, some Southern congressmen wanted a chance to reap military glory in their spare time, by doing battle with the Yankees between quorum calls. As Howell Cobb of Georgia told an Atlanta crowd, "We wanted to be near our brave boys, so that when we threw off the badge of Legislature, we might take up arms and share with them the fortunes of war."[43]

On May 20, the Confederate Congress voted to move the government to Richmond. The next day it adjourned, to reconvene there on July 20. With that, Virginia's capital had become the very symbol of the Confederacy, and the ultimate prize in a bloody war.

Davis might have taken the next train north from Alabama, but he waited until his cabinet officers and their retinue were ready for an orderly departure. In Richmond, anticipation mounted as agents sought quarters for another layer of officialdom, and a home for the man of the hour. On May 23, polling places buzzed with excitement over Davis's coming as roughly half of Richmond's adult white male citizens cast their ballots in Virginia's secession referendum.

Considering what had already happened, that vote was barely an afterthought. Balloting was not secret but viva voce, so the margin in favor of secession was overwhelming; in Richmond, though many still had reservations about what was happening, the recorded count was 3,632 to 4.[44] The incorrigible John Minor Botts, who did not dare to vote, called the whole thing "a contemptible farce." He argued that although secession had now been ratified, joining the Confederacy had not been. He was unheard against the raging wind. The South had counted Virginia within the Confederacy a month earlier, and the North considered the state's decision irrevocable as soon as the referendum was over.

The morning after the vote, Union General in Chief Winfield Scott sent troops from Washington across the Potomac to invade his native Virginia.

CHAPTER FOUR

WE SHALL SMITE THE SMITER

*A*long the tracks from Montgomery, crowds cheered Jefferson Davis northward as if he were going to drive away the Yankees with his own sword. At Atlanta and Augusta in Georgia, and Wilmington and Goldsboro in North Carolina, he gave in to their pleas for a speech and pledged that the invaders would meet a terrible fate. He kept asking for situation reports, sending telegrams to Lee, "What news today?" But when at last he reached the James River, there was no suggestion of war in his first view of the new citadel of the Confederacy.[1]

On the morning of May 29, the presidential train eased through the suburb of Manchester, into the railroad cut in the south bank of the river. From there Davis could see across to the Capitol inspired by the great democrat for whom he was named. It was not the city's tallest building, and a foreign visitor thought that while it "looks noble in the distant view, [it] is mean and paltry upon near approach."[2] But on its hilltop, its columns recalled the Parthenon on the Acropolis, signifying ancestry and authority. It stood for the colonial and Revolutionary tradition that pervaded the city and state where this outsider was coming to take power.

From the high, spindly railroad trestle above the rapids of the James, Davis saw the river curve back southward to left and right of the track. He looked down on the treetops of Belle Isle and Brown's Island, then on the smokestacks of the busy Tredegar. Approaching the depot below the city's ship basin, his special train slowed. Only then did the president of the Confederacy realize that his new capital was as eager to greet him as backwoods whistle-stops along the way had been.[3]

Richmond had expected Davis on each train for the past two days. His well-wishers in Georgia and the Carolinas had dragged out his journey so long that he was on the edge of exhaustion. Now, at 7:25 in the morning, word passed that at last he was crossing from Manchester, and cannon boomed a fifteen-gun salute to signal his arrival.

Davis stepped erect from the train as civilians and soldiers pressed around him and his entourage of close friends: Colonel Louis Trezevant Wigfall of Texas, a hero of Fort Sumter; Colonel Lucius B. Northrop of South Carolina, the Confederate commissary general, and Lieutenant Colonel Joseph R. Davis of Mississippi, the president's nephew and aide. Bands serenaded the president aboard an open carriage behind four splendid bay horses. Governor Letcher joined him with Mayor Mayo, who had met the train at Petersburg. Thomas W. Hoeninger, manager of the Spotswood Hotel, was there to escort Davis to his temporary home.

Uphill through the crowd, the four blocks to the Spotswood at Eighth and Main streets seemed much farther. Women lined the way, waving handkerchiefs and tossing flowers. Brightened by their cheers, Davis forced down his weariness and offered the smiles and handshakes of a practiced politician.

Five days short of his fifty-fourth birthday, he had been congressman, gubernatorial candidate, secretary of war and twice U.S. senator, as well as soldier and planter. By level and variety of experience, seemingly by every measure except temperament, he was far better qualified for his office than the new president in Washington. But Davis was never the ebullient politician who thrives on street campaigning. His pale everyday face spoke more truthfully than that morning's outgoing gestures: eagle eyes and nose, high cheekbones, sunken cheeks, firm thin mouth, neat chin whiskers—every angle sharp, projecting pride and certainty.

Only close up could those cheering see that his left eye was filmed over, nearly blinded by a herpes condition that recurred in times of stress. He was often plagued by attacks of malaria, dyspepsia, and rheumatism. The sternness of his portraits reflected both his character and his health. Always dignified, almost always courteous, on public occasions he could also be personable and talkative, even as he drove himself near collapse.

Outside the Spotswood, the crowd clamored for a speech. Davis, at a flag-draped window, pleaded fatigue. This is not the time for talk but for action, he said, then talked on for ten minutes. Virginia's secession reminded him that the Old Dominion was the cradle that had rocked Washington, Jefferson, Madison, Monroe, and a galaxy of other leaders. "We inherited a beautiful model government from these great statesmen and patriots," he said, "but it has been perverted by a faction whose purpose it is to deprive us of the constitutional rights bequeathed us by the fathers. . . ."

When Davis turned inside for breakfast, the crowd in the street below shouted for Wigfall, who had quit the U.S. Senate in April. Now everyone knew his name: As aide to Beauregard, he had rowed out to Fort Sumter to prevail on the Yankees there to show the white flag of surrender. Only too willing to speak, Wigfall said he was glad at last to address Virginians as fellow citizens, as he had been unable to do when passing through a few weeks earlier. "Lincoln was your president then," he said. "Davis is your president now"—and unlike Lincoln en route to Washington, "your President has not come secretly and disguised in a military cloak and Scotch cap. He is not a man of disguises, but bold, brave and open."

The Northern press, said Wigfall, had "slandered the men of the Cotton States by asserting that they only desired to drag the border States out of the Union, so that the brunt of the war might fall on them, and the Cotton States might escape. Do not the legions of brave men now here, and on their way from the far South to fight on Virginia soil, give the lie to these slanders?"

The crowd roared yes. Then those with claims or pretensions on Davis's time pushed inside. There, after very little rest, the president spent the afternoon shaking hands, trying not to make promises of jobs and generals' stars. At 5:30 he rode out to the fairgrounds to inspect the troop training center that awaited still more volunteers. Soldiers from all over the South hurrahed as he told them they were "the last best hope of liberty." His long first day in the new capital ended with the announcement that on the morrow, he would receive well-wishers formally at Governor Letcher's mansion—ladies from 11:00 to 12:00, gentlemen from noon to 1:30.[4]

For one girl in her teens, that reception made May 30 "one of the most memorable days of my life." After being presented to the president, she decided that he was "a very nice man, not tall, about middle-size, and about the lower part of his face he is something like Governor Wise . . . he is turning gray; we had all read of him as being a formal stiff man but he does not seem so at all. I think there is a great deal of grace and suavity in his manners. . . ."[5]

* * *

Varina Howell Davis arrived in Richmond three days after her husband, accompanied by their three children and ten weeks pregnant with another. On the same train came an assortment of Confederate officials and the president's horse, whose military saddle had a compass set in its pommel. When word of that got around, patriots felt sure that when Davis rode to battle, he would always point north toward the enemy.

Mrs. Davis's arrival set off yet another celebration, with street crowds and flowers along the way. One girl threw a bouquet that fell short; Richmonders watching oohed with pleasure when the president halted the carriage lined with yellow satin, ordered a servant to pick up the flowers, and presented them to his lady.[6]

In time the Spotswood Hotel would be "as thoroughly identified with Rebellion as the inn at Bethlehem with the gospel." It was to wartime Richmond what Willard's famous hotel was to Washington—"a miniature world," the place where politicians, generals, profiteers, spies, and the gentry communed amid gossip and bourbon. "In this wild confusion," wrote a South Carolina guest, "everything likely and unlikely is told you—and then everything is as flatly contradicted." The Davises were assigned Rooms 121 and 122, the best in the house, while Room 83 was decorated with Confederate colors as the president's parlor.

The hotel was their home while the city prepared a stately residence at Twelfth and Clay streets. Davis walked three short blocks each day to his office in the former U.S. Custom House, on Bank Street facing Capitol Square. He and his family ate at their own table in the hotel dining room. During the evenings Varina rustled through the gas-lit public rooms, dropping a quiet word to those with whom Davis would like a private talk upstairs.[7]

As carpenters subdivided space in downtown buildings, making little offices out of big ones, arriving Confederate bureaucrats wedged themselves into whatever corner they could commandeer. They were, in fact, a fourth layer of government, spreading atop city and state officials while the Virginia secession convention also continued to meet for months after the fundamental question was decided. Richmonders waited with curiosity on Davis's cabinet ministers, the court of the new sovereign.

The secretary of state was Robert Toombs, a burly, blustery Georgia planter whose conviviality limited his diplomacy. Secretary of War Leroy Pope Walker of Alabama, a hot secessionist, had no military training, but neither did some of those clamoring to be generals. Navy Secretary Stephen R. Mallory of Florida, a Trinidad-born former chairman of the U.S. Senate committee on naval affairs, was one of the two cabinet members who would stay in the same office throughout the war; the other was Postmaster General John H. Reagan, a rugged Texan who had been on the postal committee of the House. At Treasury was a German native, the devout Christopher G. Memminger, a reluctant but fully persuaded South Carolina secessionist. And as attorney general from Louisiana came Judah Philip Benjamin, born in the British West Indies, as smart and diplomatic and loyal to Davis as any man in the Confederacy.

Not one of them was a Virginian, because when the Confederate government was formed at Montgomery, Virginia was still in the Union. Indeed, despite the fanfare surrounding the transfer of government, many Richmonders still resented what the secessionists had forced upon their Old Dominion, and eyed the newcomers with more than simple curiosity. The flood of Deep South job-seekers and profiteers, to be followed by dispossessed refugees and battle casualties, would soon overwhelm the city and submerge its conservatism. But that hardening of attitude was just beginning; now there was a "vague, lingering suspicion," as much social as political, about joining the Confederacy, which meant bringing in all these outsiders. Nevertheless, since the government was the city's invited guest, it had to be received politely.

The memoirist T. Cooper DeLeon, a broad-minded South Carolinian recently from Washington, thought Richmond society had "a sort of brotherly-love tone that struck a stranger, at first, as very curious." Its social circle "had been for years a constant quantity, and everybody in it had known everybody else since childhood." So, as the excitement of arrival wore off, this circle inspected the newcomers, including the president and his wife, as if considering them for membership in an exclusive club. Mrs. Davis might be the First Lady of the Confederacy, but F.F.V.'s—the First Families of Virginia—had their own standards.[8]

Sallie Brock Putnam, applying these standards, assessed the thirty-five-year-old Varina as handsome but not beautiful. At a glance, one would never think to couple the first lady with her taut, angular husband. Her skin was slightly olive, her eyes dark and often brooding, her lips full and curved. She had lost her girlish slimness, and one admirer thought that gave her a "noble mien and bearing." Among her Richmond neighbors, her mother's family roots in Virginia did not fully offset the fact that her paternal grandfather had been a Northerner, a post-Revolutionary governor of New Jersey.

Varina was smart, strong-willed, and experienced; brought up and mainly educated at the Howell plantation, "The Briers," near Natchez, she had become a conspicuous hostess in Washington. In time all her

skills would be tested in defending her husband against increasingly bitter political criticism, and herself against the microscopic scrutiny of social Richmond.[9]

Mrs. Davis was as subtle as a fine needle in recalling how the ladies of
Richmond greeted her. On first introduction, she said, "I was impressed
by the simplicity of their manners, their beauty, and the absence of the
gloze acquired by association in the merely 'fashionable society.'" They
ran their households, showed little interest in small talk, and "were full
of enthusiasm for their own people."

Toward strangers, however, they showed "a certain offishness . . . they
seemed to feel that an inundation of people perhaps of doubtful standards, and, at best, of different methods, had poured over the city, and
they reserved their judgment and confidence, while they proffered a
large hospitality." They had the English manner toward strangers, "no
matter how well introduced—a wary welcome." Where she had grown
up, Varina said, "frontier hospitality" was necessary. But "in Virginia,
where the distances were not so great, and the candidates for entertainment were more numerous, it was of necessity more restricted."[10]

But most of the dainty advances and rebuffs so carefully calibrated lay
ahead. Outwardly, in those first days, enthusiasm seemed contagious,
even among the city's blacks, who did not yet fully realize that their fate
was at issue. Several hundred of them, sent to dig defensive lines on the
surrounding hills, returned in the evening carrying flags, brandish-
ing tools and tree branches like muskets, and singing "Dixie" as they
marched up Main Street. When the new president rode out to oversee
their work on Marion Hill, the surprised ditchdiggers there gave him "a
hearty three times three."

Ladies' sewing circles, having done what seemed enough Confederate
banners, turned to making uniforms and tents in homes and churches.
At the end of May, when the Fairfield Jockey Club ended its spring
meet with a mule race, very few devotees were on hand. By then the
city's premier entertainment was the trainloads of soldiers arriving from
every region of Virginia and every state of the South.[11]

Five railroads served Richmond—and ended there, because each had
its separate depot, no two of them connecting within the city. From
north came the Richmond, Fredericksburg & Potomac. From west
came the Virginia Central, which connected with the Orange &
Alexandria, reaching the Potomac opposite Washington. From east
came the Richmond & York River. Stretching southwest was the Richmond & Danville, which stopped at the Dan River because North Carolina's provincial governor would not approve a link across the state line.
The Richmond & Petersburg linked the capital to the port of Norfolk,

the West, and the Deep South. Without direct connections in Richmond, every crate and every passenger had to be unloaded there, even if destined onward. Only over hot protests from hotels, hack drivers, and draymen did the City Council soon permit temporary tracks to be laid through the streets. But in the spring of 1861, everybody wanted off at Richmond, anyhow.

On their way, troops seemed "as jubilant as if they were going to a frolic, instead of a fight."[12] They knew not what to expect in Richmond but were full of the confidence of ignorance. They sang jaunty songs rather than the sentimental favorites that would touch them later in the war. They had already adopted "Dixie" as their own, and often gave it words to fit their new world. The Bienville Rifles, coming on from Louisiana, sang it this way:

> From home and friends we all must go,
> To meet a strong but dastard foe.
>   Look away, look away, look away to Richmond town.
> And ere again those friends we see
> We vow to die or all be free;
>   Look away, look away. . . .
> We'll meet old Abe with armies brave,
> And whip the lying scoundrel knave.
>   Look away, look away. . . .
> As he pleads for terms and whiskey,
> We'll give him hell to the tune of Dixie.
>   Look away, look away, look away to Richmond town.[13]

Such high-spirited soldiers drew hundreds of citizens out from the city to the fast-growing camps each late afternoon to watch them parade, to admire their precisely aligned white tents and bold uniforms, then to socialize when drills were over. Regimental camps like that of the First South Carolina "had more the air of a picnic than of a bivouac." Romantic girls picked their favorite companies and formed crushes on young men they had never met. "8 hundred and fifty South Carolinians came yesterday, with 400 Tennessians, and the Washington Artillery of New Orleans," wrote one such admirer. "I had rather go to the S.C. camp than any where else. I feel just like some of my old friends had come back since they arrived. Oh! I do love S. Carolina so dearly almost as much as dear Old Virginia; we are *all* so proud of Virginia now."[14]

Those watching the arriving regiments were sure they could tell one state's marchers from another by their varieties of manhood, not just their flags and uniforms: "Here the long-haired Texan, sitting his horse like a centaur. . . . The dirty gray and tarnished silver of the muddycomplexioned Carolinian; the dingy butternut of the lank, muscular Georgian. . . . Alabamians . . . nearly all in blue of a cleaner hue and neater cut; while the Louisiana troops were, as a general thing, better equipped and more regularly uniformed than any others in the motley throng."[15]

Troops who brought arms came with an ordnance officer's nightmare of rifles, pistols, muskets, and duck guns, on horses large and small, on saddles to fit every whim, and all of them seemed to have bowie knives. The most spectacular sartorially were also the most uncontrollable after hours: the Louisiana Zouaves, with billowing red trousers, embroidered blue jackets, and tasseled Turkish fezzes, made hospitable Richmond think twice about its open doors. A hodgepodge of Mississippi River boatmen and recent convicts, they roamed the city, making off with chickens and garden vegetables as defiantly as they walked into saloons, drank what they wanted, and walked out telling the proprietor to charge it to the government.[16]

Richmonders were more comfortable with the Washington Artillery, a New Orleans battalion of bluebloods like the soldiers in the city's own time-honored F Company, the Howitzers, and the Light Infantry Blues. "High privates" in such companies took pride in refusing commissions, setting an example of unselfishness meant to encourage the lower classes to volunteer for the ranks. They did not miss out thereby on the social whirl; indeed, they were admired for their sacrifice. Many of them did later become officers, and many, whatever their rank, did not return from the war.

One gentleman private was George Cary Eggleston, born in Indiana, who at seventeen had inherited a plantation in Virginia's Amelia County. Charmed by Old Dominion gentryhood, he saw it with greater detachment than many who had been born directly into it. He admitted that upon enlistment, his ideas of soldiering had mostly been gathered from the romances of the South's favorite novelist in antebellum days, Sir Walter Scott.* As volunteers, Eggleston and his friends felt that they could follow the rules they liked and ignore others. Their battalion drill "closely resembled that of the music at Mr. Bob Sawyer's party, where each guest sang the chorus to the tune he knew best." They shrugged at military rank, but they recognized social rank from the beginning.

"The line of demarkation between gentry and common people is not

---

*Only half-jokingly, Mark Twain wrote in *Life on the Mississippi* that Scott had set the South "in love with dreams and phantoms . . . with the sillinesses and emptinesses, sham grandeurs, sham gauds, and sham chivalries of a brainless and worthless long-vanished society. He did measureless harm. . . . [He] had so large a hand in making Southern character, as it existed before the war, that he is in a great measure responsible for the war."

more sharply drawn anywhere than in Virginia," Eggleston wrote. "To come of a good family is a patent of nobility, and there is no other way whatever by which any man or any woman can find a passage into the charmed circle of Virginia's peerage." He cited a case in which a young private asserted his social standing to demand and get an apology from a lieutenant who had assigned him double duty, and occasions when privates declined dinner invitations "from officers who had presumed upon their shoulder-straps in asking the company of their social superiors." While training for the First Virginia Cavalry, Eggleston recalled, some privates rented nearby homes, brought their families and servants, excused themselves from early morning roll calls, and had lackeys do their menial assignments while they sat by on rail fences, watching.[17]

Out of this motley of lords and knaves and innocent, willing country boys, in time there would emerge a coherent army. But not yet.

*   *   *

On the night Varina Davis arrived, crowds outside the Spotswood had serenaded her and called on her husband yet again to speak. He told them that Virginia was ordained to be "the theatre of a great central camp, from which will pour forth thousands of brave hearts to roll back the tide of this despotism. . . ." The Confederacy began "under many embarrassments," the president said, because the enemy's government had the fruits of seventy years of Federal taxation. Thus, "we must at first move cautiously," and then "when the time and occasion serve, we shall smite the smiter with manly arms, as did our fathers before us and as becomes their sons."

The crowd cheered, and begged to hear something about Buena Vista. There, fourteen years earlier, Davis as colonel of the Mississippi Rifles had won fame and been seriously wounded. "Well, my friends," he declared, "we shall make the battle fields of Virginia another Buena Vista, and drench them with blood more precious than that shed there. We will make a history for ourselves."

With that accurate prediction, he stood aside while Mississippi's Lucius Quintus Cincinnatus Lamar and Virginia's Henry Wise turned up the rhetorical heat. Wise, who had never been a soldier, exhorted the crowd as if he had not forgotten his political ambitions: "Though your pathway be through fire, or through a red river of blood, turn not aside. . . . Your true-blooded Yankee will never stand still in the presence of cold steel. Let your aim, therefore, be to get into close quarters, and with a few decided, vigorous movements, always pushing forward, never back, my word for it, the soil of Virginia will be swept of the Vandals who are now polluting its atmosphere!"[18]

Three days later, Davis made Wise a brigadier general, to mount an expedition to hold the Kanawha Valley, in the state's western mountains. But the first clash of the war came from the other direction, the historic Peninsula between the James and York rivers.

In early June, Confederate forces were guarding the three major invasion routes into the heart of Virginia. Brigadier General Joseph E. Johnston had taken over from Colonel Jackson at Harpers Ferry, at the mouth of the Shenandoah Valley. Brigadier General Pierre G. T. Beauregard, cheered in Richmond as the victor at Fort Sumter, was above Manassas, astride the rail route from Washington to the Confederate capital. And Colonel John Bankhead Magruder was in charge on the Peninsula, watching Federal troops who still held Fortress Monroe, less than seventy-five miles from Richmond.

The presence of a single Yankee anywhere on Old Dominion soil was more than John Moncure Daniel and his colleagues at the *Examiner* could tolerate. Still contemptuous of Letcher and others who had resisted secession, Daniel wrote that there was "unutterable disgust and loathing for the wretched clique who have paralyzed the power and degraded the spirit of Virginia. . . . Up to this point, not one blow has been struck to teach the invader that the conquest of Virginia is not a holiday excursion." But now that Davis had arrived, "the reins are in other hands, and in future if we are forced to retreat, it will be when we are beaten, and not when we are afraid to fight."[19]

A week after this Daniel diatribe, Union Major General Benjamin F. Butler sent troops probing up the Peninsula from Fortress Monroe. On June 10, about 4,400 of them struck a Confederate outpost at Big Bethel, a church just above the town of Hampton. In a sharp skirmish, Magruder's 1,400 infantrymen plus the Richmond Howitzers taught the Federals that the war was not a holiday excursion, throwing them back with seventy-six casualties. It was not much of a battle, but it was the first of the war, so Richmond made the most of it.*

Store windows flaunted captured banners. When the first prisoners were brought to Richmond, a crowd jostled around the Custom House, where they were held temporarily. When the captives were sent to the city jail, white and black men and boys ran alongside, getting a good look at "live Yankees" as the prisoners were turned away from the over-full jail, sent back to the Custom House, then on to the Henrico County

---

*On June 3, Union Major General George B. McClellan had surprised a Confederate force in bivouac at Philippi, in western Virginia, and chased it away into the night. But "the Philippi Races" hardly qualified as a battle.

jail. Citizens who believed heaven would protect the Southern cause saw Big Bethel as clear confirmation.[20]

In private, some of the orators who waved the flag so bravely in public were more realistic, trying to squelch the popular idea that any Rebel soldier could lick a dozen Yankees. Even Davis did so, chatting at the Spotswood with Mary Boykin Chesnut, with whom he and Varina had become friends in Washington. Mary, the daughter of Stephen Decatur Miller, a former South Carolina governor and U.S. senator, was 38 that spring. She had come to Richmond to join her husband, James Chesnut, Jr., a planter who had resigned his seat in the U.S. Senate and become a Confederate congressman. Mrs. Chesnut, who often called on morphine to see her through headaches and depression, would become one of the Confederacy's most acute and sophisticated memoirists.[21]

Ex-colonel Davis assured her that Southern troops would do all that "dash and red-hot patriotism" could do, but his tone was more sober than sanguine. He predicted a long war, with "many a bitter experience." Only fools, he said, doubted that Northerners would fight with courage.[22] But the calm counsel of experienced soldiers could not discourage half-trained troops in the ranks, or the women who flattered them as heroes before they had heard a shot. After Big Bethel the youngsters were sure that they would win—fast. They wanted to rush into battle, to get in their licks before the whole thing was over.

Long wars often start that way.

CHAPTER FIVE

WE HAVE BROKEN THE
SPIRIT OF THE NORTH

S creamersville was a scraggly neighborhood that allegedly got its
name from the pitch of its inhabitants' voices, a place "Where
hungry dogs from hungry children steal / And pigs and chickens
quarrel for a meal."[1]

When fortune dumped thousands of soldiers at nearby Camp Lee,
some Screamersvillians, like other Richmonders in Bacon's Quarter,
Shed Town, Butcher Town, Darby Town, Scuffle Town, and Penitentiary Bottom, saw better ways to get along than squabbling over bones.
George Gormly, for example, kept a little grocery that for a while did a
big business. He had a system: When neighboring troops tossed a rock
into the road it signaled that they were thirsty, and he promptly smuggled to them whatever spirits they wanted. Afterward, full of fight, the
soldiers would go rumbling into town to stir up an evening's excitement
or nap on the sidewalks, or both.[2]

General Lee himself complained to Mayor Mayo, who shut Gormly
down. But Gormly's was just one of between fifty and a hundred con-
fectioneries about Richmond "where a few pounds of fly-specked mint
stick, a dozen or so indigestible horse-cakes, and a considerable show of
superannuated peanuts [were] used as a blind for the masked battery of
a bar room located in a back apartment."[3] Whenever the mayor shut
one, another popped open, because the demand was insatiable.

While a few hundred Confederate soldiers were fighting at Bethel,
many thousands were still training in and around Richmond—and after
the manual of arms, close-order drill, and camp inspections, some still

had youthful vigor to spare. With or without official permission, they sought outlets in the city.

In ribald revelry as in chicken-stealing and saloon brawling, Louisiana troops showed the way. A detachment of the McCulloch Rangers of New Orleans, in the nominal charge of a certain Lieutenant Jones, was ushered into Mayor's Court after being entertained at the house of Clara Coleman. There, the *Examiner* reported, the soldiers "blew out the parlor and passage lights, broke up the furniture, scattered the shrieking women like New York Zouaves before the bristling bayonets of North Carolina infantry, and to crown their unfortunate exploits, committed, it is alleged, an outrage upon the person of a 'phrail phair one,' named Eliza Liggon."

From Miss Coleman's they moved on to the establishment of Lizzie Hubbard, who would not let them in. "Nothing daunted, they climbed in by a front window, and were reenacting the same dangerous play, when the cries of 'murder,' 'help' &c attracted a sufficient number of the police to eject them from the house." As they left, the Rangers let fly a few bullets and brickbats at the police, and headed for A. J. Ford's bar. Eventually Governor Letcher was notified and sent a detail from the State Guard, but by then the troops had gone into bivouac.

In court, Lieutenant Jones said he had been trying all along to march his soldiers away. But Miss Coleman denied his plea of innocence by swearing that "in an interview which he sought with her on Sunday, he had knowledge of, and an instrumentality in, the outrage perpetrated upon a little 'unfortunate' in her house." Because police had a hard time pinning specific offenses on specific soldiers, only three of Jones's men were held for rape. Miss Hubbard was charged with operating a disorderly house and ordered to move out of the neighborhood. Ford was charged with violating the new ordinance against operating a saloon after 10:00 p.m., despite his plea that the soldiers had forced him to stay open.

The adventures of Jones's men were exceptional only because a full squad was involved, and because they tangled with the wrong women. A few days later, Miss Hubbard was accused of shooting a soldier, at which the soldier's comrades returned and threatened to tear her house down. A guard was posted for her protection. About the same time, a member of the Ouachita Blues of Louisiana was arrested for "attempting an outrage" upon a woman tending store while her husband was away in the army. At Mary Gleason's house, a lusty Irishman was picked up for assault, drunkenness, and fighting, and charged later with "injuring a cell of the cage in which he was confined."[4]

Day after day, the mayor dealt with cases of drunkenness, prostitution, rape, and assault, and the newspapers treated them with attempted humor. The light approach was standard as long as the defendants and victims were madams like Coleman and Hubbard, "phrail phair ones" like Eliza Liggon, or Irish by name or brogue.

Mayor Mayo, a vision of Dickensian dignity in his high wing collars, with wavy gray hair draped from his bald dome, had presided over the city's police court for eight years. At 65, "Old Joe" had the air of a man who had seen all since turning from medical school to law back when James Madison was president. In Richmond, he had served as commonwealth's attorney for ten years, then city councilman and state legislator before his election as mayor.

By wartime, Mayo was tolerant of the madams and their girls as long as they did business quietly. In those cases, he usually accompanied guilty verdicts with trivial fines and gentle scolding. He knew his capital, which had hosted commercial and political travelers and winked at brothels ever since it became a city. Now, as the industry boomed in service to soldiers and free-spending speculators, polite Richmond looked the other way, toward the suburban training camps where order prevailed. Among the nice girls who fluttered their lashes at well-behaved boys there, the mildest flirtatious conversation, well short of holding hands, was described as "making love."

Soldiers who had come hundreds of miles to defend Virginia were disappointed when some Richmonders treated them less like saviors than like sheep to be shorn. A few troops, of a bibulous evening, reacted like those who had disturbed the peace of Madams Coleman and Hubbard. Others who had been clipped in broad daylight were more puzzled and hurt than raging.

Edward Budget, not long on the scene with South Carolina's Hampton Legion, vented this feeling in a handwritten camp newspaper he called the *Family Budget*. So far, he admitted, he and his friends had met few of "the better classes," but they had seen enough of shopkeepers to call them "knaves and consummate swindlers." As Exhibit A he cited a comrade who had stopped in a restaurant for a small plate of batter cakes, a cup of coffee, and two mint juleps, for which he had been charged $1.25. In Charleston, Budget said, that would have cost him barely 30 cents: "This I consider a swindle. . . . his military coat marked him out to be fleeced and fleeced he was."

Such treatment provoked from him the ultimate insult: "The people you meet on the street are more like Yankees in their names than like Southerners. There is a rudeness and flippancy in their manner that is very revolting to a South Carolinian." Not only that, but even "the negroes are impudent and disobliging." Altogether, Budget said, "I am inclined to dislike the people of Richmond. It strikes me that there is too much of the Yankee element in their midst. The city itself I admire more than any I have ever seen but the people less."*⁵

Obviously Richmonders of the "better classes" would have been dismayed to hear such complaints. They were as concerned over troop morale as the generals and the president himself.

Jefferson Davis, a graceful rider, usually with a cigar clamped between his teeth, trotted his sleek gray horse out to the camps almost every evening. He liked not only to ride but to talk about horses; James Chesnut, the diarist Mary Chesnut's husband, said Davis knew more about them than any man he had ever met. Lee sometimes accompanied the president on his rides, along with the ever-present Davis retinue of aides and politicians. Here Davis promised a newly arrived Tennessee outfit that it would soon have weapons; there he surprised the Palmetto Regiment at parade and addressed it "in eloquent and felicitous language." The first lady also made conspicuous outings to the "champ-de-Mars," in a stylish open carriage with friends of her close circle.⁶

On those evening rides Davis often crossed paths with a lean, intense preacher named Moses Drury Hoge. Hoge, who would serve as pastor of Richmond's Second Presbyterian Church for more than fifty years, was one of many Richmond clergymen who did their best to warn soldiers away from temptation during their first time far from home. He had opposed secession, but once the issue was decided he was as militant as any prewar fire-eater. Without being asked, he began devoting all his spare time to the incoming troops. Speaking at Camp Lee every Sunday afternoon and at least twice during the week, Hoge also set up a religious reading room in a big tent there. Eventually he sermonized to more than 100,000 men.

"It was almost like preaching to an army from the wayside as they marched past," Hoge's son recalled. "The men before him one Sunday would by the next be on the march or in the field. . . . There was no time to lay foundations, or to prepare the ground for seed-sowing. The truth must be like their own shots—quick, vivid, unerring." That was Hoge's style, and in time his dedication to the Bible and the troops would take him on adventures far beyond the training camps.⁷

The Baptist minister A. E. Dickinson not only preached to the troops

---

*Budget's comments may also have reflected the traditional competition in snobbery between Virginia, where the Tidewater aristocracy was considered the apex of society, and South Carolina, where Charlestonians and Low Country planters ranked themselves as the crème de la crème. For generations, *North* Carolinians have described their state as "a vale of humility between two mountains of conceit." It was an old-family Charlestonian who explained to the author why he had not inquired of his roots: "Never ask a man if he's from Virginia; if he is, he'll tell you, and if he's not, you don't want to embarrass him."

but put nearly a hundred colporteurs to work distributing tracts like "The Evils of Gaming," "We Pray for You at Home," and "A Mother's Parting Words to Her Soldier Boy." They circulated at least a quarter million copies of this last title, a tear-jerking favorite written by the Reverend Jeremiah B. Jeter of Grace Street Baptist Church.[8]

*   *   *

After the *Pawnee* panic and the fight at Bethel, defensive planners' earliest priority was to block the river routes inland from the Chesapeake. Guns taken from the Gosport naval base opposite Norfolk were positioned at forts along the James, York, Rappahannock, and Potomac rivers. And at 1105 East Clay Street in Richmond, a ruddy, potbellied 55-year-old officer with a game leg experimented with ways to apply modern science to river defenses.

He was Matthew Fontaine Maury, the "Pathfinder of the Seas," oceanographer, astronomer, explorer, and controversialist, whose charting of winds and currents had helped cut six weeks off the voyage from New York around the Horn to San Francisco. In 1855 he had burnished his international reputation by publishing the first textbook of modern oceanography; his expertise had guided Cyrus Field in laying the first transatlantic cable. Now, after resigning from the U.S. Navy, he was reduced for the moment to puttering in a bathtub.

When war broke, the Confederacy had no organized navy. Though 126 officers and 111 midshipmen of the U.S. Navy defected to the South, not one captain at sea tried to run his vessel into a Confederate port. Only ten Union ships were taken in the seven original Confederate states, and a few more in Virginia waters. Secretary of the Navy Mallory realized that the South, starting with so few ships and without a factory capable of producing marine engines, needed unorthodox weapons and tactics to compete with the Federals at sea. One of its most unorthodox assets was the inventive Maury.

Commissioned a commander, Maury focused on perfecting what were then called "torpedoes," actually naval mines, to supplement shore batteries. His home was at Fredericksburg, near the Spotsylvania County Wilderness where he was born. But now he was staying at his cousin's Richmond townhouse, less than a block from the mansion being redone for Jefferson Davis. Amid a clutter of pipes and wires, with batteries borrowed from Richmond Medical College, he ran bathtub experiments on ways to explode these torpedoes against Union ships. When he was ready to graduate from the tub, he ordered barrels for gunpowder made watertight with tar, and later iron kegs custom-built by the Tredegar and by Talbott Brothers' works.

With foundry, machine shop, and the only sizable rolling mill in the South, the Tredegar was the new nation's most valued industrial plant, indispensable to both army and navy. In the next four years its works beside the James River & Kanawha Canal would produce more than 1,600 siege guns and field pieces, hundreds of thousands of artillery shells, armor for ironclad gunboats, and machinery to make other weapons. Its heterogeneous work force included skilled local, British, and European mechanics, free blacks and slaves, some hired and some owned by the company. Just east of the Tredegar, the long brick Virginia State Armory became the Confederate States Armory. Using machinery salvaged from the shops at Harpers Ferry, it would turn out more than 350,000 small arms and some 72 million rounds of ammunition. No other city in the Confederacy would come close to matching the arms output of these few acres on the Richmond waterfront.

In mid-June, Maury invited Mallory, who was skeptical of his experiments, to accompany Governor Letcher and assorted political and naval officials to witness the first full-scale demonstration of his naval torpedo in the James River. This version consisted of two explosive kegs, weighted to sink just below the surface, with sensitive triggers linked by a long line. When the apparatus drifted downstream the line was supposed to catch the enemy vessel's anchor chain or bow, swinging the kegs against the vessel, where the pressure of the current would trip the triggers.

With the official crowd watching from the steamship wharf at Rocketts, Maury and his son Richard set the device adrift. It caught but did not explode—until young Maury gave the line a tug, at which the torpedo burst and splashed stunned fish over the inventor and his crew. The officials, including Mallory, applauded.

Soon afterward, with muffled oars in the night, Maury himself set his first working torpedo adrift against Federal ships off Fortress Monroe. It failed; the Yankees recovered it, studied it, and soon began arranging small boats and nets to protect their ships against drifting mines. Still, Maury kept trying. Soon he had sown key stretches of the James with contact mines. Later he and his successors put out more advanced versions set off from shore by hard-to-get electric line, some using insulated wire from an underwater Union telegraph link blown ashore by a Chesapeake storm.[*9]

*   *   *

*After the war, U.S. Secretary of the Navy Gideon Welles said that his side had lost more vessels to torpedoes than to all other weapons combined. Yet the deterrent effect of Maury's inventions, helping to keep the Union navy out of Southern rivers, was more important to the Confederacy than all the ships they sank or damaged.[10]

One Sunday in late June, the Sabbath seemed more serene than it had been for weeks—no exciting new rumors, hardly any arrests of off-duty troops. Secretary of the Treasury Memminger had actually proposed that war work be suspended on Sundays, but that idea got nowhere. The calm was only temporary.[11]

Better discipline in the surrounding camps may have helped restrain hell-raising by then. So might the exhortations of Richmond's concerned preachers. But the main reason for the relative calm in streets and saloons was the growing Yankee threat: "the ruffian hordes, gathered from the bar-rooms and gutters of the North, about to be precipitated upon our homes and firesides."[12] The capital's first great wave of incoming Confederate soldiers was through its hasty basic training and off to the front.

General Johnston, fearing that Union forces would cut off his exposed force at Harpers Ferry, had pulled it back up the Shenandoah Valley to Winchester. East of the Blue Ridge, reinforcements rushed from Richmond to General Beauregard's army above Manassas, facing the Federals massing under Brigadier General Irvin McDowell.

North and South, newspapers were remarkably generous in informing the public—and therefore the enemy—about such troop movements. The *Examiner* reported that the Third South Carolina, "1,000 strong, Colonel Williams commanding, left this city late Saturday evening for Manassas Junction. They are a splendid soldierly-looking body of men, and finely officered. As the trains moved off in the moonlight, their loud, long continued and enthusiastic cheering awakened such echoes in Adams Valley as may not shortly be heard again."[13] The next day the paper told how two companies of the Washington Artillery headed the same way, "carrying with them a battery of two large howitzers, two rifled cannon and four twelve-pounders. The remaining half of this crack corps is to follow in a few days."

A little later, Union spies would risk their lives for that kind of specific information—and alongside those reports the newspapers reprinted comparable news about Federal moves, from Northern papers just arrived. The *Examiner* surmised, "The plot is evidently thickening to the Northward."[14]

It was, indeed, and Richmond could hardly wait for the coming explosion. "This summer will be signalized by battles such as America has never yet witnessed. . . . The result will decide the duration of the war," said Daniel's paper—cynical about many men, but stubbornly naïve about what lay ahead: If the South chanced to lose, there would be a long war, "but if the victory is ours, the war is at an end. The immediate consequence will be the occupation of Washington, the flight of the

Lincoln government, and its subsequent resignation, or a revolution in the Northern states. In either of these last cases, peace between the two Confederacies must speedily follow."[15]

Though it was unpatriotic to suggest that victory might be anything but speedy, Richmonders went about adjusting their economic lives to the possibility of a long war. Those who dealt in the old standby of tobacco had no other choice. Daniel von Groening, a city merchant, advised his customers abroad that the Virginia tobacco crop would be lean; with the Union army in every direction, planters could not import guano or expand acreage, and without guano they could not make decent crops on old land. Von Groening was already tied into the clandestine mail service that operated across the armies' lines, suggesting to a Boston firm, "Should you write please send your letters to Messrs. Jacob Heald & Co. of Baltimore. They have an opportunity now and then to forward them."

Responding to a German firm's concerns about tobacco already bought but not shipped, Von Groening said it was "perfectly secure," because "the enemy cannot come here and as regards a negro insurrection you will agree with me that that is out of the question when I tell you that we have a permanent camp here in Richmond of 25,000 troops, 500 men would be ample to keep our negroes in check even if they had a disposition to revolt which they have not."[16]

Now munitions had replaced tobacco as the city's main product, and learning the skills of the new trade could be dangerous. At the state armory a thunderous blast killed a technician named Joe Laidley, who had been working with highly sensitive fulminate of silver. Just before Big Bethel, a freelance chemist named Edward T. Finch was preparing badly needed percussion caps for the army when powder exploded, knocking down a wall of his house next to Clay Street Methodist Church and seriously injuring Finch and a servant.[17]

And all the while civic life proceeded as it had in peaceful decades before all this excitement descended. A slave named James, belonging to Isaac Walker, was sentenced to thirty-nine lashes for "living on terms of improper intimacy" with a white woman named Sarah Hall. For associating with James, Sarah was sent to jail because she could not raise bail. But the *Examiner*, so flippant about women who commercialized sex, was tender toward her. "She is young, and not of unpleasing person," it said, "but misfortune and low association have done their worst to rob her countenance of its graces. She is low and fallen, but we insult not her wretchedness; we only regret we have no institution among us where she, and such as she, could be consigned and taught to appreciate the blessings of a purer and loftier life."[18]

* * *

Insisting that the Declaration of Independence now spoke more clearly for the sovereign South than for the old Union, Richmond looked forward to the Fourth of July in a mood of tense optimism. News was just in about the daring capture of the Union steamer *St. Nicholas* and three other prizes in Chesapeake Bay. They were taken by a band of Confederates led by Colonel Richard Thomas, a Southern Maryland planter who called himself Zarvona; he had boarded at Baltimore masquerading as a French lady.[19]

That special Fourth of July started with an eleven-gun salute, one round for each of the Confederate states, fired by the Thomas Artillery at its camp at the Baptist College. At 10:00 a.m., the Tredegar Battalion, 300 strong, commanded by the ironworks' proprietor, Major Joseph R. Anderson, paraded at Capitol Square. An hour later the State Guard fired another eleven-gun salute at the square. Banks and businesses were closed.

There were fewer drunks on the streets than on earlier Independence Days; perhaps there had been so much drumming and fifing around Richmond that topers did not realize when the day to celebrate had come. But some, inevitably, got into the spirit of the occasion: A young Carolinian galloped his horse through the barroom of the Spotswood, scattering tables and customers right and left. "Intoxicated, of course," said an admiring captain—"but a splendid rider."[20]

News from beyond promptly wiped away any lingering urge to celebrate. In Washington, Lincoln sent a July 4 message to Congress, asking for 400,000 troops and $400 million to prosecute the war. In western Virginia, Federal troops under Major General George B. McClellan trounced Confederates at Rich Mountain, making "the Young Napoleon" a hero across the Union. Northern papers cheered the Federal army on. "Forward to Richmond! Forward to Richmond!" bugled Horace Greeley's New York *Tribune*. "The Rebel Congress must not be allowed to meet there on the 20th of July! By that date the place must be held by the national army!"

The Confederate Congress was due to reconvene on that date, as agreed when it adjourned in Montgomery. Its arrival would put still heavier strain on Richmond's accommodations and hospitality. But Davis, advised of an imminent Union advance, was paying more attention to military than to civilian concerns. The president repeatedly made clear in letters and conversation that he meant to take active part in the coming fight, and others encouraged him. "Civil affairs can be postponed," Johnston wrote.[21]

Lee rode out to inspect fortifications around Richmond; though he predicted that the Yankees would move on Manassas, he could not rule out a swift thrust at the capital from another direction. Assigning Richmond's street-cleaning crews to work on the defenses had not been enough. Lee, alarmed at the slow progress, asked for more laborers and formation of home-defense units to guard against the unexpected.

Four days after getting authority from the City Council, Mayor Mayo began impressing free blacks. After hundreds were rounded up by police and soldiers, he gave them a pep talk, telling them they had a duty to their country just as whites did, and since they could not fight they should work. They would get plenty of food—and, for good performance, something special to drink, too. The blacks had little choice but to respond "with cheer and good-humored acquiescence." They would draw $11 a month, the same as army privates, but that would go nowhere near as far in the booming capital as it did in the military ranks.[22]

By then Davis and Lee knew what to expect from the enemy: On July 10, a young woman had crossed the lines to Beauregard's field headquarters near Manassas and shaken from her long hair a secret message that said Union General McDowell would advance in mid-July. That information confirmed what the Confederates were picking up from Northern newspapers and casual travelers. It was sent by a bold Confederate spy named Rose O'Neal Greenhow, a widow who lived across Lafayette Park from the White House in Washington and hobnobbed with Federal generals and politicians.

Beauregard, after his overly elaborate plan for taking the offensive on three Virginia fronts in sequence was rejected by Davis, asked Greenhow for more specific intelligence. On July 16, she sent another message, saying that McDowell's divisions were on their way toward Manassas via Fairfax Court House and Centreville. Beauregard waited anxiously for Johnston to arrive with reinforcements from the Shenandoah Valley.[23]

In Richmond, "a hushed, feverish suspense—like the sultry stillness before the burst of the storm," hung over all. Then, late on the eighteenth, came news from Beauregard that his troops had won the first skirmish along Bull Run. Richmond rushed doctors, ambulances, and bandages his way.[24]

Davis, immersing himself in the minutiae of every problem, got up from bed, where he had been sent by the strain of long hours dealing with politics, logistics, and impending battle. He wanted to rush to the field, but first he was obliged to deliver a "state of the Confederacy" message to Congress when it convened on Saturday, July 20. As the legislators arrived, a huge Confederate flag flew from a new, fifty-foot flagstaff above the former Custom House, where Davis had his office. It suggested that though they would deliberate in the historic old Capitol, power resided in the executive branch, in its imposing stone building just downhill.

The president hurried through his speech, skimming the surface of what had happened since the capital moved from Montgomery and belaboring Lincoln once again. The next morning Davis took the train north, leaving an aide—R. E. Lee's son, Captain George Washington Custis Lee—in charge of his office.[25]

All that sunny day, Richmond awaited news. In late afternoon Varina Davis rode in a carriage to the funeral of a friend's child. One of the ladies with her noted how excited those on the streets seemed, but Mrs. Davis said that if anything had happened they would have heard about it. Back at the Spotswood, the first lady asked an idler if there was any news. "Yes, ma'am," he said, "they have been fighting at Manassas since six o'clock this morning."

At the hotel, the wives and relatives of soldiers tried to reassure one another in their anxiety. One woman's husband, two sons, brother, and brother-in-law were at Manassas. At the depot the first scuffed returnees told of regiments cut up, medical supplies badly needed—but these turned out to be rear-area stragglers, passing on what they had heard early in the fight. After nightfall the whole cabinet jammed Secretary of War Walker's office, where bulletins were expected. Walker strode up and down, cursing himself for being in Richmond rather than in the field.

The longer the wait, the higher rose speculation of disaster. Attorney General Benjamin detached himself to the Spotswood, where Mrs. Davis and the waiting wives had refused to go to bed. Soon Benjamin was back. Mrs. Davis had just got the first news from her husband, and it said: "Night has closed on a hard-fought field. . . . Our forces have won a glorious victory."[26]

Because that first telegram was signed by the president, rumors flew that he had been out front in the fighting. Deep in the night, Mrs. Davis eased into Mary Chesnut's bedroom and whispered, "A great battle has been fought—Jeff Davis led the center, Joe Johnston the right wing, Beauregard the left. . . ." She named generals and colonels who had reportedly been killed and wounded.

The next morning the first lady felt it her duty to inform the wife of Colonel Francis S. Bartow of Georgia that she was now a widow. She knocked at her door and entered. When Mrs. Bartow saw who it was she started to stand, but "then there was something in Mrs. Davis's pale face that took the life out of her." She stared at Mrs. Davis, who stared back. Mrs. Bartow covered her face.

"Is it bad news for me?"

Mrs. Davis did not speak.

"Is he killed?"

Mrs. Davis did not have to speak; Mrs. Bartow said later that she knew the truth as soon as she saw her face.[27]

It would happen hundreds of thousands of times, and would never be less painful to sudden widows than it was in those first hours after First Manassas.

*   *   *

There were no bonfires, artillery salutes, or parades that Monday morning.

At the Capitol, rumors and speculation bubbled as congressmen waited for details of the battle in an atmosphere of "deep and solemn joy." When they met at noon they heard Davis's messages from the field, where he remained throughout the day, conferring with his victorious generals. At City Hall a citizens meeting dispatched a committee headed by Mayor Mayo to Manassas to see what could be done for casualties. Another committee would organize hospitals and care for the wounded in the city, and a third would raise funds. At the Virginia Central depot, hundreds joined the next of kin waiting in a downpour till after 10:00 p.m. for the train from Manassas, still hoping for word of their soldiers.[28]

The news came slowly, some of it on the Tuesday train with Davis, who spoke to one crowd at the depot, then another at the Spotswood. He told how the Confederates had turned back the Yankees and sent them fleeing toward Washington. Generals Johnston and Beauregard had been in command; General Jackson's brigade had stood like a stone wall at the climax of the fight. When Davis arrived on the field the wounded cheered him, and stragglers rallied to the front.

In fact, the president had gotten there late in the day, when the battle had already swung in the Confederates' favor. In his black suit he rode forward well behind the advancing lines, congratulating the victorious troops and consoling the casualties. But from his speeches and hearsay from the field, stories grew that he had arrived just in time and turned defeat into triumph.[29]

Whoever led it, the victory was enough to inspire new daydreams in the press: "By the work of Sunday," said the *Examiner*, "we have broken the back bone of invasion and utterly broken the spirit of the North.

Henceforward we shall have hectoring, bluster and threat; but we shall never get another such chance at them again on the field."[30]

But a few, not committed to public cheerleading, were afraid that success would be a liability. William Trescot, one of Mrs. Chesnut's wealthy South Carolina friends, predicted that the victory would lull the South into "a fool's paradise of conceit," and the Union troops' shameful flight would "wake every inch of their manhood. It was the very fillip they needed."[31]

Mrs. Chesnut may have taken that to heart, because for the past two days she had watched military funerals, seen warhorses in procession with their empty saddles—"and now it seems we are never out of the sound of the Dead March in *Saul*. It comes and it comes until I feel inclined to close my ears and scream."[32]

For every such ceremonial funeral there were dozens of unmourned dead soldiers being brought to Richmond for burial or for shipping farther south in plain pine boxes. There were hundreds of walking wounded and stretcher cases, flowing back to Richmond homes, schools, hotels, and warehouses that had been turned into hospitals. And within days there were almost as many hundreds of Yankees, more prisoners of war than anyone had planned for. Among them was U.S. congressman Alfred Ely of New York, who had come out to Manassas to witness the show and had been captured when his carriage got lost in the panic of McDowell's army.

The count of Southern soldiers who had lost their lives, and the sight of Yankees who had surrendered rather than die, inspired even intelligent men to believe the worst was over. At Second Presbyterian Church, Moses Hoge offered thanks that "we are at last separated from a government . . . whose perfidy, injustice and tyranny is unparalleled in the history of the Anglo-Saxon race. . . ." Describing the kindness of the victors to their captives, Hoge repeated the story of a wounded Union soldier who said to a Confederate officer, "Sir, my leg is not only broken, but my heart is broken, that I ever come to fight such a people."[33]

But not all Confederates were kind to prisoners, and not all those who were kind were Confederates at heart. In the week following Manassas, the *Examiner* focused on "two ladies, mother and daughter, living on Church Hill, [who] have lately attracted public notice by their assiduous attentions to the Yankee prisoners confined in this city."

While every "true woman" in Richmond has been comforting Confederate sick and wounded, it said, "these two women have been expending their opulent means in aiding and giving comfort to the miscreants who have invaded our sacred soil, bent on rapine and murder, the desolation of our homes and sacred places, and the ruin and dishonour of our families." The Yankee prisoners are under competent medical care, the paper stated; thus "the course of these two females, in providing them with delicacies, buying them books, stationery and papers, cannot but be regarded as an evidence of sympathy amounting to an endorsation of the cause and conduct of these Northern Vandals."[34]

Southern patriots had hinted at such suspicions before, as when the *Examiner* warned in April that there were secret enemies who wore "petticoats as well as pantaloons." Since secession, most of those spring-time enemies had turned into summer patriots or had at least concealed their colors. But a hard core would never abandon the Union and did not care who knew it.

CHAPTER SIX

THE PERFECTION OF
TRUE WOMANHOOD

*A*s boys and men shouldered muskets and marched away, conscientious Virginia churchmen thought women should understand that petticoat wearers, too, had important duties in time of crisis. A country preacher on the Northern Neck outlined women's role in remarks so timely that the Baptists' weekly *Religious Herald* circulated them statewide. He reminded his Female Missionary Society that it was the Apostle Paul who said, in First Corinthians, that a woman's place is in the home.

At home, said the Reverend, "she should have the largest liberty compatible with the righteous authority of husband or father . . . in this position of beautiful humility and dependence, she may exercise the highest faith in her capabilities and attainments." But, he said, "nowhere else may she attain to the perfection of a true womanhood, or accomplish her mission. True, her position is one of limitation and subjection, yet it is not the limitation or subjection of inferiority, but of order and nature. . . .

"When . . . we say to her, you must not follow us into public life, you must not preach, you must not enter into the competitions of business, or take part in the disgusting strifes of the political arena—we do so, not from any feeling of conscious superiority, but because we believe that by doing so, she transgresses the bounds of womanly propriety and modesty, does violence to her own nature, and greatly impairs, if she does not totally destroy, her influence for good."

The preacher assured the ladies that in so saying, he was not debasing

woman, but placing her "upon a throne, in her hands an invisible scep-
tre," to do good by "helping, blessing, purifying and saving man by the
enduring meekness and unselfish sacrifice of her love and friendship."[1]

That order of things was already well understood across the South,
and those who most needed reminders of it were least likely to heed the
preacher's advice. Amid the stress and opportunity of war, many Richmond women like Maria Mason Tabb Hubard still lived by this gospel,
humbly devoted to their husbands.

Maria, who had grown up on a comfortable Tidewater plantation,
now sold garden produce to help support her family while her husband,
the English portraitist and sculptor William James Hubard, struggled
to succeed in war work. Earlier, he had cast his first brass cannon in the
foundry that he had converted from producing bronze statuary. Maria
confided to her diary how "my heart leaped with joy, that he has succeeded after his toil and difficulties he has had to encounter in raising
the money these war times, necessary for such an enterprise." One early
fall morning, she awoke full of hope: "This is my 48th birthday and
Wm. is going to celebrate it by casting his eighth cannon and if permitted by the government will honor me by calling it after me! Most sincerely I do trust it will be a perfect one in every respect, and give more
satisfaction and be of greater use than I have been in my worthless life!"[2]

Thousands of Virginia women did not consider their lives worthless
as they ran plantations and businesses in place of departed soldiers.
Some defied the pulpit and became camp followers, making the most of
the assets God had given them. Others, like Elizabeth Van Lew, ignored
homilies about the meekness of women and plunged into the "disgusting strifes" of the world around them.

Elizabeth and her mother could hardly have been more clearly identified if the *Examiner* had pointed to them by name, rather than dis-
guising them thinly as enemies in petticoats. They had never made a
secret of their loyalty to the Union. After all, two-thirds of the Virginia
convention had voted the same way until after Sumter, and more than a
third stood firm even then.

Perhaps because the Van Lew ladies were established and well-to-do,
perhaps because Richmond thought them a bit addled, they got away
with their loyalty. Once Virginia seceded, however, tempers ran high
and the attitude of the Van Lews' neighbors went from barely polite to
barely controlled. On the street Elizabeth's erstwhile friends looked
away without speaking. Few callers came to the Van Lews' Church Hill
mansion, with its terraced garden of boxwood, oleander, and magnolia
overlooking the James. After the first fighting, this icy disdain was replaced by something more menacing.

"Loyalty now was called treason," Elizabeth wrote. "If you spoke in your parlor or chamber to your next of heart you whispered. You looked under the lounges and beds. . . . I have had brave men shake their fingers in my face and say terrible things. . . .

"We had threats of being driven away, threats of fire, and threats of death. Some wished all Union people could be driven into the streets and slaughtered. Some proposed the hanging of all persons of Northern birth, no matter how long they had been in the South. . . ."[3]

And the war was just beginning.

In earlier decades the Van Lews had enjoyed all the social respect that comes with prosperity, though they could not buy the standing that came with birth into the right families. They were, after all, Northerners.

John Van Lew, Elizabeth's father, of Dutch blood, had come to Richmond from New York early in the century. After starting a hardware business he traveled north again and married Elizabeth Baker, daughter of an honored Philadelphia mayor. They made their Richmond home a salon of the arts, a way station for traveling celebrities. There Edgar Allan Poe recited "The Raven"; Jenny Lind, "the Swedish nightingale," sang at the peak of her career; famous men of church and state dined and gossiped about world affairs. There were balls and garden parties, and summer journeys to White Sulphur Springs in a carriage drawn by four white horses.[4]

Elizabeth, born in 1817, grew up amid this, and took it all in. Her parents thought the Richmond schools were not good enough for her and sent her to study in Philadelphia. When she returned she was certain forever that the main thing that made Richmond different from the North, the institution at the core of "the Southern way of life," was morally wrong. More than anything else, this may have been why such a vivacious and wealthy young woman did not marry. She was quick and direct, her features were sharp, her hair kept in ringlets, her blue eyes alight with curiosity. She was also sure of herself and used to having her own way. Southern swains did not queue up to court a girl with such strong convictions.

She had been in her early thirties when Fredrika Bremer, the Swedish novelist and feminist, stopped with the Van Lews during the tour she described in her two-volume work, *Homes of the New World.* In showing Bremer around, Elizabeth made sure that she saw the city's most impressive tourist attractions, the slave auctions and the tobacco factories. Bremer wrote that Elizabeth, "a pleasing, pale blonde, expressed so much compassion for the sufferings of the slave, that I was immediately attracted to her." They listened to black tobacco hands singing "Hallelujah, Amen!" at the end of a long workday, and "Good Miss Van L. could not refrain from weeping."[5]

When the elder John Van Lew died before the war, the centerpiece of his estate was the three-and-a-half-story mansion with its six-columned portico, diagonally across the street from old St. John's Church. He also left enough capital for the family to continue to live in the grand style. At the 1860 census, Elizabeth's mother was sixty-two years old, and valued her real estate at $90,000, her personal holdings at $27,000—and these were hard prewar U.S. dollars. Elizabeth's personal property was $10,000. Her brother John Newton Van Lew, 36, then managing the hardware business of Van Lew & Taylor, reported $2,000 in real estate and $20,000 in personal assets. Before the war was over, almost all of that family fortune would be spent in the Union cause.

Soon after Big Bethel, a delegation of ladies who sewed clothes and banners for the Confederacy came calling to ask Mrs. and Miss Van Lew to join them in making shirts for the gallant troops from South Carolina. They must have known before they came that there was little chance that Elizabeth and her mother would offer any help to the Confederate side; this was obviously a test to force the Van Lews to show their true colors. Elizabeth had talked with young Southern soldiers, and she longed to tell them not to be like "dumb driven cattle." When they told her they had come to protect Virginia, she asked why. "They kindly informed me that Mr. Lincoln had said he was coming down to take all our negroes and set them free, and they were going to protect us women." She felt for those innocent soldiers, but she despised the Richmond women she had heard urging them to "kill as many Yankees as you can for me" or to bring back "Mr. Lincoln's head, or a piece of his ear," or some other such precious relic.[6]

When the Van Lews refused to sew for the Confederate troops, they merely confirmed their standing as outcasts. But when the first Union prisoners arrived, both Elizabeth's heart and mind responded; those soldiers in distress gave clear purpose to her life.

*   *   *

With so many unfamiliar faces crowding in, taut suspicion gripped the city after Manassas. Three men had been fired from the Tredegar Iron Works just before the battle for "supposed disloyalty to the South," which may have been mere careless talk. But one night in May three separate fires had been started at the works, hardly by accident.[7]

Journalist George W. Bagby wrote that Richmond was swarming with office-seekers, "all of whom are hungry as leeches."[8] W. M. Clark, a Tennessee lieutenant escorting a prisoner to the capital, stayed to gawk on his first visit to such a metropolis. To his wife, Clark wrote: "It is quite amusing to stand about in the Bar rooms of the Hotels and hear the plots and plans laid for Mr. Lincoln's Army by our Hotel politicians and there are a great number of them. I think they must be office seekers. . . . They talk as if the direction of the Army should be with them. Certainly if they act as they talk some big guns will go off for they use such great swelling words about Beauregard, Davis and Johnston that one would think they were mere pigmies in the hands of these intellectual giants."[9]

Hinting at a lack of enthusiasm for the Confederate cause could mean trouble for anyone, whether in street, church, or tavern. Carping at Jefferson Davis was already becoming a sport among generals and politicians, but for a stranger in town to talk that way in a public place was imprudent. To do it and admit being a relative of Abraham Lincoln, if only by marriage, was dangerous. In the bar of the St. Charles Hotel, during the evening after the battle, a newcomer managed to combine these provocations.

The following morning, one Robert Still testified in Mayor's Court that he had been celebrating the victory when another celebrant introduced a stranger to him as Dr. George Rogers Clark Todd, Lincoln's brother-in-law. Ever the hospitable Virginian, Still offered to buy the stranger a drink anyway. But before it could be served, Dr. Todd announced aloud that he had been treated "damned rascally" by both President Davis and his aide, Colonel Louis Wigfall.

At a later day, in some other company, this might have inspired a toast in agreement. But Still was a Davis man, and he concluded that the stranger could hardly be "sound upon the goose" if he talked that way. Thus he personally arrested Todd for "making use of what was considered incendiary language."

Various witnesses appeared to support Dr. Todd, who explained that he had come to Richmond to be appointed a Confederate surgeon, as Davis had promised, but had been getting the runaround. He also noted that his connection with the Lincoln family had been "a source of constant and most vexatious annoyance" as he traveled in the South. After a brief stay in jail, Todd was released, and after all the publicity, his appointment came through and he served the Confederacy well.[10]

Those Todds of Kentucky did tend to lean Southward. One of Mary Todd Lincoln's full brothers, three half brothers, and three brothers-in-law were Confederate soldiers. Mrs. Lincoln herself, because of her family and her own sometimes erratic behavior, was the victim of Washington gossip that she was a Confederate spy. Her half sister's husband, Benjamin Helm, was a Southern general, who would be killed at

Chickamauga. Another of her half sisters later admitted smuggling quinine and a gift uniform and sword for General Lee through the lines from Washington to Richmond. And barely a mile from Richmond's City Hall, where Dr. George Rogers Clark Todd explained his allegiance to the Confederacy, there was another brother-in-law of Abraham Lincoln's. Suddenly that summer, he became the object of Elizabeth Van Lew's calculated attention.[11]

*   *   *

At 9:00 on the second evening after the battle at Manassas, about a thousand bedraggled Union prisoners arrived at Richmond's Virginia Central depot. They waited an hour before being marched through moonlit streets to Liggon's tobacco factory, a brick structure on Main Street between Twenty-fifth and Twenty-sixth streets. There, four blocks from Van Lew's house, they were so tightly jammed into the second and third stories of the dark 35-by-70-foot building that they could hardly lie down. The next morning, after the prisoners had a breakfast of dry bread, boiled beef, and coffee, the Confederate inspector general came to apologize for the rough quarters, saying Richmond had not expected so many prisoners so soon. He assured the officers that separate quarters would promptly be ready for them in an adjacent building.[12]

The moment Elizabeth Van Lew heard that the Federal captives were there, she hurried down to see them. She remembered how her heart beat as she approached the officer in charge, Lincoln's brother-in-law, young Lieutenant David Todd. She told him that she wanted to become the hospital nurse. Todd took down her name, then realized who she was and looked up in surprise. He told her that she was the first and only lady who had thought of such a thing, and sent her away.

Elizabeth had no intention of staying away. Bustling from office to office, she remembered something about the deeply reverent treasury secretary Memminger, and stepped up to his desk in the old Custom House. When she told him she wanted to see the prisoners, the South Carolinian glared at her and said this was unthinkable: "Such a set and such a class—they aren't worthy or fit for a lady to visit!"

"Mr. Memminger," Van Lew purred, "in peacetimes, I once heard you speak beautifully on the subject of religion." The secretary's face softened, and she pressed on. "Love," she said, "is the fulfilling of the law, and if we wish *our cause* to succeed, we must begin with charity to the thankless and unworthy." Relenting, Memminger wrote a note recommending her to Brigadier General John H. Winder.[13]

Winder had been inspector general of the Richmond area camps, responsible for policing their soldiers, for just a month. Every related job that did not automatically fall to another office—chasing deserters, issuing passes, enforcing curfews, housing prisoners—became his responsibility. Born on Maryland's Eastern Shore, he was 61 that summer. His was a distinguished Maryland family that included judges, prosperous planters, and a governor—but his father, William H. Winder, had been the general whose troops fled British invaders at Bladensburg in 1814, opening the way for the sacking of Washington.

Thus John Winder had inherited something to live down, at West Point and in the regular army. He taught tactics at the academy when Jefferson Davis was a cadet, and though breveted twice in the Mexican War, he was not promoted to permanent major until 1860, forty years after his graduation. By 1861 he had married and lived in North Carolina for many years, and most of his family identified with the South, though at the outbreak of war his oldest son remained a Union army captain. Winder resigned his U.S. commission and offered himself to Davis at just the right time; with drunken soldiers roaming the streets, spy fever raging, and the first prisoners arriving, Davis put him to work with a brigadier general's commission.[14]

Bulky, silver-haired, and imposing, Winder was capable of elaborate courtesies, but he was not a born diplomat. The abrupt ways of his four decades in the army were just being felt in Richmond when Elizabeth Van Lew showed up at what she called his "shanty office."

Winder received her politely, and she took his measure in a few minutes of chitchat. "General," she said as she gazed at him, "your hair would adorn the temple of Janus; it looks out of place here." Gradually she worked around to asking permission to bring the prisoners something to eat and read.

Duly flattered, Winder wrote out a generous pass allowing her "to visit the prisoners and to send them books, luxuries, delicacies and what she may please."[15]

That interview was the start of a long, semiflirtatious cat-and-mouse game between Van Lew and Winder, which grew less playful as the war wore on. Van Lew and her mother soon appeared at the prison with books and flowers for the Union soldiers. At first it was "very innocent aid and comfort," Elizabeth conceded, but "it added much to our own comfort." She might have gloated when she returned to Lieutenant Todd with the pass from his commanding officer, but she was thinking ahead. Instead of gloating, she plied Todd with buttermilk and ginger cake.[16]

* * *

On the evening of the battle of Manassas, St. James's Episcopal Church in Richmond was filled with worried worshippers. They knew there had been a fight at last, but they did not know yet who had won. Among them was tiny, devout Sally Louisa Tompkins, recently come to Richmond from her family's Mathews County plantation. She listened to the Reverend Joshua Peterkin as if to memorize his every word. Before his sermon, Peterkin prayed for the president and for deliverance from the enemy. After it, he prayed for victory.

The minister's words seemed to get quick results. As the congregation broke up, the streets were alive with news of what had happened along Bull Run. Sally heard bright cheers as she walked back to the Arlington Hotel; a fresh regiment was marching to the depot. At the hotel she heard President Davis's victory bulletin. Awake in her excitement long past midnight, she tried to describe that evening to her absent sister. "I felt," she wrote, "that we could indeed say 'thy right hand, O lord, is become glorious in power; thy right hand, O Lord, hath dashed in pieces the enemy.'"[17]

The brave predictions of editorial columns and training-camp oratory had been proven right; those soft-handed urban clerks from the North had fled before true-bred Southern manhood. Sally Tompkins, like thousands of others, could not imagine that after such a defeat the Union would still fight on.

But Davis, Johnston, and Beauregard immediately began arguing over who had done what at Manassas. Colonels, wives, and politicians from one state asserted that its men had led the way while others had hung back. South Carolinians quibbled over which of their regiments had been most heroic. The press demanded to know why the Confederates had not marched on to Washington to end the war. Officers who had been there blamed this reticence on lack of supplies, and blamed that in turn on Colonel Lucius B. Northrop, the presidential favorite assigned as commissary general. All the wrangling settled nothing, but the acrimony it stirred would last long past the war.

And then the casualties began streaming back from Manassas, and reality set in.

If Richmond was unprepared for nearly a thousand Federal prisoners from Manassas, it was even less ready for half again as many Confederate sick and wounded. Homes became impromptu hospitals, and women who had been busy sewing uniforms and knitting socks became nurses. These, some of them, were the same ladies who had called for Lincoln's head. Now it was time to do something more useful than talk. Sally Tompkins set an example.

Sally, then 27, knew how to run things. Though she came of an old, cultured Tidewater family, she was neither social nor bookish, except for her devotion to the Bible. She had learned as a girl to deal with births and deaths, to administer to family, servants, and neighbors in the plantation country between Mobjack Bay and the Piankatank River. When her father died she came to Richmond with her mother and sister, and when mangled boys began arriving from Manassas, she responded as if they were her own brothers.

Those early casualties were sent to the Medical College Hospital and to what had been the City Almshouse, to the Richmond Female Institute, the Second Market, the St. Charles Hotel, the Springfield Masonic Hall, to converted tobacco warehouses, and dozens of private homes—and still there was not room for them all.[18]

Judge John Robertson, who had moved his family to the countryside, offered his townhouse at Main and Third streets. Sally Tompkins promptly stepped in to manage it. Ten days after the first casualties reached the city, her Robertson Hospital was in business. It would treat 1,333 patients—with only seventy-six deaths—before Sally shut it down two months after the war.

Dr. John Spotswood Wellford volunteered as Robertson Hospital's first surgeon. But there was never any doubt about who was in charge. The serious, straight-lipped Tompkins expected society matrons volunteering as nurses to serve as obediently as uniformed privates. With a satchel of medicines at her waist, she moved among her patients' beds dispensing drugs and religious encouragement. Each evening she led a prayer service. Day and night, she insisted on clean blankets, clothes, floors, bodies, and minds.

She played no favorites. When Mary Chesnut dropped in and asked, "Are there any Carolinians here?," Tompkins said, "I never ask where the sick are from." Chesnut wrote in her diary: "I was rebuked. I deserved it."

When the handsome widow Martha Carter reddened at a rough compliment paid by one of the patients, Tompkins said, "If you could only leave your beauty at the door and bring in your goodness and faculty!"

When a soldier sneaked out into town and overcelebrated his improved condition, Tompkins took away his clothes until he apologized and promised never to try it again. She fought the bureaucracy successfully for medical supplies and provisions—and paid for everything out of her own funds.[19]

Eventually Confederate officials realized that they could not keep track of patients scattered among so many private hospitals. With no central control, supplies disappeared without accounting, and relatives from far away had trouble finding their ailing kin. Too often, fully recovered soldiers found it congenial to stay on and be pampered, or to slip away home. Thus all private hospitals would be closed, and all military patients sent to hospitals run by the Confederate government or the states.

Sally, who had thrown her whole being into her work, shed tears for only a moment. The daughter of William Crump, assistant treasury secretary, wrote that Sally quickly recovered and persuaded Judge Crump to accompany her in a direct appeal to Jefferson Davis. Displaying her records, Sally said that no other hospital had returned such a high percentage of patients to active service. The president was sympathetic, but an order was an order; he could grant no exceptions. According to Crump's daughter, Davis pondered Sally's case, then offered to make her an army officer—which would make her hospital official and so keep it going.

On September 9, 1861, Sally became Captain Tompkins, the only woman knowingly commissioned as an officer in Confederate service.* (Several women served as medical officers or chaplains in the U.S. Army, and on both sides there were women who masqueraded as men, a few of whom held commissioned rank.) Tompkins was nominally assigned to the cavalry because pay in that branch was higher, but she never accepted her government salary and stayed on at her own expense. During most of the war she worked with Dr. A. Y. P. Garnett, who had practiced earlier in Washington. Sally's diligence gave little Robertson Hospital such a reputation that ranking officers often sent her their most serious cases.[20]

Unquestionably, Elizabeth Van Lew would have turned her home on Church Hill into a hospital for suffering Yankees if such a thing had been permitted. Though General Winder's pass allowed her to call on and comfort the Federal prisoners, only in extremity would they be able to call on her.

* * *

When they arrived in Richmond, some officers among the Yankee prisoners from Manassas expected to be treated as gentleman visitors, as if they were defeated knights of some medieval war, surrendering their

---

*Tompkins's commission as captain was dated months before the government formally moved to centralize the hospitals. When she became a captain in September, her little hospital had been in operation only five weeks. Her military rank helped maintain the hospital's independence, but it was apparently awarded in anticipation of the government order rather than in reaction to it.

swords and exchanging toasts with their captors. Both sides were so un-used to the new realities that a Confederate major promised his captives that in Richmond they would be introduced to the secretary of war, then paroled with the freedom of the city—and at the start there were ges-tures in that direction. But instead of checking into Richmond hotels the captured officers slept on the floor of Liggon's. A day later, some were moved to one floor of Atkinson's tobacco factory next door. That gave them sleeping room but barely improved the conditions of their existence.

The diaries and memoirs of Federal prisoners are among the most numerous accounts of life in wartime Richmond. Understandably they dwell on the hardships, and some extend the cruelties and negligence of individual captors into a blanket condemnation of all Confederates who had any place in the prison system. Many accounts published by re-turned prisoners during the war were blatant propaganda. But cruelty and negligence there surely were, along with kindness and diligence, even at the beginning. Nevertheless, a Massachusetts lieutenant who was held at Liggon's wrote long afterward that the treatment he got there, compared with that in notorious Confederate prisons later in the war, "bears about the same relation to them as purgatory does to hell. . . ."[21]

Congressman Ely and Colonel Michael Corcoran of the Sixty-ninth New York, both captured at Manassas, and Colonel Charles DeVilliers of the Eleventh Ohio, brought from western Virginia, were senior pris-oners at "Rocketts No. 1," as the Liggon factory complex was labeled. They had hardly arrived when Ely drafted a petition to Abraham Lin-coln, informing him that about 40 officers and 900 enlisted men were held and asking for quick steps to free them.

The next day, with Ely as president, the officers formed the Rich-mond Prison Association, "for mutual improvement and amusement." Under the circumstances, the emphasis fell on amusement, which helped to improve morale. The association's "official seal" depicted a circle of body lice with the motto "Bite and Be Damned." Elaborate ceremonies were arranged in which the prisoners awarded pseudo-decorations for pseudogallantry. Occasionally the Yankees were sub-jected to harangues by visiting Confederate politicians. They found this amusing, too.

At first, prisoners who had greenbacks were allowed to send out to buy supplemental food in the Richmond markets. But Lieutenant Todd halted this practice because they had been sneaking spirits into the prison. A Union surgeon, Dr. Lyman Stone, got rowdy after such a delivery and caused a ruckus that brought Todd rushing in with drawn pistol to order Stone locked in irons.

While this enforcement may have been necessary, one Union soldier asserted later that Todd was "singularly vicious and brutal," that he always entered the prison with drawn sword and at least once had struck a captive with the flat of his blade for not falling in fast enough. Some insisted that Todd encouraged guards to shoot at prisoners who leaned innocently out of windows.[22]

Todd may have drawn special criticism because of who he was, but in the long run his name barely made the list of Civil War villains, far below that of his orderly sergeant that summer, a Swiss-born Louisiana physician named Henry Wirz.

Though Elizabeth Van Lew did not spare most prison officials in her journal, she said she knew of no unkindness on Wirz's part while he was in Richmond.[23] But New York prisoners spoke of how they defied Wirz when he tried to question them about how someone had escaped.

"Tell me," said Wirz, "or I shall keep you tree days on pred and wasser."

"Oh, ho!" his charges would shout. "Three cheers for Wirz! He will feed us three days on bread and butter!"

"No, no!" screamed Wirz. "You tam villains; I say pred and wasser; *wasser,* not busser!"—and *wasser* is what they got.*[24]

Calvin Huson, Jr., a Rochester lawyer defeated by Ely in the 1860 congressional election, had ridden out to Manassas and had been captured with him. He soon fell ill with typhoid fever, and his comrades petitioned General Winder to send him home. Only weeks later, when Huson's condition became critical, was his transfer approved. He and his nurse, a Yankee private, were moved—not home to New York or to an established Richmond hospital, but into the care of Elizabeth Van Lew.

Soon afterward Elizabeth hurried in her carriage to the prison. In tears, she told Ely that his friend Huson was dying, and asked the congressman to go to him. Twenty minutes later, as Ely prepared to leave escorted by the new prison commandant, a messenger came to say that Huson was dead. Ely went to the Van Lew house to oversee arrangements with an undertaker, and there a Union chaplain from the prison conducted a funeral service.[26]

---

*Wirz was transferred to line duty and wounded in 1862; he then served as a Confederate agent and courier. In 1864 he was made commandant of the prison camp at Andersonville, Georgia. For his role there, he became the only Confederate prison official tried and executed by the U.S. government after the war.[25]

If all this coming and going of prisoners seems strange, considering that others were shot for merely leaning out a window, it is due partly to Ely's status as a civilian rather than a military prisoner, and partly to the confused state of protocol. In an international conflict, he and Huson as civilians might have been interned under comfortable conditions. But because Washington did not acknowledge the Confederacy as a sovereign power, diplomatic protocol was inoperative. At that stage of the war, irregularity was the rule, and nowhere did it apply more haphazardly than among the prisoners, the authorities, and the Van Lews.

By the time Huson died, Lieutenant Todd had been replaced as officer in charge of the prison by Captain George C. Gibbs. As soon as Gibbs took over, Elizabeth Van Lew cultivated him. She even helped him solve the housing problem met by everyone who arrived in Richmond: She took the captain and his family into her home as temporary boarders. Gibbs promised her free access to the prisoners, but more than once she was turned away by others.[27]

Many Richmond ladies were angry at Van Lew's kindness to enemy soldiers. They gossiped among themselves about her sheltering the Union politician Huson and hosting his funeral. Along with Winder and his police, they grew suspicious of what Van Lew took into those prisons. Gradually they also began to wonder whether she was bringing anything out.

CHAPTER SEVEN

OUR AFFAIRS IN THE
HANDS OF NOODLES

*J*efferson Davis was, by his wife's admission, "a nervous dyspeptic" of "supersensitive temperament . . . even a child's disapproval discomposed him."

The backbiting and finger-pointing that began when the South realized that Manassas was just the beginning of war seemed to close in around the Davis family at the overcrowded Spotswood. Newly arrived congressmen and their wives, refugees from downriver and upstate, women from farther south seeking their missing husbands, others come to tend their sick and wounded, hundreds waiting in the capital to comfort their soldiers at nights and on weekends—all added to the crush at city hotels. With great relief, the Davises moved on August 1 into the mansion that had been renovated for them at Twelfth and Clay streets.[1]

Immediately, some labeled it "the White House of the Confederacy," though proud others would not deign to copy the informal name of Lincoln's mansion in Washington. They preferred "Gray House," which described the stucco that covered the building's brick walls. Day to day, it was simply the "President's House" or the "Executive Mansion."

The building was substantial, three and a half stories, 52 by 67 feet, with a small stoop at the front and a classic columned portico at the rear, looking down on Shockoe Valley across a steep terraced garden with fruit trees. Its halls and fireplaces were elaborately decorated, and its stairways wound into airy rooms above. Varina wrote: "One felt here the pleasant sense of being in the home of a cultivated, liberal, fine gentleman," and in the garden there "came to my mind's eye a lovely woman, seen only in the eye of faith, as she walked there in 'maiden meditation.'"

That vision was inspired by visitors' descriptions of Mary Brockenbrough, the adopted daughter of Dr. John Brockenbrough, the banker and politician for whom the building was completed in 1818. Later the house was owned by James A. Seddon, who would become an important figure in Davis's cabinet, and then by Lewis D. Crenshaw, operator of one of Richmond's major flour mills. When President Davis came to town the city bought the house for $35,000, intending to present it to him; when he refused the gift, the Confederate government rented the house as his official residence. Although Varina would have liked more and smaller rooms—some were 40 feet square—here, at least, the family felt "somewhat more at home."[2] But nowhere could Davis escape the carping that arose in army, Congress, and press.

The week after Manassas, Beauregard the aspiring Bonaparte wrote to congressional friends, asserting that Davis's old friend Lucius Northrop had botched his job of supplying the army, thus preventing a triumphant march on to Washington. This early in the war, Commissary General Northrop was already a candidate for most despised civilian functionary in the Confederate government; one gentleman soldier would call him "a crotchety doctor, some of whose acquaintances had for years believed him insane. Aside from his suspected mental aberration, and the crotchets which had made his life already a failure, he knew nothing whatever" of the commissary business. "It was nothing to him that in the midst of plenty the army was upon a short allowance of food. . . . System was everything. . . . Red tape was supreme, and no sword was permitted to cut it."[3] Northrop had met Davis when they were young lieutenants on the western frontier, and received a medical discharge after being wounded in 1839. Though Davis as U.S. secretary of war had reinstated his commission, Northrop remained a civilian doctor in Charleston until secession.

At the Capitol, Congressman William Porcher Miles of South Carolina read aloud Beauregard's complaining letter about Northrop, setting off a testy exchange between admirers of the hero general and those of the hero president.

When Davis headed for the battle at Manassas, he had left behind his aide, Colonel Wigfall. It is unlikely that he simply forgot him; the man lived virtually under the president's feet at the Spotswood and was at his elbow in daily rides about town. He had been a Davis colleague and a pugnacious secessionist in the U.S. Senate; a duelist who had killed one man, wounded another, and been wounded himself; a hero of Sumter;

and nominal commander of a Texas regiment. He also drank heartily. Embarrassed at having missed Manassas, Wigfall joined the complaint raised by Beauregard.

In May the Confederate Congress created the rank of full general. But not until the end of August did Davis finally decide which brigadiers would be promoted, and in what order of seniority: first, 63-year-old Samuel Cooper, who would serve as adjutant general in Richmond; second, Albert Sidney Johnston, whom Davis idolized but who was just returning from the Far West and was not yet in Confederate uniform; third, Robert E. Lee, then assigned to western Virginia; fourth, Joseph E. Johnston; and fifth, Beauregard.

When that list was disclosed, Joseph Johnston exploded in "surprise and mortification." *He* was senior general in the army, he insisted—and he had a case. Congress had specified that the rank of officers coming over from the U.S. Army would determine their relative standing in Confederate service. Joe Johnston had been a brigadier general, while the first three named had been colonels, and Beauregard a mere major.

Johnston declared that ranking him only fourth served "to tarnish my fair name as a soldier and a man." Davis told him that his "arguments and statements [were] utterly one-sided, and [his] insinuations as unfounded as they are unbecoming." Johnston, said the president, had been a U.S. brigadier only as quartermaster general, a staff position which did not entitle him to command troops; as a line officer, he had been just a lieutenant colonel.[4]

Davis might have mentioned that he and Johnston had had other disagreements down through the years. At Manassas, Johnston had refused orders sent from his friend and West Point roommate, Lee—refusals that the president twice labeled "insubordinate." And like Beauregard, Johnston had complained aloud about the president's crony, Northrop.

Ex-Secretary of War Davis might have admitted, too, that he listed the low-key Cooper first because he did not want an argumentative general in chief challenging his judgment in Richmond. He could have said that he chose A. S. Johnston next, to be senior general in the field, because decades earlier, as an upper-classman, Johnston had befriended Davis when he was a plebe at West Point.[5]

Instead, Davis stuck to his formal reason for passing over Joe Johnston. He thus assured himself of sometimes sulkiness, other times outright disobedience, from a skillful general who was one of the few men anywhere with skin as thin as his own. Wigfall became a Johnston champion. Partisans in Congress and the press were glad to keep up the squabbling even as Davis tried to smooth relations and the principals themselves temporarily submerged their grudges against the president.

Before the summer was out, Davis also lost two cabinet members, Robert Toombs at State and Leroy Walker at War.

He replaced the grumbling, hard-drinking Toombs with R. M. T. Hunter, the first Virginian in his cabinet. Gossip turned even this appointment into a negative for the president, as when one bystander explained the switch by citing "Incompatibility of temper. [Toombs] rides too high a horse—that is, for so despotic a person as Jeff Davis."[6]

Walker quit after Davis appointed another presidential friend, Colonel A. T. Bledsoe, to a senior job in the War Department without bothering to consult the secretary. To replace Walker, Davis turned to the most controversial member of his cabinet, Attorney General Judah Benjamin, with whom he had served in the U.S. Senate.

Although Benjamin was faithful to Davis and efficient in office, many around the president already resented him. Anti-Semitism was part of it; in the politest circles of the day, casual bigotry was common, and as economic times tightened it became nastier. Many memoirs of the period, even without explicitly mentioning that Benjamin was Jewish, focused on his olive skin, his soft round face and form, his mental agility and social suavity, as if any knowing reader would get the point. Jealousy also played a part in the resentment; those jostling for presidential favor were dismayed by Benjamin's quick entrée to Davis's confidence. The surest way to the president's heart was to agree with him, and War Department clerk J. B. Jones predicted that the new secretary would exert great influence, for he had studied the president carefully—learning not only what and whom Davis liked but especially those he didn't.[7]

In the military lull after Manassas, when much of the South believed it should already have won the war, these disputes swelled out of all proportion to their substance. Griping was heard from Southern capitals where governors who had preached states' rights to justify secession now cited states' rights to justify balkiness toward the secession government. On the North Carolina coast, Federal forces took Fort Hatteras, cutting off an important passageway for vessels running the Union blockade and scoring a propaganda triumph that loomed large in the absence of other strategic news. Davis immersed himself even more deeply than usual in details of politics and government that should have been left to subcabinet bureaucrats.

The result was mental and physical exhaustion, which broke the president's health and sent him to bed in his darkened chamber for days at a time. While he was ailing, one of Mrs. Chesnut's friends said, "The president is ill—and our affairs are in the hands of noodles. All the generals away with the armies—nobody here. . . ."[8]

Between breakdowns, Davis visited the army in the field, encouraging his generals and still stirring cheers from the soldiers. In early October he was called back by word that a carriage with his wife and Mrs. Johnston had overturned. Though Varina's injuries were slight, she was seven months pregnant—one more in the growing list of concerns that crowded in upon the president.[9]

Another was the forthcoming election.

Davis and the one-house Congress were branches of the merely provisional government that had been organized in haste at Montgomery to serve no more than a year. Within that year, a "permanent" president, vice president, House, and Senate must be elected. All the grousing about Davis might have tempted someone of stature to challenge him seriously in the voting set for November 6. Indeed, after Manassas some touted Beauregard as the strongman the new nation needed. There was conversation about Davis's new secretary of state, Hunter, a politician of national reputation and ambition.

There was much more talk, even agitation, about finding someone new for vice president: Alexander Stephens had been a reluctant secessionist and was still halfhearted in his commitment—what would happen to the Confederacy if the fragile Davis should die in office?

*   *   *

In those days newspaper correspondents were paid by the column inch of type, and since type was small they blatantly padded their facts with inches of easy reading. One who sometimes signed himself "Hermes" combined a crumb of economic news with his amusement at the efforts of eager Richmond women doing their bit for the soldiers.

"Visit them when you will, they meet you knitting in hand," he wrote for the Charleston *Mercury*. "The formation of some of the socks which they have produced does not indicate a very exact knowledge of human anatomy. I saw one last evening which, I am told, was intended for the foot of the entire Southern Confederacy. From its size, I judged it would make a rather loose fit. Socks are costly luxuries now-a-days. The coarsest yarn costs two dollars a pound, and a pound of yarn will not quite make five pairs of socks."

This was the work of George William Bagby, whose lasting legacy is his humorous, sentimental essays on old Virginia, but who was better read during the war as a stylish and opinionated daily journalist. Bagby had started his career in Lynchburg, and before the war had reported the oncoming crisis from Washington. Amid the secession debate, he returned to Richmond to take over the monthly *Southern Literary Mes-*

senger from John R. Thompson. His satirical essay "The Virginia Editor" portrayed others more accurately than it did himself.

"The Virginia editor is a young, unmarried, intemperate, pugnacious, gambling gentleman," he wrote. "Between drink and dueling-pistols he is generally escorted to a premature grave." The editor's "attainments may be summed up in the word 'politics,' for while he does not underrate those who understand and take interest in Belles Lettres and the Arts and Sciences, he frankly confesses that he knows and cares nothing about them himself."

To the contrary, Bagby did know and care, not only as an author but as a certified doctor of medicine. But from the day he stepped in at the *Messenger*, hard-edged politics replaced the poetic Thompson's high literary standards and efforts toward North-South accommodation. Bagby's first issue had explored "The Difference of Race Between the Northern and Southern People," featured a piece titled "Hannibal: a Nigger," and taunted the memory of John Brown in a poem entitled "The Mock Auction, or Ossawatomie Sold."[10]

The *Messenger* was closely read, but its circulation was limited. The 33-year-old Bagby reached a much wider audience when he returned to civilian life after a brief sojourn as a private with the Eleventh Virginia Regiment at Manassas. Soon he was corresponding from Richmond for the *Mercury*, then for other papers in the major cities of the South. Writing over pen names like Hermes, Pan, Malou, XY, and Gamma, he gave readers in Charleston, Atlanta, New Orleans, Memphis, Mobile, Knoxville, Columbus, and Chattanooga a running account of high and low life in the Confederate capital. Continuing to edit the *Messenger*, he also did occasional unsigned pieces for the *Examiner* and the *Whig*. In all those outlets, he joined the rising and falling chorus of dissatisfaction with Davis and his friends. Sometimes he led it.

By lashing Commissary General Northrop and other presidential favorites, Davis's critics were lashing the president by proxy. Bagby wrote that "Our commissariat in Virginia is still 'all of a muck.'" He also wrote that the Post Office was full of "Lincolnites," and perhaps General Winder's passport office as well, since it was issuing passes for "absquatulating aliens" by the hundreds to depart for the North.[11]

Bagby reflected what was heard in Richmond's hotels and saloons when Robert E. Lee failed in early fall operations aimed at retaking western Virginia. After being frustrated at Cheat Mountain in September, Lee took over a campaign that had bogged down under two squabbling ex-governors turned brigadier generals, Henry Wise and John Floyd. Steady rains flooded the valleys, and while Lee awaited Union

attack, Brigadier General William S. Rosecrans's Union force con-
fronting him slipped out of reach. The Confederate effort to retake
the mountainous western counties sank into the mud. Lee—and thus
Davis, too—got the blame.

"Poor Lee!" wrote Bagby. "Rosecrans has fooled him again. . . . Are
the roads any worse for Lee than for Rosecrans? The people are getting
mighty sick of this dilly-dally dirt-digging, scientific warfare: so much
so, that they will demand that the Great Entrencher be brought back
and permitted to pay court to the ladies. . . ."[12]

Davis needed good news, and on October 21 it came—from the Potomac border, where a Federal expedition had ventured into Virginia at
Ball's Bluff above Leesburg. Rebel troops drove it back into the river,
killing or capturing hundreds of Yankees before they could pile into
boats to escape. All the South cheered, though Davis was still concerned
about threats to western Virginia, the Carolina coast, the Yorktown
Peninsula, and Confederate states beyond the mountains. On October
24, in fact, western Virginians voted to split their counties off into a separate state of the Union.

Despite the discontent, no one dared formally to challenge Davis for
the presidency. Nor did anyone do more than talk about replacing
Stephens as vice president. Both were elected, without opposition, for
six-year terms.

The prevailing feeling was summed up after the election by William
H. Semple, of the New Orleans *Crescent,* when Bagby sent him reports
that the Louisianian found too personally critical of Davis. Semple
wrote back saying that while the paper also urged bold military action,
"bitter attacks on Davis and the Administration don't suit the stomachs
of our people. . . . To break down the Administration now would be to
break down the Government itself in the crisis of its fortunes. It would
encourage the North and play hell generally. . . . Growl about the policy, but please do not try to shake confidence in the President. If this be
done, I tell you, the Government goes to the devil. . . ."[13]

(That the editor and Bagby were more than casual professional acquaintances was suggested when Semple wrote later asking Bagby to
deliver a letter to "Josephine De Meritt, or Josephine Demarest, or
Josephine D. Merritt," at a "maison de plaisir" at Twelfth and Cary
streets. Semple said he didn't know the lady, he was just doing a favor for
a friend—and that if Bagby didn't want to deliver it in person, would he
please get someone to do so?)[14]

* * *

The victory at Ball's Bluff brought another batch of live Yankees to be jammed in with those taken at Manassas and in scattered skirmishes elsewhere.

"What are we to do with these creatures?" Bagby asked. "The officers might be kept, in case retaliation becomes necessary. Some people think we ought to feed them on fodder or mixed horse feed, while others say the cheapest plan would be to destroy them outright. It is becoming a serious question how to dispose of them. . . . They are an insolent set."[15]

Although Bagby was not quite serious in his proposals, the question was serious indeed. Far and near, especially in the mountains of western Virginia and eastern Tennessee, civilians openly loyal to the Union were arrested for treason and sent to prison in the capital. As the war progressed, Richmond suffered more and more from the routine shipment of military prisoners to its care, no matter where they were captured. Already, because of overcrowding and short supplies, hundreds were being transferred from Richmond prisons to states farther south.

The subject of retaliation did not simply pop up in Bagby's lively imagination. Davis had promised an eye-for-eye response to Federal treatment of captured Confederate privateers—civilian mariners commissioned by the government as high-seas raiders. On November 9, General Winder appeared at Liggon's prison and read an order from Secretary of War Benjamin, directing him to choose a ranking Federal prisoner by lot. That officer would be held for execution if the Union carried out a Philadelphia court's death sentence against a Confederate privateer captain taken at sea. Thirteen other officers would be picked as hostages, to be treated the same as privateer crewmen held in the North were being treated.

As tense prisoners gathered around him, Winder handed Colonel W. Raymond Lee of Massachusetts six slips of paper bearing the names of Union colonels then in Confederate prisons. Lee dropped the names into a cylinder, and Winder told Ely to draw one. The congressman balked, but then pulled out the name of Michael Corcoran of the Sixty-ninth New York, who by then had been transferred to Charleston. The thirteen others chosen the same way included Major Paul Revere of the Twentieth Massachusetts, grandson of the Revolutionary rider. The next day the thirteen were thrown into Richmond's Henrico county jail to be treated as common criminals.[16]

Before the war was over, Richmond would see a series of prisoners executed, but Michael Corcoran would not be among them. This selection of hostages was Davis's winning move in a clear contest of wills with Lincoln. Although the United States had insisted in earlier conflicts that its own privateers be treated as prisoners of war under international law, Lincoln classed Confederate privateers as freelance pirates, for which the punishment could be death. Davis's response was an effort not only to save the Southern sailors but to force the Union to deal with Confederate personnel as if they served any other warring nation. Davis meant his threat to retaliate. Lincoln knew it, and quietly backed down.

While that threat was still alive, it stirred Elizabeth Van Lew to step up the number and riskiness of her contacts with Union prisoners. To Major Revere, she slipped letters from home and money to bribe his way out. When his close confinement ended he did not try that route, but his family would not forget Van Lew's help. Revere, like Colonel Corcoran, was soon exchanged, only to die later in the war. With each venture into the prisons, Van Lew's commitment grew deeper and more dangerous.

* * *

Letters like those passed on by Van Lew flowed north and south, through and around the lines of two armies, past a tightening naval blockade. As soon as war cut regular mail service, a flock of private letter carriers went into business. Some were motivated purely by profit. Others were spies working for one or both sides. War Department clerk Jones reported that couriers charged $1.50 a letter, carrying an average of 300 letters per trip. They supplemented this service by smuggling "diverse articles they sell at enormously high prices," raising their income to perhaps $1,000 a trip, twice a month.

Jones was unhappy that under Benjamin he had to issue special passports to these messengers, as well as to Baltimore entrepreneurs who bribed officials on both sides to let them cross the lines to sell hard-to-get merchandise. He was suspicious of the fact that the dispatch riders got passports just as freely from Northern officials as they did from him. They brought Northern newspapers, but "they seem particularly ignorant of the plans and forces of the enemy," Jones wrote. "It is my belief that they render as much service to the enemy as to us."[17]

Secretary Benjamin told Thomas Bragg, who had replaced him as attorney general, that he feared War Department correspondence was being seen by unfriendly eyes. "Persons of very doubtful loyalty" had infiltrated some departments, Bragg wrote in his diary, and they should be deported. "We have spies in Washington & Maryland, and they no doubt have them here—some perhaps are cheating both sides."[18]

Weeks earlier, Bagby had written that the Confederate Post Office was full of "Lincolnites," and if the Post Office was, why not the passport office, too? The problem, he said, "is in the character of the Southern people. Southern people are fools—that is, they are fools enough to believe other people are as sincere and honest as themselves. They are a noble race, but it is the easiest thing in the world for a Yankee or any other liar or hypocrite to outwit them."[19]

Neither Jones, Benjamin, Bragg, nor Bagby was suspicious enough.

CHAPTER EIGHT

THE HORRORS OF
A POLITICAL CAPITAL

*T*he first year of the Confederate political experiment neared its end in the postelection doldrums.

Jefferson Davis was still quibbling over the past, asking Joe Johnston's support against Beauregard's insistence that the president had prevented a triumphant march on Washington after the victory at Manassas. Robert E. Lee was sent to oversee South Atlantic coastal defenses, but before he reached Savannah, a Federal landing force had taken nearby Port Royal, South Carolina, and was threatening the town of Beaufort. The Confederate capital waited to know how soon Lincoln's appointment of the young, seemingly vigorous Major General George B. McClellan to succeed old, immobile Lieutenant General Winfield Scott as general in chief would bring the next Union march "on to Richmond."

Then, two days after Davis's reelection, an encouraging surprise came from offshore. Outside Havana, a Union warship halted the British mail packet *Trent* and from it removed Confederate envoys James M. Mason and John Slidell, who had run the blockade from Charleston to Cuba, en route to England and France to urge diplomatic recognition for the South. This Union offense outraged the British and raised Southern hopes that it would bring on war between Britain and the North, or at least London's formal recognition of the Confederate government.

Argument over the *Trent* affair mildly boosted spirits in Richmond for weeks. In the end, however, dreams of British involvement proved just as vain as the invocations offered by the Reverend Hoge at each sitting of the Confederate Congress. As the *Trent* crisis mounted, Hoge prayed yet again for heavenly intervention: "We beseech Thee [to] interpose for our defence. Stretch forth Thy hand against the swarm of our enemies—do Thou defeat their councils, disappoint their designs & fill them with confusion & dismay."[1]

If any mortal was doing more than praying at the Capitol, the rest of the capital saw little of it. Missouri's breakaway government was admitted to the Confederacy, but that did not deliver its territory into Confederate hands, and congressional discussion of the issue was not considered the people's business.

"Congress and the Virginia Convention are both so hermetically sealed that [one] would never dream they were here in our very midst," Bagby wrote—"unless he should chance to walk by the *Whig* office about dinner time, when he would certainly encounter a crowd of people, whose angular and elongated frames, shabby overcoats, and deliberate strut, indicate unmistakably that inward consciousness of greatness which beams only from the visages of 'Members.' A few drops of information are dripped occasionally into the public ear from the cans of wisdom in the Capitol. . . ."[2]

This Confederate Congress was still provisional, the single house whose members had not been popularly elected but originally sent to Montgomery by each state's secession convention. This was the last of its five sessions, which would end just before Davis's formal inauguration on George Washington's birthday in 1862. The elected House and Senate that moved in to replace it were different in organization, and many faces were changed, but most of their habits were the same.

Not quite a third of these Confederates had served in the Congress at Washington. Citing the precedent of early U.S. congresses, the legislators insisted on meeting in closed session when dealing with things that mattered. "The discussions of the Confederate Congress must be secret," the *Examiner* had declared that first summer. "Its halls must not become the theatre of polemic oratory nor the banquet of popular curiosity."[3] Less than a year later, the paper had lost its enthusiasm for legislative secrecy. "The members of the old Provisional Congress locked themselves from the newspapers that they might drink whiskey and give their votes, excluded from the observations of the world," it said.[4]

Perhaps John Daniel of the *Examiner* wanted to reserve polemic oratory for his own columns, in which he lashed Governor John Letcher so meanly that the governor's brother, Lieutenant Colonel Sam Houston Letcher, tried to goad the editor into a duel.

Neither did Daniel allow personal sympathy to dilute his tirades. In the days after the governor's 3-year-old daughter died of diphtheria in

November, the *Examiner* actually sharpened its criticism. Red-haired Sam Letcher ran a "card" (personal advertisement) in the rival *Whig* calling Daniel "a mendacious slanderer and coward"—the verbal equivalent of slapping him across the face with his gloves. Daniel, still under the peace bond imposed by Mayor Mayo after his springtime run-in with Marmaduke Johnson, did not rise to the challenge. On his behalf, his colleague, Edward A. Pollard, denounced the colonel while the paper continued its running assault on the governor.[5]

But whether Congress was provisional or "permanent," its sessions open or closed, it spewed polemic aplenty and provoked more in return. Vice President Stephens would call it "a weak and contemptible body," and a Georgia editorialist would one day label congressmen as enemies of liberty who, if they did not resign, should "be hung like egg-sucking dogs!"[6] Impatient criticism of a revolutionary body trying to organize itself while improvising solutions to urgent problems was not entirely fair, but Southern press and politicians had played the role of critic for so long in national life that any other attitude seemed unnatural. Anger against Congress arose first in the original seven-state Confederacy, where provincial politicians resented Richmond's war-driven encroachment on individual states' rights. Indeed, in December there were rumors in the deeper South of moving the Confederate capital away from Richmond, perhaps to New Orleans or Nashville.

* * *

"Not so," Bagby told his Crescent City readers with the authority of one who had just spoken with someone who knew someone who should know. Viewing Richmond from the Spotswood or the Exchange Hotel, "the number of dram shops, lager beer houses, billiard rooms, faro banks, oyster cellars, etc., etc., is literally innumerable and appalling. Get down on your knees and pray that New Orleans may be delivered from the horrors of a political Capital."[7]

Earlier, Richmond's after-hours recreation had been concentrated in certain neighborhoods from which the righteous averted their eyes. But booming demand spread drinking, gambling, and whoring all over downtown.

At first, games of chance for wartime sportsmen were organized upstairs above the stores on Main Street; later, faro parlors and less specialized gambling operations broke out in every direction, and prospered despite raids by ax-wielding policemen. These "hells" operated on two levels, with separate rooms for high rollers and riffraff. Wine, food, and cigars were on the house, and inevitable overenjoyment of this hospitality brought on knife fights and at least one fatal duel.

Despite the raids, the dens prospered. "You can't suppress these nuisances," wrote Bagby. "The best plan would be to license them." He had heard that one "great faro dealer" had offered to pay the state's entire tax bill in return for a protected monopoly of the game. Bagby predicted that the gambling raids would shorten the session of the General Assembly and make winter dismal for congressmen and officers on leave. (One local reporter wrote that state legislators made so much noise cracking and eating peanuts that he was unable to hear the reading of a bill.)[8]

The mayor issued repeated declarations against vice, but they produced little but laughs. Prostitution erupted beyond the prewar array of bordellos along lower Cary Street, and discretion became a thing of the peaceful past. In good weather, fancy women strutted the streets, promenaded on Capitol Square, and were accused of crowding proper ladies off the sidewalks. Some 300 of them—white, black and mulatto—gathered around a coroner's inquest that was looking into a murder at Alice Hardgrove's house on Fifteenth Street. Mayor Mayo was indignant that while respectable citizens were on their way to church the indomitable Clara Coleman paraded in a carriage drawn by yellow horses, "making mouths at the ladies and bowing and kissing and flirting her hand at military officers."[9]

When a brothel opened opposite the YMCA Hospital on Tenth Street near Main, its girls flaunted themselves in upstairs windows, inspiring miraculous recovery in some patients, who crossed the street to say hello. Such comfortably housed businesses, with bawdy displays for window shoppers, had competition from individual enterprise of a lower order in parks and alleys. The predictable result was a rate of gonorrhea and syphilis that further overcrowded Richmond hospitals.

On the dark streets, muggers roamed despite increased patrols by the city's force of night watchmen. Still, night life boomed. At the Richmond Theater, rowdies jeered performers—perhaps with cause, since the theater manager himself admitted that the best professional actors had fled north and he had only managed "to collect enough of the fagends of disabled companies to open . . . with a passable exhibition of novelty, if not of talent."[10]

* * *

War, blockade, dissension, and disorder together could not suppress that Christmas in Richmond.

Coffee was selling for $1.50 a pound, turkeys for as much as $4 each, apples $20 a barrel, ice cream $9 a quart, "French candy" $1 a pound. Salt was going for the "tremendous price" of $1.40 a sack, and a few Richmonders were hoarding it till the price went higher, which it would surely do. One man reportedly had 8,000 sacks stowed away; another on Broad Street had a three-story houseful. Bagby's *Southern Literary Messenger* had to publish on dingy gray paper.[11]

But the essentials of holidaying were still available; the whiskey distiller Franklin Stearns was making a $4,000 profit a day, to hear Bagby tell it, and "could make five thousand if he would exert himself." Bagby may have exaggerated; Stearns, a former New Yorker and an unrepentant Union sympathizer, was not among his favorites. But Bagby did not stretch the truth when he added that the demand for whiskey was such that every gallon was sold as soon as it was made.[12]

Thus there was eggnog aplenty to go with turkey and plum pudding, firecrackers, rockets, drum-beating, horn-tooting, and assorted bloody noses and cracked skulls. Black Richmonders especially had more freedom and fun from Christmas to New Year's than at any other time of the year. Their owners and employers were traditionally tolerant in the week leading up to January 1, when the custom of hiring out slaves and servants reshuffled the lives of many.

In mock complaint, Bagby wrote that at one major hotel a lone black waiter showed up at dinner, "and at night not a black rascal was to be found to hand round the refreshments provided for the dancers." But while Christmas lasts, he said, "all boys, dogs and darkies ought to be allowed to have their swing."[13]

There was a soft, springlike breeze on New Year's Day. Bagby strolled past the *Dispatch* office and inspected a display of new flags proposed for the young Confederacy. He thought he could do better: "Hah! How would a buzzard sitting on a cotton bale, with a chew of tobacco in his mouth, a little nigger clasped in one claw, and a palmetto tree in the other, answer? Nothing could be more comprehensively Southern." All around him, residents and businesses were hiring black labor for 1862— women for as much as $150 for the year, men usually for $100, with experienced cooks of either gender at a premium.

For the first time since moving into their mansion, the Davises held a full-fledged New Year's Day levee like those they had attended on Pennsylvania Avenue in Washington when Davis was senator and secretary of war. For more than three hours the president greeted hundreds of visitors, from John Tyler to painstakingly dressed ladies of the Richmond bourgeoisie. They chatted cheerfully despite the fact that news was just in about the end of the *Trent* affair—Lincoln had finally released Mason and Slidell, cooling the crisis between London and Washington.

Thomas Bragg, the North Carolinian who had been attorney general for less than six weeks, insisted on imagining a bright side: "Though it may prevent a [U.S.] war with England, the moral effect of the action of the Lincoln government must be greatly to their prejudice and our advantage and it is highly probable that England will soon recognize our Independence."[14]

A Methodist preacher defied protocol and the gasps of proper ladies by bringing his three small children to meet the president—and Davis gave them more attention than he did many more dignified callers, summoning his own children to entertain them.[15] The convivial John Letcher was there, too, before departing to be host at the traditional Virginia governor's reception—where apple toddy flowed by the gallon, and so perhaps there was more realism than at Davis's levee.

* * *

That night the Richmond Theater opened its 1862 program with a production of *The Log Fort*, which included a make-believe battle with real smoke and gunpowder. The entrepreneur who kept theatrical melodrama flowing was John Hill Hewitt, a New Yorker who had attended the U.S. Military Academy, studied law and written plays, songs, reviews, and poetry, along the way befriending, then offending, Edgar Allan Poe. He was in Richmond teaching music when war came. As a former West Pointer, he asked Jefferson Davis for a job but got none.

Thus, in November, Hewitt became manager of the Richmond Theater. He did it with a certain feeling of guilt: "I had always considered myself a gentleman, and I found that, in taking control of this theatre and its vagabond company, I had forfeited my claim to a respectable stand in the ranks of Society—with one or two exceptions, the company I had engaged was composed of harlots and 'artful dodgers.'" One of those dodgers was his chief assistant, Richard D'Orsey Ogden.[16]

Some Richmonders must have thought that the sham combat in *The Log Fort* was anticlimactic compared with the offstage action at Hewitt's "den of inebriety and iniquity." In and around the theater, the season's excitement had included a homicide and a gang fight between a crew of "Baltimore Plugs" and a Butchertown crew defending its local turf.[17] But Hewitt turned in at his theater apartment that January night confident that he was off to a year of sensational profits.

Then, sometime after midnight, a series of explosions stirred him. He woke surrounded by flames, and was badly burned as he escaped.[18] The towering fire brought hundreds out of bed at 4:00 a.m. to watch the "scene of appalling grandeur," and scared thousands by cascading sparks onto the roofs of downtown Richmond. Bagby suspected that the fire had been set intentionally. On the wall of the theater's ruins somebody had painted the words "Alas, poor Yorick." Hewitt immediately rented the empty Trinity Church and reopened there as the Richmond Varieties. Everyone in Richmond recalled that early-morning fire and assumed that it would be the most memorable of their lives.[19]

*   *   *

At the depot a few days later, a thin, soldierly young man wept like a child as he clung to an infantry captain, begging him over and over not to leave. Except for his Confederate army overcoat, the young man was dressed like an undertaker, in black suit and hat. The train gathered steam to depart, and the captain gently pulled himself away. He boarded, and waved from a car window as the train took him back to his regiment.

The young man turned to the street. "My good, dear brother," he thought, "my splendid hero brother—Oh! God!" He walked back to his boardinghouse, shaking his head, puzzling over how the twists of war had left him walking the streets of Richmond while his brother headed for duty in the field.

"Oh! God! I may have parted from him forever. He goes to battle against his people, his kinfolks and the flag that has watched over him since infancy. Is it not strange, is it not passing all understanding, the inscrutable ways of Providence! To think of it, brother against brother. . . ."[20]

The brother who departed was Confederate Captain John Donaldson of the Kanawha Riflemen. The brother left behind in Richmond was not a Confederate but Union Sergeant Francis A. Donaldson, of what was called the California Regiment, later the Seventy-first Pennsylvania.

Before 1861, John had moved from the family's home in Philadelphia to Charleston, in western Virginia, where he adopted the Southern cause. When war came, he had joined a company organized by Captain George S. Patton, a Virginia Military Institute graduate who was one of Richmond's "kid glove soldiers" and the grandfather of a more famous twentieth-century officer of the same name. Frank Donaldson enlisted in Philadelphia and was among nearly 700 Yankees who were captured in the October fiasco at Ball's Bluff.[21]

Taken to Richmond, Frank hoped to see John there. "You can imagine with what joy I looked forward to a meeting with a brother I love so well, and one who has gone so far astray as he has done, even to lifting up his hand against a government which has protected him from his youth up," he wrote from prison to another brother in Philadelphia. But John's regiment had moved back to the mountains, and he got leave to go to Richmond only after Frank had spent weeks in captivity.[22]

Once there, however, Captain Donaldson used all his influence to free his brother. He looked up his regimental adjutant, Noyes Rand of the Twenty-second Virginia, who as a student at Washington College in Lexington had known future Governor Letcher. Through Rand, John was able to get a letter from the Confederate War Department setting his brother free on parole. John and Rand, sharing quarters at the Spotswood, hired a carriage, proceeded to Libby Prison, and picked up Frank, thus transporting him "from hell into heaven."

John found Frank a room in a private home with a gentlemanly ex-soldier of the Kanawha Riflemen, Levi Welch, with whom he had good-natured political arguments. Yet another of John's friends, a civilian official named Joel Shrewsbury, offered Frank a job in the Post Office Department if he would stay in Richmond. But John urged him to return to duty under the U.S. flag he had sworn to uphold, advice that only confirmed his brother's intention.

Meanwhile, however, Frank was free to stroll the streets, watching troops come and go, listening to hotel gossip, making mental notes. He attended St. Paul's Church, where he looked down from the balcony on Jefferson Davis at worship. At first, passersby jeered him because his only clothes were his Federal uniform. To stop this, Rand swapped overcoats with him. Frank was so grateful that he pledged that if either John or Rand was ever captured by Union forces, he would "crawl on his hands & knees to Washington if necessary to secure our release."[*23]

But in late January Frank had to face the "sore trial" of John's leaving for the field. He feared that the scene at the depot had made him "quite contemptible" in the eyes of bystanders, but "I could not help it—my feelings got the better of my manhood. . . ." Part of those feelings was gratitude, and part was the fact of separating again to fight on opposing sides. This separation had not been so painful the first time, when John was far away in Charleston and Frank joined the army in Philadelphia.

"To think of it," Frank wrote—"brother against brother.

"Still for all that, I love him so tenderly and had he been less honorable than he is, this very heart's tenderness could have been worked

---

*Frank Donaldson was exchanged by flag-of-truce boat on February 19, 1862. Wounded at Fair Oaks, he later became captain of Company H, 118th Pennsylvania Infantry—the "Corn Exchange Regiment." When Noyes Rand was captured and taken to Johnson's Island in Sandusky Bay, he was unable to find out where Frank's unit was to ask him for help. Later, John Donaldson was also captured, and held at Fort Delaware. He did correspond with his brother, but Frank was unable to free him without John's taking the oath of allegiance to the Union, which he refused to do.[24]

upon to have had me remain here, and awaited the termination of the bloody embitterment of war. Even now, I am utterly powerless to express my feelings and as I write my eyes are blinded with the tears that refuse to be stayed and I write I know not what."[25]

Frank told his family that he would be an ingrate if he later told Federal officers what he saw and heard every day in Richmond, because he was deeply grateful for the way he had been treated.[26] Other, less naive Union loyalists in Richmond were also treated with great consideration. But they were more secretive than Donaldson, who as he awaited exchange made no pretense of who he was, except to shed his provocative blue overcoat.

* * *

Frank Donaldson's sadness on parting with his brother matched the mood of Richmond around him that winter. The weather darkened the prospect for anonymous diarists in puppy love as much as for politicians in charge of the lives of thousands.

Near midtown a teenager daydreaming of a fickle medical student complained to her diary:

"Rain, rain, all the time. . . . I cannot imagine why Mr. H. has not been, he used to come so often . . . maybe he will come to-morrow night, I hope, I hope he will. . . . Well I must not think any more about it, but wait until he comes, and if he dont come, I shan't care anything about it. . . . It has just struck 10 o'clock I must go to bed, I hope I will dream pleasantly about him, Oh! I had such a sweet one last night; I thought that he took me in his arms and kissed me."

The next morning she looked out: "Really, it almost seems as if it will never be clear again. Last night it commenced snowing, then turned to hailing, and now, I believe it is snowing, raining, and hailing, all at the same time. . . ."[27]

From the president's house the view was no brighter. After talking with Davis and other cabinet secretaries, Attorney General Bragg summed up the situation: "Upon the whole, we have much to apprehend."

The tightening blockade was beginning to cut the supply of military essentials and medicine as well as consumer goods like coffee and tea. Measles, typhoid, pneumonia, and dysentery were sweeping through the army. Richmond was flooded with officers dissipating on furlough and dispirited soldiers heading home, perhaps not to return in the spring. Many troops who had enlisted for three months, six months, or a year were balking at signing up for the duration of the war. The governors of Georgia, Florida, and North and South Carolina were demanding the return of any arms sent from their states that had not already been issued to their own troops.

"The President was much irritated" by this, Bragg wrote. Davis declared that if the states held this course, carrying on the war would be impossible—"that we had better make terms as soon as we could, and those of us who had halters around our necks had better get out of the country as speedily as possible. . . .

"I have not seen him so gloomy. I wish he was a dictator. He is an able and honorable man—somewhat irritable when opposed—wants to have his own way, but left to himself he would conduct things more wisely, safely and energetically than he can now. . . ."[28]

In mid-January, 71-year-old John Tyler, tenth president of the United States and the sixth from Virginia, died after a public career that reached back to the War of 1812. Last of the golden-era Virginians who led the country between Revolution and Civil War, he had become president upon the death of William Henry Harrison; the two were born barely six miles apart in Charles City County, just downriver from Richmond.

During the secession crisis Tyler had represented Virginia's strained conscience as faithfully as any man. Though he declared himself morally opposed to slavery, he was a plantation slave owner and defender of states' right to decide the issue for themselves. After resisting secession and working desperately for compromise, he supported his state when it came to war. He was Richmond's delegate to the Provisional Congress, and had been elected to the Confederate House of Representatives. Now, state and new nation paid him homage.

His body lay in the Capitol before being taken to St. Paul's, where a crowd had gathered in the rain. After the funeral, the State Guard, a military band, and carriages bearing the president, the cabinet, Congress, and the state legislature followed the hearse and the family to Hollywood Cemetery, west of town by the river. There Tyler was buried near James Monroe, whose body had been brought home to Virginia in 1858 on the centennial of his birth, after lying for twenty-seven years in New York. State funerals were becoming a matter of practiced routine in Richmond.[29]

And still it rained.

Judith Brockenbrough McGuire, forced out of Alexandria, had moved away from the Yankees to one Virginia town after another. At last her husband, the Reverend John P. McGuire, principal of Alexandria's Episcopal High School, got a clerk's job in the Confederate Post Office, so she went looking for quarters in the overcrowded capital.

Judith was not just another of the thousands of undistinguished refugees. She was one of the Richmond Brockenbroughs, the family of bankers and judges that had built the mansion where President Davis now lived. Still, she was turned away repeatedly at hotels and boarding-houses, because there simply was no vacancy. After slogging through the downpour for three days, she heard from a friend of a friend about a place at Mr. Lefevre's school on Grace Street; he was renting out rooms because enrollment had dwindled so. Having seen how others had to live, McGuire was grateful for what she got.[30]

Few arriving in a capital "full from cellar to roof" could put on a jaunty face like that of the carefree 24-year-old bachelor Burton Harri-son. A Phi Beta Kappa at Yale, he had been an assistant professor at the University of Mississippi when he was recommended as the president's private secretary, replacing the jovial and bibulous Robert Josselyn. Har-rison was lucky to be able to board with relatives while earning the af-fectionate confidence of both Jeff and Varina Davis. New in Richmond, he wrote to a university friend that he was delighted to meet "all the po-litical and military grandees . . . then too I meet all my old flames, and am utterly distracted with uncertainty as to which one it behooves me to cultivate. . . . what will become of me is a mystery which Cupid and fu-ture alone can determine."[31]

The burdens of office sat lightly on young Harrison that gloomy win-ter, but officials like Robert G. H. Kean, soon to be chief of the War Bu-reau, knew enough to empathize with soldiers in the field. Kean left the capital to visit the army and reported: "For nearly a fortnight there has been but two days in which the sun has shown. Rain, hail, snow, sleet, mist have succeeded each other in dreary round—pitchy dark nights, dismal days, the whole earth one mud hole. . . . There seems to me to be a more general feeling of despondency prevailing at this time than ever before since the war began."[32]

Less than two weeks after Kean's assessment, news from west and south plunged Richmond deeper into despond. Union forces under Ulysses S. Grant had taken Fort Henry on the Tennessee River, giving the Federals a water route into the Deep South that bypassed the Mis-sissippi. That same day, another thrust came closer to home: Roanoke Island on the North Carolina coast fell to a Federal amphibious force, clearing the way into Albemarle Sound and opening the back door to Norfolk and potentially to Richmond.

More than 2,500 Confederates were captured at Roanoke Island, among them a thousand of the Wise Legion. The Legion's commander, Henry Wise, was bedridden with pleurisy at Nag's Head, so he missed the fighting. But among the dead was his son and champion, Jennings, captain of the Richmond Blues, dueling editor of the *Enquirer,* darling of the Confederate capital.

A steamer bringing young Wise's body from Roanoke Island stopped at Currituck. There General Wise had the coffin opened, leaned to kiss his son's face, and moaned the truth: "Oh, my brave boy, you have died for me, you have died for me."[33]

At Richmond there was another crowded funeral, this one at St. James's, and another long procession of carriages in the rain. And there Jennings Wise's brother John, now fifteen, "gazed for the last time in the cold, calm face . . . saw the black pageant which testified to the general mourning as they bore him to his last resting-place in beautiful Hollywood," and vowed to "bury these hands in the heart of some of those who wrought this deed!"[34]

*   *   *

Not all of those mourned were public heroes. On one of the president's days of fast and prayer, Maria Hubard stayed home at Rose Cottage, on the city's western edge, rather than go to church. She joined a congregation of servants singing and praying over "poor little Temple, our little coloured boy," who had died after she tended him in a long illness. The next morning, after a sad procession to the cemetery, Maria planted a hyacinth and named it for "poor good little Temple."

"Ella and I really wept as much as though he was some relative instead of a poor slave," she wrote in her diary. "What would the Northern Abolitionists say could they have witnessed the scene?"[35]

Maria would need a reservoir of tears.

Her husband, the painter, had worked up and down the Atlantic coast before settling in Gloucester, Virginia, on the Chesapeake Bay. Moving to Richmond with his bride, he was befriended by Edward A. Peticolas, then the capital's leading artist, and Mann Valentine, Jr., a patron of the arts who later created the city museum named for his family, where many of Hubard's works were preserved.

In the 1850s Hubard switched his talents to sculpture, gaining the exclusive right to make bronze replicas of Jean Antoine Houdon's marble statue of Washington, which graces the rotunda of the Virginia Capitol. But he had managed to sell only six Washingtons when war came, and he turned to producing cannon instead of statues.

Learning to cast twelve-pounders at his home foundry on Grove Street was a slow process. Maria sold strawberries and other garden produce in season, but their winter income was almost nil. Though they could buy no presents at Christmas, they invited friends in for eggnog.

William, who had experimented with explosives before the war, broadened into the production of artillery shells.[36]

One late afternoon during gray February, Maria stepped into their storeroom to draw whiskey for bottling. As she turned off the tap there was a crash in William's workshop. She ran out. There came another report, and a scream.

"Oh! God! How shall I tell it?" she asked later. "I saw my idolized husband coming out of his gate, his hair standing up high all over his head, and his face bleeding . . . his dear hands stretched out on either side, shattered and bleeding!!!" She ran and threw her arms about him.

"My precious husband, are your beautiful eyes out?"

"No, my darling," he whispered. "I can see you and my beautiful children."

Though William's coat was afire, he was calm as she pulled him inside, ripped off the coat and plunged his mangled hand into a bucket of water. Then he fainted. A doctor came and amputated part of three fingers and a thumb; William would be an artist no more. They did not tell him yet that his painful leg was broken and would also have to be amputated. In the self-possession of shock, he told Maria that the night before, he had looked at her sleeping and knelt beside her:

"How I prayed, how I prayed, how I prayed to smooth your pillow free from care, and that I might give you the luxuries of life. . . ."[37]

That night he slept, and the next day Sally Tompkins came from her hospital to see him, and urged Maria to sleep, too. Maria later wrote in her diary: "Oh could I have known the next day would have been his last on earth, no power could have induced me for one moment to have left his dear side."[38]

Three weeks later, the widow Hubard wept again as her 18-year-old son departed for Virginia Military Institute to learn to be an officer.[39]

CHAPTER NINE

YOU'LL HAVE YOUR
HANDS FULL

*T*was a grave and great assemblage," wrote one onlooker. "Time-honoured men were there, who had witnessed ceremony after ceremony of inaugurations in the palmiest days of the old confederation; those who had been at the inauguration of the iron-willed Jackson; men who, in their fiery Southern ardour, had thrown down the gauntlet of defiance in the halls of Federal legislation, and, in the face of the enemy, avowed their determination to be free, and finally witnessed the enthroning of a Republican despot in our Country's Father's Chair of State. All were there; and silent tears were seen coursing down the cheeks of gray-haired men, while the determined will stood out in every feature."[1]

At 11 o'clock Saturday morning, February 22, 1862, the Confederate Congress and the Virginia General Assembly gathered in the Capitol for Jefferson Davis's inauguration as president of the "permanent" government. The galleries were reserved for ladies, and were full despite the downpour outside. Male spectators crammed the rotunda. Mrs. Davis and the cabinet sat facing the president's chair.

When Davis arrived he was pale as always and tense with the significance of the moment. Dressed in plain black, he sat in the Speaker's chair until officials formed up to move outside. Mounted men had to clear a path through the crowd. As the president stepped onto the bunting-draped stand at the base of the Washington Monument, he could see few of the roughly 2,000 faces beneath a forest of black umbrellas, covering the muddy Capitol grounds and streets close by.

Davis had carefully planned this ceremony for this day on this spot. If anything could inspire the new nation to persevere, the recollection of George Washington should do it; to insist on the link between the first American Revolution and this one, the Great Seal of the Confederacy portrayed this statue of the first president. But what the South had done in the year just past overshadowed the memory of what the colonies had done eight decades earlier.

Since Davis had taken provisional office, Confederate victories at Big Bethel, Manassas, and Ball's Bluff had lifted morale unrealistically high, so that when reverses followed, it had far to fall. Brass bands and orators had hailed the secession of Virginia, North Carolina, Tennessee, and Arkansas, and the motions of secession by rump governments in Kentucky and Missouri.

Maps and casualty lists, however, spoke more meaningfully than music and speeches. The early expectation that a show of stiff resistance by the South would persuade a halfhearted North to back down was now forgotten. Those first Confederate victories had instead determined the Union to mobilize men and material for a war of political survival. Now most of Virginia east of the Chesapeake and west of the Shenandoah was in Yankee hands. Six days before Davis's inauguration, a no-nonsense U.S. general named Grant demanded and got the unconditional surrender of Fort Donelson on the Cumberland River. This took away Kentucky and much of Tennessee; Confederates immediately began evacuating Nashville, moving the Tennessee capital to Memphis.

As if military setbacks were not enough, Davis was hearing troublesome noises from an enlivened legislative branch. The newly sworn Confederate Congress was in session, debating demands for the resignation of Secretary of War Benjamin, scapegoating him for the loss of Roanoke Island and urging a congressional role in strategic planning. When someone argued that "Congress should not usurp the military power," a waspish member from Tennessee drew laughs by declaring, "If simply to express an opinion is to be styled and considered usurpation, I want to go home."[2]

Now, as Davis stood in the rain, the carping recessed for a while. He waited minutes for cheers from beneath the umbrellas to die down. Then he took the oath of office, lifted and kissed the Bible, and opened his address with an unnecessary reminder of why the crowd stood where it did:[3] "On this, the birth-day of the man most identified with the establishment of American independence, and beneath the monument erected to commemorate his heroic virtues and those of his compatriots, we have assembled to usher into existence the permanent Government of the Confederate States. Through this instrumentality, under the favor of Divine Providence, we hope to perpetuate the principles of our Revolutionary fathers. The day, the memory and the purpose seem fitly associated."

Retracing the reasons for secession, Davis said that any possibility of rejoining the Union had been wiped out by the North's "malignity and barbarity" thus far in the war. In seeming sincerity, he cited Union disregard for "all the time-honored bulwarks of civil and religious liberty." He decried "Bastilles filled with prisoners, arrested without civil process . . . the writ of habeas corpus suspended . . . civil officers, peaceful citizens, and gentle women incarcerated for opinion's sake. . . ."

Confederate loyalty to the original Constitution had been proven, he said, by "the fact that through all the necessities of an unequal struggle, there has been no act on our part to impair personal liberty or the freedom of speech, of thought or of the press. . . ."

Davis admitted that "the tide for the moment is against us," and that his "permanent" government was taking over at "the darkest hour of our struggle," brought on by recent serious disasters. But he said that "the final result in our favor is not doubtful." Soon the North would sink under the immense debts that it had contracted. Even the blockade of the South had its bright side: "It is fast making us a self supporting and an independent people."

Then, as Reverend Minnigerode had urged, Davis called on "Him whose favor is ever vouchsafed to the cause which is just." Lifting his eyes and arms, he concluded: "With humble gratitude and adoration, acknowledging the Providence which has so visibly protected the Confederacy during its brief but eventful career, to Thee, Oh God! I trustingly commit myself, and prayerfully invoke Thy blessing on my country and its cause."[4]

* * *

In the predawn darkness, little more than a week after Davis's inaugural criticism of the suppression of civil liberties in the North, a pounding at the door woke John Minor Botts at his home on the western edge of Richmond.

Armed deputies surrounded the house as Captain A. C. Godwin, assistant provost marshal, arrested the 59-year-old ex-congressman. Botts's son fainted; his family was frantic. Without a warrant, Godwin took Botts in a buggy to what his prisoner called "a filthy negro jail" in downtown Richmond.[5]

Three hours earlier, a posse had arrived at Tree Hill, Franklin Stearns's estate just beyond Rocketts, southeast of Richmond. When

Stearns opened the door and saw the detectives, he said, "I suppose you're arresting me because I'm a Union man."

"Right," said a captain.

"Well, you'll have your hands full," said Stearns.[6]

Davis had castigated the North for filling prisons without due process and jailing citizens "for opinion's sake." He had boasted that despite the war, the South had committed no such outrages against civil liberties. Five days after he spoke, a bill was rammed through both houses of the new Confederate Congress, allowing the president to suspend the writ of habeas corpus. Davis signed it and quickly placed endangered Norfolk and Portsmouth under martial law.

Two days later he issued the same order covering Richmond and ten miles beyond, effective at midnight of March 1, 1862. General Winder, named provost marshal, was charged with enforcing the edict in Richmond and Henrico County. Before dawn his men started their roundup of citizens suspected of disloyalty.[7]

In their first sweep they took in Botts; Stearns; Valentine Heckler, a butcher; John M. Higgins, a grocer; Burnham Wardwell, an ice dealer; Charles Crouse, a city night watchman; August Brummell, a lieutenant in the Wise Legion, and assorted others, for such offenses as "uttering incendiary sentiment." They arrested Charles Tickwell for saying in the presence of two black men that "the Yankees will soon be here, and all the Negroes will be free." They brought in a slave named Allen, property of Richard Whitfield, for "treasonous language." What Allen had said was, "Jeff Davis is a rebel," and "I acknowledge no man as my master." The Mayor's Court sentenced him to thirty-nine lashes and indefinite imprisonment.[8]

Winder's police locked their prisoners in what had been "McDaniel's negro jail," a holding pen for slave dealers in an alley off Franklin Street opposite Wall. The newspapers made it seem cozy: "thirteen clean and well-ventilated rooms, comfortable beds, accommodations far surpassing nine out of ten of the cheap boarding houses of Richmond." Renamed Castle Godwin for its commandant, it would soon be jammed overfull, and earn its reputation for being less than hospitable to guests.[9]

Winder confiscated Stearns's and other distilleries and ordered a halt to all sales of alcohol. As chief of police he named Samuel Maccubbin, who, like many of Winder's other detectives, came from Baltimore. Three guard detachments with muskets patrolled the streets, in addition to the city's regular night watchmen.

The crackdown on alcohol thinned out the number of street drunks, and the city's taverns seemed shut tight when seen from the street. But inside, glasses still clinked and laughter rang as business proceeded through the back door. The papers complained that while saloons for ordinary soldiers and workmen were nominally closed, plush faro parlors catering to senior officers and bureaucrats rollicked on undisturbed.[10]

The enabling act gave Davis power to suspend habeas corpus "in such cities, towns and military districts as shall, in his judgment, be in such danger of attack by the enemy as to require the declaration of martial law for their effective defense." Norfolk and Portsmouth were in imminent danger. The Federal invasion of eastern North Carolina, combined with the force long established at Fortress Monroe, raised the threat to Richmond.

Davis knew that the redoubled Northern army under General McClellan was trained and waiting to move with the spring. In his first message to the new Congress, he admitted that in the year just past, "events have demonstrated that the government had attempted more than it had power necessarily to achieve. . . . In efforts to protect, by our arms, the whole territory of the Confederate States, sea-board and inland, we have been so exposed as to encounter serious disasters."[11]

To nudge Congress, on the day it acted Richmond papers reprinted a Baltimore item quoting a paroled Union soldier, who had served as quartermaster clerk in the Richmond prisons. This Yankee, George W. Walker of Pennsylvania, had been less scrupulous about honoring the terms of his parole than Philadelphian Frank Donaldson had been when wandering Richmond as he awaited exchange.

Walker told Northern friends that "a strong and gallant band" of Union men in Richmond was "willing and anxious to welcome the old flag." He said it was 3,000 strong, and could turn out a trained regiment on an hour's notice. He added that "Union ladies are also very numerous," spending their means to help Federals in the capital's prisons and hospitals.[12]

From a Yankee safely across the Potomac, such unsettling talk might seem a mere scare tactic—but Stearns also heightened concern in Richmond when he told his captors they would have their hands full if they were rounding up all the city's Union men. That he was one of them was known by everyone in town. The *Enquirer* reported that his house was suspected of being "a rendezvous of Lincoln sympathizers." The *Examiner* said, "It is the universal conviction that Franklin Stearns, by means of his whiskey, has killed more of our men and done more to disorganize our army than all the balance of the Yankee nation put together."[13] (A little later the *Dispatch* would josh that some whiskey seized by the police was poured into the street and split the cobblestones for a quarter mile, sounding like claps of thunder and making some Richmonders think a general engagement was under way.)[14]

The police recorded further evidence against Stearns when they arrested the Reverend Alden Bosserman, pastor of the Universalist Church two blocks east of the Capitol. Born in Maine, Bosserman had come from Baltimore to take over the Richmond mission in January 1861. When President Davis proclaimed a day of thanksgiving after Manassas, Bosserman had refused to open his church. He refused again when Davis proclaimed February 28 a day of fasting.[15]

As Elizabeth Van Lew wrote, these official fast days, when markets and stores were closed, were "more scrupulously observed than the Sabbath," because they were considered "test days of [Confederate] loyalty." Van Lew thus made a contrary point of having a better dinner on those days than usual—"and as it was a holyday, it was a great comfort to see and talk with any fellow [Union] loyalists, if that were possible."[16]

Obviously Bosserman failed the Confederacy's loyalty test. On the Sunday before his arrest he allegedly had prayed that "this unholy rebellion be crushed out." He was quoted as saying that he did not observe fast days because Stearns had urged him not to—and Stearns contributed more money to his church than the rest of the congregation together.[17]

Spy fever escalated amid the great roundup of suspects, many of whom were guilty of nothing more dangerous than loose lips and unfashionable opinions.

Winder's attitude toward these civilian Unionists may have been harshened by what had happened to his brothers William and Charles, arrested in the North and held for months because of their Confederate sympathies. William Winder was almost as outspoken in Federal prison as John Botts was in General Winder's captivity. He wrote from Fort Warren in Boston Harbor that "the illegal, unconstitutional & oppressive rule which forbids our discussing military or political matters induces me to forego any expression of my sentiments. . . . There is not much choice in going out of here in the silence of death or into our land divided & distracted, embittered, desolate, subjected to despotism which would seem to be the fate now being foreshadowed. . . ."[18]

But here and there, on both sides, fire was found beneath the smoke of disloyal rhetoric. Some of those arrested by Winder had done more than talk. And public fears seemed justified when the newspapers disclosed that the provost marshal's men had cracked the first serious spy operation uncovered in Richmond.

*   *   *

Luck had a lot to do with it.

One night in late October 1861, a 40-year-old mail carrier named Timothy Webster had sneaked across Chesapeake Bay in a blockade runner's log canoe. A few days later, he reached Richmond aboard a steam packet from the lower James. He checked into the Spotswood and set about delivering dispatches he had brought from the North. Among them was a letter of introduction to a former Baltimorean named William Campbell, a leather contractor with the Confederate War Department. With Campbell, Webster drove around the defensive batteries surrounding the city, then stopped at the Confederate ordnance department for a chat with the officer in charge. The next day he returned to the fortifications alone, strolling about, making notes and sketches. A day later he went with Campbell to John B. Jones's office and got a pass to Manassas and Centreville. He proceeded there, looked over the disposition of the Confederate army, and stopped in Warrenton before returning to Richmond.

Without being questioned, Webster got another pass to recross the lines via Fredericksburg and Yorktown, delivering mail northward for Confederate officials. Back in Washington, he handed over an immense batch of intelligence information to General McClellan.[19]

All this happened while John Jones himself was complaining about the ease with which passes north were being issued, Confederate cabinet members were commiserating with one another over the likelihood that someone was reading their mail, and journalists were blaming the trusting character of Southerners for the widely suspected infestation of Yankee spies.

Official laxity and native naïveté did, indeed, help Northern agents penetrate Richmond. But Timothy Webster could never have operated as effectively as he had without savoir faire, courage, and years of undercover experience. He was "a Pinkerton"—working for Allan Pinkerton, who ran the famous Chicago detective agency. Pinkerton had recommended Webster as a confidential dispatch carrier for Lincoln within a week after the start of war. When McClellan took command of the Union army and asked Pinkerton to set up a Secret Service, Webster had already worked himself into the busy Confederate underground in Baltimore. There he collected letters for delivery in Richmond. Thus, when Southern sympathizers sneaked him through the lines, they believed they were helping their own cause.

In Richmond, Webster posed as an Englishman, hung around the War Department and the newspapers, and ingratiated himself with officials high and low. Both Winder and Judah Benjamin trusted him enough to use him as a dispatch carrier going north again.[20]

Webster was only one of the agents dispatched to Richmond by Pinkerton that first fall and winter of war. In his memoirs, the spymaster related that in November, shortly after Webster's first trip, he sent Mrs. E. H. Baker, a former resident of the Confederate capital, back to visit old friends there. Her mission was to discover what she could about Southern success with "torpedoes"—naval mines. Her host was a Captain Atwater, a secret Union sympathizer.

With him she toured the Richmond fortifications and bluntly asked to visit the Tredegar Iron Works, where torpedoes were being built. Atwater agreed, but first he was scheduled to watch a submarine test in the river below Richmond. Mrs. Baker invited herself along, heard a complete account of how the secret weapon worked, and witnessed the destruction of a scow by a charge mounted on a spar extending from the submarine's bow. A larger model was under construction to combat the Union blockade at the mouth of the James.

According to Pinkerton, Mrs. Baker went the next day to the Tredegar and saw the full-scale submarine nearing completion. Then she said goodbye to the hospitable Atwater and returned to Washington via Fredericksburg. Pinkerton said that alerted Federal seamen soon afterward spotted a submarine's breathing apparatus and disabled the vessel before it could attack.[21]

Pinkerton's and other accounts make it seem that Northern agents, professional and amateur, were almost tripping over each other in Richmond as both sides prepared for the Union spring offensive.

The spymaster, who used the cover name of "Major E.J. Allen," also related his operatives' night rides and narrow escapes in southern Maryland and the Virginia Peninsula. They moved through Henrico County east of Richmond with the help of a friendly innkeeper. Webster returned to Richmond, working with a pretty matron named Hattie Lawton, whose husband, Hugh, was another Federal agent. John Scobell, a talented ex-slave from Mississippi, had been recruited as a spy after fleeing north. He posed as Mrs. Lawton's servant.

When Webster fell ill with painful rheumatism, Mrs. Lawton tended him in his hotel room. But Webster was so immobilized that he let weeks go by without reporting to Washington. Early in March 1862 Pinkerton, worried about his best agent, sent two experienced detectives to find out what had happened to him. They were Price Lewis and John Scully, who made it to Richmond carrying a letter from a fictional volunteer spy for the South, and checked into the Exchange Hotel. When they asked about Webster at the *Enquirer,* for which he had carried mail, they were sent to the Monumental Hotel.

There they found Webster with Mrs. Lawton and a Richmond acquaintance. That conversation was guarded and brief. When they came back, Webster had another visitor—his carefully cultivated friend Samuel Maccubbin, General Winder's chief detective. Maccubbin genially told them to be sure to register with the provost marshal. On reporting there, they were questioned by Winder himself. Lewis pretended to be an Englishman and Scully an Irishman, both hoping to prosper in blockade running.

It seemed their cover story had succeeded when they returned to Webster's room to tell him all about it—but suddenly one of Winder's men appeared, to inquire exactly where they came from across the sea. The moment this detective departed, Webster warned them to leave town immediately. They hardly had time to react before two more men entered. One was a detective. The other was Chase Morton, son of the ex-governor of Florida.

A few months earlier, Lewis and Scully had searched the Morton family's Washington house looking for evidence of pro-Southern shenanigans. Now young Morton identified them as Union detectives. They denied it, but Winder ordered them jailed.

Three days later Scully was taken away, leaving Lewis in the cell. Lewis joined an escape scheme already under way and got out with about twenty other prisoners—only to be retaken, hungry and chilled, in a mid-March storm. Scully, meanwhile, had been tried, identified by the whole Morton family, and convicted. Two days after Lewis was recaptured he, too, was quickly convicted, and the two were transferred from Henrico jail to separate cells in Castle Godwin. A day later, both men were sentenced to be hanged.

But Winder was more interested in Webster. With threats of death and promises of mercy, his men broke first Scully, then Lewis, just before the date of their scheduled hanging. The spies told all about Webster's mission and their own. Webster, after lying quietly for days wondering what had happened to his colleagues, had improved enough to move to the home of his sympathetic friend Campbell. Then, after Scully and Lewis uncloaked Webster, Philip Cashmyer, another of Winder's men, arrived to carry out what he called his "painful duty" to arrest Webster and Hattie Lawton. Not until much later would the truth of Cashmyer's regret become clear.[22]

Webster and Lawton were locked in Castle Godwin; by then, some 232 allegedly disloyal citizens, 9 deserters, 25 other Confederate offenders, and 9 blacks had joined the Union captives in Richmond's political prisons.[23] Still among them were John Minor Botts and Franklin Stearns, arrested in Winder's first sweep at the beginning of martial law.

* * *

Since that early March, Union forces had begun to move on every front.

Joseph Johnston surprised President Davis by withdrawing his army from around Manassas to the Rappahannock River, only fifty miles from Richmond. Stonewall Jackson pulled back up the Shenandoah Valley. Confederates lost New Bern on the North Carolina coast. Federal troops probed out of Fortress Monroe toward Yorktown. Most alarming to Richmond, there was a historic naval collision downstream that first raised, then ended, Southern hopes of breaking the Union blockade.

The Confederates had lifted the sunken Union steamer *Merrimack*, armored her sides with iron plate from the Tredegar works, boosted her firepower, rechristened her the CSS *Virginia*, and sent her out against the Federal fleet in Hampton Roads. There she attacked and sank or ran aground several wooden-hulled Union warships before retiring for the night. During that night, however, the Federal ironclad *Monitor* arrived from New York to challenge her.

Early the next day, March 9, 1862, "the modern era of naval warfare began" when the two clumsy vessels blasted and rammed each other for hours before at last backing away. Superficially, it was a drawn battle, but the *Monitor* had neutralized the *Merrimack*. By doing so she eliminated any Confederate naval threat to McClellan's latest strategic plan, to approach Richmond from the east by moving his main army up the Peninsula between the James and York rivers. Eight days after the battle of the ironclads, the first ships of a long procession began moving Union troops down the Potomac from Alexandria.[24]

Someone in Richmond had to be held responsible for all this bad news. The morning after McClellan began shifting his army, the increasingly anti-Davis Richmond *Whig* declared that "Our president has lost the confidence of the country." The paper did not aim at cabinet officers, who were widely blamed for Confederate misfortunes; they were "merely headclerks," while the president tried to do everything himself.[25]

That very day, Davis switched Judah Benjamin from the War Department to the State Department, replacing him with George Wythe Randolph of Virginia. R. M. T. Hunter, who had been secretary of state, took a seat in the new Senate.

Benjamin, like Commissary General Northrop, was a whipping boy for those seeking reasons to attack Davis. As Congress dragged out its investigation of the Roanoke Island disaster, legislators faulted Benjamin for inadequately reinforcing the island before its fall. Others criticized him because he had overseen the pass system by which suspicious travelers came and went so freely. Moving him from War to State Department only annoyed those critics more.

But Benjamin seemed "secure in his own views and indifferent to public odium . . . with perfectly bland manner and unwearying courtesy . . . his rosy, smiling visage impressed all who approached him with the vague belief that he had just heard good news, which would be immediately promulgated for public delectation." And that, predictably, annoyed his assailants still further.[26]

From the other direction, Botts in Castle Godwin blamed the "corrupt and contemptible little vagabond, Benjamin," for the excesses of martial law. As soon as Benjamin was transferred from the War Department, Botts wrote to Randolph as one old-family Virginian to another. He insisted that since failing to hold the state back from secession, he had "determined to retire from the field," and voiced his opinions only when asked. Since his arrest he had been kept in solitary confinement, and his family and lawyers had been refused permission to visit. Winder had told him that he was charged not for his private opinions but for heading an organization intended to undermine the Confederate government.

"Ridiculous," said Botts. When Winder alleged that he had been informed of this by Franklin Stearns, Botts laughed and noted that Stearns was being held prisoner only thirty feet away, and that he would be glad to rest his case entirely on Stearns's testimony.

"Great God!" Botts wrote, citing the arrest of so many without benefit of hearing or counsel. "Can a Virginia gentleman witness such scenes as these, and not have the blood curdle in his veins?" He demanded a fair trial for himself and all those others, declaring that "The consequences growing out of this communication will serve to show whether or not the Star Chamber, the Inquisition . . . have been really transferred from the Old World into the heart and capital of Virginia."[27]

Though he had hired three lawyers, in April the irrepressible Botts argued his own case before a military tribunal. After eight weeks in prison, he was paroled on condition that he move away from Richmond to the interior of Virginia, stay there, and keep his mouth shut for the duration.[28]

Botts's account of a peculiar exchange during his time in jail drapes more mystery about one of the feared figures of wartime Richmond: Captain George W. Alexander, who took charge of Castle Godwin after escaping from Federal captivity in Baltimore's Fort McHenry.

Alexander, born in Pennsylvania, had quit the U.S. Navy to enlist as a

Confederate army private. He had become a lieutenant by the time he accompanied Colonel Richard Thomas when Thomas masqueraded as a French lady to seize the Union vessel *St. Nicholas* the previous summer. While attempting another such coup, Alexander and Thomas were captured on the Eastern Shore and taken to Baltimore. There, Alexander would say later, he was "kept in a cell seven by four for three weeks, that cell underground with no window." With the aid of his wife, he escaped by leaping from the fort, injuring an ankle, and was smuggled back across the lines by the Maryland underground.[29]

Because of his game ankle, Alexander was assigned to prison duty in Richmond. But he was still mobile enough to lead a raid that swept up eighty-nine suspects and a batch of illegal liquor along Hughes Row, in the neighborhood of Richmond's Seventeenth Street, the Old Market and the docks. This contingent was too much for the already over-crowded Castle Godwin to handle, so Winder locked the captives in a three-story brick tobacco warehouse nearby.[30]

With Alexander as commandant, that warehouse became "Castle Thunder," the most dreaded political prison in the South.[31] John Caphart, a veteran detective from Norfolk, helped Alexander make it so.

Unionists like Elizabeth Van Lew understandably hated Alexander. If she knew that he had kept up his prewar avocation as songwriter and dramatist, that only raised her contempt for his other works.* She said he "had written his name high in the annals of cruelty to prisoners . . . was a desperate Brigand-looking villain and I have heard of his having gold by the bag full."

But she hated Caphart more, reviling "his long heavy & grey beard all stained with tobacco juice, his head deep buried in his old greasy high crowned broad brimmed felt hat, his tall figure, his stoop, his forward shouldered dottering gait, his profanity, his infidelity, of wh. he exult-ingly boasted, his general misanthroppy, his fine & squeaking voice, his heavy club an unfailing companion, his cursing every thing that was Yankee & every thing and every body that wd show sympathy for a suf-fering Northern man, his often expressed wish that he might have the power to consign every man woman & child to hell equalling if not ex-ceeding Caligula. . . . The sight of him made humanity sick & strong men to shudder as he passed."

So low was Caphart's reputation in Van Lew's circle that behind his back he was called "the anti-Christ." Van Lew alleged that he brutally attacked a young black woman who heard this and innocently spoke to

---

*Alexander anonymously wrote *The Virginia Cavalier*, which became the greatest hit of the Confederate stage despite reviewers' opinion that "the dialogue is stupid, the incidents are stale, and the plot ridiculous."[32]

him by that name. "G—d— your black nigger soul I'll anti-Christ you!" he yelled, clubbing her as she begged, "Oh please Mr. Anti-Christ don't beat me what have I done Mr. Anti-Christ?"[33]

Eventually even many of those who worked with Alexander and Caphart would testify to their cruelty at Castle Thunder. But Botts's encounter with Alexander was not so blunt. According to Botts, soon after Alexander arrived he came to his cell, said it was a pity such a distinguished citizen was behind bars, and offered to free him immediately— if he would accept a commission as brigadier general in the Confederate army.

Botts asked if Alexander realized who he was, and declared that if he were given command of 10,000 men, "Before the sun went down, I would hang every scoundrel of you from Jeff Davis down to you." But then he thought he might make something of the proposition; he told Alexander he would consider it if he could see the commission first. After days of back-and-forth, the purported deal was still undone when Botts was paroled and exiled.

The whole exchange might seem a flight of Botts's imagination were it not for hints of other Alexander intrigues yet to come.[34]

*　*　*

The perceived danger that provoked martial law and Winder's wholesale arrests had become real.

To deal with it, Davis had brought Robert E. Lee back as his military adviser after Lee spent months strengthening defenses along the southeastern coast. The president vetoed his critics' bill to create a general-in-chief position, which would have weakened his own hand in military affairs. Then he effectively gave Lee the role without the title.

On the Peninsula, George McClellan joined his massive Union army and laid siege to Yorktown. The Northern public was so confident that the "Young Napoleon" would take Richmond that on the day of his move, five Yankees had applied to the U.S. secretary of war to operate hotels in the Rebel capital. Half a dozen wanted to open printing shops. Many had filed for permission to farm the Virginia "waste lands" recently occupied by the Union army. Washington heard rumors that the Confederate cabinet had decided to burn Richmond on the approach of McClellan's army.[35]

Lee started hurrying Joseph Johnston's troops south to reinforce Major General John B. Magruder against McClellan, although other Union forces under Irvin McDowell renewed the Northern threat along the Rappahannock. To divert them, Stonewall Jackson in the Shenandoah Valley dazzled a series of Union generals contesting inland Virginia. In

the western theater, Confederates under Albert Sidney Johnston surprised U. S. Grant's army at Shiloh, Tennessee. But the Federals there
recovered and in bitter fighting, Johnston, Davis's favorite, was mortally
wounded. Union troops captured Island No. 10, opening another breach
in Southern defense of the Mississippi, while Federal gunboats advanced against the river forts near the Gulf, setting the stage for an advance on New Orleans from north and south.

At Yorktown, Magruder's thinly stretched troops held the Confederate line while Joe Johnston rushed reinforcements through Richmond
and down the Peninsula. Near noon on the first Sunday in April,
word spread through the capital's churches that three trainloads of
Longstreet's men had come in from Fredericksburg, famished after
twenty-four hours without eating. Before services ended, people began
slipping out, heading home to share their dinners with the troops.

Broad Street was promptly jammed with women, children, and servants bringing baskets of food. As regiments marched down Ninth
Street, almost every man could be seen eating something, carrying a half
loaf of bread or here and there a severely lacerated ham stuck on a bayonet. A teenage girl watched them and gushed to her diary that despite
all, they "were very cheerful, but their appearance was enough to bring
tears to one's eyes. Sunburnt, ragged, stained with clay as if they had
been living in it, they presented a sad contrast to the time when clad in
their neat uniforms, and untouched by the toils of war, they left their
happy homes for the trials and hardships of the camp. Poor fellows,
what have they not been through! God bless, protect, and reward them
all, now and forever more!"[36]

Davis himself went down to Rocketts wharf to see off troops em-
barking on steamboats. Standing on a balcony, he waved his hat to passing Mississippians. "God bless you, boys!" he shouted. "Remember
Mississippi!" They cheered him as they headed downriver.

For days more thousands marched through, many laughing, with
spring flowers stuck in their hatbands. The New Orleans gentlemen of
the Washington Artillery sent word that they were coming, asking that
the ladies who had presented them their battle flag the year before
please be on their Franklin Street veranda at a certain hour. There the
Louisiana cannoneers came, officers saluting the ladies with their
swords, band playing "My Maryland," soldiers cheering as the travel-
stained flag dipped low in passing. "One must grow old and cold indeed
before such things are forgotten," wrote Constance Cary, a young
refugee from near Washington.[37]

As one battalion marched past, heading down into Shockoe Valley, its
wisecracking troops saw a pale young man beside a lady watching from

a window. "Come right along, sonny!" a soldier shouted. "The lady'll spare yer! Here's a muskit fur ye!"

The young man, a veteran, shot back in the same spirit: "All right, boys!" He propped the stump of his leg on the window sill. "Have you got a leg for me, too?"

The battalion halted, turned, and brought its muskets to salute, filling the long street with the Rebel yell. Then it marched on.[38]

The Sunday after Longstreet's hungry troops arrived, the teenage Richmond diarist noted that a year had passed since Fort Sumter. "Oh! how fraught with light and darkness, with happiness and sorrow!" she wrote. "How swiftly has it passed away! So many hearts that beat high with life & hope then, and so many that joined in that battle, now sleep cold upon fields of glory, or rest beneath the soil of soldier graves, far away from home and friends. Is not this enough to stir any one's heart? How cruel, cruel is this war that causes so much desolation.

"But do they sleep forgotten? Oh! no, their memory shall brighten the pages of history, and the soft eyes of many a maiden will grow tearful, as she reads the story of their toils and suffering, in this great struggle for our independence! These thoughts make me feel so sad, I cannot better express my feelings than in these two words, 'sad remembrance.'"[39]

At her age, at that stage of the war, she found flowery words that would be echoed by many a gray veteran at commemoration ceremonies in decades to come. But in that early April, neither she nor they had any idea how much darkness and sorrow, cruelty and desolation, there yet would be, or how many soldier graves would be dug in the weeks just ahead.

On April 14, at a long evening strategy session in the presidential mansion, Lee and Davis prevailed over Johnston, who agreed halfheartedly to confront McClellan far down the Peninsula rather than falling back close to Richmond.

But with Yankees in all directions, near and far, Southern manpower stretched thinner and thinner. One-year enlistments begun in the fervid spring of 1861 were about to run out, and new volunteers were scarce. Facing this, Lee persuaded Davis to approve a law to draft white males between 18 and 35 years of age for three years of armed service. A great howl went up from those who called conscription a violation of civil liberties, most of them citizens who feared that they would be drafted. Within five days, a companion act exempted a long list of occupations. Nowhere was the contrast between warlike words and willingness to serve more vivid than in Richmond's press.

In late winter Virginia had rehearsed this mobilization with an act conscripting able-bodied militiamen to meet the state's unfilled volunteer quotas. The *Examiner* reported that the muster rolls then handed in by colonels of two Richmond militia regiments were "the most ridiculously curious documents it has ever been our luck to encounter. . . . Hundreds of the men have attached to their names the record of some permanent injury or horrible distemper. The great number of one-eyed and deaf men, the prevalence of chronic diarrhea and rheumatism in all its varieties, is truly astonishing."

The same paper, perhaps the same writer, made fun of the crowd seeking exemptions from the draft board, which convened at the office of the city gasworks. But the reporter conceded that he himself was there awaiting two doctors to testify on his behalf. Editorials wailed at the idea of conscripting editors. One argued that if the legislature did not exempt ten men on each daily newspaper, it would destroy the free press.[40]

As fancied threats to the city hardened into military fact, the government did start commonsense security restrictions. Belatedly guarding against spies, the War Department installed soldiers with fixed bayonets at its doors, barring visitors accustomed to casually copying reports and inspecting documents. The *Examiner*'s man, furious at this, declared that "we refuse to make application to the departments on the footing of news-beggars, ante-room waiters and eaves-droppers."[41]

When the *Whig* asserted in the wake of the martial-law crackdown that Davis had "lost the confidence of the country," Winder threatened to shut the paper down if it continued "its vicious habit of uttering unpalatable truths." Answering Winder, the *Whig* alleged that suppression under Davis was almost as bad as that under Lincoln. Southerners were ready to risk everything to resist such "despotism," it said; the administration was treating Richmond as "a hostile city taken by storm."[42]

But press freedom was never in serious danger. Despite the guards at War Department doors, despite the bluffs of General Winder, Richmond's papers still packed their columns with dense type about what was on the public record and what their reporters could see in the public streets.[43]

Undercover Unionists became bolder as McClellan marshaled his army. One morning the city awoke to find that the walls of shops and warehouses had been scrawled with "traitorous and incendiary legends," including strained allusions to *Macbeth:* "Southern boasters grasp the dust / In the Lord you vainly trust / For the Lord you fain would chat / With Halcyon lips and Pluto's feet / The cry is *still they come.*"[44]

* * *

At 6:00 a.m. on April 29, Captain Alexander set out in a carriage to take the Union spy Timothy Webster to Camp Lee, the former fairgrounds now used for executions. Leaving the prison, the detail stopped for the Reverend George Woodbridge of Monumental Episcopal Church. But Webster rudely rejected the minister's attentions, so when the carriage arrived at the camp, Woodbridge walked away from the condemned man.

Webster had sat up all night. Now, in a holding cell, he lay down to sleep for half an hour. At about 9:00, troops formed a cordon around the camp; another fifty encircled the scaffold erected in one corner. Webster was still cool, talking about everything except what was happening around him. "It was very evident . . . that he did not, at this time, believe he was really to be hung," said the *Examiner*. "He thought the whole demonstration was gotten up to intimidate him, and that, like Lewis and Scully, he would be reprieved before the arrival of the fatal moment."

So, apparently, did the rest of Richmond; on the day Webster's two colleagues had been scheduled to hang, the road to Camp Lee was thronged, and a dozen carriages bearing fancy women rode out to enjoy the show. But now there were only soldiers, officials, and perhaps 200 civilians who had climbed trees and roofs around the camp, and "these were for the most part negroes and boys."

At about 10:00, Webster realized that the proceedings were not a sham, and according to the *Examiner* he broke down and wept, and asked for a chaplain. The Reverend Moses Hoge quickly came to his side, and Webster begged him to ask that he be shot like a soldier rather than hanged like a criminal. He also was unhappy that there was no crowd, for he had imagined making a Nathan Hale–style speech before dying.[45] (Pinkerton's Union version was that the prisoner fully understood what was about to happen, and met his fate bravely. Pinkerton got his account from Hattie Lawton, who, like Scully and Lewis, was later released. She said she had tried to reach President Davis to ask mercy for Webster, then appealed to Mrs. Davis, who sympathized but would not intervene. Mrs. Lawton said she had sat up with Webster all that final night in his cell, after Webster asked General Winder the day before that he be shot instead of hanged, and Winder had refused.)[46]

Finally, when Alexander came to escort Webster for the final 200 yards, the prisoner was calm. Wearing a black suit and silk dress hat, he strode erect up the steps to the gallows. Jailers tied his hands and legs. Hoge spoke "a prayer of solemn and touching eloquence." The black hood was placed over Webster's head, the trap was sprung—and he plunged straight to the ground "with a dreadful thud."

Picked up, helped up the stairs again, he said, "I suffer a double death." When someone said the rope was too short, he muttered, "Oh, you are going to choke me this time," and spoke no more. He hung for half an hour before detectives took him down, then cut up the rope for souvenirs among themselves.[47]

CHAPTER TEN

SHELL AND BE DAMNED!

*I*t was curious, wrote Constance Cary, how most exciting war news struck Richmond on Sundays, just as preachers were winding down their morning services. She was right. On the last Sunday in April of 1862, word came that New Orleans, biggest city in the South, grand portal of the Mississippi, had fallen to Union gunboats steaming upriver from the Gulf of Mexico.

This was the worst blow yet suffered by the Confederacy—and it was partly Jefferson Davis's fault, because he had insisted that the Federals would approach the city from the other direction, downriver. But New Orleans was a thousand miles away, and official concern about it was soon distracted by Federals closer to Richmond. Only sixty miles down the Peninsula, McClellan had assembled at Yorktown the most powerful army the nation had ever seen, while two other Union forces pressed south along the Rappahannock and in the Shenandoah Valley.

Six days after New Orleans fell, Joe Johnston, commanding the reinforced Confederates on the Peninsula, surprised Davis by advising that after holding McClellan at Yorktown for a month, he must pull back toward Richmond. That meant abandoning Norfolk and the lower Peninsula—and that meant opening the mouth of the James River, the waterway to Richmond.

On May 3, the same day Johnston withdrew from Yorktown, the Yankees got close insight into Davis's reaction to such news. William A. Jackson, a slave whom Davis had hired and trusted as his coachman,

crossed the lines and turned up at a Union army camp at Fredericksburg. There he was greeted "as though a Rebel general had been
bagged." The Federal commander, Irvin McDowell, promptly questioned him and telegraphed his answers to Washington.

Jackson was literate and talkative. His most important intelligence
was that some Confederate officials had packed up government property, ready to flee to Danville when the invaders threatened Richmond.
He told of quarreling between Davis and Johnston—Davis grumbling
that "while he was making plans for holding positions, his generals were
making plans to evacuate them." Jackson had lived in the Davis household almost as a member of the family; according to him, the Rebel
president was more quarrelsome and pessimistic than ever. Sometimes,
he said, Davis met news of setbacks by stretching out on the floor before
the fire and mumbling half-asleep about what should have been done.[1]

When Yorktown fell, Davis agonized over how to evacuate Norfolk
with minimum losses. Coming home late from his office, he dragged
himself upstairs and fell on a sofa. He would not eat. After daylong conversations with his staff and hours more with his wife, he moaned that
he would give anything to have someone to share his burden. Varina saw
his plea as an opening; for weeks, she had encouraged him to talk with
the rector of St. Paul's, the Reverend Charles F. E. Minnigerode. Now
Varina asked Minnigerode to pay her husband a visit.

Early on May 6, after a sharp clash the previous day with Johnston's
rear guard, Union forces moved into Williamsburg. At 9:30 the same
morning, the 47-year-old, German-born Minnigerode arrived at the
president's house to talk with Davis "on the subject of confessing Christ."

The president "met me more than half way," the minister wrote.
"That he must be a Christian he felt in his inmost soul. He spoke very
earnestly and most humbly of needing the cleansing blood of Jesus and
the power of the Holy Spirit; but in the consciousness of his insufficiency felt some doubt whether he had the right to come. All that was
natural and right; but soon it settled this question with a man so resolute
in doing what he thought his duty."

There in the intimacy of the Davis home, within its wine-red parlor
walls, Minnigerode baptized the president "hypothetically," because
Davis was not sure whether he had been christened as an infant. Then,
that noon, Davis was confirmed at St. Paul's. Minnigerode said, "It was
quite in keeping with his resolute character, that when the Bishop called
the candidates to the chancel [Davis] was the first to rise, and, as it were,
lead the others on, among whom were General [Josiah] Gorgas and
several other officers. From that day, so far as I know and can judge, 'he

never looked back.'" As Varina put it, "a peace which passed understanding seemed to settle in his heart."[2]

It could not last long.

Three days after Davis's baptism, Confederates abandoned Norfolk and its naval base. Abraham Lincoln himself had come down to Hampton Roads to urge his generals on; he and two members of his cabinet boarded small craft to seek out a landing place for Union troops.

That evening in Richmond, Davis was entertaining at a reception when a messenger called him away. As the president returned to the drawing room, Varina cut her eyes at him and he whispered that enemy gunboats were headed up the James. The unsuspecting guests partied on, and when they left, Davis told Varina that he hoped the gun batteries, torpedoes, and sunken vessels along the river would block the enemy's approach—but in case they did not, she must be ready to leave Richmond in the morning. She had already packed the family's personal needs and valuables. On May 10, she and the Davis children took the train 150 miles south to safety in Raleigh.[3]

A day later, off Norfolk, Confederates scuttled the CSS *Virginia,* the former *Merrimack,* which some citizens believed was worth 50,000 troops in the field.

"And so perished the naval glory of the Confederacy, after effecting a revolution in the naval history of the world," wrote Moses Hoge. The *Examiner* said the fall of New Orleans itself "has not given a more painful shock to the public mind than the melancholy fact that the Confederate government has found nothing better to do with the *Merrimac*—that great gift of God and of Virginia to the South—than to take her out into the river and blow her timbers to atoms. . . . It is a confession of impotence, mismanagement and wretchedness too painful for consideration."[4]

The Rebel warship was scuttled because when Norfolk was abandoned, she had no home; with her twenty-two-foot draft, she could not navigate shallow river waters. But the *Monitor* and her sister Federal ironclads *Galena* and *Naugatuck* could. With an escort of gunboats, they were on their way to Richmond, with orders to "shell the city to a surrender."*[5]

---

*In June a court of inquiry heard testimony on the *Virginia*'s scuttling. Pilots had told the ship's master, 66-year-old Flag Officer Josiah Tattnall, that because westerly winds had lowered the tide his vessel could not ascend the James to Westover, where he wanted to go. He scuttled her at Craney Island, where he had undergone his baptism of fire as a midshipman half a century earlier. The court said he should have brought the *Virginia* to a narrow bend below Jamestown, where she could have blocked Federal passage. But it conceded that amid the evacuation of Norfolk and the burning of the navy yard, Tattnall could not consider all such options. Though it did not recommend a court martial, Tattnall demanded one, and in July that proceeding cleared him.[6]

More than two weeks earlier, "in the very crisis of the country's agony, when the existence of the nation which it pretends to represent is trembling in the balance of fate," the Confederate Congress had voted itself a pay raise and abruptly decamped from the capital.

The *Whig* sent the lawmakers away with scorn: "For fear of accidents on the railroad, the stampeded Congress left yesterday in a number of the strongest and lowest canal boats. These boats are drawn by mules of approved sweetness of temper. To protect the stampeders from the snakes and bullfrogs that abound along the line of the canal, General Winder has detailed a regiment of ladies to march in advance of the ranks, and clear the towpath of the pirates." After escorting Congress to safety, the paper said, the ladies would "return to the defense of their country."[7]

* * *

Now columns of rural Virginians were swarming into the city ahead of McClellan's advance up the Peninsula. As these hundreds arrived in Richmond, others departed, hurried by Varina Davis's example and the sight of packing cases of vital archives stacked outside government offices, addressed to Columbia, South Carolina. "It is remarkable," the *Examiner* said, "that people in the country, whose nerves are weak as regards the approach of our invaders, think if they could just get to Richmond they would be safe; while citizens of Richmond of the same class are selling all they have preparatory to taking to the piney old fields of Pittsylvania."[8]

Some fled the capital in fear that they would be dealt with as harshly as defiant citizens had been treated by Union Major General Benjamin Butler in New Orleans. Businesses shut down. Many houses were left deserted. Wagons heading south and canal boats heading west were packed with people, piled with suitcases and trunks. Riflemen in and out of uniform hurried down to the riverbank to repel the invaders.[9]

The guns of the advancing Union flotilla quickly silenced a Confederate battery at Rock Wharf, and three hours of heavy fire from the *Galena* covered the other vessels as they steamed past Hardin's Bluff. On they came, up the broad, winding James, past the ruins of the original Virginia settlement at Jamestown, past old river plantations like Westover, Berkeley, and Shirley. As they approached, the Virginia legislature called on Davis to defend Richmond "to the last extremity."[10]

The cabinet asked Lee where Johnston's army might next draw a defensive line if the capital was abandoned. At the Staunton River, nearly 100 miles away, Lee said dutifully. But with tears in his eyes he declared that "Richmond must not be given up; it shall not be given up!"[11]

Rich men and patriots said they would torch their homes and the Capitol, even blow up the magnificent statue of Washington, to keep them out of Yankee hands. The *Dispatch* said that to lose Richmond was to lose Virginia, the key to the Confederacy. Governor Letcher and Mayor Mayo rallied citizen volunteers, forming a Home Guard of boys 16 to 18 and men over 45 years old. The 66-year-old mayor told a cheering crowd that he was ready to take up a musket himself. When the long-expected rumble of heavy guns sounded faintly from the south, Letcher declared that if the Yankees called on the capital to surrender or be shelled, he would say "Shell and be damned!"[12]

Undeterred by Matthew Maury's few torpedoes set in the channel, the Yankee gunboats chugged toward Richmond until they came to a bend in the river seven miles below the city. There the Confederates had sunk a collection of old steamers, sloops, and schooners, driven pilings and built cribs of stone, leaving open only a narrow, crooked passage. On the south bank, an abrupt hill dominated these obstructions from ninety feet above the river.

This was Drewry's Bluff. On it the Confederates had mounted eight heavy guns, a position the Yankees called Fort Darling. Along both banks below, companies of sharpshooters awaited the intruders. It was Richmond's last line of river defense—"our only chance for safety," wrote Sallie Putnam.[13]

As the Federal vessels approached early on May 15, they had no room to maneuver past the bluff; they would have to fight their way through. In no time, the *Monitor*'s skipper realized that he could not elevate his guns enough to fire on the defending batteries. The *Naugatuck*'s Parrott gun burst after a few rounds, and she dropped out. The burden of the job was left to the *Galena*. Though skillfully handled, she was overmatched. In a fight that lasted for three hours and twenty minutes, the expertly sighted Confederate guns under Commander Ebenezer Farrand battered the *Galena* with forty-six hits, forcing her to retreat downstream. Her escort of wooden gunboats, peppered with shells and musket balls, pulled away with her.*

The Yankees steamed out of sight, hurried along by three cheers from the heights. One of the sharpshooters' officers yelled as the *Monitor* passed, "Tell Captain Jeffers that is not the way to Richmond!"[15]

But there were other ways.

---

*Navy Captain Sydney Smith Lee, older brother of Robert E. Lee and father of cavalryman Fitzhugh Lee, had been ordered to replace Farrand on May 15. Because the engagement had already started when he arrived, he stood aside until it was over. Smith Lee, whom some ladies thought more handsome than his famed brother, was the prewar chief of the U.S. Navy's Bureau of Coast Survey. He did routine duty in Richmond throughout the war.[14]

* * *

While the Yankee flotilla thrust up the James, hoping to shell Richmond into surrender, other gunboats had opened the York River on the other flank of the Peninsula. Between the two rivers, Johnston's Confederates fell back steadily, and McClellan's troops sloshed through the spring mud behind them. Official Richmond did not realize how far Johnston had withdrawn until Davis and his aides switched their attention from the naval threat on the James.

Johnston, who would never stop smarting from having been passed over by Davis in 1861, refused to keep the president informed of what he was doing. Two days before the fight at Drewry's Bluff, Davis had ridden out to consult with him at his headquarters, then more than twenty miles from Richmond. Shortly after the river battle, he asked for a situation report, but Johnston did not answer, so the president went again to see him in person.

Riding with Postmaster General Reagan, Davis was shocked to find Confederate regiments tented in the Richmond outskirts, well south of the Chickahominy River, within five miles of the Capitol.

Johnston was there because he did not want to confront McClellan with that river at his back—and further, he explained, the water of the muggy Chickahominy was probably unhealthy for his troops. He did not need to point out to Davis that by withdrawing to fight on Richmond's doorstep, he was doing just what he had proposed weeks earlier, when he was overruled by Davis and Lee. Now Davis, stuck with Johnston and reluctant to change generals on the verge of battle, rode out almost every day to see what was happening; if things got worse, he might have to take command himself.[16]

Reinforced and supplied via the York River, McClellan's grand army pushed along behind Johnston's tired, hungry troops. When the Federals arrived at White House plantation, where the York River Railroad crossed the Pamunkey River, they found a note tacked to the door of the house. It said: "Northern soldiers who profess to reverence Washington, forbear to desecrate the home of his first married life,—the property of his wife, now owned by his descendants. [signed]—A Grand-daughter of Mrs. Washington."

The granddaughter who had left the note was Mrs. Robert E. Lee, who had found refuge at White House after fleeing Arlington and had departed just ahead of McClellan's advance guard. Her note did not mention that the plantation was now the property of her son, W. H. F. "Rooney" Lee, a colonel in Jeb Stuart's cavalry. McClellan posted guards to keep soldiers out of the farmhouse, but White House Landing be-

came a huge supply base for his army as it marched on Richmond, guid-
ing along the railroad.[17]

McClellan, always mistakenly certain that he was outnumbered,
wanted McDowell's army at Fredericksburg to come down and join him
to take Richmond in short order. McDowell had already started south
when he got orders to turn around: Stonewall Jackson had outfoxed and
outfought three separate Union commands in the Shenandoah Valley,
and was marching north to the Potomac. Lincoln reacted just the way
the Confederates wanted him to, by drawing McDowell back to protect
Washington. Thus, when McClellan's army started crossing the Chickahominy to lay siege to Richmond, it outnumbered the Rebels by only
about three to two.[18]

As the Union army and gunboats pressed toward Richmond, Constance Cary and others there "had begun to feel like the prisoners of the
Inquisition in Poe's story, cast into a dungeon of slowly contracting
walls."[19]

"Richmond may fall," George Bagby conceded. Yet, especially since
the repulse at Drewry's Bluff, "there is a wonderful composure manifest
in every one you meet. . . . if we fail, the decree of fate will be met as becomes a brave race. Resentment against imbecile officials is swallowed
up in the patriotic desire to defend the capital to the last." And later: "If
we are to go through a regular siege, and be reduced to mule meat, boot-
top soup and saw dust puddings, we are very cool about it."[20]

Defiant as usual, the *Examiner* roared that defending Richmond "is
worth a year of random skirmishing in other quarters. In a moral point
of view, its holding at this hour is all-important—equal to the sacrifice
of an hundred thousand men and the demolition of the city itself. A
monument of ruins hereafter will claim more veneration and respect
than a city unscathed, but tamely surrendered to the invaders. . . ."[21]

As if making his will, Davis sent away his most cherished books and
the Mexican War pistols he had used at Buena Vista, with a letter telling
Varina: "These articles will have a value to the boys in after-time, and to
you now." Women who had been sewing sandbags for fortifications at
Yorktown, then Williamsburg, then Richmond itself, switched to
rolling bandages. And at her home on Church Hill, Elizabeth Van
Lew's mother had "a charming chamber with new matting and pretty
curtains all prepared for Gen. McClellan."[22]

*   *   *

Late in May, after repeated urging, Johnston promised Davis and Lee a
counteroffensive against McClellan. For days it did not materialize.
Then, with the Union army straddling the rain-swollen Chickahominy,

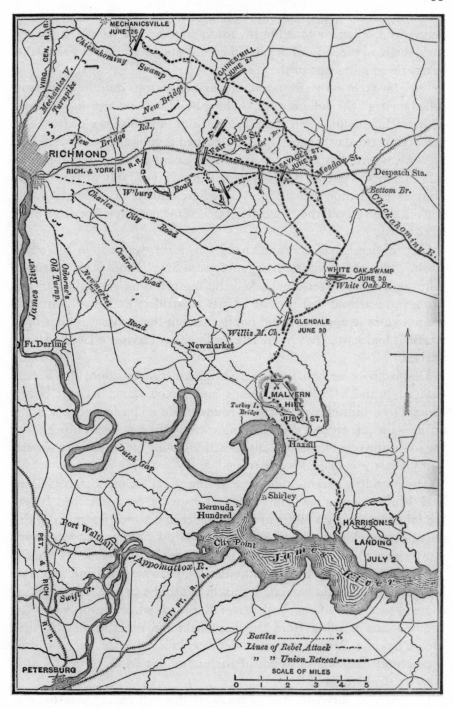

SPRING AND SUMMER, 1862

Johnston decided to attack the Federals south of that swampy stream before McClellan could bring his forces together. He would strike toward the road junction of Seven Pines and the rail station at Fair Oaks, barely seven miles east of the Capitol.

On May 31, in early afternoon, the "awfully grand" thunder of cannon rolled through the dull overcast, shaking buildings and rattling windows all over Richmond. Soon the popcorn sound of musketry drifted into the city. As the day advanced, people rushed to hills and rooftops, looking east, where they could see gunsmoke drifting. They asked one another for news, but all they got were rumors, inevitably of triumph or disaster. Each time the firing swelled, excitement swept the crowds; when it dropped off, they speculated that some tactical victory had been won.

Old soldier Davis, more anxious than most, was not in his office awaiting dispatches but riding again toward Seven Pines. Lee, already at Johnston's headquarters, had asked the commanding general about the firing and was told that it must be just an artillery exchange. Johnston did not know it, apparently did not hear it, but that firing was his army's attack. It had started five hours late, and neither Davis nor Lee had been advised.

Despite poor reconnaissance, timing, and coordination, the Rebels charged into McClellan's divisions and forced them back at Seven Pines. Davis himself was where a president had no business being, amid artillery fire just behind the attacking waves, acting as a staff officer, trying to shuffle brigades about. But as action swung late in the day toward Fair Oaks, the course of battle turned.

The president and his aides were trying to rally Confederates falling back when troops approached carrying someone on a stretcher. It was Joe Johnston, hit by a bullet in the shoulder and a shell fragment in the chest. He would be out of action indefinitely. Command of Johnston's army automatically fell to his next-senior general, Gustavus W. Smith.

That evening long lines of ambulances, farm wagons, and ox carts, loaded with dead and wounded, trundled into the city. Other casualties came aboard cars of the York River Railroad, while Union wounded jammed cars heading from the battlefield the other way, to White House landing. Among the wounded was Juliet Hopkins, organizer of the Second Alabama Hospital in Richmond, hit while caring for soldiers on the battlefield.[23]

Confederate survivors told of breaking through enemy breastworks, of capturing boxes of lemons, oranges, brandies, and wines, "all the luxuries of distant lands which enter the unrestricted ports of the United

States."[24] Richmond hospitals overflowed with casualties. Hundreds of patients were taken into warehouses and into homes abandoned by Richmonders who had fled when the Yankee gunboats approached. Others were unloaded onto the sidewalks, making the city seem one vast emergency ward.

Richmond's women—young and old, rich and poor—turned out to comfort and feed the wounded. Constance Cary and her sister, searching for a young friend, stepped into the St. Charles Hotel, which had been turned into a crude hospital.

"Such a spectacle!" she wrote. "Men in every stage of mutilation lying on the bare boards, with perhaps a haversack or an army blanket beneath their heads—some dying, all suffering keenly, while waiting their turn to be attended to. To be there empty-handed and impotent nearly broke our hearts." When one of the volunteer nurses consoled a grievously mangled Georgian, he whispered as he died, "God bless you, God bless you, kind stranger"—sentiments that would be repeated thousands of times before the war was over. Sallie Putnam spoke for many when she wrote: "It was woman's duty to minister thus to the suffering and dying, and to place upon the breast of the youthful unknown hero the flowers of summer, to be borne with him to his last resting-place in the burial-ground of the soldier—love offerings of national gratitude."[25]

Davis had no confidence in General Smith, who seemed solid until he came under stress, when he tended to melt down. When the president pressed him for information about his next moves, Smith was uncertain. Davis rode with Lee back to Richmond that evening. Before they arrived, he confided that when this fight was over, Lee would be the army's new commander. The next day, June 1, the battle that the Rebels called Seven Pines and the Yankees called Fair Oaks resumed, tapering off when Smith could not will himself to follow through on his attack.

Hundreds of freelance citizens headed out from the city that Sunday morning—to help somehow, to share the glory, to pick over the field for salable booty, or at least to find out what had happened. Among them were George Bagby and four friends, who left behind the eager spectators crowding Chimborazo Hill on the city's eastern edge. They met swarms of stragglers, sometimes a whole squad of soldiers escorting one slightly wounded comrade to the rear. They passed farmhouses used as aid stations, one with a pile of amputated arms and legs reeking outside an open window. Ambulances struggled through "an almost endless mud puddle."

"Everybody in Richmond seemed to be in the road," wrote Bagby. "All the great civilians"—president, governor, secretary of war, ministers of the gospel, clerks, editors—"a whole city as it were, turned loose on a fine Sunday morning, and rushing to the field of battle, as to a race-course, or a country preaching."

Then word came that the battle was about to begin again; a shell was fired somewhere ahead; a squad of Yankees rushed out to capture a mired double-decker omnibus that had been commandeered from the Spotswood Hotel to bring in the wounded. At that, civilians, horses, buggies, and ambulances "were struck on a sudden as by a white squall, and the living tide began to flow backward with precipitancy and evident signs of alarm." Another one or two shells "would have made another Bull Run affair of it," Bagby recalled, "and the citizens of Richmond would have been forever deprived of the pleasure of laughing at the Washingtonian stampede" the summer before.[26]

But the battle was ending, not beginning again. Before noon it was over, a bloody draw. At about 2:00, Robert E. Lee joined Davis and Smith at field headquarters. There, for the first time in his thirty-three years as an officer, Lee took command of an army in the field.[27]

* * *

So far in this war, Lee had been honored more for who he was than for what he had done. His Mexican War exploits were brilliant, but they were now history. Although he had performed at a high professional level in mobilizing Virginia's forces and organizing Southern coastal defenses, his 1861 excursion against the enemy in western Virginia had failed and the Yankees had taken key points along the Atlantic shore. Lee's acquaintance with Davis ran back to their cadet days at West Point, yet they had never been close, even when Davis was secretary of war and Lee superintendent of the U.S. Military Academy in the early 1850s. But during the months when Lee had been at Davis's side as adviser in Richmond, the general's calm judgment had won respect from the president. So had his tact.

Besides, who else was there?

Lee outranked every officer in seniority except 64-year-old Samuel Cooper, who had settled in comfortably as adjutant general. Davis could have chosen Beauregard, but the Creole not only was out west, he was as contentious as Johnston, and more vain. The president could have promoted Smith to full general, or reached down to John Magruder, James Longstreet, D. H. Hill or A. P. Hill, all major generals active in the current fight. Instead, he did what he may have decided on privately weeks earlier.

Because Johnston's wounding at Seven Pines gave Davis the opportunity to appoint Lee, it was one of the luckiest events in the history of an often unlucky Confederacy. As Johnston lay recovering at a friend's home on Church Hill, even he conceded as much, telling a caller, "The shot that struck me down is the very best that has been fired for the Southern cause yet, for I possess in no degree the confidence of our government, and now they have in place one who does. . . ." Lee was at hand, and he was ready. Indeed, frustrated in staff duty, he had sent a personal message to Johnston the day before the battle, offering to serve him in any role.[28]

In his order assuming command, Lee designated his force the Army of Northern Virginia, and the significance of the adjective was not lost on his soldiers. Then, before planning his first move, he made a point of asking Davis what he would do. This contrast with Johnston's secretiveness made clear Lee's understanding of the insecure Davis, his realization that diplomacy can be an essential element of generalship. Before every major decision, he would keep Davis informed of at least his broad intentions. Because he did, the two would be able to work together in a way that Davis found impossible with any other general, effectively reversing the situation in which Lee had been the president's adviser. More often than not, for the duration of the war, Lee would have his way.

Confederates called what had happened at Seven Pines "a glorious victory"—but so did McClellan, and his army was still there, on Richmond's outskirts, 100,000 strong, its observation balloons still visible, its big guns audible in the city. When Lee moved from the Spotswood into his new field headquarters, he was barely a mile and a half out of town. And while some called Lee's appointment "a harbinger of bright fortune," others demanded bolder action, faster.[29]

Lee understood that if McClellan's still-growing army brought Richmond under its heavy artillery, the city must eventually fall. He had to drive the Federals away before a classic siege began. At a council of war two days after taking over, he listened to the doubts of a younger general, W. H. C. Whiting, about holding Richmond against such odds. Lee quickly squelched such thinking: "Stop, stop! If you go to ciphering, we are whipped beforehand."

Outnumbered as he was, he would strengthen Richmond's thinly manned earthworks to hold off McClellan while gathering his brigades for a counteroffensive. As rain turned the Peninsula into a deeper mudhole and the Chickahominy surged higher, he ordered construction of a belt of mutually supporting strong points facing the enemy. By the time soldiers had been digging for two weeks, they were complaining about doing slaves' labor and calling Lee the "King of Spades." The *Examiner* sneeringly compared his apparently static strategy with Stonewall Jackson's fast footwork in the valley.[30]

At about this time, Major E. Porter Alexander, who had been on Johnston's staff, rode out to look over the fortifications with Colonel Joseph C. Ives, an aide to Davis. Alexander noted that Lee seemed to be saying, in effect, "Whenever you are ready, Mr. Enemy, we propose to give you the hardest kind of fight, but you can take your time about getting ready." With inferior forces, the major said, "our only hope is to bounce [the enemy] & whip him somewhere before he is ready for us, and that needs audacity in our commander. Has Gen. Lee that audacity?"

Ives knew Lee, and he knew something of what Lee was planning. He reined up and turned to face the young officer. "Alexander," he said, "if there is one man in either army, Federal or Confederate, who is, head & shoulders, far above every other one in either army in audacity, that man is Gen. Lee, and you will very soon have lived to see it. Lee is audacity personified. His name is audacity. . . ."[31]

CHAPTER ELEVEN

THE DAZZLE OF IT
IN THEIR EYES

*A*s they scraped away the mud and blood of Seven Pines and Fair Oaks, Yankee infantrymen like Horatio Staples of the Second Maine could still hear the church bells of Richmond. Some, from a high, clear spot, could see the city's steeples. But Richmond was not as alluring to men in the lines as it was to staff officers and politicians who viewed it at the point of clean broad arrows on headquarters maps. Staples's regiment had fought desperately against charging North Carolinians trying to take a pair of Federal cannon. After what he had been through, he wrote "Richmond and the Loon, or the Peninsula Side-Step":

> When a loon, on our northern lakes, sees a bright object, something that glistens, he straightway wants it. Not that it would do him any good. Not that he knows what he would do with it if he had it. But he wants it. And the harder it is for him to get it, the more that fool bird wants it.
>
> There was a good deal of the loon in our commanding generals. . . . They thought the city of Richmond was a shining mark—a glittering prize. It wasn't. It was just an ordinary little cobble-stone, hubbly, tobacco-saturated municipality; as full of humps as a caravan of camels. But these Federal commanders had the dazzle of it in their eyes.[1]

George Brinton McClellan certainly saw the dazzle of it; he told his troops that they had brought the Confederates to bay, and "the final and decisive battle is at hand." He was sure that capturing Richmond would end the war and emblazon his name in history. It might even make him president of the United States.

Lincoln, despite his own impatience with the general, accepted Mc-Clellan's strategy; he even agreed to send McDowell's army south to strengthen him for his next move. McClellan insisted that those reinforcements were urgently needed, because Secret Service director Pinkerton had reported that Lee's defending force was superior to his and still growing. The general was always glad to hear Pinkerton's overestimates of enemy strength; they gave him an excuse to wait, plan, refit, reorganize, retrain, to demand still more men and supplies—to do everything except attack.

Robert E. Lee did all he could to provide McClellan with further excuses.

In the Shenandoah Valley, in late May and early June, Stonewall Jackson had conducted a brilliant display of fast marching and elusive tactics, making himself the Confederacy's hero of the moment. With only 15,000 "foot cavalry," he had outmaneuvered and outfought three separate Union forces, keeping Washington in a state of nerves and thus preventing reinforcement of McClellan. Now Lee proposed to bring Jackson secretly to join him in striking McClellan outside Richmond.

First Lee would set up that move with one of the tricks that helped win him the nickname "Gray Fox." Assuming that Union spies, observation balloons, and escaped slaves kept McClellan informed of all troop movements in and out of Richmond, Lee sent two brigades through the streets, conspicuously marching to join Jackson. To give the transfer a veneer of mystery, he asked Richmond newspapers not to mention it. The move was calculated to prevent McDowell from coming to reinforce McClellan; by giving the impression that Lee had troops to spare, it also strengthened McClellan's belief that he was outnumbered, so he had better dig in deeper and wait longer.

As the two sides dug and waited, McClellan saw to it that he would not be outdone by the Confederates in old-fashioned chivalry.

Mrs. Robert E. Lee, when she fled White House plantation ahead of the Yankees, had taken shelter at another farm that was promptly overrun by McClellan's advancing divisions. She moved again to Edmund Ruffin's Marlbourne plantation, below the Pamunkey River, and it, too, fell to the Federals. McClellan posted guards there to protect her, but she had become grouchy and crippled with arthritis, and did not appreciate such courtesies from Yankees. She heard wild rumors that Richmond had fallen, that a vast army of Yankees was chasing fleeing Confederates. Worried, she demanded that McClellan send her to

Richmond. As soon as he and General Lee could arrange it through flag-of-truce exchanges, McClellan ceremoniously dispatched her across the lines to her husband. With a Yankee cavalry escort, she rode in a carriage to Meadow Bridge, where she crossed the Chickahominy into Confederate hands.

Lee's troops cheered as he greeted his wife; he had not seen her in fifteen months, since he rode away from Arlington for the last time. Since then, seeking one place of refuge after another, she had aged alarmingly; her graying hair had turned nearly white, and her face was drawn and angular.[2]

Lee could spare very few hours to make up for those lost months. Calling in his gaudy brigadier, J. E. B. Stuart, he issued orders that would launch Stuart's reputation as the most irrepressible of cavalrymen. Lee needed to know how far McClellan's positions extended north of the Chickahominy, where he intended Jackson to strike. He sent Stuart with 1,200 horsemen to find out.

Stuart, alert to the dramatic potential of every situation, saw that if the chance developed, he might ride all the way around the Union army—and that is what he did. Up from Richmond to the North Anna River, then east, then down across Totopotomoy Creek and the Chickahominy to Charles City Court House, then northwest back to Richmond, he encircled McClellan's mighty host. He also embarrassed his father-in-law, Brigadier General Philip St. George Cooke, a Virginia Unionist who commanded the Federal cavalry. Zigzagging, burning Yankee supplies, charging surprised outposts, building makeshift bridges, capturing men and horses, narrowly escaping, Stuart made it back—losing only one man.

That man was Captain William Latane, shot down at the head of his squadron in a skirmish at Old Church. When Union pickets refused to pass a minister to give Latane a formal funeral, ladies and slaves at nearby Summer Hill plantation buried him properly. Latane soon became a beloved martyr, thanks to a poem by John R. Thompson published in the *Southern Literary Messenger* (". . . Gently they laid him underneath the sod / And left him with his fame, his country, and his God . . ."). A painting of the burial, copied in engravings, soon decorated many a Southern parlor.

But the latest hero of the moment was Jeb Stuart, who trotted victoriously into the capital with 145 Yankee prisoners, 16 recaptured slaves, and 200 mules. Governor Letcher presented him a sword, and a few days later Stuart lifted Richmond's spirits with typically gallant remarks to a crowd in Capitol Square. "What a change!" wrote War Department clerk Jones. "No one now dreams of the loss of the capital."[3]

* * *

The cavalry ride around McClellan was the most spectacular battlefield intelligence effort of the war to date. Stuart brought back the kind of hard, immediately useful information that other, more stealthy spy projects merely hoped for.

In April the Confederates had formalized an office comparable to Pinkerton's Federal Secret Service. Major William Norris, another of the Marylanders so busy in Southern spy and counterspy work, had been getting Northern newspapers regularly by courier and delivering them daily to President Davis. From them Lee pieced together important conclusions about which Union forces were where, and what they might do next.

Norris, a Baltimore lawyer, had been a judge advocate with the U.S. Navy, where he learned something about signal operations. In the run-up to war, he tried unsuccessfully to organize a secession party in Maryland. When fighting started, he came south as a civilian and devised a signal system for General Magruder on the Peninsula. Magruder was so impressed that he urged the War Department to commission Norris to operate on a wider scale.

As McClellan's army started toward Richmond, Norris set up what was called the Signal Bureau, with quarters on Richmond's Bank Street, between Ninth and Tenth streets. He was chief signal officer, in charge of Confederate ciphers, of sending, receiving, coding, and decoding classified messages, and monitoring Union communications. He sent signalmen to the field, with flags to wigwag messages from towers and hilltops. From shoreline stations they blinked lights telling blockade runners when it was safe to head into port. But Norris's franchise was broader than its title suggested; it involved espionage as well.

Expanding briskly after its April start, Norris's bureau organized a network of safe houses, reliable helpers, and transportation to slip agents and messages to and from Washington, Baltimore, New York, and abroad. It also kept an eye on enemy movements along the Potomac, above and below Washington. And almost immediately after Norris started his bureau, Yankee agents apparently became aware of it.[4]

Pinkerton wrote that as the Peninsula campaign began, he dispatched to Richmond one of his "keenest and shrewdest operatives," a former New York infantryman named George Curtis. Curtis allegedly bluffed his way through the lines, into the capital and the good graces of Secretary Benjamin, by pretending to be a dealer in contraband goods. Over drinks and cigars he quickly made a partner of a trusting Southerner who took him to the "subterranean headquarters" of what Pinkerton called "the bureau of intelligence," which actually was on the third floor of their hotel.

Curtis reported that this bureau was operated partly for the government and partly for wealthy Richmond and Baltimore merchants doing business across the lines. Its manager gave him a small badge that would admit him in the future, and introduced him to everyone there. Soon thereafter, Curtis left Richmond with a pass and contracts for goods from Benjamin—and bearing confidential dispatches to Magruder, which he turned over first to Pinkerton's field network.

According to Pinkerton, Curtis carried out repeated missions to Richmond before the war ended. But Curtis's adventures are much harder to document than Pinkerton's story about Timothy Webster and his associates, which is essentially confirmed by Confederate records. In any case, whether Curtis actually penetrated the Norris bureau or not, both sides heightened their efforts to find out enemy intentions as the Union army moved up the Peninsula.[5]

For weeks, as McClellan advanced from Yorktown to and across the Chickahominy, brightly lacquered Union observation balloons advanced with him. Day after day, Rebel officers with spyglasses watched Yankee aeronaut Thaddeus S. C. Lowe and his colleagues watching them.

One afternoon Lowe invited the New York *Herald* correspondent, young George Alfred Townsend, to go aloft with him in a basket dangling from the U.S. balloon *Constitution*. Townsend gasped as the earth seemed to widen beneath them. "Richmond lay only a little way off, enthroned on its many hills, with the James stretching white and sinuous from its feet to the horizon. We could see the streets, the suburbs, the bridges, the outlaying roads, nay, the moving masses of people." The Capitol, the smoky Tredegar works, and riverboat docks were in clear view, and the two men picked out hotels and neighborhoods they knew.

Lowe was busy sketching Confederate defenses when they saw a puff of smoke below, then heard the dull boom of a cannon, then the shriek of a shell passing close by. Then came another, closer. Lowe shouted down to the troops manning his mooring lines, and they began to haul him in. Then another Confederate battery opened fire, and Townsend afterward admitted that he fainted before the balloon was safely down.[6]

When a Union officer told the mistress of a plantation within McClellan's lines that he could see all the capital from the balloon, she was not impressed. "Yes," she said, "Moses also viewed the promised land, but he never entered there."[7] Those balloons were a curiosity to Richmond civilians, a challenge to Confederate gunners, and a nuisance to Confederate officers, forcing them to try to conceal fortifications and movements from Professor Lowe. The aircraft would have been more of an asset to Union generals if McClellan had always sent experienced officers aloft and paid more attention to what they reported. The Southern army also had used balloons earlier in the campaign, but technically the Northern models were far superior. Lowe had devised a portable apparatus to produce hydrogen in the field, which gave his balloons more lift and endurance than the hot-air versions used by the South.

Now, in Richmond, the Confederates were rigging an improved model of varicolored silk sewn together in Savannah and varnished to make it airtight. They would inflate it not with hot air but with illuminating gas, at the municipal gasworks just below Chimborazo Hill. Lee ordered Porter Alexander to take charge—the same Alexander who had so recently questioned Lee's audacity, and earlier had been General Johnston's signal specialist. Alexander planned to moor the new balloon behind a Richmond & York River locomotive, ready to follow the rail line eastward when Lee made his move.[8]

*　　*　　*

On the afternoon of June 23, an exhausted Stonewall Jackson—the man, not his army—rode into Lee's headquarters outside Richmond. There Lee outlined his plan of attack for his generals, then walked away, leaving them to work out the details. The Southern counteroffensive would begin with a Jackson surprise. After a swift march from the Shenandoah, his army would strike the Union flank north of the Chickahominy, joining the commands of A. P. Hill, James Longstreet, and D. H. Hill to drive the Yankees back toward the York River. When the four-hour council of war was over, Jackson rode back into rain and darkness to fetch his army.

All this was wrapped in utmost secrecy—if McClellan suspected it, he might concentrate his superior numbers against the flank attack or use them to storm Richmond's thinned defenses. Lee had shut down comings and goings from his army, provoking complaints from the newspapers but cheers from war clerk Jones: "Officers returning from furlough cannot ascertain in the Adjutant-General's office where their regiments are! . . . No man with a passport from Gen. Winder, or from his Provost Marshal, can pass the pickets of Gen. Lee's army. This is the harbinger of success. . . ." But Jones himself added that "there are some vague rumors about the approach of Stonewall Jackson's army. . . ." And if Pinkerton's agents had heard the gossip in and around Richmond, they must have given the Union commander fair warning.[9]

Though some of Lee's brigade commanders did not yet know his intentions, the wives of politicians apparently did. As the city waited and wondered, Mrs. Louis Wigfall, whose husband had resigned his generalship to become a congressman from Texas, wrote to their daughter on June 25: "Gen. Jackson is to move into position tonight. . . . This was agreed upon last night . . . Jackson and his forces are to make the attack on the rear. . . ."[10]

As she wrote, Union divisions drove in defending pickets and started a brisk but inconclusive fight at Oak Grove, a mile closer to the city than the Seven Pines–Fair Oaks battlefield. Confederate resistance there encouraged McClellan to believe persistent reports that Beauregard's army had arrived in Richmond from the West, boosting Lee's army to 200,000 men—more than double its actual strength. The following morning, the *Dispatch* said in black and white: "It is generally expected that operations of great moment will take place today."[11]

Roger Pryor, former editor and congressman, had won battlefield promotion to brigadier general, then fallen ill with malaria during the fight at Seven Pines. His wife, Sara, brought him from the field back to the Spotswood to administer cool buttermilk and kindness. On the hot morning of June 26, she was fanning him and reading the papers aloud when a message arrived:

> Dear General, put yourself *at once* at the head of your brigade. In thirty-six hours it will all be over.—Longstreet.

Despite his fever, Pryor rose and rode away with other officers, and shortly afterward Mrs. Pryor and a captain's wife followed to the brigade's camp to say goodbye. As they turned back to the capital, they saw smoke billowing from Federal cannon beyond the lines.[12]

The city listened as still, oppressive hours passed with no news. At Powhite plantation, near the Yankee lines, a family cook came in from the yard and said, "Miss Jane, did you know that Jackson's men are up here at Mechanicsville?" Her mistress scoffed. "Go away," she said. "You are a triplet and haven't your share of brains."[13]

Davis, Secretary of War Randolph, and Secretary of the Navy Mallory rode out toward the Chickahominy to see what was happening. The afternoon wore on without action, and with each hour the officials looked gloomier. Nearby, Lee waited as his planned attack fell seven, then eight hours behind schedule; his restless eyes gave away the anxiety beneath his usual calm.

At last, near 4 o'clock, a dozen guns sounded beyond the Chickahominy.[14]

In Richmond the curious crowded onto rooftops and the hills north and east. Soon the booms merged into thunder—"detonations of cannon could not be counted, yet were full, round and perfectly distinct, while incessant charges of musketry struck upon the ear like great drops of rain on a tin roof. . . ."[15]

Yet downtown a British traveler stepping off the train in Richmond for the first time could hardly believe the war was so near.

Second-class militiamen shuffled about the streets, as if the weight of their muskets were a cruel burden. In Capitol Square, Alabama soldiers lolled, awaiting orders. Men with pale faces, crutches, and slings clustered about many doorways, clearly labeling those buildings as hospitals. Shops and bars were closed. A group of stragglers did their best to misunderstand directions to their unit; a band of idle blacks laughed, passing the time. To the traveler, no one seemed excited. Soldiers wounded and furloughed sat smoking and talking on hotel steps; women chatted on porches and stoops, fanning themselves against the heat. McClellan had been so close for so long that "an engagement within hearing of Richmond produced, perhaps, less excitement here than it did next morning at New York. . . ."[16]

Before evening, from atop the Capitol and the president's house, those watching could see gunfire flashing like heat lightning across the darkening horizon. Occasionally a shell arced red above the trees. When the sound and light seemed to shift eastward, shouts swept the watching crowds: "Stonewall is behind them! We are driving them back!"[17]

But Stonewall was too far behind them, so far that he was not even in the fight. Fatigued by the long forced march, confused by vaguely mapped roads through the thick lowlands, and apparently misunderstanding how much Lee's plan counted on close timing, he was still miles away when A. P. Hill attacked toward Mechanicsville without him.

Random shells exploded around Lee as he tried to follow the action from a cleared knoll. Surprised to see Davis and his retinue of aides and politicians rein up close by, he rode over, saluted, and asked, "Mr. President, who are all this army of people, and what are they doing here?"

Davis looked guilty. He said, "It is not my army, General."

"It is certainly not *my* army, Mr. President," said Lee—"and this is no place for it."

Almost sheepishly, Davis lifted his hat: "Well, General, if I withdraw, perhaps they will follow me." With his entourage behind, he rode away, stopping just out of Lee's sight. As he did, a shell killed a soldier at his feet.[18]

Other accounts had Lee asking Davis whether he as general was in command there, and on being assured that he was, forcefully forbidding the president to stay in such danger. Whatever his words, on that occasion the general spoke to the president as if Davis were a junior officer.

No one else addressed Jefferson Davis that way, and Davis did not respond to anyone else that way. Usually Lee was careful to defer to the president, but that exchange under fire may have given a quick glimpse at the heart of the relationship that meant so much to Southern prospects.

In various versions, the story quickly circulated in Richmond; war clerk Jones wrote in his diary: "Yesterday the president's life was saved by Lee." Some still thought that Davis was directing every major move, but those who had seen him afield reported that "he issued no orders; but awaited results like the rest of us, praying fervently for abundant success."[19]

Some Richmonders, if they prayed at all, knelt in the other direction. Elizabeth Van Lew rode with a friend on another errand as the battle escalated. She found the excitement along the Mechanicsville Turnpike "more thrilling than I could conceive—men riding and leading horses at full speed—the rattling of their gear, their canteens and arms—the rush of the poor beasts into and out of the pond at which they were watered—the dust, the commotion . . . the ambulances—the long lines of infantry awaiting orders." A picket stopped them and said the Confederates were whipping the Yankees all across the front. "The roar of the guns grew louder and louder. . . . The rapid succession of the guns was wonderful. . . . No ball could be as exciting as our ride this evening. . . ."

It was a scene that would have made some Richmond ladies feel faint. Van Lew called it "thrilling," suggesting that if she were a man, she would be in the midst of the fight. Few knew that in her way, perhaps that very afternoon, she was living a life almost as dangerous as marching with the infantry.[20]

* * *

After driving the Federals back through Mechanicsville, six miles from downtown Richmond, A. P. Hill's furious opening assault ground down against strong Yankee positions. The next day Lee, with almost all his army committed to the counteroffensive, attacked McClellan's right again to keep the Yankees from marching into the capital. "Prince John" Magruder, a master of deception, commanded the skimpy Southern force facing the Union left, directly between McClellan and Richmond. He busied it marching and countermarching, making a racket and stirring up clouds of dust to persuade the Federals that hordes of Rebels were spoiling for a fight there. Porter Alexander was up in the new Confederate balloon above the York River Railroad tracks, and his presence also fed McClellan's misimpression.

In an ill-coordinated assault at Gaines's Mill, eight miles from town,

Lee's troops broke the Union lines and drove the enemy south of the Chickahominy. Again, Jackson lagged behind, and again, the cost was high, but after each clash the rumble of guns sounded fainter in the city. McClellan, still sure he was hopelessly outnumbered, burned White House plantation and his huge supply base there, and started pulling back toward the James, away from Richmond.

On June 29, Lee drove in the Union rear guard at Savage's Station, ten miles from the capital. The next day he sent his men through the morass of White Oak Swamp against the Federals at Frayser's Farm, thirteen miles out.

Lee hoped to break the Union army in two and block its way to the James, but once again command confusion and faulty maps worked against him. The Federals, with the river at their back, arrayed their cannon fourteen miles from Richmond on Malvern Hill, an open plateau ideal for defense. There, on July 1, they cut down thousands of Confederates who kept up fruitless piecemeal attacks until after dark.

For Lee, Malvern Hill was a tactical defeat, his worst performance as a general until a year later, on a July afternoon in Pennsylvania. But the Seven Days campaign was a major strategic success. McClellan pulled back to Harrison's Landing, nineteen straight miles from the city, much farther by crooked roads or winding river. Never again would soldiers doubt Lee's audacity. Against the odds, it had saved Richmond.

The capital rejoiced at the news, lifting Lee to the highest pedestal among Confederate heroes. And then the dreadful cost of that decisive week became clear: more than 20,000 Confederate casualties—including 3,300 dead and 16,000 wounded—compared with almost 16,000 Federals, of whom some 1,700 had been killed, 8,000 wounded, and 6,000 taken prisoner.[21]

Nearly all those Southern wounded, most of the dead, the prisoners, and hundreds of Northern casualties trickled into the already overpacked capital by train, ambulance, oxcart, muleback, and every kind of transport. "Every family received the bodies of the wounded or dead of their friends, and every house was a house of mourning or a private hospital," wrote Sallie Putnam. "Death held a carnival in our city."[22]

For a while the very streets became hospitals as Richmond dealt with more than three times the casualties of Seven Pines and at the same time tried to find shelter, food, and medical attention for thousands of new captives. Those efforts inspired moments that Richmond would remember with pride, and forced others that it would rather have forgotten.

CHAPTER TWELVE

CAN'T YOU WAIT
UNTIL WE'RE DEAD?

Sara Rice Pryor had turned down Mrs. Letcher's invitation to join her family and friends, watching for signs of battle from the roof of the governor's mansion. She could not bear to think that somewhere beneath those clouds of gunsmoke her husband might be lying helpless, or dying. She stayed in her room at the Spotswood, sitting up all that night after the fight at Mechanicsville, looking down on streets lit by a full moon.

Very late, she watched two shadowy figures sitting on a doorstep singing a sad, sad song and found herself in tears—"not for my own changed life, not for my own sorrows, but for the dear city; the dear, doomed city, so loved, so loved!" Sara remembered how as a country preacher's daughter from Halifax County she had come to visit, and in the scary stillness of the night looked out upon what seemed "the splendor, the immensity of the city," and heard watchmen cry "All's well." "Never, never again," she reflected, "could all be well with us in old Virginia. Never could we stifle the memories of this bitter hour. . . ."

Before dawn, a courier arrived to say that her husband was safe but had much more fighting to do. Without sleep, but with new resolve, she left the Spotswood, heading for the makeshift hospital set up in Kent & Paine's dry-goods store, three blocks down Main Street.

Wounded men already filled cots lining the broad first floor, and more were being laid out upstairs. Sara volunteered her help to a skeptical matron. As she was walking through the ward to sign up, the sight of a freshly amputated arm made her faint. The matron, standing over her when she revived, told her she was clearly too young and delicate for such service. But Sara insisted that she had fainted only from lack of sleep. She came back the next day, determined to help; the matron gave her a post near the door, where she could breathe fresh air. Sara served on, putting in twelve hours or more a day. Soon one of her servants brought a basket with bandages she had ordered made from all her household linens at home in Petersburg.

With each battle of that long week, another surge of casualties flowed in, and with each a messenger came to assure Sara that her husband was still safe. When she asked one whether the general had had a comfortable night, the messenger said he certainly had: "He slep' on de field 'twixt two daid horses!" Many wounded died because there was not enough medical help to go around. "Very few men ever walked away. . . . They died, or friends found quarters for them in the homes in Richmond. . . . None complained!"

Back and forth between hotel and hospital, Sara veiled her eyes against the walking wounded, the ailing prisoners, and especially the open wagonloads of dead soldiers bound for burial. At last, days after Malvern Hill, her husband dragged himself into the Spotswood covered with mud and dust. When he saw Sara he burst out, "My men are all dead!" and fell on the bed weeping.[1]

Not all Roger Pryor's soldiers were dead; 170 had been killed outright, 681 wounded, 11 were missing—a total of 862 casualties, nearly half of his brigade.[2] They had been with Longstreet's division in the thick of the fighting. But Pryor's was only one of the grievously damaged commands in Lee's army. Back to Richmond the victims came, maimed and limping, too many for the hospitals both established and makeshift; too many for the volunteer nurses, the hollow-eyed surgeons, and overworked gravediggers.

Out at the eastern end of Broad Street, Chimborazo Hospital, at times one of the most efficiently managed institutions in the Confederacy, could not come close to handling the caseload that swamped it in those stifling days of late June and early July. When ambulances bearing suffering men were turned away from one crowded hospital after another in the city, many drove back to Chimborazo, whose 3,000 beds were already full. Rejected again, some drivers dumped their wounded in the hospital streets and hurried away to pick up more. Attendants stretched surplus patients on the floors, then in hastily requisitioned tents, then in the open around those tents. Flies swarmed everywhere. Doctors had to make triage decisions wholesale, ruling at a glance on who would have surgery and who would have to die.[3]

George Bagby, returning from a month's well-timed vacation, felt "the dread of infection" as his train neared Richmond. Across the river in Manchester, he was already struck by "the odor of suppurating wounds," which grew stronger as he came closer. He found "a strange stillness" in the night streets as he passed the temporary hospitals with their "ministering angels passing to and fro."[4]

A physician wrote later that "To be wounded in this war meant to be dead or an amputee." Too often, it meant both. Of 541 amputations recorded in Richmond hospitals after the Seven Days, 40 percent of the patients died; with thigh amputations, the death rate was 59 percent. Despite such prospects, surgeons kept sawing, because infection made not amputating much more risky.[5]

Jennie Harrold, a young girl whose hospital duties were limited to bringing in delicacies and staying to fan patients, told of watching two black attendants move a pair of critically ill amputees from Seabrook's warehouse, at Seventeenth and Grace streets.

One of the soldiers asked, "What are you going to do with us?"

"We want to make room for those coming in," said one attendant.

"Can't you wait until we are dead?"

"No."

As those hopeless cases were carried away to the "dead house," another soldier lay dying nearby chanting, "Retribution, retribution, retribution. . . ."[6]

There was not enough soap, not enough bandages, drugs, equipment, help—not enough of anything a hospital needed. Like every other Richmond hospital, Seabrook's and Chimborazo were simply overwhelmed by the results of the Seven Days campaign. Chimborazo Hospital spread across a forty-acre plateau atop the hill for which it was named, overlooking Rocketts and the York River Railroad. Between Chimborazo and Church Hill ran the deep gulch of Bloody Run (whose name suggested what went on at Chimborazo in the 1860s but dated back to a clash with Indians there more than 200 years earlier). The hospital was set up after Manassas, on the orders of newly appointed Surgeon General Samuel P. Moore, an old-army veteran. He realized that the city's scattered smaller hospitals, many of them organized to treat casualties from particular states, could not handle a serious war.

As chief surgeon of Chimborazo, Moore appointed a native Richmonder, James B. McCaw, whose father, grandfather, and great-grandfather had been physicians before him. A 39-year-old New York–trained professor at the Medical College of Virginia, McCaw had studied typhoid fever and understood something of the value of clean surroundings. He was an ingenious administrator who got his way with gentlemanly persuasion rather than martial bluster.

McCaw's hospital had five divisions, nominally one each for soldiers from Virginia, Georgia, North Carolina, Alabama, and South Carolina. In less crowded weeks, patients were housed in 150 rough-sided, white-washed, one-story buildings laid out in neat rows across the plateau, in addition to about 100 army tents. Under McCaw, Chimborazo bought its own canal boats, which shuttled into the country to bring back fresh produce. It ran its own bakery, soup house, and soap factory. It had its own hundreds of cattle and goats, pastured on the nearby Tree Hill plantation of the distiller whom one writer called "the patriotic Mr. Franklin Stearns."

Only Winder Hospital, on the city's western border, challenged Chimborazo as the largest hospital in the South and perhaps in the world. Amazingly, in a time of rocketing inflation, McCaw ran Chimborazo fiscally in the black, drawing funds only for the daily rations of its patients. But all forty-four of the city's large and small hospitals together could not accommodate the flood of mangled men coming back from the battles that drove McClellan down the Peninsula. Neither, indeed, could Richmond's cemeteries.[7]

*   *   *

On a plank at the head of a Union soldier's shallow grave east of the city, some Southerner had lettered an epitaph:

> *The Yankee host with blood-stained hand,*
> *Came southward to divide our land.*
> *This narrow and contracted spot*
> *Is all that this poor Yankee got.*[8]

But that poor Yankee buried on the field was handled better than hundreds of Confederates who were killed there and brought into the city, or who made it to Richmond's hospitals before they died. At first, as after earlier, lesser battles, there were individual funeral processions for officers, with riderless horses with boots reversed in the stirrups and bands playing dirges through the dusty streets. But now ceremony was overtaken by numbers. The bodies of enlisted soldiers were taken straight to burial, perhaps in the greenery of Hollywood Cemetery, west of Oregon Hill, or at Oakwood, north of Church Hill. Their graves were marked by wooden shingles stuck upright, their names scrawled in pencil. As more and more bodies came, services were held far into the night, and many soldiers were buried with no service at all.

The dead arrived faster than gravediggers could make places for them; at one time about fifty bodies waited for burial, swelling in the heat and choking blocks of the city with the smell of death. The *Exam-*

iner demanded to know why the authorities could not enlist enough cemetery workmen from among "all loaferdom around Richmond, both white and black." When Hollywood used up all its own ground, workers started burying soldiers beyond its boundary, on land near the city reservoir. Waterworks officials appealed to the City Council, worried that graves might taint the water supply, and asserting that the space was needed for another reservoir to service a city whose population had tripled in little more than a year of war.[9]

That tripling did not include the families of soldiers who swarmed in after battle trying to find and help their sons and husbands. Day after day the newspapers ran columns of agate type naming hundreds of casualties, hospital by hospital and regiment by regiment. Kinfolk bought advertisements to seek news of lost soldiers. Nor did the population boom count the Yankee prisoners who marched wearily into a city already unable to care for its own. One of those Yankees was Brigadier General John F. Reynolds of Pennsylvania, caught at Glendale and greeted in the capital by an official he had known in happier times.

"General," said the Confederate, "this is in accordance with McClellan's prediction; you are in Richmond."

"Yes, sir," said Reynolds. "And damn me, if it is not precisely in the manner I anticipated."[10]

Trainloads of captives had been sent to states farther south, but that only briefly eased crowding in the buildings commandeered for prisons after Manassas. Libby warehouse, a ship chandler's loft beside the canal at Twentieth Street, would become the most famous prison in the city because most of its occupants were Union officers, better-educated soldiers who wrote uncounted letters and memoirs about their life in Rebel hands. But now Libby was overfilled with wounded Yankees; by July 9, there were 5,250 prisoners of all ranks in the city, and more coming.[11] They had to be kept somewhere, and there were few troops to guard them.

General Winder considered putting enlisted captives at Camp Lee but rejected the idea because two regiments would be needed to make the camp secure. He had to find a safe place immediately. He chose Belle Isle, surrounded by the swift-flowing James, along the city's western edge near Hollywood Cemetery. In the July heat the island was a welcome change from the packed, sweltering warehouses in town. The newspapers made it seem a holiday resort:

> Seeing a Good Time—The prisoners on Belle Isle are encamped on the lower ground of the island, within convenient distance of the water, and at all times in the full face of the breezes that almost continually sweep along the river. They pass away time in exercise such as wrestling, jumping, and tumbling about generally,

apparently caring for nothing and nobody, and quite as contented as they can be under the circumstances. They are supplied with excellent tents, and have a plenty to eat. . . .[12]

Bagby thought the 4,600 Yankees on Belle Isle in late July were lucky to be in their "beautiful encampment, regularly laid out, with a wide long street, which they call Broadway." They had dug plenty of wells and were allowed to bathe in the river under guard. By then only one had escaped, and he had been retaken.[13]

*   *   *

The Seven Days campaign was the biggest, most costly yet fought, and strategically a major Southern success. But just as after Manassas, fervent cheerleaders in Richmond managed to overstate what it meant.

With almost every local household taking in one or two wounded and sick Confederates, the beer-hall keeper Gottfried Lange wrote that "my pen is too weak to describe the great lamentation that had befallen the city of Richmond." Yet when the guns had been silent for less than forty-eight hours, the *Enquirer* asserted that the victory had opened the way to end the war, though "the Yankees will protract it for a while." The South's independence was now assured, the paper said, but it must fight to hold its rightful boundaries and secure permanent independence. There would be negotiations, in which the Confederacy must be sure to retain Maryland, Kentucky, and Missouri.[14]

Below Richmond a more realistic Jeff Davis had met with Lee and his generals in a lashing rainstorm after Malvern Hill. They decided that the weather, the hopelessly muddy roads, and the gunboats protecting the Union army at Harrison's Landing must postpone further attacks. Lee still did not realize how hollow McClellan was beneath his Napoleonic posturing. The Federal general claimed that his command's performance against "vastly superior forces" had placed it "among the celebrated armies of history." He solicited praise for his withdrawal tactics, for changing his base of operations from the York to the James River.[15]

"Changing my base" inspired jokes among Rebel soldiers for months afterward:

> *Henceforth, when a fellow is kicked out of doors,*
> *He need never resent the disgrace;*
> *But exclaim, "My dear sir, I'm eternally yours,*
> *For assisting in changing my base!"*[16]

Assuming that McClellan must be planning other ways to get at Richmond, Lee ordered Jeb Stuart's cavalry and Porter Alexander's balloon to reconnoiter Federal positions. Since the campaign had turned south away from the York River Railroad, this time Alexander inflated his balloon and moored it not to a train but to an armed tugboat named *Teaser*. Aboard this primitive aircraft carrier, he set out from the Richmond gasworks, steaming down the James to Malvern Hill. After a successful scout, he descended and the boat's captain put him ashore to report to Lee. Then as the tide pulled out, the *Teaser* ran aground on a mud bank. Before she could get off, both vessel and balloon were captured by a Federal gunboat. Alexander escaped, but that was the inglorious end of the Confederate balloon corps in Virginia.[17]

McClellan's resounding claims of success were as transparent to his own army as they were to Lee's. In late July a New York soldier named Theodore Smith was so distraught that he hardly slowed to punctuate as he gave his father the facts of life in the Army of the Potomac:

> There is gloom where before there was confident hope. There is sorrow where before there was almost exultation. . . .
>
> All last winter in camp you could hear nothing but going down to Richmond. It was the song of every soldier through out the Potomac army. While we were at Alexandria my regt. serenaded Gen Mcclelland at his headquarters. The song that was sung was the one I have just mentioned, "going down to Richmond." The general came out and made a short speech yes says he we are going down to Richmond and soon to and I think we can get there without much trouble I think we can take it. Every soldier seemed to place so much confidence in his plans what ever they might be.
>
> Well he has marched us to Richmond safe in sight of the confederate capital within four miles of it after the labor of two months the horrible sickness of thousands of our men poisoned in the swamps of the Chickihominy the loss of probably more than ten thousand as noble fellows as ever lifted a hand to defend their country he finds himself twenty five miles from the city wagons burned ammunition trains blown up parks of artillery captured no entrenchments and with an army so small that it is not pretended that he can reach Richmond.
>
> It was the opinion of every soldier that we would spend the fourth day of July in Richmond now there is no prospect of spending it there in the year 1863 unless something is done and done quick we are gone up we will have fighting in another direction but I hope not. I want to see this war closed there has been blood enough shed 20,000 brave fellows fell on the field on our side during the seven days battles. The enemys loss is estimated at four times that amount. . . . We are throwing up entrenchments and strengthening our lines the weather has been extremely hot for a few days but it is very sickly here.[18]

In Washington, Lincoln and Secretary of War Stanton were about as sick of McClellan's excuses as infantryman Smith was sick of summer on the Peninsula. In early August, they officially ended the "Young Napoleon's" grand plan to take the Confederate capital and ordered him to start withdrawing his army, to try another day on another road to Richmond.

CHAPTER THIRTEEN

AT WHICH ANGELS
MIGHT WEEP

Sunday services had already begun when a bearded officer with jingling spurs arrived at the Second Presbyterian Church on Fifth Street between Main and Franklin. Few noticed as he quietly took a seat in the light filtering through high Gothic windows. But as soon as the preacher said "Amen" to the closing prayer, worshippers turned around and recognized the latecomer. They crowded about his pew, ignoring and squeezing away the younger officers who had arrived with him.

The welcome visitor was Stonewall Jackson, whose lapses in the Seven Days campaign had done nothing to hurt his standing with the worshipful public. Particularly in this church, he was admired as much for his Presbyterian zeal as for his generalship. He was all modesty as he thanked the congregation for its praise. When Henry Kyd Douglas and Jackson's other staff officers somehow led him outdoors, the crowd pressed around again, until the general mounted his sorrel horse and headed back to camp outside the city.

On that second Sunday after the Seven Days, Stonewall got orders to march his troops north again; he would not return to Richmond until the following spring, under very different circumstances. But already he had become friends with his spiritual brother, the man in the pulpit. Before his force departed, Jackson gave the pastor a note saying: "Permit the bearer, the Rev. Moses D. Hoge, to pass at pleasure from Richmond to any part of my command."[1]

Moses Hoge would use that pass. He was still conducting services regularly at his church, opening sessions of the Confederate Senate, and preaching to regiments coming and going at the camps around Richmond. Beyond that, he tried to help in the field whenever there was action nearby. During the Seven Pines fight he rode, with a colonel friend, so close to the battle that his horse was hit and spooked by a spent musket ball. On the way, he chastised a civilian for cursing passing prisoners, telling him that "the best way of showing his hatred of the enemy was to fight them in the ranks, and not to abuse them when in our power." He gave up his horse to a wounded soldier long enough for the soldier to reach an ambulance; helped a grieving servant find out that his master had not been wounded after all; gave troops behind the line a pep talk. "It helps men to be able to go in cheerily to battle," he said later.

At an overcrowded aid station he walked in on "a spectacle at which angels might weep! No one knows what war is who has not seen military hospitals; not of the sick only, but of the cut, maimed and mutilated in all the ways in which the human body can be dishonored and disfigured." There amid the groaning casualties, he knelt to ask God to ease their pain and spare their lives.[2]

Day and night, Hoge was hyperactive. Job-seekers, distraught widows, and unpaid soldiers came to him as if he were their congressman. So did friends, and friends of friends, looking for shelter. In a city where four or six strangers might share a room, many moved into Hoge's boxy stucco house beside the church. Politicians and judges stayed for months; Vice President Stephens, cabinet secretaries, and generals came to call.

Hoge's wife, Susan, was away in Prince Edward County that summer because two of their children were sick. Hoge tried to list the outsiders in residence for her, but he did not know all their names. "Last night people were calling on various errands until after 12 o'clock," he wrote. "I am glad to be of use and comfort to so many people, & while I have anything to eat, or anything to buy with, I mean to keep an open house for all comers." Before many months, that openheartedness would bring complications.[3]

Not all those who offered quarters to refugees, to next of kin seeking missing soldiers, to bureaucrats and congressmen, were as hospitable as Moses Hoge.

Mary Chesnut, who had gone home to South Carolina for a year, returned with her husband, now newly appointed as an aide to President Davis. After a brief stay at the Ballard House hotel, they had to move in with "decayed ladies" forced by unaccustomed straits to accept boarders. The ladies' ancient house was "a dreadful refuge of the distressed," Mrs.

Chesnut wrote—comfortable, with decent food, but extravagantly priced, and "you were forced to assume the patient humility of a poor relation. So fine was the hauteur and utter scorn with which you were treated."[4]

Mrs. Chesnut was charmed by that other Davis aide, Joseph Ives, a native New Yorker who as a young U.S. Army officer in the 1850s had explored the Colorado River and been engineer of the Washington Monument. She admired his style, his slashing boots, the way his spurs rattled. As a colonel, he was a "handsome creature . . . quite the picture of a soldier"—but also suspected by a few of being a Northern spy. Porter Alexander's sister urged Varina Davis to tell the president of Ives's alleged disloyalty, but Alexander said such suspicions clearly were unfounded, because the Yankees were so astoundingly ignorant of Confederate strength. "They never had a spy worth a cent," Alexander maintained. There were things going on around him that he did not know.[5]

Ives served loyally throughout the war. Doubts of his trustworthiness may have been encouraged by his reputation as a toper—and other whispers about now-forgotten "social scandals," whispers that would poison his reputation with some ladies but make him fascinating to others.

That late summer Ives's wife and children were in Lexington, and his mother far away in Boston. He had not heard from his mother in eighteen months and wrote to her joking about trying to find a place for his family: "I am making desperate efforts to get up a panic in Richmond, in order to get a furnished house, but the stupid people won't have a panic, and the city is crowded, and when I endeavour to represent the danger of staying here, after the million of men come to attack us, they invariably find out that I am trying to settle my own family in the city, and refuse to put faith in my hypocritical predictions."

He hoped to get a little cottage outside town, and when he did so he would send for his mother. Then, he wrote, "you will have the advantage of learning how little people can get along with, and yet be comfortable and merry, or you can, if miserable without tea, coffee, shoes, clothing & such luxuries, practice self-denial and become, according to our Catholic notions, better prepared than ever to take those 'wings of a dove.' "[6]

* * *

One reason why self-denial was on the minds of Richmonders was General John Henry Winder. Winder, forty-two years an army officer, was not educated in the fundamentals of economics.

In the spring of 1862, with the blockade tightening and McClellan advancing along the Peninsula, the price of produce shot up in city markets. Winder responded with a frontal attack, expanding his martial-law authority by ordering price ceilings on such staples as fish, butter, eggs, and potatoes. The combination of shrinking access to the countryside and fixed prices to farmers cut the supply so deeply that in less than a month he was forced to back off this experiment. But by then genuine scarcity had sent prices rocketing. Butter cost consumers almost triple what it had before Winder clamped down, eggs five times as much. In summer he tried again, ordering ceilings on corn and fodder, and when supplies promptly dried up he was informed by the War Department that he had stepped beyond his authority.[7]

Salt was so short that the city began buying it directly from Saltville in far southwestern Virginia and rationing it, a pound per person per month, at 5 cents a pound. War Department clerk Jones said "extortionists" were selling it for 70 cents. In early fall, he tracked the climb of other prices. Wood was up to $16 a cord and coal $9 a load when it was available, but as cold weather approached, there was none. Flour was $16 a barrel, bacon 75 cents a pound, potatoes $5 a bushel, scrawny chickens $1 each, butter $1.25 a pound. When Jones's wife returned from refugeeing in Raleigh, he bought a pound of sugar for 80 cents, a quart of milk for 25 cents, four fist-size loaves of bread for 20 cents each. Coffee was $2.50 a pound—when there was any. Mrs. Jones had learned to make substitute coffee by toasting cornmeal to a burn, which Jones said he liked, perhaps because it cost only 5 or 6 cents a pound. "How can we live here?" he asked. "How shall we subsist this winter?"[8]

In truth, Jones and Richmond still had only a nodding acquaintance with self-denial and inflation. Intimate experience was yet to come.

* * *

General Winder's other most resented initiative was his bringing in dozens of detectives, mostly from Maryland, to enforce his decrees and investigate political offenses. For jobs that demanded high integrity, Winder hired "a coterie of vagabond refugees from Baltimore, the habitués of brothels and gambling houses," the *Examiner* said. They were called plug-uglies after the rowdies who had given Baltimore the reputation of being "Mob City." To Richmond, the newspaper said, they had brought "a carnival of crime" in which detectives were accused of bribery, extortion, and fraud. One of them, arrested for bribery, coolly offered $50,000 for bail.

Winder, responding to an indignant public and perhaps to presidential orders, fired the whole crew as of November 1, "down to the messenger and a vicious-looking dog." That included his chief detective, Samuel Maccubbin of Baltimore, although three of Maccubbin's children had died of diphtheria in the month just past. The only exception was Winder's right-hand man, another Baltimorean, Captain Philip Cashmyer.[9]

The detectives were not the only Marylanders who had flocked to Richmond; many Southern sympathizers crossed the Potomac to escape Lincoln's martial law, among them refugees bearing some of Maryland's most illustrious family names. But there also were gangs of gamblers, muggers, and whores from Baltimore's netherworld, and later, dodgers of the Federal draft.

As Winder laid off the detective force, Mayor Mayo announced that he was going to start enforcing city vagrancy laws and sentencing men with no legitimate job to the chain gang. The mayor said that he and the police spent 70 percent of their time dealing with "scoundrels who have immigrated from Baltimore, Washington or New Orleans." But Captain Alexander of Castle Thunder, himself a Baltimorean, resented such broad accusations and protested that every criminal caught "lied and said he was from Baltimore."[10]

Winder also pledged to crack down again on sales of alcohol, which had boomed since his prohibition edict. As demand grew the quality of the goods diminished, and retailers used ever more ingenious ways of bringing spirits in from the countryside. The police caught women who rode railroad cars hiding beef bladders of bad liquor under their full skirts, smuggling them from Coalfield to "low Irish groggeries" in the city.[11]

But renewed pressure had almost no impact on drinking, private or public. The extent of it was "appalling" to the *Examiner,* and "only a chemist familiar with the most horrible secrets of his calling" could describe the product. "Apart from its terrible nauseousness to the undebauched palate and nostrils, the properties are said to be more deadly to the health of body and mind than that fatal and filthy compound which in times of peace used to circulate among the negroes. . . . This is the vile stuff which not only ruffians of beastly and depraved appetites, but well bred, well educated, influential gentlemen are now swallowing with avidity. . . ."[12]

* * *

When congressmen left town with their famously alleged escort of ladies to protect them against snakes and bullfrogs, the Federal army was on the city's outskirts and Lee was being questioned about where he would fall back from Richmond. When Congress returned in mid-

August, Lee had driven McClellan down the river and Jackson had already confronted the latest Union thrust from the north at Cedar Mountain, in Culpeper County seventy miles away.

Though civilians by the train-, wagon- and boatload had fled the capital along with the lawmakers in the spring, a few had donned uniforms and headed for the approaching front lines. One such was John Moncure Daniel of the *Examiner*.

Mentally, the 36-year-old, 120-pound Daniel was as martial as men come, but he was a frail bundle of nerves, hardly constituted for rough life in the field. When he served briefly as aide to general and ex-governor John Floyd in the unsuccessful 1861 western Virginia campaign, he had set out with accoutrements grand enough for a Southern McClellan, including valet, cook, and complete kitchen. Then, when Richmond was threatened in 1862, he joined A. P. Hill's staff as a major. Hill so admired Daniel's vehement views that he read *Examiner* editorials aloud with his general orders, to inspire his officers to fight. In the Seven Days' campaign, a musket ball damaged Daniel's right arm. With this "honorable wound" he retired to editorial combat, which he waged almost as aggressively against the Davis administration as against the Northern enemy.

Even when Daniel was absent, the *Examiner* did not give politicians a holiday. During the editor's weeks away in 1862, his associate in charge was Edward A. Pollard, whose criticism of the president and Congress was as merciless as Daniel's. But close readers of the *Examiner* could always tell when Daniel was there, for then the paper had a character that no one else could instill. Its articles, written by a varied cast of contributors, were unsigned; with a few strokes and inserts, Daniel made them all his own.

George Bagby told of sending Daniel a satirical piece at mid-war and looking for it in print day after day, then being asked to come in to be paid for it. When he protested that it had never run, Daniel pointed to the files. There Bagby found an article "twice as long and twice as good as the one I had written—my own ideas, but so enveloped in Daniel's fine English, and so amplified that it was hard to recognize them."[13]

Daniel offered to make Bagby his assistant editor, but Bagby by then had the same title at the *Whig*, besides editing his *Southern Literary Messenger* and corresponding for his myriad out-of-town clients, so he settled on writing two or three editorials a week for the *Examiner*. This further strained Bagby's endurance, but not his conscience, for though he was less mean-spirited than Daniel, their prejudices ran parallel.

Early in the war, the capital's major papers had chosen sides. The *Examiner* under Daniel and Pollard, and the *Whig* under Alexander

Mosely and James McDonald, competed in lashing the president. But the *Enquirer,* edited by the late Jennings Wise's partner Nathaniel Tyler, then by Bennett M. De Witt and Richard M. Smith, stoutly defended the administration except in increasingly impatient editorials by the Irish expatriate John Mitchel. James A. Cowardin's politically unaffiliated *Dispatch,* which had the greatest circulation, spoke out loyally and safely for soldiers in the Confederate ranks.[14]

Occasional journals mushroomed, then folded in the wartime capital. Two weeklies that lasted were the *Southern Illustrated News,* started in September 1862, and *Southern Punch,* first published in August 1863. With poems, cartoons, and admiring portraits of Southern heroes, they did not come up to the standard of their models in London.

Gradually, decent newsprint became as hard to get as imported consumer goods, and Richmond's newspapers shrank to one tabloid sheet, front and back. They were often blurry, printed with battered type on gray, mottled stock. Still, they crammed their columns with news, gathered firsthand and reprinted from other papers North and South. What set each apart from its competitors was not so much its coverage as its opinions, and how vividly they were expressed. The only hint of objectivity in Daniel's editorials, for instance, was the impartial way they assailed both Congress and the president.

Daniel's associate, Edward Pollard, later wrote of "that extreme intellectual degradation which made the Confederate Congress a peculiar stock of shame in the war—actually one of the weakest and most inane bodies that ever met under the title of a legislative assembly. . . . the history of the Confederate Congress is scarcely more than . . . the reflection of the will and temper of President Davis—a mere servile appendage to an autocracy the most supreme of modern times."[15]

* * *

Because Pollard's half-dozen cruelly critical books were published during and soon after the war, they overinfluenced other assessments of the Davis government; flawed as Congress and president were, neither was as abysmal as Pollard maintained.

Davis was torn between his determination to win the war and his reverence for the Confederate constitution, which was much like the one under which he had served the Union as soldier, senator, and cabinet member. The strain of trying to save the Confederacy and uphold strict constitutionality racked him from the beginning. Though often accused of aspiring to dictatorship, he did not dare to ignore his constitution as cavalierly as Lincoln sometimes did his.

In four-plus years, fifteen men occupied the six seats in Davis's cab-

inet, and since the same two headed the Navy and Post Office throughout, the turnover in the remaining four departments was still more impressive. Yet the president stayed on cordial terms, coming and going,
with most of those men, often defying popular censure to retain them.
Some left because of other political ambitions, some because of congressional rather than presidential displeasure, but only his War Department secretaries had consistent reason to complain of interference
from ex-colonel, ex-secretary of war Davis.

In Congress it was Davis's opponents who lit the most memorable
rhetorical fireworks, and in closed session they even talked of deposing
him—if only Alexander Stephens were not vice president. Yet Davis
prevailed more often than not. Legislators tried repeatedly but failed to
intrude on his strategic management of the war, and their investigative
efforts to embarrass the president were feeble compared with what Lincoln endured in Washington. In four years, Davis vetoed thirty-nine
bills passed by Congress, and while occasionally House or Senate voted
separately to override, the two houses joined to turn back only one of
those vetoes. That was on a measure to authorize free delivery of newspapers to soldiers.

Even amid crisis, squabbling was endemic in Richmond—not only at
the Capitol but between press and government, between rival newspapers, between the national administration and the state capitals, between the branches of government,* and between grand egos within
each branch. The overworked president, sensitive as he was to every syl-
lable of criticism, tried hard to contain his resentment, though occasionally those feelings seeped out through his close circle. More and
more he worked sealed in private behind his six aides, who defended
him from time-wasting visitors. Callers who got through often found
him cold and distant, which offended many who wanted to be his
friends and drove those who already held grudges to extremes of
vituperation.

Some of those grudges ran back a long way. In Washington in 1847,
still limping with a leg wounded in Mexico, Davis had gotten into an argument that became a fistfight and stopped just short of a duel with his
fellow Mississippi senator, Henry S. Foote. Slight and bald, a lively
stump speaker, Foote opposed Davis on fundamental issues in the Senate, then defeated him for the Mississippi governorship in 1851. During
his tumultuous career, the Virginia-born Foote survived duels with four
other men, plus uncounted less formal scrapes. And now he was a Con-

---

*At the highest level, this intragovernmental squabbling was between two branches rather
than among three, because Congress never created the Supreme Court authorized by the
Confederate constitution and supported by Davis.

federate congressman from Tennessee, who seemed to think his main duty was to bedevil the president.[16]

All around Davis were men who believed they should be president instead, or at least commanding general.

Robert A. Toombs of Georgia had reluctantly entered the Confederate cabinet as secretary of state, soured on Davis, and resigned to become a brigadier while still in the provisional Congress. At Malvern Hill he challenged Major Gen. D. H. Hill to a duel when Hill reprimanded him for his conduct under fire; in reply, Hill merely slapped him with another reprimand. After acquitting himself well in a later battle, Toombs would resign again because he had not been promptly promoted. Frustrated that professional soldiers ranked above him, he suggested that the epitaph for the Southern army should be "died of West Point," and that if the Confederacy won, it would be despite Davis, not because of him. He tossed off such comments, often over drinks, while opposing the president publicly on conscription, martial law, and other emergency measures.[17]

Louis Wigfall of Texas, the man who had prevailed on Fort Sumter to surrender and then had come to Richmond proudly at Davis's side, also indulged a hostility to Davis and a friendship with the bottle. The burly, thick-bearded Wigfall handled that friendship less discreetly than Toombs did, and his wife, Charlotte, spoke spitefully of Varina Davis.

The president made a conciliatory gesture by appointing Wigfall a brigadier, but the Texan shed his uniform in early 1862 to enter the Senate. At the Capitol and in the barrooms of Richmond, he berated Davis. At a party at Mary Chesnut's, while others stood respectfully to greet the president, Wigfall's daughters sat and turned their backs. "A remarkable episode," Mrs. Chesnut called it. She had long since decided that Wigfall was Davis's worst enemy in Congress.[18]

Competition for that distinction was vigorous. Foote, Toombs, William Lowndes Yancey of Alabama, and, increasingly, Vice President Alexander Stephens were all contenders.

Stephens had opposed secession but had gone along with Georgia and then helped persuade Virginia to follow. At 60, he was thin, pale, and pockmarked. A journalist wrote: "If he were to draw his last breath any instant you would not be surprised. If he were laid out in his coffin, he need not look any different, only then the fires would have gone out in those burning eyes."[19]

As vice president, Stephens was presiding officer of the Senate, where he stood against Davis on habeas corpus, conscription, martial law, and almost any conflict between national and states' rights. But he became so discouraged by what he saw as Davis's growing "despotism" that for months at the height of the war, he stayed at home and would not set foot in Richmond. Stephens felt deeply for victims of the war, often visited military hospitals, and, more than any other ranking Confederate official, sought ways to negotiate peace. He insisted that he did not oppose Davis personally; his opposition was founded on issues, however specious, rather than on petty jealousy. But the record supports those who charged that he "was more concerned with the maintenance of the constitutional rights of the people than with winning the war. . . ."[20]

By reflex, most Confederate politicians of the era were opponents rather than advocates of presidents and policies. For decades, in Washington and their state capitals, they had fought against the inexorable trends of nationalism. Now that the showdown had come, in theory they stood together in their new confederation. But, though nominally Democrats, they were as fractious as ever. Old-time Democrats still resented the ex-Whigs among them, but attitudes toward Davis had replaced party labels in dividing the legislature.

While Congress was at work the steps of the Capitol were lined with idle, tobacco-puffing, tobacco-squirting kibitzers. The corridors were full of visitors and politicians. At stands in the halls women sold apples, peaches, and peanuts at tables "like the money changers of biblical lore, making the place, with Congressional sanction, a place of merchandise."[21]

In this atmosphere many congressmen made it clear that they were less committed to the wartime needs of the Confederacy than to the fancied rights of their own states. Some, indeed, were less concerned for their states than for their personal glorification. Fire-eaters and conservatives refused to forget their prewar feuds over secession. They complained about Confederate requisitioning of troops and arms from their states. They complained when Davis did not appoint them and their friends to political generalships, and when he did appoint and promote his own favorites. They complained that there were too many generals from Virginia, and whenever an officer from any other state commanded a regiment or brigade from their own. And they second-guessed strategy and tactics, even after clear-cut Southern victories like those at Manassas.

*   *   *

Late in August of 1862, Lee left the capital lightly defended and joined Longstreet and Jackson to smash Union major general John Pope's on-to-Richmond dreams on the familiar fields by Bull Run. That second battle of Manassas was another triumph; after it, Lee took his army across the Potomac into Union territory for the first time. All Dixie rejoiced—yet even then, as frightened Pennsylvania officials evacuated state archives and treasure from Harrisburg and Philadelphia, the Confederate Congress spent the day debating whether Lee should have invaded the North.

Soldiers debated it, too, after Lee again met McClellan, who had brought his army north from the Peninsula and taken command outside Washington. Because Union soldiers had found a lost copy of Lee's complex campaign order, McClellan reacted with uncharacteristic vigor. Along Antietam Creek, outside the Maryland village of Sharpsburg, the armies fought a seesaw battle that made September 17, 1862, the bloodiest single day of the war.

At about that time the surgeon general reported that since war began, Richmond's military hospitals had received 99,408 sick and wounded. That was two and a half times the city's prewar population. Of those, 7,603 had died, a rate of nearly 8 percent. Chimborazo had taken in 24,895 patients, of whom 2,033 had died, and Winder Hospital 22,874, of whom 1,271 had died. In hospitals staffed by men only, the death rate was about 10 percent; in those run by women, it was less than 6 percent. As of that report, there were 10,200 patients in the city's hospitals. But several hundred more had just arrived, and many hundreds more were on their way from Maryland.[22]

Before those fresh casualties could be treated, when there had hardly been time to argue whether Lee's outnumbered force had won or lost at Antietam, news came from Washington that momentarily united even the Confederate Congress.

Lincoln, after mulling over the emancipation of slaves for months, had secretly presented a draft proclamation to his cabinet in July. His secretary of state, William H. Seward, cautioned that he should hold it until after a Union victory, lest it seem a gesture of desperation. On September 22, the president decided that the costly standoff at Antietam would serve the purpose. He announced that as of January 1, 1863, the Federal government would consider all slaves within the states still in rebellion to be free.

Reaction to Lincoln's stroke was far from unanimous, even in the North. To the white South, it seemed a raw effort to inspire 4 million bondsmen to rise up while their masters were away. To the rest of the world, it cast the war in clear moral terms that made foreign intervention less likely than ever. For Union soldiers, it gave new meaning to lyrics that Julia Ward Howe had written months earlier: ". . . As he died to make men holy, let us die to make men free. . . ."

CHAPTER FOURTEEN

A SCHEME SO ATROCIOUS

*T*hat late summer and fall, when budgets were increasingly tight for most Richmonders, Silas Omohundro bought his beloved Corinna a pitcher and goblets for $85, a black dress for $22.50, a tea set for $30, a toilet set for $25, and a pair of gaiters for $20, not to mention an occasional bottle of brandy.

He could afford to be generous, since he had prospered in the slave trade for more than a decade, and just that year had put $1,000 into partnership with a sutler following the army. At Christmas he gave Corinna a $100 diamond ring, while spending $1.50 on candy for their children and dividing $4 among the house servants.[1]

Sometime before mid-century, Omohundro had come to Richmond from up the James River, near the Fluvanna-Albemarle county line, where his family had put down roots in the eighteenth century. Long before war came, he was firmly established in the capital. Altogether his real estate was valued at only $3,000 in 1860, but his personal worth—mostly in slaves—was $75,000. L. T. Slater and T. H. Jones, traders staying with him, were even more comfortable, with $32,000 in real and $125,000 in personal property each.[2]

One reason for Omohundro's business success, aside from the hungry demand for field hands in the Deep South cotton states, was his meticulous record-keeping. Corinna ran the household, paying the washerwoman and repairmen, buying clothes for the children, and marketing. Omohundro's ledger lists carefully what was paid for such items as candles, candy, apples, rat poison, and cleaning the family clock. Sometimes strictly business items were recorded among the domestic trivia: "Aug. 21—pr. handcuffs $10. . . . Oct. 13—Telegraph dispatches for runaway negroes, $3.75; advertising 3 runaway negroes in *Dispatch*, George, Moton and Dick, $5.50." The only spending not separately itemized was Corinna's marketing, for which Omohundro recorded lump sums of hundreds of dollars each month.[3]

The previous summer, Corinna had presented Omohundro with their sixth child. By then their oldest son, in his teens and soon to die, and their only daughter apparently were not living with the parents. Another boy had died in infancy. Two younger boys, ages 8 and 3, were at home with Silas and Corinna. In 1863 there would be still another boy. Altogether, Omohundro fathered at least fourteen children, seven of them by his first two wives.*[4]

Omohundro's home and business were in the heart of Richmond's old slave-trade neighborhood, just east of the Capitol and downhill toward Shockoe Creek. He had an office on Seventeenth Street at Broad, near Seabrook's warehouse, and a "jail" on an alley off Wall (Fifteenth) Street between Main and Franklin, two blocks from Capitol Square. Five other dealers worked out of offices in the nearby Exchange Hotel, and several ran their auctions at Odd Fellows Hall.

The "jails" kept by larger traders were so called because they penned up slaves, but they were run more like boardinghouses. Before wartime inflation, they kept slaves for 30 cents a day and put up their owners and visiting buyers at lower rates than nearby hotels charged. Lumpkin's, in the alley off Wall Street that eventually took the proprietor's name, was typical: a low, two-story brick house facing an open courtyard. Guests there ate at a long table, family style.

Although Lumpkin's had the nickname "Devil's Half-Acre" among local blacks, some slaves were treated better in these "jails" than they had ever been before. They might arrive from the country droopy and ragged, but to bring top dollar they were fed, cleaned up, and dressed neatly before going on sale. Both buyer and seller preferred to make private deals without proceeding to auction; it was considered more discreet and gentlemanly.[6]

In 1860, typical prices for "negro boys" had run in the $1,100–$1,300 range, and the broker's commission ranged from 7.5 to 10 percent. Though volume dropped after the war began, slave prices rose, pushed by both diminishing traffic and general inflation. As refugees crowded into Richmond, Omohundro and other traders opened their boarding-

*The Omohundro genealogy says Silas was born in 1807; the U.S. Census says he was 40 in 1860. The genealogy says Corinna was born in 1823; in her later years, she said family records showed that she was born in 1835. The U.S. Census says she was 32 in 1860.[5]

houses to the public. Immediately after secession, before the outlying army camps were organized, volunteer companies arriving from the counties might spend a night or two in a "negro jail." By mid-1862, transient officers, refugees looking for permanent housing, and a few long-term boarders were paying Omohundro $3 for bed and breakfast and $5 a day or $50 a month for full board. At the time, the average government clerk was making only $1,200 a year, which was raised that fall to $1,500, not quite $4 per workday.[7]

* * *

Slave traffic had slowed not only because the Union occupied parts of Virginia and the farther South but because there was now heavy local demand for the sweat and skills of Virginia blacks, who before the war had become a surplus commodity. Thousands of slaves were in occupied territory or had slipped away across the lines. At the same time, thousands of pick-and-shovel laborers were needed to improve the deepening fortifications around Richmond, to build and maintain roads and railroads, and to mine coal and ore.

Most nurses, attendants, and cooks at the proliferating hospitals were slaves and free blacks. Someone had to feed, do laundry for, entertain, and otherwise service the swarms of strangers who converged on the city. Teamsters and longshoremen had to move the commissary and quartermaster material shuttling through depots, docks, and warehouses. War factories like the Tredegar and the armory were running multiple shifts.

In the city that was capital, military headquarters, transportation hub, industrial heart, prison, and hospital center of the Confederacy, black labor was a vital necessity, and suddenly it was not in surplus but in shortage.

Within less than a year, the government saw that recruiting free black volunteers for war work would fall far short of needs. Thus, weeks before the Confederacy drafted whites for military service, Virginia began drafting free blacks for labor. The legislature in February 1862 required state courts to list free black males between 18 and 50 years of age. Military commanders could requisition their service for up to six months. Then in October, the state enacted a similar system to impress slaves for up to two months. The Confederate government would pay their owners $16 a month per slave and provision the laborers as if they were soldiers. Owners would also be compensated for slaves who died or were hurt while serving, or ran away to the enemy. In time, Congress would pass laws putting the Confederate government in charge of labor impressment throughout the South.[8]

Despite the emergency, and broadened opportunities for profit in what had previously been business sidelines, Richmond's dealers clung to the familiar slave trade as long as slavery existed. While McClellan was on Richmond's doorstep, agents were still scouting the hinterlands for salable commodities.

J. Wimbish Young wrote from Clarksville, in southside Virginia, that he had bought 6,000 pounds of first-rate bacon and 700 pounds of very nice lard in North Carolina, and was shipping it to E. H. Stokes in Richmond along with a Negro family: "Man, woman & child . . . cost eighteen hundred Dolls ($1800.00). Man Good Carpenter & Shoe Maker. I want you to do the best you can with them I think we can make money on them."

J. H. Burnett at Williamston, in eastern North Carolina, asked Stokes for current slave prices and whether the trend was up or down. "I could have invested $10,000 in negroes near the Yankee lines at fair prices and good profits had I the money," he said. "I can get negroes 30 miles from here and run no risk. I may be on this week with a boy 22 years old 5 ft 10 inches high weighs 180# healthy. What is he worth?"[9]

*　*　*

But motives other than cold profit drove some of the new business created by war. About the time the casualty lists from the Seven Days battles were coming home, John Robertson wrote to Stokes from Yanceyville, North Carolina, near the Virginia line:

"I have got my poor brother at home I have now concluded to get a substertute for myself so you will oblige me very much if you will see if I can get one in Richmond. . . . My mother is very Sick so much so I cant possibley leave Home if I can get a Subberstute right so see the chance to get one for me and low as possible."[10]

Robertson may not have been able to afford a substitute, but if he could, there were plenty of potential takers among the capital's horde of drifters. Some of them took the money, went into the army, deserted, then did it again and again, risking the whipping post or even the firing squad if they were caught. If the broker did find a substitute, he charged an inordinate commission on each deal.

The very existence of the substitute law revived a complaint heard since the first shots were fired—that this was "a rich man's war and a poor man's fight." The draft act allowed potential conscripts to hire stand-ins on the theory that some men valuable in civilian roles might not be covered by the long list of exemptions. Despite the fact that inflation and increasing casualties drove the going rate for substitutes from $500 to as much as $5,000, beyond the reach of ordinary citizens, thousands of Americans on both sides bought their way out of service.

Unhappiness about favoritism rose in October, when Congress created another loophole that favored rich planters over non-slaveholders. Its critics called it "the 20-negro law" because it exempted one white man on each plantation with as many as twenty slaves. Jefferson Davis defended it as providing necessary protection and supervision on the home front, but Senator James Phelan of Mississippi spoke for soldiers as well as the majority of civilians when he said that no law had ever inspired more "universal odium."[11]

In his anger, Phelan may have forgotten about Federal laws; at any rate, he spoke before Lincoln had formally proclaimed emancipation. When that happened, a roar of fury erupted in Richmond and swept the South—but it had an undertone of fear. Visions of Nat Turner uprisings in every county had long plagued the white South. Now, the more excitable politicians and editors seemed sure that Lincoln's proclamation would bring the frightful dream to reality. "A scheme so atrocious and infernal," Phelan declared, "is unparalleled in the blackest and bloodiest page of savage strife, surpasses in atrocious cruelty the most signal despotism that ever disgraced the earth, and reveals the design of our enemy to be, regardless of the laws of God or man, the annihilation of the people of these Confederate states." Benjamin H. Hill of Georgia urged in the Confederate Senate that from then on, all Yankee prisoners should be treated as if they had come to incite "insurrection and murder," making them liable to the death penalty. Some congressmen said the South should raise the "black flag"—take no prisoners.[12]

The *Whig* wanted revenge, too, saying the proclamation meant that "We can no longer be held to the practice of civilized war," that the South should create raider regiments to dash into Union territory and destroy towns and villages without mercy. The *Examiner* blew back and forth. At first glance the proclamation was a "call for the insurrection of four millions of slaves, and inauguration of a reign of hell upon earth." But four days later it meant little, because "beyond the ground [the Yankees] stand on, it will have about the same force and effect as an edict from the vermillion pencil of China's Emperor." Actually, the paper suggested, the proclamation would help divide opinion in the North, so perhaps it was a positive development. But this assessment did not last long.[13]

* * *

Main Street in peacetime. *Soon after this view, looking east toward Shockoe Bottom and Church Hill, was drawn, the streets of Richmond were filled with brass bands and marching men.*

Citizen-soldiers of the Richmond Grays. *Uniforms were grand and spirits high as the city's militia companies responded to John Brown's raid at Harpers Ferry.*

Standing tall. *Drum Major C. R. M. Pohlé of the First Virginia Regiment epitomized the strutting style of troops North and South in April 1861, before their serious soldiering began.*

(above right) Henry A. Wise. *After speaking and conniving for Virginia's secession from the Union, he became one of the many politicians on both sides who acquired general's stars without benefit of military experience.*

John Letcher. *Wise's successor as governor did all he could to hold Virginia in the Union, until Lincoln issued his call for troops to put down rebellion in the Deep South.*

John Minor Botts. *After struggling against secession, the stubborn ex-congressman refused to shut up until he was arrested and exiled to Virginia's interior.*

Capitol of state and nation. *The symbol of Virginia and the Confederacy is pictured at war's end. The wings on each end of the Capitol today were not added until 1904–05.*

Jefferson Davis. *This portrait of ex-soldier, ex-senator Davis as Confederate president captures the pride and stubbornness that characterized him all his life.*

Varina Davis. *By the time she became first lady of the Confederacy at the age of 35, her youthful face and figure had rounded; her lips and eyes suggest the wit and intelligence with which she defended her husband.*

(*above left*) Alexander H. Stephens. *Although he had resisted secession, the wizened Georgian was chosen as Confederate vice president. For much of the war he stayed at home, championing states' rights against Davis and the Richmond government.*

LIBRARY OF CONGRESS

(*above right*) Judah P. Benjamin. *Successively Confederate attorney general, secretary of war, and secretary of state, the former U.S. senator from Louisiana was one of Davis's steadiest supporters and the only Jewish member of his cabinet.*

LIBRARY OF CONGRESS

Sally Tompkins. *President Davis made the tiny, devout Tompkins a nominal captain of cavalry so she could continue to operate her Robertson Hospital.*

COOK COLLECTION,
VALENTINE MUSEUM

Joseph C. Mayo. *Every day in Richmond's police court, the hardworking old mayor dispensed rough and often uneven justice to offenders white and black.*

Brigadier General John H. Winder. *As inspector general and then provost marshal, Winder sometimes overreached as he clamped harsh military rule on the capital. He was widely blamed for conditions in Richmond's war prisons.*

Defending the James. *Confederate artillerymen used transplanted naval guns to turn back Union gunboats steaming up the river toward Richmond.*

Preparing to spy from the sky. Union aeronaut Thaddeus Lowe's arm is visible at right as his ground crew, using a portable hydrogen generator, inflates an observation balloon during the Peninsula campaign.
PATRIOT PUBLISHING COMPANY

"Changing his base." This drawing suggests the size of the Union army and fleet as Mc-Clellan, in the face of Lee's fierce counterattacks in the Seven Days campaign, abandons White House on the Pamunkey River and shifts to the James.
LESLIE'S ILLUSTRATED

Moses Drury Hoge. *This Presbyterian minister, one of the South's great pulpit orators, served the Confederacy diligently on missions at home and abroad.*

George W. Bagby. *The editor of the* Southern Literary Messenger *held an M.D. degree, but won his reputation with his fluent pen, corresponding for a string of newspapers throughout the South.*

John Moncure Daniel. *The brilliant and misanthropic Daniel's diatribes against the Davis administration made his* Examiner *perhaps the most carefully read newspaper in the Confederacy.*

Tredegar Iron Works. *The wartime bustle is missing from this post-occupation view of the factory that produced most of the South's heavy weapons and other essential hardware. The vital Tredegar was one reason why Richmond became the Confederate capital.*

Chimborazo Hospital. *With Bloody Gulch in the foreground, the huge complex where Phoebe Pember practiced the healing arts sprawls across Chimborazo Hill above the James River and Rocketts landing.*

Libby Prison. *The warehouse below Church Hill became Richmond's best-known military prison, though captives fared much worse on Belle Isle. The U.S. flag flies in this photograph, taken soon after the city's occupation by Union forces; on close examination, imprisoned Confederate soldiers can be seen at windows.*

Rescue in the suburbs. *Prisoners who
have escaped by tunneling out of Libby
Prison rejoice on meeting roaming
Union cavalry outside Richmond.
Almost half of the 108 tunnel escapers
were recaptured and punished.*

LESLIE'S ILLUSTRATED

Colonel Ulric Dahlgren. *The young
Union cavalryman met his death in an
ambush after leading one wing of a
daring but unsuccessful raid to free
Richmond prisoners and perhaps to
assassinate Confederate leaders.*

MEMOIRS OF ULRIC DAHLGREN

Elizabeth Van Lew. *Praised by U. S.
Grant after the war as the most important Union spy in Richmond, the
seemingly eccentric spinster slipped
secret messages through the lines and
sheltered escaped prisoners.*

Van Lew at home. *Long after the
war, an elderly Elizabeth sits outside
her Church Hill mansion. The secret
chamber in which she hid escaped
Federals was located where the roof
of the columned portico met the main
structure.*

Grant's greatest blunder. *The Union commander (with blotch on coattail) leans forward to inspect a map at a council of war outside Bethesda Church, 10 miles northeast of Richmond. Grant was planning the next day's attack at Cold Harbor, where he lost thousands of men within minutes.*

LIBRARY OF CONGRESS

A matter of values. *Southern alarm over Lincoln's Emancipation Proclamation inspired this Northern cartoon, in which the Rebel planter says, "Yes, my son, you must go to the War. I can't spare Pomp; he cost me Twelve Hundred Dollars, and he might get shot. Besides, you know, you couldn't stoop to work like a field-hand!"*

HARPER'S WEEKLY

WHO ARE THE NIGGER WORSHIPERS?

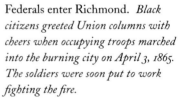

Federals enter Richmond. *Black citizens greeted Union columns with cheers when occupying troops marched into the burning city on April 3, 1865. The soldiers were soon put to work fighting the fire.*

Major General Godfrey Weitzel. *As commander of the Union occupying force, Weitzel moved into the mansion evacuated only hours earlier by Jefferson Davis. Weitzel was criticized by Northern radicals for trying to carry out Lincoln's policy of leniency.*

After the fire. *A lone Union soldier stands among cannon balls strewn beside the canal basin. The Capitol is in center background; the Custom House, also spared by the flames, is below and to the right of it.*

LIBRARY OF CONGRESS

The legacy of war. *The former capital was a city in mourning. Women in black pass the shells of burned buildings in downtown Richmond.*

LIBRARY OF CONGRESS

The day of Jubilee. *As Lincoln toured the fallen city, thousands of blacks surrounded and praised him. Though most whites stayed indoors behind drawn blinds, some joined the welcoming celebration.*

View from the Capitol. *The city was still smoldering when Lincoln visited on April 4. Union cavalry horses are tethered to the fence bordering Capitol Square; the Custom House is at right.*

Freedom in the ruins. *A group of recently liberated slaves poses beside the canal; others, in the background, have climbed a fence to get into the photograph.*

To war no more. *Just returned from Appomattox, Robert E. Lee, despite his obvious fatigue, still had the look of command. He had to be persuaded to pose for Yankee photographer Mathew Brady at the rear of his home at 707 East Franklin Street.*

Between Lincoln's preliminary and formal proclamations, Davis, Richmond, and the South cheered Robert E. Lee's latest triumph, halfway between Washington and Richmond.

On December 13, 1862, at Fredericksburg, the Army of Northern Virginia shattered repeated attacks by Major General Ambrose Burnside's Army of the Potomac. Another Federal offensive was turned back—yet the Union force, still growing, was still there along the Rappahannock, rebuilding and planning still another drive "on to Richmond."

Within the Confederate bureaucracy and beyond the mountains, things were less encouraging. Davis had wanted to go to the Rappahannock to be with Lee when the long-expected battle began. But when he got word of fighting at Fredericksburg he was in Chattanooga, four days out of Richmond on an urgent western journey.

The news came to him in a telegram from James A. Seddon, the recently appointed secretary of war. George Wythe Randolph, who filled that post after Judah Benjamin was shifted to the State Department, had quit in November—frustrated, he said, by Davis's indecisiveness, his inability to discriminate between what was important and what was not, and his refusal to take advice. After replacing Randolph for three days with Major General Gustavus Smith, the president turned to Seddon, a lawyer who had no military background but did not talk back. Besides, Seddon, like Randolph, was a Virginian, and choosing him headed off renewed controversy about geographical balance in the cabinet.

Davis did not need any more controversy. He set out hoping to reassure his nation and boost enlistments in the West, where jealousy and confusion among Generals Joseph E. Johnston, Braxton Bragg, John C. Pemberton, and others had shaken the confidence of soldiers and citizens. When he returned to Richmond early in January, Davis heard of new Confederate successes in the territory he had just visited. A band welcomed him back with "Listen to the Mockingbird," and he stood on the steps of the president's mansion to give an upbeat account of his travels. But shortly thereafter, the good news from the West turned sour. Bulletins of victory had been premature; the generals out there were squabbling again.

Davis spoke to the reconvened Congress on January 12. He was not amused when he was accidentally introduced as "the President of the United States"; then he had to strain to sound optimistic. Though the enemy had marched to the gates of Richmond and been driven away, though Lee's army had repeatedly outfought bigger Union forces, as the new year began the outlook for the Confederacy was no brighter than it had been at the gloomy start of 1862.

With little to be cheerful about domestically, Davis aimed much of his address beyond his listeners, across the sea to Britain and France. He retold how the South and the Continent depended on each other economically, and asserted again that the Union blockade was an offense against both the Confederacy and her would-be partners in trade. But after the Emancipation Proclamation, the chance of European diplomatic recognition for his government was much dimmer than it had been thirteen months earlier, when Davis hoped that the *Trent* affair would drag Britain out of its neutrality.[14]

* * *

If anything might persuade London to move, it was less likely to be Jefferson Davis's rhetoric than firsthand British journalism about prospects for the South. And no reports were ever more obviously written to influence government than those printed by Britain's most influential newspaper, the *Times* of London. They came from correspondent Francis Lawley, who ran the Potomac River blockade to Richmond in late 1862. Before war's end he sent about a hundred long, detailed letters describing the Confederacy, its battles, and its leaders in the most favorable light.[15]

In his first report from Richmond, Lawley said the only shortage the city faced was that of ice; though the South was "sorely vexed" by the Union blockade, four-fifths of the craft slipping across the Potomac made it safely, as did two-thirds of those running into coastal ports. He found widespread confidence that "no Northern army will ever capture Richmond without such an effusion of its own blood as would change the howl of Northern exultation into a nation's wail of woe."

Two weeks later he wrote: "In the annals of civilized warfare such harmony in support of a war has never been approached." The women, the clergy, the press, even the blacks detest the Federals, he said: "Again and again the slaves have fled from the Yankee army into the swamp to escape from compulsory freedom . . . if a being so morally weak and nerveless as the African could be made to fight for anything, he would fight for slavery much rather than for liberty."[16]

Lawley, a former member of Parliament, had come to America to replace William H. "Bull Run" Russell, whose usefulness to the *Times* was limited after he angered official Washington with his exuberant description of the rout at First Manassas. Traveling south with British colonel Garnet Wolseley, Lawley immediately fit into the circle of European officers and writers who gathered to lift glasses and tell tales at restaurants like Madame Zetelle's, on Main Street near Twelfth in Richmond. They took the field together to witness—or sometimes join in—major battles.[17]

In between, their songs and accents enlivened night life in social Richmond. Some were remembered years later for their intrepidity, as when Frank Vizetelly of the *Illustrated London News,* red-whiskered Colonel George Gordon, and a certain nobleman called Lord Cavendish entertained at a lavish dinner that lasted from 2:00 p.m. until midnight and for which they never paid. Vizetelly, a talented writer and artist, left a reputation as "reckless, aimless . . . a boon companion," but not a man to whom the wise lent money. "Lord Cavendish," who swaggered in and out of town with tales of adventures at the front, turned out to be an imaginative Irishman named Short. But Gordon, aside from being a spirited gambler and freeloader, was an authentic soldier, who served with North Carolina infantry and as volunteer aide to various generals.[18]

Before year's end, Lawley had visited Lee, Jackson, and Longstreet in the field, and dispatched enthusiastic portraits of the generals and their troops. "Any battle into which these men enter is half won when the first shot is fired," he wrote before the fight at Fredericksburg. Eighteen months of war had given the Confederates such confidence that "the day of battle is surely and triumphantly looked on as necessarily the day of victory."[19]

Lee's success at Fredericksburg was so lopsided that it made Lawley's assessment seem credible. But neither Lawley's propaganda in the *Times,* nor Vizetelly's articles and drawings in the *Illustrated London News,* nor any other report from Richmond, could persuade Britain and France to take sides.

Conclusive proof that the South was about to win the war might have done it. But there was little remaining of the Confederate hope that the blockade cutting off Southern cotton from British mills would do it. From the beginning, Britain's Tory aristocracy had leaned toward the South, perhaps recognizing the parallel between slavery and Britain's own class system. But English mill workers saw the parallel, too. Cotton-state secessionists had assumed that those workers, their jobs threatened by a cutoff of raw materials, would demand action against the Union. But Southern cotton, it turned out, was not king. Britain had a sizable inventory when the war began, and imported more from its colonies. And now Lincoln's proclamation won the emotional cheers of those British textile workers.

Davis's recital to Congress of why breaking the blockade made economic sense for Europe was rather wistful, since the longer the war went on, the tighter the blockade became and the clearer it was that restricting Southern trade did no vital harm to Britain or France. When he shifted his attention to the Emancipation Proclamation, he still seemed to be speaking to listeners afar, but his tone turned to anger.

Common humanity could pass judgment, he said, on "a measure by which several millions of human beings of an inferior race, peaceful and contented laborers in their sphere, are doomed to extinction, while at the same time they are encouraged to a general assassination of their masters. . . . Our own detestation of those who have attempted the most execrable measure recorded in the history of guilty man is tempered by profound contempt for the impotent rage which it discloses. . . ." In response to Lincoln, he promised to turn all Union officers captured in the South over to local officials, to be prosecuted under state laws against "exciting servile insurrection."

But Davis's threat of reprisal was never carried out. The great slave uprising he warned of never took place. As the new year began, battalions of black workmen building Richmond's defenses still marched through the streets singing, tools over their shoulders, sounding as docile as they had in days of peace. And Silas Omohundro and his colleagues in the slave trade went on with business, unaffected for the moment by the grand proclamation that Abraham Lincoln had issued in Washington.

CHAPTER FIFTEEN

ALL THE PATRIOTISM
IS IN THE ARMY

*T*here was little merriment at Moses Hoge's on that second Christmas of the war; as in so many Richmond families, the man of the house was away. In the evening Susan Hoge tucked the children in, then sat and wrote to her husband.

"My darling Mody," she began: "I tried to be brave & to keep up a good heart the last few precious hours we were together, to encourage you & cheer you in your good work, but after you left I experienced the meaning of the words 'bitterness of spirit.' "

Susan told her husband how she had been unable to sleep, and how their son had come into her bed and asked for his missing father. "I was the next morning feeling very poorly & sad," she wrote. "I went to breakfast but when I saw your seat I had to leave the table. I went out to camp as usual & the men seemed very sorry to hear you had gone. Thompson the consumptive man said he would see your face no more, but he knew God would bless you & prosper you in your work. . . ."[1]

In a winter with twenty-seven recorded snowfalls, the shortage of fuel, food, medicine, and shelter cut deeper each week. In Lee's army along the Rappahannock, hardtack and fatback were sparse, and hundreds of soldiers went without shoes or overcoats. Stonewall Jackson encouraged his troops to pray as a religious revival swept through Confederate ranks. But even when they sought strength in Scripture, hungry soldiers confronted wartime shortage again.

Moses Hoge's brother William, a Charlottesville minister, often preached to Jackson's troops. Just before Christmas he wrote to Moses with the idea of asking churchgoers in Britain to send thousands of Bibles to the Confederate army. The blockade, he said, had cut the South off not only from food and medicine but "from the very word of God."

Moses was enthusiastic, but thought someone should go to Britain to ask in person. William was willing, but he could not get to Charleston in time to catch a certain steamer that was about to run the blockade. Moses volunteered to go instead, and within hours he was on his way.[2]

The very idea of effectively blockading the South was a "farce," British correspondent Lawley wrote when he visited Charleston. In the age of steam, such an operation was almost impossible: "Swift vessels of light draught, painted lead color, so as scarcely to be visible at a distance of 30 yards, and consuming coal which emits only a light vapoury smoke, laugh the blockade to scorn." Some such ships have run in and out fifty times and scarcely heard a shot fired, said Lawley.[3]

But the idea was no joke to Moses Hoge, or to the skipper of his ship. Moses wrote to his brother, but not to Susan, that the captain had orders never to surrender and if halted to scuttle the vessel and set his passengers adrift in boats. This prospect in midwinter did not cheer Moses, who told another friend that thirteen Federal steamers were now guarding Charleston Harbor.[4]

Getting past them was as exciting to Hoge as the battles he had witnessed outside Richmond: "Amid lowering clouds and dashes of rain, and just wind enough to get up sufficient commotion in the sea to drown the noise of our paddle wheels, we darted along, with lights all extinguished, and not even a cigar burning on the deck, until we were safely out, and free from the Federal fleet." They made it to Nassau, hired a little schooner to go to Havana, and from there took passage on the Royal Mail Steamship Line to St. Thomas and Southampton. When Hoge arrived in England, his adventures had just begun.[5]

*   *   *

Wartime is hardship and sacrifice to many but adventure and opportunity to others. Along the Rappahannock, soldiers were scavenging for firewood and catching barn rats to eat. In the capital, strangers got used to sharing beds and society matrons learned to entertain with ersatz. On Broad Street, others had somehow found a way to rebuild the Richmond Theater within thirteen months after it burned to the ground.

The New Richmond was a gleaming four-story structure with promenade, dress circle, and cast-iron scrollwork. Above its curtain was a heroic portrait of Robert E. Lee.[6] On the Sunday before the grand February opening, the theater got a free publicity boost from the Reverend John L. Burrows of the First Baptist Church.

The round, energetic Burrows was impressed with what builders and artists had done—it would even deserve praise "if, in any sense, their work were useful in these pressing times. . . ." To his congregation he noted that the theater company included twenty gentlemen of the chorus and ballet: "No cripples from the battlefield are these—they can sing and dance; they can mimic fighting on the stage. For the serious work of repelling a real enemy they have neither taste nor heart. But they can sing while the country groans, and dance while the cars are bringing, in sad funeral procession, the dead to their very doors and the dismal ambulance bears the sick and the wounded under the very glare of their lights and within the sound of their music."[7]

Burrows's contempt for play soldiers may have been sharpened by the fact that during the year when the company was operating off-site as the Richmond Varieties, D'Orsey Ogden had replaced John Hewitt as manager. Hewitt, after departing, remembered his successor as "a fawning sycophant, with just brains enough to know how to fascinate a frail woman and keep himself from the clutches of the conscript officer, by swearing allegience to the Queen of England when it was known and proved that he was born in this country."[8] But the preacher's indignation was more moral than patriotic, based on what he had seen, or at least heard, of scandalous behavior in Richmond's wartime theaters.

The New Richmond, he said before it had even opened, "is a public assignation house where any vile man may be introduced to an infamous woman by paying the price of a ticket." He charged that the theater's third tier was designed expressly for harlots, a place where Richmond's sons would be "drawn into the very depths of debasement and vice."[9]

In fact, Richmond's sons were a minority of the patrons exposed to such risks. Before the New Richmond opened, the *Enquirer* had called for a higher order of theater, maintaining that "flash productions" might please "the mob," but Richmonders were "a reading and reflecting class" who deserved something better.[10] But the theater operators were well aware that their main clientele was precisely the mob, the thousands of transients, soldiers, and speculators who were out for amusement, not enlightenment.

Nevertheless, at least on opening night, there were stodgy grandfathers, young cavaliers, respectable ladies, and ranking politicians in the audience, as well as diamond-studded gamblers and troopers with spurs like circular saws. The evening began with a poem produced especially for the occasion by the South's best-known versifier, Henry Timrod.

Then came "The Marseillaise," to which Dixie-flavored English lyrics had been written, and then the feature production, *As You Like It*. The *Southern Illustrated News* ended its astringent review with the wish that the New Richmond would be a place where clients might come "without the fear of having the blush brought to their cheeks by the imprudence of plain-jack actors. . . ."[11]

Despite snobbish criticism and perhaps because of disapproving preachers, soldiers often left the humdrum of camp life to slip into town for a few bright hours at the theater. But Jeb Stuart, who personally liked to laugh and sing, did not like his troopers to be absent without leave, whatever their motive. One night, with a squad of horsemen, he swooped down on the theater and picked up every cavalryman in the audience.

Instead of applauding this contribution to military order, General Winder was embarrassed that anyone presumed to arrest soldiers in Richmond without his instructions. He threatened to arrest Stuart if he dared to do such a thing again. Stuart, predictably, replied that he would be in again the next night with thirty horsemen, looking for missing troopers, and that Winder was welcome to arrest him if he could. When Stuart and his men came clattering through the streets as promised, Winder was nowhere to be seen.[12]

* * *

The New Richmond, Metropolitan Hall, the Varieties, and every other showplace in town prospered because "the mob" could afford nightlife. But for the many, the cost of everyday life was climbing beyond reach. In January of 1863, War Department clerk Jones estimated that a hypothetical grocery bill for a small family was ten times higher than it had been in 1860. Bacon had gone up from 12½ cents to $1 a pound; butter from 23 cents to $1.75; soap from 10 cents to $1.10. Trying unsuccessfully to pass a state law "for the suppression of extortion," a Virginia legislator reported that coarse shoes had risen from $1.50 to $15 a pair, wool hats from 7 cents to $7 apiece, and good gray wool from $2 to $28 a yard. Coffee, like all imports, had zoomed upward—from 12½ cents to $5 a pound.[13]

No one was better positioned to watch this inflation, and imagine its profit potential, than a clerk in the Confederate army's clothing bureau.

There, in early 1863, sat Philip Whitlock, erstwhile private in the Richmond Grays. After standing alongside John Wilkes Booth to witness the hanging of John Brown in 1859, Whitlock had gone into Confederate service with the Grays, which had become Company G, Twelfth Virginia Infantry. In Brigadier General William Mahone's brigade, he enjoyed light duty at Norfolk until the city was evacuated. Still, he thought, "this life did not suit me . . . I was ambitious and did not see any chance to improve my condition as the profession of a 'sodier' was not to my taste. . . . and [in 1862] I could see there was no chance as we were getting week and the other side were getting stronger. . . ." He decided to get out of the army, "honerably if possible."

Whitlock had tried to hire a substitute but could not afford one. When he became sick his brother got him a timely "discharge" from General Winder and he went to the country to recuperate, thus missing the Seven Days battles. After returning to his company, Whitlock reported sick again and "through the activity and intercidence" of his brother and brother-in-law was sent to Chimborazo Hospital. From there, "through the kindness" of a Dr. Smith, he was allowed to go to his brother's home and was then recommended for duty in the quartermaster department.

Orders for his 9 a.m. to 3 p.m. job there had to be renewed every month, but "by being friendly with the Dr. this was mannaged so that I got extention every time." His pay was only $3 a day, not enough to live on, so he "did some speculating in merchandise by buying at auction sales and selling again." That whetted his appetite. When he got a thirty-day leave, he and his brother-in-law Ellis Abram resolved to run the blockade north to buy "some goods that was then very high & scarce here which could be sold here at a large profit." Thus they set out on a business venture considerably riskier than anything Whitlock had experienced while in uniform.[14]

They were not alone. Despite the sporadic efforts of authorities on both sides, clandestine traffic between North and South ran on throughout the war. It was winked at, even encouraged, by some officials who used it to move both official and personal mail, as well as intelligence agents. Onlookers thought the pass system overseen by Winder was "a very marvel of annoying inefficiency." It repeatedly blocked the way of soldiers trying to travel legally to and from their regiments, "while it gave unconscious but sure protection to spies, blockade-runners, deserters and absentees without leave. . . ."[15]

Whitlock and his brother-in-law were joined by four such fellow travelers when they reached the Potomac and had to wait to hire a boat to sneak them across at night. Tracking them step by step illustrates how busy the underground route between capitals was, despite traps along the way:

At the river they found a black man who was willing to row them past picketing Federal gunboats. Moving with muffled oars, they spotted a gunboat when they were halfway across, and the oarsman started to turn back. One of his passengers put a pistol to his head to persuade him to keep going, and they slipped by in the darkness thirty yards from the Yankee vessel. Then the frightened oarsman put them out short of the Maryland side and they had to wade ashore.

Barely missing a Union cavalry patrol, they paid a farmer to take them to Leonardtown, where they arrived at daybreak and had breakfast at a hotel. Whitlock recalled that they hired a wagon to the railroad, then took a train to Washington.* He and Abram registered under false names at the Metropolitan Hotel and could not get a room but were assigned to cots in a dormitory full of Union soldiers coming and going at all hours, cursing "the damned Rebels."

The next day they took the train to New York, where they stayed for nearly a week, buying notions that would fit into their hand luggage. "No matter what we bought we could make a profit," Whitlock said. They filled their bags with fine-toothed combs, tobacco pipes, pins, needles, pencils, and various concealable goods, then headed south.

The trip was dangerous in both directions; in the North they could have been arrested as Confederate spies, and in the South without a pass, Whitlock could have been charged as a deserter from the army. For Whitlock and his brother-in-law, coming back with merchandise was harder than going out with cash, which could always be used to ease the passage.

In Washington they got a sympathetic hack driver to take them to Surrattsville in southern Maryland. With their bags covered by lap robes, they were held up at the Navy Yard bridge. After tense waiting, the driver somehow persuaded the guard that they were in such a hurry to attend a wedding that they had no time to apply for passes. They made it to the tavern kept by Mary Surratt (who had the bad luck to befriend Whitlock's acquaintance, John Wilkes Booth, the following year in Washington).

Waiting to hire another wagon, Whitlock and Abram amused themselves shooting at targets with Mrs. Surratt's son John, postmaster of the village and a courier for the Confederate underground. That wagon took them to a farmer, who was nervous because Federal soldiers were searching the area. He hid the travelers in a tobacco barn with several other line-crossers, one of whom knew how to roll cigars. They "sat and smoked day after day for about two weeks" until the soldiers went away and an oxcart took the travelers to the Potomac.

---

*There was no railroad from southern Maryland to Washington during the war. If Whitlock's memory is correct, they probably caught the train at a stop between Baltimore and Washington, perhaps Bladensburg on the capital's outskirts. That would involve a long wagon ride from Leonardtown but would avoid sentries suspicious of travelers from rebellious southern Maryland.

They crossed without trouble, but as soon as they landed in Virginia a Confederate captain arrested them and took them to his headquarters to examine their baggage. When he released them, they found that half the goods they had bought in New York had been stolen. Afraid to complain, they returned to Richmond and sold what was left. Despite their high markup, they "just got out about even" after all their exertion.[16]

Back at the quartermaster department Whitlock had a hard time keeping his job in the clothing section because of the rising demand for able-bodied men in the field. Every month he had to report to the doctor, but "my Dr. was my friend for a certain reason—he inveribly extended my detail. . . ."

In his account, Whitlock never uses the word *bribe,* but repeatedly hints at it in explaining how he crossed the lines and retained his safe assignment. He says he was "in constant fear and anxiety, not that I was any way unpatriotic but in the way things looked to me then, that it was a *lost cause,* and every human being that lost his life was a useless sacrifice." But his friend the doctor made him so secure that later that year Whitlock got married and bought a tobacco shop at Franklin and Locust streets while still holding his quartermaster job. He and his wife ran the store through the rest of the war, while his brother and family fled north for the duration.[17]

* * *

For those who knew their way across the lines, through the bureaucracy, and around the sublegal economy, there was opportunity to prosper in Richmond. For the young at heart, there was ample chance despite shortages to laugh and love, for romance was made keener by the depression that clutched the capital. Burton Harrison, the president's secretary, who on arrival had been unsure which lucky belle merited his poetic fancy, found himself helpless before the Cary girls, heavily courted refugees of an old Virginia clan. He even signed himself "Captain Cary" when he wrote "A Paean to My Pipe," which ended:

> *Thus living with Loves*
> *And flocks of Doves*
> *The shafts of Care shall not wound me*
> *While down life's vistas*
> *The musical sisters*
> *In their airy courses float o'er me*
> *And golden halos*
> *and tinted rainbows*
> *Envelop the future before me.*

Those musical sisters were Hetty and Jennie, the Baltimore Carys, who brightened many a dreary winter evening with their songs. But time would show that Harrison was looking past them to their reddish-blond 19-year-old cousin from Alexandria, the gifted amateur actress and future author Constance Cary.[18]

While the young held back the night with parlor theatricals and songfests, wartime Richmonders with personal fortunes or rich inland plantations managed to entertain more substantially. Though they might be sharing space more intimately than they had ever expected, with effort they sometimes drank and dined as if war were no more than a distant rumor.

Mary Chesnut's bibulous but indispensable man Laurence, for example, could find delicacies when there were none. Scoffing at the idea that starvation existed in Richmond, he told her that given enough money he could bring home whatever she wanted. His findings supplemented monthly shipments of wine, rice, ham, eggs, butter, and vegetables from the family plantation in South Carolina. When the Chesnuts were not out at parties, concerts, and private entertainments, the parlor of their rented quarters was full of guests, from president to gentleman private.

Once the lawyer James Lyons spread a grand display of Virginia hospitality at his home, Laburnum, a mile outside the city. At dinner Mary was seated beside a dark, intense guest whose name she did not catch. The wine was excellent, and she talked. When her dinner companion proved sharp and clever, she suggested that he be gentler—he sounded "as bad as the *Examiner.*"

He teased her into talking on. She chastised the press for being so critical of the government—"they are splitting us into a thousand pieces." She spoke of the casualties, the soldiers sleeping in the snow—the newspapers might convince them that they were fighting and dying in vain. As for Daniel of the *Examiner,* she did not know him, but perhaps he should be hanged for "fomenting direst division." When the party dwindled, she discovered that she had been talking to Daniel all evening.[19]

But if John Daniel could be slyly gracious in conversation with such a lady, he stonewalled workers who organized to defend themselves against inflation at his expense.

Richmond printers, craftsmen who set each letter of tiny type by hand, were exempt from the draft because their skill was deemed essential. Now they had banded into a Richmond Typographical Society, seeking higher pay because "cabbages were worth a dollar a head." Daniel hauled them into court. When his suit was thrown out, he insisted that it had not been tried on its merits and should not set a precedent: "Let the opinion get abroad that 'trade unions' are beyond the reach of the law and we shall soon have 'unions of cord wainers,' 'associations of white washers,' and 'united oyster-openers' organized to tyrannize over persons of their calling and to extort money from the rest of the community."[20]

Though printers had organized in some American cities as early as the 1790s, any trade unionism was an unwelcome Yankee concept in Richmond. But wartime inflation drove workers to try to keep up with prices. Among others, local postal clerks walked out for higher pay. Once the military draft began, the government did not hesitate to use it against strikers. When troops detached from uniformed service to the Richmond armory struck for a raise from $3 a day, they were sent back to the front at privates' pay of $11 a month. Lithographers exempt from conscription were jailed when they attempted a strike. Irish gravediggers who stopped work were replaced by blacks; when they drove the blacks away, officials replaced both with penitentiary convicts.[21] But when Irish foundrymen at the Tredegar struck for better pay in September of 1861, they got it—and their success lifted daily wages for other skilled hands in the vital factory from $2.50 to $3, followed by another raise in mid-1862.[22]

The Tredegar was a special case. When war came, it had immediately shifted to a seven-day schedule to meet rush orders. One of the first was for 200 eight-inch, 150 ten-inch, and 20 fifteen-inch coastal defense guns; in peacetime, producing a single ten-incher had taken two months. The plant cast armor for the *Merrimack* and other Southern ironclads, built torpedoes and a prototype submarine, turned out tens of thousands of cannonballs, and tried to meet the demands of the South's overused railroads for track, bridges, and rolling stock.[23]

The ironworks operated its own mines, oceangoing blockade runner and commissary, and for years had employed slaves, owning some and hiring the rest. But because the works furnished these slaves' food, clothing, and housing, using them added expenses when wartime inflation began. Most of the Tredegar's approximately 1,000 workers were white, and many of them—indeed most of Richmond's iron-workers wherever employed—were either Northern or foreign-born. Just when the Tredegar needed more skilled hands, dozens of its experienced workmen had headed north to their former homes. Too many others had volunteered as soldiers.[24]

Proprietor Joseph Anderson, of the West Point class of 1832, had kept some eager patriots on the job by organizing a Tredegar militia battalion as an outlet for their martial spirit. Anderson commanded the battalion briefly, until his own zeal pressed him into Confederate service as a brigadier general. He returned in 1862 after being slightly wounded; he was far more valuable at the Tredegar than in the field.

The shortage of expert hands for industry grew more acute despite the glut of applicants trying to squeeze into draft-proof high-skill jobs. But North and South there were plenty of the untaught and unskilled, working for long hours under crude, often dangerous conditions. Before inflation, their wages were just enough to live on; when prices took off, they still had to eat.

By mid-March of 1863, beef was up to $1.25 a pound, butter $3, bacon $1.50, cornmeal $6 a bushel, potatoes $12, flour $40 a barrel, molasses $1.50 a pint, and turkeys $15 each. War Department clerk Jones said with disgust, "All the patriotism is in the army; out of it the demon avarice rages supreme. Every one seems mad with speculation. . . . we have at the same time, and in the same community, spectacles of the most exalted virtue and of the most degrading vice." He sold a cherished watch for $75 to help support his family group of seven.[25]

He was lucky to have a watch to sell. Unlucky others had to rent out their children.

*   *   *

On Friday, March 13, 1863, Eliza Willis was 10 years old. Mary Archer, Alice Johnson, Mary Zerhum, Virginia Mayer, and Mary Ellen Wallace were all 12. That morning, as usual, they reported to their jobs at the Confederate States Laboratory on Brown's Island at the foot of Seventh Street.

The Reverend John H. Woodcock, a former schoolteacher, was in charge of the long, low frame building where they worked. A single coal stove barely warmed the room against the dreary winter. At least seventy workers were busy there, loading cartridges with gunpowder, packaging percussion caps, and filling sensitive friction primers used to ignite the charge in Confederate cannon. Each employee made an average of 1,200 cartridges each twelve-hour workday, for which girls were paid $1.50 and women $2.40.[26]

That morning Captain Wesley N. Smith, the superintendent who had organized this "general ordnance laboratory of the South," walked past the work station of an 18-year-old Irish girl named Mary Ryan and routinely reminded her to take care with what she was doing. Shortly afterward, Lizzie Dawson was breaking up cartridges and Mary Cordle had just emptied a box of powder. Both of them looked up when Mary Ryan, as she had done many times before, tapped a board containing primers against her work bench.

In the next seconds, Richmonders blocks away heard and felt a low rumble that was different from the frequent reports of cannon being tested at the Tredegar. Thick smoke poured upward from the riverside.

Mary Ryan's tapping had set off the primer, which had exploded the loose powder in the air, and the coal stove had completed the blast. The building's roof blew up, the walls collapsed, and then the roof fell onto the workers. Ten or twenty died outright. Some leaped into the river. Many more were horribly burned, wailing for help with their clothes and hair in flames. Workers from other laboratory buildings ran to rescue them. Ambulances shuttled with victims to military hospitals in the neighborhood. Relatives panicked as they searched for their daughters, charred and unrecognizable in the chaos.[27]

At least forty-five workers were killed by the laboratory explosion, and another twenty-three were injured. All but two of the dead, Woodcock and 15-year-old Robert Chaple, were women and girls like Eliza Willis. The oldest was 67, the youngest 9. Twenty of the twenty-nine victims buried in Hollywood and Shockoe Hill cemeteries were 16 years old or younger.[28]

A city that had been proud to nurse and bury the casualties of war felt shame beneath its sadness as the bodies of so many children were carted through the streets to their graves. Jones called the day "a great calamity," and added in dismay, "Most of them were little indigent girls!"[29] Colonel Josiah Gorgas, the chief of ordnance, wrote in his diary: "It is terrible to think of—that so much suffering should arise from causes possibly within our control." He ordered a formal investigation, which did not have to look far to learn of Mary Ryan's way of loosening primers, which certainly was within the control of her supervisors. Only chance had kept the explosion from happening long before; stricter rules and oversight kept it from happening again.[30] Mayor Mayo organized a committee to raise funds for the victims' families, Mrs. Gorgas spent many hours ministering to the grieving, and the business of war went on.[31]

* * *

The women who replaced the victims of the ordnance laboratory explosion held out later in 1863 for a 60-cent increase in their $2.40 daily wage, and got it. But the following year 300 were fired when they struck for another raise in an effort to keep up with inflation.[32] Meanwhile, another echelon of women, called ladies partly because they were literate enough to sign their names, were making $500 a year for doing just that. They were clerks at the Treasury Department on the first floor of the Custom House, below the president's office. Despite their modest pay, in their way they were contributing to inflation in the Confederacy.

Scarcity of goods was only one reason prices soared. The other major factor was the oversupply of money. Many blamed mismanagement of Confederate finances on Christopher Memminger, the secretary of the treasury. The *Whig* would call him "a second rate lawyer in Charleston, famous for the energy and persistence with which he collected small bills and dunned petty debtors. . . . He has done his best, but he has been overtaken—that is all."[33] That was correct; Memminger did his best. But even if his uncertain advice had been carried out to the letter, it would not have solved the problems built into the Southern economy.

Before Confederate paper money was in wide circulation, Virginia had issued its own, and soldiers and refugees arriving in Richmond brought money printed by other Southern states. "One did not know was it good or bad," wrote beer-hall keeper Gottfried Lange. "But it all was accepted as payment."[34]

To deal with the new nation's debts and overcome this confusion of currency, Congress ignored Memminger's pleas for restraint and authorized huge amounts of unsecured bills and bonds. It assumed that the excess currency would soon be soaked up by sale of the 8 percent bonds, but potential buyers saw that speculation in almost anything was a better bet.

Congress ruled that to make counterfeiting harder, each individual Confederate bill, whatever its denomination, must be signed and numbered by a Treasury clerk. Though this did not prevent copying, it kept a battalion of lady clerks busy, signing and numbering and telling themselves they were doing their bit for the cause.

Because the Confederacy never minted its own coins, and small U.S. coins were hoarded, making change was a constant annoyance; so many postage stamps were sold for use as petty cash that Postmaster General John Reagan's system actually ran in the black during the war's latter years.* But the South could not print nearly enough stamps to meet the demand. Soon states, cities, railroads, merchants, taverns, even individuals, began issuing small paper bills in denominations of from 2 to 50 cents. Thus, Lange said, "the paper fraud was on."[35]

Richmond was snowed under by these ubiquitous little "shinplasters." The *Examiner* asserted that even "Loaferdom" was surfeited—"beggars have ceased to beg for [them]. The enterprising newsboy . . . will break you a Fifty if your change is scarce, and forthwith produce a wallet bursting with shinplasters. The little pickanniny, to whom you throw

---

*After operating at a deep deficit in 1861 and 1862, the Post Office ran a sizable surplus, aided by the use of stamps as currency and by an influx of low bids for rural delivery routes from men seeking draft exemption as postal employees. Reagan was criticized for not channeling this surplus back into improved service.[36]

your bridle reins at the hotel entrance, when you come to cast him the pittance he expects, disturbs your gravity by whipping from his pocket, with a look of business, a wallet of overpowering size, and adding the shinplaster to his collection. The market women reek with shinplasters, the shopkeepers lazily draw them over their counters, as though tired of raking shinplasters into their tills. . . ."[37]

The classic engine of inflation, too much money chasing too few goods, was accelerated by the tightening blockade. Sellers of items unaffected directly by the blockade, even farmhands selling scrawny chickens, used it as an excuse for jacking up prices. Existence in every city cost much more than in the country, and with New Orleans in Union hands, Richmond was by far the most expensive, corrupt, overcrowded, and crime-ridden city in the Confederacy. At one point prices in Columbia, South Carolina, were only a fifth of those in Richmond; cane syrup selling for $1 a gallon in rural Georgia was $50 in the capital.

The outlook everywhere seemed bleak in the dark months of winter and early spring, raising doubts of whether, in the long run, the Confederate dollar would be worth anything at all. Gold and the Yankee greenback seemed safer—and when cheap Confederate dollars began chasing those commodities, the Southern currency became even cheaper. In March the Virginia legislature completed an investigation of war profiteering: On capital of $200,000, Richmond's Crenshaw woolen mills had declared 1862 dividends of $530,000; on capital of $41,000, the Belvidere paper company declared dividends of $175,000. But they were capitalized with pre-inflation currency, and paid shareholders in shrunken Confederate dollars.[38]

In a time of endemic anti-Semitism some diarists, politicians, and editorialists alleged that Jews, along with Yankees and foreigners, were the most notorious speculators and draft dodgers in the South. (In fact, about one hundred Richmond Jews—a higher percentage than among their coreligionists nationally, North or South—served in the army.) War Department clerk Jones spattered such disparaging remarks throughout his journal. In Congress the splenetic Henry Foote asserted that in Richmond "four out of five of the tradesmen in our principal thoroughfares" were Jews. He cited rumors that "by official permission . . . this swarm of Jews from all parts of the world had come to this country invited to trade with us, and permitted in many cases to conduct illicit traffic with the enemy. . . ." Foote said that "an eloquent gentleman of Virginia" had told him that "if the present state of things were to continue the end of the war would probably find nearly all the property of the Confederacy in the hands of Jewish Shylocks."[39]

Among the capital's daily newspapers, only the *Dispatch* spoke out against such charges, as when it voiced disgust "in this age of universal speculation and extortion, with the slang of 'Jew, Jew', a cry akin to that of the practical pickpocket, when he joins the cry of 'Stop, thief!' to direct attention from himself."[40] The *Examiner* seemed impartial when it said that "every man in the community is swindling everybody else, and everybody else is swindling him." That applied to the many who hoarded attics full of goods until the price was high enough to make a sufficient killing. But the mass of Richmonders were not buying and selling; they were offering honest labor for sums that were a bare living wage one week and an insufficiency the next.[41]

* * *

In midwinter Lee had sent a quarter of his army to block Union forces probing toward Richmond around Suffolk, inland from Norfolk. Lee's move was logistical as well as strategic; it meant two fewer divisions to feed along the Rappahannock, and those divisions' secondary mission was to scour relatively untouched southeastern Virginia for provisions for the rest of the army.

Things were so desperate in the army that Commissary General Northrop was authorized to seize flour, corn, and meat for military use, which sent a "somewhat senseless panic" through the city. Though his agents had to pay a fair price, what they considered fair was far below the going rate, so farmers stopped bringing food into town. The *Whig* said the public was being "gouged by heartless extortioners and robbed by official rogues."[42]

The harsh fact of impressment was resented all the more because Northrop was behind it. Since his early run-ins with Joe Johnston and Beauregard, he had managed to make enemies of most high-ranking Southern officers—including Robert E. Lee, who usually stayed above the conflict of sensitive egos.

As Lee's troops got hungrier, Northrop urged the general to send them to impress food from the countryside. With scurvy showing up in the ranks, Lee ordered regiments to scavenge the greening woods and fields for sassafras buds, wild onions, garlic, and pokeweed sprouts. Responding to Lee's vain requisitions for more food, Northrop seemed to think he had done his duty by saying in effect, "I told you so," while also blaming the weather and the railroads. If Lee had cut his troops' meat ration as directed, the available supply would have lasted weeks longer, he added.[43]

At the time, the daily ration for Lee's men was already down to eighteen ounces of flour and four ounces of questionable bacon, with occasional supplements of rice, sugar, or molasses. Nevertheless, Lee dutifully ordered his soldiers to observe another of Davis's official days of fasting and prayer on March 27. "No portion of our people have greater cause to be thankful to Almighty God than yourselves," he told them.[44]

To cold and hungry troops, this must have suggested that conditions were even worse on the home front. For some civilians in Richmond, this was true, because they had no saintly general assuring them of their good fortune, no chain of command to see that they got a measured though meager ration each day—and cornmeal was up to $12 a bushel. John Jones spoke for them: "Fasting in the midst of famine! May God save this people!"[45]

*   *   *

As the weather began to soften, Sara Pryor's friend "Agnes," a colonel's wife, took a morning stroll in Capitol Square. There on April 2, among the new dandelions and trilling birds, several hundred people assembled quietly. One of them, a pale, emaciated young woman, came to sit beside Agnes on a bench, saying she could no longer stand. When she raised her hand to her bonnet, Agnes gaped at her bony arm. The girl pulled her sleeve down, saying with an apologetic little laugh, "That's all that's left of me!"

Asked if this gathering was a celebration of some kind, the girl said yes—"We celebrate our right to live. We are starving." When enough people arrived, she said, the women were going to the city's bakeries and take one loaf each—"That is little enough for the government to give us after it has taken all our men."

As the crowd in the square grew, a delegation strode to the governor's house to ask for food. Their leaders had decided to make this appeal, at least as a gesture, when they met earlier at a Baptist church on Oregon Hill. Letcher, caught at breakfast, said he would try to help if they came to his office later. But things were moving too fast. In the square a black maid came to snatch her wandering charge away because the child might "catch something from them poor white folks."

The angry but still controlled mass flowed out of the square, down Ninth Street to Main. Letcher ordered guards to ring the alarm bell in the tower. John Jones watched the passing throng and could not help offering his best wishes, telling the marchers they were headed the right way to "find plenty in the hands of the extortioners."[46]

William P. Munford, head of the Young Men's Christian Association, tried to head them off, telling them that he would issue food if they came to the YMCA office.[47] Some did, but most surged along behind their leaders. Mary Jackson, "a tall, daring, Amazonian-looking woman," conspicuous with a long white feather in her hat, was out front with Minerva Meredith, who flaunted a pistol. Their followers pushed into the government commissary, then turned on shops, grabbing bread, flour, hams, and shoes, loading them into carts and wagons commandeered along the curbs.

When merchants began shutting their doors the crowd turned into a mob, smashing windows with hatchets and taking not only necessities but silks, bonnets, jewelry, tools, whatever was attractive. Hundreds more arrived, well-fed men and women among them. Some watched; others joined what had become a full-scale riot.

Firemen hosed them down, which only made them angrier. The alarm bell brought the Public Guard, a company of armory workers organized by Colonel Gorgas, running to the square. With the Guard, Letcher confronted the crowd and had Mayor Mayo read the Riot Act. Then the governor gave the protesters five minutes to disperse or the Guard would open fire. The looters halted, waiting, but did not go away.

As tense seconds passed, Davis arrived. He was not in a conciliatory mood that morning. For weeks he had been so ill that he seldom worked in his office, and only the night before one of his favorite horses had been stolen. There had been a demonstration in Salisbury, North Carolina, that probably inspired this one. If such riots spread from the capital across the South, they could be disastrous to the cause.

Stepping onto a wagon turned sideways across the street, the president told the rioters to go home so the bayonets facing them could be aimed against the invaders. Disorder would only mean famine, he said, because farmers would refuse to bring food to the city. He offered to share his last loaf with them but said they must bear their trials with courage and stand united against the enemy. According to Varina Davis, he reached into his pockets and flung all his money into the crowd, then took out his watch. "We do not wish to injure anyone," he said, "but this lawlessness must stop. I will give you five minutes to disperse, otherwise you will be fired upon."

A new five minutes started ticking off. The captain of the Guard scanned the crowd before him. He recognized some of the women as wives of men in his command. He warned that they were risking "two balls and a buckshot." Davis held his watch, waiting. And then the crowd began to drift away.[48] (Some contemporary accounts credit Davis, some Letcher, and some Mayo with finally quelling the bread riot. Considering the likely bias of each source, this is the most plausible sequence.)

That afternoon, Assistant Adjutant General John Withers urged

Richmond newspapers to "avoid all reference directly or indirectly to the affair," lest it "embarrass our cause and encourage our enemies."[49] But such news could not be contained.

Hall Tutwiler, an excitable private at the Signal Office, was an eyewitness but not a precise reporter. He wrote to his sister that what seemed 5,000 protesters filled Cary Street and another 5,000 were on Main and Broad streets. "I was right in the middle," he said. "It was the most horrible sight I ever saw." Another visitor, Margaret Brown Wight of Hanover Court House, wrote in her diary that "men of the worst character" were among the rioters, and "no doubt they were at the bottom of this infamous proceeding. . . . This is but one of the disgraceful attendants upon this unholy, & in my opinion, unnecessary, War."[50]

Despite Withers's appeal for self-censorship, the *Examiner* held off only a day before publishing its account, based on Mayor's Court hearings of thirty-eight persons arrested, almost half of them men. The protesters, the paper alleged, were "a handful of prostitutes, professional thieves, Irish and Yankee hags, gallows birds from all lands but our own . . . with a woman huckster at their head." They robbed shops of everything but bread, and those who had gone to the YMCA threw the rice and flour they got there into the street. Concluding with a predictable jab at the administration, the *Examiner* said the mob "deserved immediate death," but that officials lacked the pluck to do their duty.[51]

The day after the riot, clusters of the unhappy gathered at street corners, still demanding food. This time the Guard scattered them without trouble, arresting nine more. The City Council issued free-food coupons to the deserving poor, and officials handed out rice and flour from government supplies.

For days Mayor Mayo worked his way through cases against at least forty-seven riot defendants. His courtroom at City Hall was full of women and "young men of the veriest rowdy class." They overflowed the prisoners' boxes and sat on barrels of flour, piles of bacon, dry goods, tubs, and other recaptured booty brought as evidence.

A market clerk testified that Mrs. Jackson had warned him before the riot that he had better stay off the street, because the women were going to shoot down any man in their way. An Oregon Hill woman said Mrs. Jackson had told her that she would be "mobbed" if she did not take part. The papers said Mrs. Jackson, a housepainter's wife, had been profiteering as a huckster. They also said she bore a grudge beyond hunger: She had been turned away from the War Office when she pleaded for an army discharge for her son.

Dr. Thomas Palmer, surgeon of the Florida brigade, was charged with not moving when the crowd dispersed. Instead, he had stood his ground and shouted, "There is a power behind the throne mightier than the throne, and that power is the people!"

The mayor was not impressed. "There is no reason why there should have been any suffering among the poor of this city," he told the courtroom. "More money has been appropriated than has been applied for. It should be, and is, well understood that the riot yesterday was not for bread. Boots are not bread, brooms are not bread, men's hats are not bread, and I never heard of anybody's eating them."[52]

From the heights of society and officialdom, there was little sympathy for those who broke the rules.

Emma Lyon Bryan, daughter of the Chesnuts' landlady, looked down her nose at the rioters as a "turgid mob with hoarse threats, the unwashed masses from the purlieus of the city." Colonel Gorgas wrote: "It was a real woman's riot, but as yet there is really little cause for one—there is scarcity, but little want." Citing current wages of $1.50 to $3 a day, he said, "With such wages and flour at $30 they cannot starve." Yet he had just talked with the president, who was more realistic. Davis said that "large as his [own] salary appeared, and altho' he lived just as he did as a Senator in Washington, he found it took all of it to defray his expenses."[53]

After the riot, Davis published an address to the Confederate nation, saying, "There is but one danger which the government of your choice regards with apprehension." To meet it, the country must plant its fields not in cotton and tobacco but exclusively in crops to feed man and beast.

"Is it not a bitter and humiliating reflection that those who remain at home, secure from hardship and protected from danger, should be in the enjoyment of abundance, and that their slaves also should have a full supply of food, while their sons, brothers, husbands and fathers are stinted?"[54]

The president clearly did not refer to those who remained at home in Richmond. Only by comparison with troops in the field were they secure from hardship, and many months would pass before they enjoyed abundance again.

CHAPTER SIXTEEN

THE AWFUL HOUR
HAS COME AGAIN

*I*t was not a likely arrangement, for mid-April of 1863:

On one side sat James T. Kirby, for months a prisoner in Castle Thunder, charged with being a Union spy.

On the other sat Captain George W. Alexander, commandant of the Castle, a man used to accusing others and punishing those who talked back.

In between sat five members of the Confederate Congress, listening as Kirby charged Alexander with "inhumanity" to prisoners in his care.

Kirby was not alone. That winter General Winder had listed him among 171 civilians kept in Richmond's political prisons. Most were farmers and artisans from border counties, who had been accused of disloyalty to the Confederate government and were being held without trial. A few were suspected spies. Then there were hundreds of military offenders, from deserters and murderers to simple stragglers held for return to their regiments.

When Congress ordered an investigation of alleged cruelty at Castle Thunder, a series of military and civilian inmates, detectives, and prison officials testified for and against Alexander. He was a hard man with a hard job; only the day before the hearings began, he had officiated at the hanging of the first Union soldier to be executed for violating his parole.

* * *

The condemned man was another Webster—Captain A. C. Webster, a name some suspicious Southerners considered an alias; they thought that since he was captured in Loudoun County, near Harpers Ferry, he might be the missing youngest son of John Brown. Alexander painted Webster as a "fiend," and the Richmond papers said he was guilty of murder, stealing horses and slaves, and other crimes too hideous to mention.

This Webster, said to be a New Hampshire native, was a Confederate soldier who had been captured by Yankees at Fort Donelson. After taking the oath of loyalty to the Union, he became a Federal officer leading a "band of desperadoes" in the bitter skirmishes along the Potomac border. Confederate partisans trapped him and his men in a church, and after a hard fight set the building afire to take them captive.

Webster was freed on pledging not to take up arms against the Confederacy again, but he was recaptured after his involvement in the killing of a Southern conscription officer in Loudoun County. Brought to Castle Thunder, he tried to escape, was injured in a fall, and apparently could not stand or walk. Sentenced to death, Webster asked that his epaulets be sent to his wife at Point of Rocks, Maryland—the one he loved best of "about eight" wives he allegedly had at the time.

Alexander was in command as guards lifted Webster into a carriage, escorted by cavalry on the way from the Castle to Camp Lee. There, after praying with the Presbyterian minister William Brown, the condemned man was helped to the scaffold and sat on a stool in his Union officer's uniform while the noose was fixed and his head covered.

Someone handed him his black hat, which he was to toss aside when ready to drop. "Hold, hold a minute while I pray," he said. Then, at 12:47 p.m. on April 10, he threw the hat and the trap was sprung. The businesslike Alexander, with the old detective Caphart, then returned to Castle Thunder, ready to face the congressional investigators.[1]

*   *   *

Considering that the prisoners who testified against Alexander were still at his mercy, some were remarkably outspoken, no doubt in hopes that appearing conspicuously before the committee would protect them against retaliation. They told of inmates being flogged up to fifty times with broad leather straps, tied up by their thumbs, forced to wear barrel shirts, confined in a windowless "sweat house," bucked and bound like calves going to market, shut in the prison yard with no shelter against the elements, and shot at for leaning out of windows.

A former hospital steward said that "some of the officers of the prison treat the prisoners as though they were dogs instead of soldiers fighting in the common cause of the Confederacy." A former warden said

Alexander and his staff were guilty of "cruel and inhuman" treatment. Detectives still working with the commandant backed up these charges.

But the boldest allegations came from the accused spy, Kirby. Once, when Alexander called him a "damned son of a bitch," Kirby had called him a "damned coward" in response. He admitted saying to another prisoner, as the commandant walked past, that "I have no more respect for Captain Alexander than I have for my royal Bengal stern." As punishment for this impudence, he was locked in a solitary cell without food for a day.[2]

For a spy, Kirby was not a cautious man. When arrested the previous November, he was carrying a pocket diary that traced his movements from Confederate Virginia to Washington and back. He had posed as a volunteer nurse, an Englishman living in Canada, and used a pass from Southern medical officers to circulate through the army in northern Virginia. He crossed the lines to Washington, then returned after Antietam to Lee's army in the Shenandoah Valley. In early October 1862 he was at Confederate Brigadier General Wade Hampton's headquarters when Hampton's cavalry rode away with Jeb Stuart to raid Pennsylvania. He made himself at home in the command tents of Lee, Longstreet, and Jackson, and got to Richmond again before being recognized and arrested.[3]

Prosecutors collected affidavits against him. But he told the committee investigating Castle Thunder that the attorney general had closed his case for lack of evidence, and he remained a prisoner only because he had refused the chance to go north by flag of truce.[4]

Captain Alexander played favorites among the prisoners, Kirby said; some men sentenced to wear ball and chain never did. "Any person or prisoner could be Captain Alexander's favorite if he would become his pimp. I could have been one I reckon." No one asked exactly what Kirby meant by "his pimp."

Repeatedly, the committee asked what had happened when prisoners tossed a canteen of gunpowder into a wood stove the previous November, causing a minor explosion and inordinate punishment. Prisoners said the incident was a joke, meant to scare other inmates. Alexander maintained that it was an escape attempt. When inmates refused to tell who had done it, he turned about a hundred of them into the courtyard. There they spent two cold, sleety days and nights without fire or shelter.

Caphart led the procession of witnesses defending Alexander. One blockade runner, who said he had served in the East India Royal Navy, testified that he had experienced military prisons abroad, and witnessed there "nothing so lenient as at Castle Thunder in America."

Alexander himself maintained that only a few of the thousands of men who passed through his prison had been punished, and then for good reasons. He recalled his own war adventures, his imprisonment and escape from Fort McHenry. He also told them of "a pale little Virginia woman—my wife" who cared for suffering soldiers at "the little hospital of the 'Angel of Mercy.' "

In the end, Speaker Thomas S. Bocock of Appomattox County concluded that both Alexander and Winder should be censured and fired. Another congressman called Alexander's punishments "illegal and improper," though not serious enough to warrant firing. But three of the five committee members found the commandant's conduct justified. After all, these prisoners were "desperate and abandoned characters . . . in the main murderers, thieves, deserters, substitutes, forgers and all manner of villains."

Thus, for the moment, Winder, Alexander, and Caphart all stayed on. But for different reasons, their days on the job were numbered.

* * *

One of the most useful witnesses in Alexander's behalf was Captain Thomas P. Turner, commandant of Libby Prison, the jail painted by many Yankee prisoners' memoirs as the worst in Richmond. Turner explained that captured enemy soldiers were treated more humanely there than Southern soldiers and civilians who fell into Alexander's care at Castle Thunder.

Turner's prisoners were, presumably, honorable soldiers captured in battle, just as thousands of Confederate troops had been captured and were now in Federal hands. They were officers, who behaved better and expected to be treated as gentlemen. But the inmates of the Castle, Turner said, were "the worst in the land." He told of sending two of his errant guards to Alexander's prison, where "they were set upon, beat, their clothing torn off and robbed of everything."[5]

Bribery was mentioned only briefly in fifty-three pages of printed testimony in the congressional investigation of Castle Thunder. By that account, it would seem that such payoffs were often tried but never completed. But bribery was an omnipresent fact of the war, the grease of commerce among passport officers, blockade runners, spies, hotel clerks, sentries, wholesalers, boatmen, railroaders, and possibly the commandants of prisons. It was particularly effective where men paid in shrinking Confederate dollars were offered gold or U.S. greenbacks. Indeed, as the Castle Thunder hearings ran down, Alexander was tipped off that one of his sentries had been bribed and a mass escape was planned. He ordered other guards to set a quiet trap, and that night when twenty-five prisoners slipped onto the Castle roof past the cooperating sentry, they were recaptured and put on a diet of bread and water.[6]

When the newspapers reported in October 1862 that a number of Alexander's personal friends had presented him an elegant $600 horse and trappings, they said the gift was in appreciation of the commandant's qualities in private and social life as well as for his official duties. But there were broader implications fourteen months later, when Alexander was charged with malfeasance in office. Correspondent Bagby had heard that Alexander's "board alone, at the Ballard House, exceeds his entire salary, to say nothing of the spanking team he sports and the cottage he has purchased. . . ."[7]

*   *   *

Whether or not greenbacks produced it, there was more accurate Union intelligence out of Richmond that spring than ever before. This was the product of the Army of the Potomac's new Bureau of Military Information, run by Colonel George H. Sharpe, formerly commander of the 120th New York Infantry and before that a sophisticated lawyer and diplomat. Rather than sending spies on vague missions to pick up whatever they might find in Confederate territory, Sharpe dispatched experienced agents to collect up-to-date strategic intelligence.

This improvement was ordered by the latest Federal commander facing Lee along the Rappahannock River, halfway between Richmond and Washington. He was Major General Joseph Hooker, who had taken over after Major General Ambrose Burnside's January effort to advance on Richmond bogged down in the great fiasco remembered as "the Mud March." Hooker's chief of staff, Major General Daniel Butterfield, said that at the change of command, "We were as ignorant of the enemy in our immediate front as if they had been in China."[8]

Sharpe quickly remedied that, giving Hooker better intelligence than any Northern commander before him had received. But Sharpe's military spies were not the only Union agents busy between the James and the Rappahannock as the April sun hardened the roads for the armies to move again.

The major supply line to Lee's army that winter and spring was the Richmond, Fredericksburg & Potomac Railroad. Lee, anything but a habitual whiner, had apologetically complained to President Davis about operation of the line before the battle of Fredericksburg. If it was not run more energetically, he said, he would have to withdraw to Hanover Junction, more than halfway back to Richmond.

Obviously the much-maligned Commissary General Northrop was partly to blame for the fact that Lee's men were hungry. But at the same time, railroad bridges went unrepaired, private shipments were given priority over military supplies, and trains arrived bearing only a fraction of the essentials they could carry. There was a constant shortage of freight cars. During Burnside's "Mud March" offensive, Lee bluntly urged Davis to replace the R.F.&P. superintendent, Samuel Ruth. But Davis stuck by Ruth, a Pennsylvania native who had settled in Richmond.[9] Only later, after lying his way out of confinement at Castle Thunder, did Ruth reveal himself to be a secret agent of the Union.

But "Fighting Joe" Hooker was after immediate and specific help as he drew up his grand plan to outgeneral Lee and end the war. Since winter, Hooker had strengthened the Army of the Potomac, reorganized and drilled it, and revived its morale. "I have the finest army the sun ever shone on," he bragged. "I can march this army to New Orleans." When President Lincoln came down to review the general's troops and his plan, Hooker spoke repeatedly of what he would do "after we have taken Richmond."[10]

Hooker's words reached Richmond but made little impression on citizens who had heard such braggadocio earlier from George McClellan and John Pope. They were paying more attention to the shad, perch, and rockfish that were beginning their spring run up the James. When plentiful fish appeared in Richmond's markets at "monstrous unreasonable prices," old men, women, boys, and girls with poles and nets soon lined the banks of the river from the city down to Drewry's Bluff. The auction price of bacon and sugar started to drop. Spirits lifted.[11]

The tonic effect of sunshine and greening trees, combined with confidence in Robert E. Lee, tempted some in Richmond to make light of Hooker's bombast. "The finest army on the planet maintains its positions, steadfast as a fixed star," said the *Examiner*, noting that Hooker seemed to rely more on threats than on cavalry, artillery, or infantry.[12]

But even as Richmond shrugged off Hooker's rumbling, twenty-one Federal infantry divisions moved toward the fords of the Rappahannock. Ten thousand Federal cavalrymen were swinging west and then south to cut behind Lee's army. George Sharpe's agent in the Southern capital was collecting just the kind of material the Yankee general needed to turn boast into action. The spy brought back numbers that staff officers could depend on, up-to-date information that they could plot on headquarters maps, the kind of hard intelligence that comes from firsthand sources, perhaps inside the Confederate military bureaucracy:

> The works around Richmond are most formidable at Meadow Bridge and Mechanicsville road. They are intended for field artillery. No guns in position. Fifty-nine thousand rations issued to Lee's army, exclusive of cavalry. . . . At Richmond are the City

Battalion and some artillery. Two thousand seven hundred rations issued to the troops in Richmond in active service. General Wise has 5,000 on the Peninsula. Longstreet has three divisions at Suffolk. . . . Their effective force, all told, not over 15,000 men. D. H. Hill ordered from Washington, N.C., to re-enforce Longstreet's corps. He may, however, take Longstreet's place at Suffolk, and Lee may be re-enforced by Longstreet. Imboden has 2,500 men at Staunton. If not sent to Jones, may go to Lee. No other re-enforcements can be brought to Lee in any reasonable time.[13]

In the event, no reinforcements at all would reach Lee, who was outnumbered by more than two to one when Hooker's lead brigades crossed the Rappahannock on April 28, 1863. At the War Department, John Jones read incoming reports and wrote that families North and South would be holding their breath at the news: "The awful hour, when thousands of human lives are to be sacrificed in the attempt to wrest this city from the Confederate states, has come again."[14]

CHAPTER SEVENTEEN

GOD HAS BROKEN OUR IDOL

*A*mid shouts and rattling muskets, hundreds of Richmond civilians swarmed into Capitol Square, falling in by companies. Army wagons racketed through the streets to the R.F.&P. depot. The iron gates of the square clanged open and shut as officers rushed in and out. On that first Sunday morning in May, worshippers at St. Paul's heard little of what the Reverend Minnigerode was saying from the pulpit. The clamor outside drew their minds to marauding Yankee cavalry and the great, as yet unnamed battle going on along the Rappahannock fifty-five miles away.

As Minnigerode talked on, the church sexton eased up the aisle and whispered to someone whose son or husband had been hit in the fight. He came back to another, and another. One by one, soldiers' relatives left their pews, their faces pale as they slipped out the rear of the church. Then the sexton signaled to Minnigerode himself, who leaned across the rail to hear him and stepped out while an assistant went on with communion.

Mary Minnigerode, the minister's 43-year-old wife, waited at the church door, her face a picture of tragedy as she looked into her husband's eyes.

"Your son is at the station—dead," she said.

They hurried three blocks to the depot to bring home the body of 18-year-old Charles. But the soldier they found was someone else's son, not theirs. Trembling, Dr. Minnigerode went back to church to complete the service. Afterward someone asked him what had happened. It was a mistake, he said, but "it came so near—it aches me yet."[1]

To other families all over Richmond, bulletins came closer, news more reliable than the false tidings that had so upset the Minnigerodes.

In the parlor of Moses Hoge's hospitable home beside Second Presbyterian Church, Mary Anna Jackson was attending private services. She had gone in late April to visit her husband, Stonewall, on the Rappahannock, taking along the 5-month-old daughter whom he had never seen. Baby Julia was baptized there, and as the stern, reserved general played with her, his heart softened. But when a messenger came with word that Hooker was crossing the river, Jackson cut short this peaceful interlude and sent his wife and daughter back to safety in Richmond. After a few days at Governor Letcher's home, Anna had stayed with Mrs. Hoge.

Now, rather than attending services at church next door, she knelt to pray with Hoge's family and friends. They must have asked heavenly remembrance of both the devout general and Hoge, who was still abroad seeking Bibles for the army. But the moment Anna arose from her knees, someone told her that her husband had been wounded the night before.

More than that, she did not know.[2]

After church Colonel James Chesnut, though an aide to President Davis, refused to tell his wife, Mary, how the battle was going. A neighboring colonel's wife told her that Yankee raiders were only forty miles from Richmond. The two anxious ladies sat for tea, waiting to hear more. Then they walked to Capitol Square and watched companies of home guards mustering in a hubbub of excitement. From there they went to the steps of the president's house, where colonels and hastening couriers came and went. Eventually Varina Davis stepped out and hugged Mrs. Chesnut, who said how awful it was that the Yankees were only forty miles away.

"Who told you that?" asked Mrs. Davis. She assured her that the enemy was much closer. The news made Mary Chesnut a little dizzy.

The president was ill, the first lady said. She asked Mrs. Chesnut to stay the night with her. Later staff officers took time to joke with them and make light of the situation. Look at us, Mrs. Davis said: "We look like frightened women and children, don't we?"

The next morning the president was up and out, though still shaky. His aides, Custis Lee and Chesnut, loaded pistols and rode on each flank of his carriage. Colonel Chesnut told Mary that if Mrs. Davis fled Richmond, she should leave with her. When guns sounded close to the city, Mary's servant Molly urged her to "burn up everything," because when the Yankees came they would print in their newspapers all that she had written. Mary destroyed much of her journal and had to reconstruct sections of it later. Soon Confederate troops from Petersburg arrived in the capital, and she thought the danger was past. But the fright had hardly begun.[3]

* * *

Early that Monday, at a plantation house two miles north of the city, John B. Young heard hoarse-breathing horses gallop into his yard. Then came voices and the sound of scuffling. Running out, Young saw three men trying to slip a halter onto his favorite buggy horse.

He shouted, "What are you people doing?"

"We're taking this horse by orders from headquarters!" one of the riders yelled back.

Only then did Young realize that the intruders wore Union blue—that suddenly there were "live Yankees," unchallenged, on Brook Turnpike, within the outer ring of Richmond's defenses. The worst had happened, he thought: Lee was defeated, Hooker was marching into Richmond.

There seemed to be Yankees everywhere. Confederate Lieutenant R. W. Brown, who had ridden out to visit the Pulaski family farther up the Turnpike, saw a swarm of cavalrymen and approached to ask who they were.

"Who are you?" a trooper demanded.

"One of General Winder's officers," Brown said.

"Well, I'm an officer in the Second New York Cavalry," said the trooper. "Get off that horse."

Surrounded by Yankee riders with pistols drawn, Brown did as he was told. They took him to their commander, Colonel Judson Kilpatrick.

Brown tried a bluff. "You know it's impossible for you Yankees to get away," he told the colonel. "All your movements are known in Richmond."

Kilpatrick laughed. "I don't care if we're captured or not, we're going to do as much mischief as we can!"

He paroled Brown and rode away, leaving him to walk back into town. When Brown got there he heard that General Winder himself had nearly been caught when he rode out and mistook the Union force for friendly cavalry. Winder and his aide escaped only because the Federals' horses were too jaded to give chase.

From out the Brook Turnpike, from every northward road and bridge, Richmond heard rumors of rampaging Yankees.[4]

The Union cavalry had swept south as Hooker pushed his army across the Rappahannock, planning to flank Lee out of his prepared defenses. If Lee retreated westward, the road to Richmond would be clear.

Meanwhile the cavalry would swing down to cut Lee off from the capital. If that forced Lee to turn and fight, superior Union numbers would crush him. Federal supply boats had orders to meet Hooker's army at the Pamunkey River.

On reaching the South Anna, Hooker's cavalry commander, Brigadier General George Stoneman, called in his officers and told them that they had dropped in that region "like a shell, and that I intended it to burst in every direction, expecting each piece or fragment would do as much harm and create nearly as much terror as would result from sending the whole shell." His regiments would scatter to cut railroads, burn bridges and supplies, and throw a scare into Richmond.[5]

Except for its timing, that part of Hooker's plan worked just as Stoneman described it. The part for which Hooker himself was directly responsible was another matter.

Crossing the Rappahannock above and below Fredericksburg, Hooker's infantry came at Lee's outnumbered Army of Northern Virginia from both directions. But when Lee sent Stonewall Jackson to confront the main Union advance, Hooker pulled back onto the defensive around the crossroads of Chancellorsville. Lee then divided his army, dispatching Jackson on a daring march through the Spotsylvania Wilderness to strike Hooker's flank. Jackson, riding ahead of his lines that night, was accidentally wounded by his own troops, and Jeb Stuart took over his command. In furious fighting the next morning, Sunday, the Confederates battered the invaders away from Chancellorsville. By early Wednesday, Hooker's "finest army the sun ever shone on" was back across the Rappahannock.

But Richmond knew little of this as it was happening. Yankee riders were slashing in and out of the city's suburbs, cutting telegraph lines, destroying rail bridges, engines, boxcars, and miles of track, taking horses and mules, burning warehouses of supplies. At Ashland, the Twelfth Illinois Cavalry captured a train of wounded Confederates coming from the battlefield, questioned the troops, and freed them on parole. When Richmond sent an engine to check the track northward, the Federals ambushed it and sent it steaming off a burning bridge into the Chickahominy.

The streets resounded with anxious questions: "Where is General Lee? Where is our army?" But this time there was no exodus like those in earlier emergencies. Perhaps there was not enough buildup to panic; perhaps Richmond's people were like soldiers who settle down after their first firefights, who learn the difference between an advancing army and a cavalry raid.

This time citizen companies filed into the fortifications prepared under Lee's order months earlier. Major John F. Wren led his Thirty-first Virginia Cavalry Battalion out to meet the raiders. Volunteers stood duty as bridge guards. From Winder Hospital, Dr. A. G. Lane brought 300 convalescent soldiers, assigned to defend the River Road. Even Congress got into the "universal exhibition of patriotism," as 120 legislators and other officials formed a company that double-quicked to the suburbs and spent the night on picket. When it returned, Governor Letcher and the proud officials exchanged congratulatory speeches, and little boys watching imitated their elders, marching about the square with stick muskets.

Major General Arnold Elzey, commander of the Military Department of Richmond, vainly trying to restore order amid the excitement, said he would rather be dead. Major General James Longstreet, responding too late to Lee's call for help from Suffolk, approached Richmond ahead of his divisions and issued orders to fell trees across roads to cut off the Yankees' withdrawal. Among the captured raiders was one who trotted through town to Libby Prison and offered himself up. Told that a major exchange of prisoners was about to go off, he said that was unfair; he had looked forward to sightseeing in Richmond.[6]

At first critics of the administration found in all this confusion another reason to complain. "The Confederacy has never received an insult so mortifying and provoking," grumped the *Examiner*: the Yankee raid "throws an unpleasant light on the improvidence of those who control the military powers of this country." News of the great Confederate victory on the Rappahannock temporarily quieted such critics of the Davis administration. Indeed, it made Richmond seem so safe that soldiers afar were eager to swap life in the field for comfort in the capital.

One of them, cavalryman H. G. Armstrong, was a remote cousin of Davis's secretary, Burton Harrison. His jocular petition to Harrison was a welcome change from the thousands of pathetic appeals that poured into the president's office from troops, some ailing, some malingering. He asked "whether it is possible, by any art, strategy or chicanery, inspired by men, angels or the devil, to procure a detail for light duty in the pleasant city of Richmond. I am firmly convinced that that place is the only suitable residence for a man of refined and indolent disposition."

Actually, said Armstrong, he suffered from a heart condition. "I am aware that you are cheek by jowl with the chief luminaries of this fire-eating, psalm-singing constellation of the south. . . . I will [serve as] anything from a general of division to a parish priest" to be removed "from the society of these infernal farmers to the delightful atmosphere of politics and rio coffee. . . . Twenty four months have I luxuriated on corn bread and middlin'. A man with disease of the heart cannot ride 35 miles a day and sleep comfortably on so barbarous an aliment."[7]

The fact that Rebels seemed so secure in their capital provoked carping from Northern editors about Yankee officials whose only strategic concept seemed to be "On to Richmond!"[8]

"Nothing short of a surgical operation will get this delusion out of the heads of our public men," wrote William Cullen Bryant in his New York *Evening Post*. They think that if Richmond is captured, "our distracted people may give themselves no further trouble about traitors or treason. Jefferson Davis and his Cabinet, when they see our armies approaching their stronghold, and likely to possess it, will, of course, remain in the place and surrender. . . . The whole bubble of revolt will then go out like a snuffed candle. . . ."

Only such naive assumptions could explain the way Generals Scott, McDowell, McClellan, Pope, Burnside, and Hooker have persisted, said Bryant. "We have tried [Richmond] in front, we have tried it from behind, we have tried it from the sides, and, though always in vain, though we have been repulsed a dozen times, and sacrificed fine armies in the effort, the official mind at Washington still clings to it as the one thing needful."[9]

Lincoln was more capable than Davis of brushing aside the complaints that whined about his ears as he tried to concentrate on urgent affairs.

* * *

The bloody battle of Chancellorsville was the climax of two great soldiers' careers; indeed, this triumph of teamwork between Lee and Jackson was the high point of Confederate military fortunes. But it was hard to celebrate when Jackson, his left arm amputated, lay in a fever at a plantation by the R.F.&P. tracks south of the battlefield. Prayers for him rose from all the South.

After the amputation Jackson sent one of his aides, his wife's young brother, Captain Joseph Morrison, to fetch her from Richmond. Morrison was aboard the train caught by the raiders at Ashland but went to ask water from a nearby well and was hidden by the woman of the house. While the Yankees were listing their captives he slipped away, and when they left he somehow got to Richmond.

As soon as the railroad was repaired, Anna, little Julia, and Mrs. Hoge went up to Guiney Station, where Stonewall rested in a plantation outbuilding. Toward the end of the week, he began to slip in and out of delirium. On Sunday morning, May 10, his doctors told Anna that he would not live through the day. He died that afternoon, murmuring peacefully, "Let us cross over the river and rest under the shade of the trees."

Letcher and a carload of dignitaries went to bring Jackson's body back to Richmond. Returning to the city, the train stopped on the outskirts for Mrs. Jackson to board a carriage with Mrs. Letcher in order to avoid the crowds ahead. Businesses had been closed since 10:00 a.m., and all the city's church bells tolled in expectation of the train's arrival at noon. That time was put back four hours, and through those hours the bells tolled on. Thousands waited at the depot, then flowed through the streets following Jackson's hearse to Letcher's mansion at the corner of Capitol Square.

Nothing else until war's end would hit Richmond so hard. "Had a visible pall overspread the city, it could not have expressed grief more profound, nor sorrow more universal, than that which fixed every heart, and sat upon every countenance," said one of the newspapers. "It was as though a death had come home to every household, and snatched the one dearest away."[10]

The next morning Jackson's coffin was covered by the new white Confederate flag, which had the better-known battle colors in its upper corner. As the coffin was lifted to the hearse, a signal gun sounded near the Washington Monument and a band struck up the too-familiar "Dead March." Two regiments of Pickett's division, the Public Guard, the Camp Guard, six artillery pieces, and Wren's battalion led the slow procession that stretched nearly a mile through the streets. Four white horses drew the hearse, which was decorated with black plumes of mourning and escorted by eight generals. Behind it came a horse with Jackson's boots strapped to the empty saddle. Then came convalescents of the Stonewall Brigade from Richmond hospitals, then Davis and Vice President Stephens, the cabinet, Jackson's staff, the governor, the city council, and a long column of friends.

Commerce had halted. The cortege wound past the brick row houses and closed shops of downtown and returned to the Capitol. Longstreet, Jackson's fellow corps commander and sometime rival, headed the pallbearers who lifted the coffin into the House chamber. There an estimated 20,000 mourners passed by, many in tears. "I looked a moment, but for a moment," wrote a grieving young woman, "when the eager silent multitude hurried me on. Only a thin glass lay between me & the grey, lifeless features of him who was our country's boast. God has broken our idol & left us desolate. The city is one house of mourning, the stores closed & crape hanging from each door & window."

Late in the day, as officials cleared the chamber and started to close the coffin, a wounded veteran who had marched with Jackson tried to push close. Held back, he raised the stump of his arm and said through tears, "By this arm, which I lost for my country, I demand the privilege of seeing my general once more." Letcher intervened and waved him through.[11]

From Richmond, Jackson's body was taken to Lexington in his beloved Shenandoah Valley, where he had taught at Virginia Military Institute, married his Anna, and found his God. Everywhere, in the papers and on the streets, people asked who could replace him, and the true answer was that no one could. Later Longstreet would write that when Jackson fell, "the dark clouds of the future began to lower above the Confederacy." But in the gloom of that funeral day, war clerk Jones, as if it were his duty, insisted that "there are other Jacksons in the army, who will win victories—no one doubts it."[12]

* * *

Just before the Jackson funeral procession, about 3,500 Union prisoners from Chancellorsville, one of the biggest shipments ever to arrive at once, shuffled along Main Street toward Libby Prison. Though more than 500 captives had been sent away on exchange during the week, there was not enough room for so many newcomers at Libby, and most of them were marched on to Belle Isle. Among them was Thomas Evans of the Twenty-fifth Ohio, who resented that "we were paraded through the streets to show us to the idolatrous people who I must say behaved like devils outright." Others, too, remarked that after Jackson's death Richmonders seemed more resentful toward captured Yankees, as if those particular enemies had killed their hero.

Compared with prisoners captured later, many of those brought in from major battles in the war's first half were lucky, because the exchange system cut short their stay in enemy hands. But at Chancellorsville, Hooker had suffered more than 17,000 casualties, with 5,729 listed as missing, some of them dead, most of them prisoners sent to Richmond. Lee's losses were almost 13,000, of whom only 2,528 were missing. An even exchange would still have left Richmond with a net addition of perhaps 3,000 prisoners to feed and house or ship southward. In a South where foodstuffs and transportation lurched in and out of crisis, the worst was still ahead for prisoners of war, as well as the citizens of Richmond.

Lee's army, half as big as Hooker's, had inflicted heavier damage at Chancellorsville than it had suffered. But in percentage terms, it had lost more. Despite the devastation, even despite Jackson's death, the morale of the Confederates was up, and Lee was determined to use the initiative he had bought so dearly. A week after Jackson's funeral, satisfied that for the moment Hooker had no intention of trying to cross the Rappahannock again, he came to Richmond to decide what to do next.

Lee and Davis agreed that moving the war onto Union territory would allow Lee to feed his men and horses while Virginians brought in their crops safely. A decisive victory beyond the Potomac, perhaps the capture of a major city, might scare Washington into negotiating for peace. The president and the general still clung to unrealistic hopes that a bold stroke might stir England and France to act.

But within days after they agreed, news came that Union forces were tightening on Vicksburg, threatening control of the Mississippi River. Davis brought Lee back and convened the cabinet to talk about sending part of the Army of Northern Virginia west to help Joe Johnston, now commanding the Department of the West. Longstreet was eager to undertake the mission in command of the two detached divisions with which he had missed the fight at Chancellorsville. Postmaster General John Reagan of Texas argued forcefully in favor. Losing Vicksburg, he insisted, would lose the West.

But Lee, fresh from victory, prevailed by saying that the president must realize that it was a choice between Mississippi and Virginia. Put that way, it was no choice at all; Lee prepared to lead his army, including Longstreet, into fat and unravaged Pennsylvania.[13]

As he did, the Yankees tried a tactic that Lee and Jackson had used so effectively—to counter the invasion of friendly territory by threatening the enemy capital. In late June, couriers brought word of Union forces landing from both the York and James rivers. For a day or so, things quieted, but then enemy troops were at Hanover Junction, cutting the R.F.&P. railroad again.

At Hickory Hill plantation nearby, the Southern commander's son, Brigadier General W. H. F. "Rooney" Lee, was recovering from a serious leg wound suffered in the cavalry clash at Brandy Station as the Confederate move north began. Before his mother's eyes, Union raiders carried Rooney away on a mattress in a confiscated carriage. His youngest brother, Rob, watched from hiding. The raiders took their prize catch past his burned plantation at White House, then by boat to Fortress Monroe.[14]

In Richmond, Mayor Mayo issued broadsides warning that the enemy was approaching. "TO ARMS!" they said. "REMEMBER NEW ORLEANS! Richmond is now in your hands. Let it not fall under the rule of another BUTLER. Rally, then, to your officers tomorrow morning [June 28] at 10 o'clock, on BROAD Street, in front of the City Hall."[15]

Departmental clerks were put on standby. D. H. Hill's division was alerted at Petersburg. The capital did not know whether to mourn or exult; from somewhere came a report that Vicksburg had fallen, and another that R. E. Lee had taken Harrisburg.[16]

When the alarm bell sounded on July 2, second-class militiaman Gottfried Lange was in his garden, planting late potatoes. He was hurrying to finish the last row when a fireman doing police duty ordered him to report immediately. His wife had readied his rifle and filled his bag with bread. As Lange's unit marched to the outskirts, his two sons and a flock of other boys ran along behind, but after three hot, dusty miles the youngsters turned back.

Lange, in his early fifties and still proprietor of a beer hall, was in no better shape than the boys. He and his militia comrades gladly broke their hike at an inviting brook, where Lange downed what was left in a flask of apple brandy. After marching what he thought was eleven miles, the troops halted and Lange and friends built a brush hut for the night. The next day, unaware of what other Southern troops were doing under the same hot sun in Pennsylvania, Lange passed up wormy army-issue beans and lost what little enthusiasm he had for soldiering.

After his unit was hauled back on flatcars, Lange got one night's sleep at home before the alarm bell called him out again, this time to slog through rain and mud north of the city. "We did not see the enemy and probably were not seen by him either," he wrote after the typical day of an infantryman.[17]

Again, the capital was excited over local threats while great events went on beyond the reach of railroad or telegraph. When Yankee cavalry burned the depot at Ashland on July 7, there still was no accurate word of what had happened in either Pennsylvania or Mississippi. The Richmond *Sentinel,* a daily newspaper transplanted from occupied Alexandria, sold a run of extras by claiming that Lee had routed the enemy at Gettysburg, taking 40,000 prisoners, and the *Dispatch* reported that Johnston had outmaneuvered Grant at Vicksburg. But later that day, Secretary of War Seddon reluctantly forwarded to Davis the official report that Vicksburg had fallen.

Crowds pressed around the War Department, anxious but hopeful. Lack of news from Lee was "beginning to create distrust," wrote war clerk Jones. "If Lee falls back again, it will be the darkest day for the Confederacy we have yet seen." Seddon wanted to believe a wild report that Lee was driving the Federals back on Baltimore, and sent it along hoping to cheer Davis. Only on July 9, six days after Lee's invasion of the North crested on Cemetery Ridge, did the truth about Gettysburg arrive. It came from Lee himself; repulsed with heavy losses, he was retreating to Virginia.[18]

Cooper DeLeon said, "The dark cloud from Gettysburg rolled back over Richmond, darkened and made dense a hundred fold in the transit. . . . And out of the thick darkness that settled on the souls of all, came up the groan of inquiry and blame. . . . Why had the campaign failed? . . . Why. . . . Why. . . . Why . . . ?" But at Libby Prison, when a black steward came dancing with news of Vicksburg, captive Yankees raised a loud chorus of "The Star-Spangled Banner" and kept their cursing guards awake by singing "John Brown's Body" until midnight.[19]

Press and public criticized Southern generalship in East and West. Yet Josiah Gorgas was one of the few who saw that week for what it was, and he confided his view to his diary. "Yesterday," he wrote, "we rode on the pinnacle of success—today absolute ruin seems to be our portion. The Confederacy totters to its destruction."[20]

Lee, who had resolutely faced away from earlier criticism, absorbed every word of it this time. On the battlefield, as his men limped back from the Union lines, he had told them it was all his fault. Returned to Virginia, he wrote to Davis asking that someone younger and stronger, who had the public's confidence, be appointed in his place. Davis promptly replied, "To ask me to substitute you by some one in my judgment more fit to command, or who would possess more of the confidence of the army, or of the reflecting men of the country, is to demand an impossibility." Lee stayed on, and in large part because he did, the war would go on as long as it did.[21]

* * *

At Gettysburg, Lee's army lost more than 23,000 men killed, wounded and missing, and the Federals lost more than 28,000. Even as the Confederates withdrew, they brought back new thousands of prisoners and casualties to Richmond.

Most of the Yankees captured at Chancellorsville had been exchanged before Gettysburg. But others constantly arrived from distant conflicts that had no relation to the capital. In May, for example, Colonel Abel D. Streight and a hundred of his officers were shut in Libby Prison after being captured by Confederate Brigadier General Nathan Bedford Forrest during their long raid through Alabama and Georgia. So were the officers of the U.S. ironclad *Indianola*, rammed and sunk by Confederate boats on the Mississippi. So were three Northern newspapermen fished out of the Mississippi after the tugboat on which they had hitched a ride past Vicksburg was hit by Rebel cannoneers.[22]

One of the journalists was Junius Henri Browne of the New York *Tribune*, Horace Greeley's fiercely antislavery organ. Browne's treatment did not improve after Richmond papers reprinted a paragraph from the *Tribune* calling Major Thomas Turner, the Libby commandant, an "infernal brute." Only gradually did Browne come to agree with that description.

Browne witnessed another of those chilling prison lotteries by which pawns were chosen for games of bluff between officials North and South. The unlucky winners were two captains, designated for execution in retaliation for Major General Ambrose Burnside's hanging of two Southern recruiting officers in Kentucky.

This time it was the Confederates who backed down, because the Federals held as prisoners not only W. H. F. Lee but General Winder's oldest son, a Confederate captain; perhaps the Yankee raiders had gone after young Lee for this very purpose. The two Union captains at Libby were released after Washington sent word that the two conspicuous Rebel generals' sons would serve as hostages for their safety.[23]

From the upper floors of Libby, inmates had a clear view of the bridges across the James to Manchester, from which trains departed south and west. During endless card games, political debates, and cootie hunts, some there kept watch from Libby's windows for things of interest to Washington.

Soon after arriving, Lieutenant Louis R. Fortescue, a Union signal officer caught by Jeb Stuart's cavalry during the retreat from Gettysburg, was helping to slip intelligence out by codes and invisible ink. "Our government was kept informed of every thing of importance transpiring within the range of our vision, or which came to us from trustworthy sources," he wrote. Fortescue told of how Union general Neal Dow of Maine deceived prison clerk E. W. Ross by writing with lemon juice, which became visible only when heated.* Another captive signal officer devised a code based on dots and minor alterations in handwritten letters.[24]

---

*Major William S. Long of the Forty-fourth Virginia, adjutant at Libby while convalescing from a wound late in the war, alleged long afterward that Ross turned out to be a Federal spy. Long described him as "a little Jew named Ross," saying, "He was a civilian claiming Eng. protection, and I told him that as a property owner in Richmond he owed it to common decency to shoulder a gun and throw his English allegiance to the dogs and join the men who were offering their lives to protect his property. . . . If I had known then that he was acting the part that he was proved to be by subsequent developments I undoubtedly would have ordered the sentinel to shoot him as I had the undoubted right to do."[25] The author has found no corroboration of the spying charge. Ross died in the fire that destroyed the Spotswood Hotel in 1870.

Breckinridge Long, a student at Princeton when his father wrote to him about Ross in 1903, later became the assistant secretary of state most responsible for obstructing admission of Jewish refugees from Nazi Germany into the United States before World War II.

Browne of the *Tribune* wrote that before he escaped, much later, he was in seven different Confederate prisons, and Libby was the "least bad" of all. Indeed, he said, the officers sent there "were in every way better treated than any other class of prisoners," particularly Southern civilians.[26]

* * *

No one gave even a "least bad" rating to Belle Isle, the enlisted men's prison in mid-river. Three weeks after Gettysburg, Weston Ferris, a Connecticut cavalryman, was marched with about 400 other captives across the James River bridge to Manchester, then over the short bridge to the island. He described his new home:

"The upper part is rough and broken. Where the camp was, is a flat sandy plain of a few acres. The prison was made by digging a ditch about three feet wide, and throwing the dirt on the outside, thus making a breast-work behind which the guard was stationed. The ditch was the 'dead-line.' If a prisoner attempted to cross that, he was shot without a word of warning."[27]

Aaron E. Bachman of the First Pennsylvania Cavalry told of how prisoners made a gesture toward getting even by stealing seven poodle puppies owned by guard officers. The last one disappeared early on the day Bachman's outfit was to be moved from Belle Isle. The officer who owned the dog announced that "Not a yank can go until the man is found who killed my dog." Eager to leave, the prisoners quickly pushed the guilty man forward. "For his punishment he was compelled to eat one pound of raw dog meat, in [the officer's] presence. The man had been stuffed with dog meat that morning, so an extra pound of raw meat was a rather severe punishment."[28]

Before and after the battles of that springtime, the *Whig* had asked the world to understand that the outlaws infesting the city were not Richmonders but "the rag, tag and bobtail which ever pursue political establishments." In the same way, Americans North and South were sure that their own kin were incapable of cruelty to helpless captured soldiers—that someone else was responsible. Yet Belle Isle existed, as did Danville and Salisbury, as did Yankee prisons like Elmira and Fort Delaware, all of them operated by someone's sons and husbands.[29]

CHAPTER EIGHTEEN

THOUSANDS OF
BAREFOOTED MEN

*M*oses Hoge's impassioned eloquence was quickly effective on his mission to England; within three weeks of landing, he had persuaded the British and Foreign Bible Society to contribute 10,000 Bibles, 25,000 Testaments and a quarter of a million bound biblical excerpts to soldiers of the Confederacy.

His appeals brought more gifts of books and cash as he spoke to religious groups and met such conspicuous sympathizers as Thomas Carlyle, who was then writing his biography of Frederick the Great. Hoge spent some of the funds on printing thousands of pocket-size tracts with the Confederate battle flag on the cover. His only failure was in trying to sell Confederate 8 percent bonds, donated by Virginia Presbyterians, for 60 cents on the dollar; a London financier told him that at the going rate of exchange in Richmond, they were not worth more than 30. But even that realistic Englishman was moved by Hoge's sincerity, and made a cash contribution to his effort.

Hoge's dedication to holy works fused with his dedication to the Confederate cause. No qualms about separation of church and state restrained him, at home or in England. His most valuable introductions abroad were through his Virginia friend, the Confederate envoy James M. Mason.

After Lucius Q. C. Lamar of Mississippi, who had been Hoge's house guest in Richmond, was appointed Confederate emissary to St. Petersburg, he came through London and tried to persuade the preacher to journey to Russia with him. Hoge refused, because he had already been away from home for months soliciting British aid and arranging shipment of tons of books through the blockade. But he did accompany Lamar to Paris for several weeks, vainly hoping to arrange an audience with Emperor Napoleon III. Back in London, at midsummer he was looking forward to the voyage home when Mason sent him a brief newspaper clipping with a penciled note expressing hope that it was not true.[1]

The newspaper reported that a woman staying at Hoge's house in Richmond had been arrested as a Union spy after writing letters to the North urging that he be captured on his way home. When detectives went to the Hoge house to arrest her, it said, they found a child of the family lying dead, so they waited until the funeral was over.

Numbed, Hoge wrote on August 12 to his wife, Susan: "I have learned that I am bereaved of one of my children. I know not which has been taken. I love them all with my whole heart, and were God to permit me to decide which one to surrender, I could not decide, but would refer it back to him. My grief is increased when I know how much you are distressed for me, that I should be thus suddenly, strangely afflicted, when far from home, among strangers. . . ."[2]

He used the rest of his brief letter to comfort Susan. He did not know then that more than three weeks earlier, she had sent him a grievingly detailed account of how their son Lacy, almost 4, had died of a painful infection after stubbing his bare toe while playing. For nine pages, she narrated in a fine, clear hand every step through Lacy's funeral, in which four ministers had taken part. Only then did she offer her puzzled explanation of why the child's death was incidentally mentioned in the press.

General Winder, she wrote, "was kind enough to bring me the most infamous letter I ever read the other day from some spy in Richmond. It was captured at our lines and sent to [Secretary of War] Seddon. It was to Rev. Morgan Dix [of New York's Trinity Church], son of the Gen. [Union Major General John A. Dix], telling him that you were expected home & he must immediately take steps to have you captured if possible & confined in a dark dungeon—that you went to England under the pretense of getting bibles &c but it was as a spy & a correspondent of the English press for the South & that you were the 'vilest rebel firebrand' in the South."

The intercepted letter alleged that Hoge had corresponded with Southern sympathizers in Baltimore and elsewhere in the North, who "ought to be imprisoned at once."

It is "a great mystery & the authorities are doing their best to find the author of it," Susan said. "Genevieve's sister sent it, but she will not tell who wrote it, as she is a prisoner at present. I pity her, but do not believe she wrote it as many do."[3]

"Genevieve's sister" was 29-year-old, Cincinnati-born Mary Caroline Allan, wife of Patterson Allan, a well-to-do Goochland County planter. He was the son of Edgar Allan Poe's foster father, the Scottish merchant John Allan of Richmond. When Mrs. Allan spent time in the capital, rather than stay at her in-laws' mansion, Moldavia, off Main Street, she lived with the Hoges. So did Mrs. Stonewall Jackson and many other dedicated Confederates.

Without doubt, as Mrs. Allan sat in the confidence of the Hoge family and such guests, she had heard hours of conversation that would anger any loyal Yankee. One Richmond lady maintained that Mrs. Allan's "simulated sympathy" with Mrs. Hoge during her troubles was treachery "more fiendish than that to the government which she had affected to sustain by her sympathy, her wealth and her influence. The indignation against her was universal. . . ."[4]

Whether Mrs. Allan actually heard anything to indict Hoge as a Southern "spy" abroad is uncertain. But the preacher's public rhetoric had long identified him as a "rebel firebrand" by Northern standards, and his every speech in Britain could be called Confederate propaganda. His close relations with Mason in London and his trip to Paris with Lamar might easily have convicted him in a Northern court.

Those questions were never settled in court, however, because Hoge made it home without being captured. In London, three weeks after he got the clipping from Mason and six weeks after Susan had written, he at last received her letter about their child's death and the allegations of spying. Shortly afterward, in early September, he sailed for Halifax, Nova Scotia. From there he headed for Bermuda to board the celebrated blockade runner *Advance,* a rakish Scottish-built side-wheeler capable of well over twelve knots under steam.

By then the Union cordon outside Charleston had tightened, so the vessel's captain made for Wilmington instead. Though the Yankees blocked the main entry into the Cape Fear River, a narrow cut through the barrier island was protected by Confederate Fort Fisher. Watched by Federal ships, the *Advance* paralleled the coast innocently before making a sudden break shoreward. The Yankees gave chase, their shells whistling through the *Advance's* rigging. It was a near thing until the pursuers came within range of the fort's heavy guns, which opened fire and held them off. Susan later reported to her sister: "Oh! you do not know what a thrill of joy was sent to my heart . . . by the telegram sent from Fort Fisher, 'Ran in this morning under heavy fire; all safe and well.' "*[5]

Hoge's return did nothing to settle the case of Mrs. Allan, which would stretch on as long as the war. Rather than confine her at Castle Thunder in the rough company of other suspected traitors, Winder provoked resentment in Richmond by sending her to the Hospital and Asylum of St. Francis de Sales, north on Brook Road—reportedly over the protests of Catholic bishop John McGill. The surgeon in charge there said Mrs. Allan was nearly crazy at the prospect of being thrown in with common criminals. Defended by a host of prominent attorneys—including former secretary of war George Wythe Randolph—she heard the charges against her in Judge James D. Halyburton's Confederate district court.[7]

Apparently she had written not one but two letters, handing them to a friend to be forwarded north. En route they reached a Richmond gambling parlor, whose operator was a dispatcher in the underground mail system. For some reason he suspected them, opened and read the enclosure to the Reverend Dix, and promptly sent it to Colonel Robert Ould, who oversaw prisoner exchanges and flag-of-truce communications. The letter also targeted Secretary of War Seddon, so Ould passed it on to him. When Mrs. Allan returned from the country to the Hoge house, Seddon ordered her arrest. Detectives arrived to find little Lacy Hoge being prepared for burial, so they backed away until after the funeral.

In court, prosecutors charged that Mrs. Allan had welcomed Yankee cavalry officers at her plantation during Stoneman's raid in May. After that the raiders departed without disturbing the Allan property, although they pillaged other farms in their path. The captured letter complained that they should have burned Seddon's plantation at Sabot Hill, twenty miles from Richmond. (His birthplace, the Seddon family seat in Stafford County outside Fredericksburg, had already been razed by invaders.) The writer pinpointed other Goochland plantations for burning because they belonged to dedicated secessionists.

But Mrs. Allan's lawyers cast enough doubt on the provenance of the letters to produce a hung jury. Eventually they persuaded the judge to free Mrs. Allan on $100,000 bond, to await retrial amid the comforts of her home in Goochland.[8]

---

*A year later, the USS *Santiago* captured the *Advance* at sea out of Wilmington when the blockade runner's flight was slowed by the smoky, low-grade Carolina coal she had to burn during the war's latter months.[6]

* * *

Soldiers' wives were everywhere in Richmond—some come briefly to tend wounded husbands, some to take their bodies home. Some stayed on because the capital was within reach of the battlefields, to steal an occasional night or weekend with loved ones long gone from home, and some went astray while waiting. Hundreds of others, like Mrs. Robert E. Lee, were refugees whose homes had been occupied or destroyed by the Yankees. There was no going back to the Lee mansion at Arlington, where Mary Custis and the general had been married and their seven children born. It had become a Union army headquarters shortly after her departure in May 1861; its collection of relics from Mount Vernon, heirlooms from Mrs. Lee's great-grandmother Martha Washington, had been taken by the Federal government.

Since being handed across the lines by McClellan during the Peninsula campaign, Mrs. Lee had spent part of the time with tobacconist James Caskie and his wife at Eleventh and Clay streets, near President Davis's house. Although she had many respectful callers, Mrs. Lee did not take part in the busy social life of the neighborhood. She had been with her wounded son Rooney at Hickory Hill plantation in Hanover County when raiding Yankees took him away. She was upset by that experience; her arthritis worsened, and she could move about only with crutches. That summer she made a laborious trip to Hot Springs in the Virginia mountains, vainly hoping that the waters would help her.

Back in Richmond, she rented a modest frame house on Leigh Street near Third, the only place that she and her daughters had had to call home since leaving Arlington. The City Council, seemingly embarrassed by her situation, agreed to spend $60,000 to buy a more impressive dwelling as a gift to the general, but he predictably refused it, urging the city to use any available funds to help the families of needy soldiers. Later Mrs. Lee insisted on moving into the brick townhouse—now 707 East Franklin Street—that her son Custis and his colleagues had called "the Mess" while using it as bachelor officers' quarters.[9]

She had become so disabled that her crutches were almost useless, and she spent her days in a wheelchair, in a back room that opened onto a little veranda shaded by ailanthus trees. "I suffer so much nothing I have taken here seems to afford me the slightest relief. I can not walk a single step without crutches & very few with them," she wrote.[10] But as she sat knitting, she received the worried wives and mourning mothers of soldiers who served with her husband. In the turmoil of marching troops and wild rumors, her quarters became a quiet sanctuary for those who needed a word of assurance.

There were times, with all four men of her family in uniform, when she herself needed such comforting. It came from her husband, who responded to what seemed unfair blows from other directions, away from the front. In November 1862, their daughter Annie, 23 years old, died while visiting friends in North Carolina. In the general's tent near Fredericksburg, his aide found him weeping at the news. But Lee tried to hide his tears from his wife. "I cannot express the anguish I feel at the death of my sweet Annie. . . ." he wrote. "But God in this, as in all things, has mingled mercy with the blow, in selecting that one best prepared to leave us. . . ."[11]

In November of the following year, when Rooney's wife, Charlotte, died while he was still being held by the Yankees, his father wrote to Mrs. Lee with the same seeming resignation: "It has pleased God to take from us one exceedingly dear to us, and we must be resigned to His holy will. . . . I grieve for our lost darling as a father only can grieve for a daughter, and my sorrow is heightened by the thought of the anguish her death will cause our dear son and the poignancy it will give to the bars of his prison. May God in His mercy enable him to bear the blow He has so suddenly dealt. . . ."[12]

Lee met crushing setbacks in the field, the loss of thousands of loyal soldiers, with a stoic "God's will be done." His inner despair was revealed only at those few moments when someone like his aide found him letting go. Though his letters were often moving, Mrs. Lee had been apart from him for so much of the war that she may never have fully understood how he suffered.

Soon after her return from Hot Springs, General Lee wrote from camp on the Rappahannock praising her for offering socks for the army and urging his daughters to send all they could knit and collect. "I wish they could make some shoes, too," he said. "We have thousands of barefooted men."[13]

Mrs. Lee was writing to friends and relations, telling them "the sooner you can send the socks to Genl Lee the better . . . I always request that they should be given 'to the most needy.'" Mary Chesnut came calling and said Mrs. Lee's room was "like an industrial school: Everybody so busy." Even casual visitors were put to work knitting socks. "What a rebuke to the taffy parties," Mrs. Chesnut sniffed, thinking of the innocent frivolities of younger women.[14]

The Union blockade cut off medicines for Southern civilians as well as the army. As the necessities of daily life grew scarcer, housewives fell back on ancient formulas learned from Indians and slaves, and stretched their ingenuity trying to fill more recently acquired tastes. Mrs. Lee, desperate to ease her ailment, wrote to her sojourning daughter about "a recipe which is said to be an infallible cure for rheumatism. I tried to get the materials at Shirley [plantation] but did not succeed." Perhaps, she said, servants where her daughter was visiting could round up the ingredients, boil them down, put them in black bottles and send them to Richmond. "I could add the whiskey and molasses here," she noted.[15]

To substitute for imported coffee, Richmonders dried and ground almost anything that would color water. Many swore that roasted rye was best, but corn, okra seeds, carrots, sweet potatoes, acorns, dandelion roots, rice, cottonseed, peas, peanuts, and other ingredients had their partisans. The sediment at the bottom of sweet-potato coffee was touted as strong soap for cleaning carpets and curtains. Besides the old standby sassafras root, women brewed wild pickings like blackberry, huckleberry, willow, sage, and holly leaves to take the place of tea.

But the most imaginative recipes were for beverages that their makers called whiskey, brandy, and wine. For generations Virginians had been producing passable home-grown potions, but government efforts to curtail the use of grain for whiskey and beer inspired bootleggers to invent fantastic and sometimes dangerous concoctions. Nevertheless, soldiers and civilians bought up anything drinkable as fast as it reached the market.[16]

When the real thing was available it was priced beyond most Richmonders' reach, and the lucky ones who partook felt like celebrating. Even into the late stages of the war, the city's opulent gambling dens still offered safe nonprescription drinks, and a few of the city's hostesses could still produce an antebellum bottle from the cellar for special occasions. But by late 1863, the only institutional dispensaries of spirits fully sanctioned by law were the hospitals, and even there the guardians of the cask were under constant siege.

* * *

"One of *them* has come."

Thus did a sneering surgeon greet the first woman to be appointed a matron at Chimborazo Hospital. She was Phoebe Yates Levy Pember, one of six daughters of a cultivated Charleston family that had moved to Savannah before the war. She went to Boston with her Yankee husband but returned to the South when he died soon after the war began. Though Phoebe was widely read and traveled, when she came to Richmond in late 1862 she was not prepared for the brutal facts of life in a military hospital, or the isolation of her first months alone with wards full of mostly uneducated soldiers. But she toughened fast.

The Levy daughters were not shy. Phoebe's sister Eugenia, wife of Alabama ex-congressman Philip Phillips, had been jailed as a suspected

Confederate spy in Washington, then sent south. In New Orleans, she stood up to Union general Butler and was locked away again for her defiance. She had been arrested for allegedly laughing at the passing funeral of a Yankee officer. When Butler demanded an apology, she refused, explaining that she had been laughing at a children's party indoors. Butler called her a "vulgar woman of the town" and ordered her confined at Ship Island, the local yellow-fever station. Glaring at him, she said, "It has one advantage over the city, sir; you will not be there."[17]

In Richmond, every day made heavy demands on Phoebe Pember's morale. That September after Gettysburg she had been at Chimborazo for more than eight months, ministering to boys maimed by Union guns, learning to love them in their roughness. Invited out for an evening among "a particularly pious set" of ladies, she returned and wrote to Eugenia: "The feelings against the Yankees here exceeds anything I could imagine, particularly among the good Christians." One woman had told of piling Yankee bones around her pump so she would readily see them, and another asked Phoebe to save her a Yankee skull for a trinket box.

As these gentle ladies tried to outdo one another, Phoebe said, "I lifted my voice and congratulated myself at being born of a nation and a religion that did not enjoin forgiveness on its enemies, that enjoyed the blessed privilege of praying for an eye for an eye, and a life for a life. . . . I proposed till the war was over they should all join the Jewish Church, let forgiveness and peace and good will alone and put their trust in the sword of the Lord and Gideon. . . ." Whether she was encouraging the ladies or sarcastically chiding them is not clear, but she reported that overall it was "a very agreeable evening. . . . and the gentlemen seconded me ably."[18]

Phoebe was matron of Chimborazo's Hospital No. 2, one of five divisions that eventually expanded to thirty rough-sided, whitewashed wards each. At first only Deep South patients were sent to her division; then in mid-1863, it was turned over entirely to Virginians, as well as a few Marylanders. This was "highly agreeable," Phoebe wrote, for [Virginians] were the very best class of men in the field; intelligent, manly, and reasonable, with more civilized tastes and some desire to conform to rules that were conducive to their health." Besides that, they were "a hardier race . . . more inclined to live than die."[19]

But because those soldiers were close to home, sometimes their entire families moved into the hospital to comfort them. Phoebe found out that the will to live was not always paired with the civilized attitude she saw at first in Virginians. She told of how an extended family of rustics arrived at the hospital to be with a soldier recovering from typhoid fever.

They sat cluttering the ward, smoking their pipes, refusing to leave until she ordered a nearby patient to change his underwear in their presence. They demanded food and lodging, and even when their soldier was sent back to the field they would not go home, the wife saying he might get wounded and return. A week later, he did exactly that.

Soon afterward the true reason for the wife's stubbornness emerged. Phoebe was surprised one morning to find that the soldier had given up his cot to his wife and a newly born child. When a surgeon suggested that the mother be moved to another ward and fed tea and toast, she said she would rather stay there and have bacon and greens. Phoebe finally sent the family away with a free rail ticket, provisions, and baby clothes made by Richmond ladies, but then the wife left the child behind. Only when the soldier was given a furlough to take the baby home was Phoebe rid of the Daniells clan. Later she learned that the seemingly unappreciative parents had named the baby girl after her.[20]

When Phoebe and other matrons arrived, there was no precedent to guide them in performing their duties. She cooked for patients, often trying to persuade them to eat by following their imaginative recipes for dishes their mothers used to make. After assistants arrived, she was able to give more individual attention to the suffering.

A young soldier named Fisher, his thigh broken in battle, became a hospital favorite for his cheerfulness during months of recovery. Phoebe and the surgeons improvised a stovepipe-like brace to slip onto his leg as he tried to walk with crutches. The night after his first successful attempt, a nurse woke Phoebe. Something was wrong with Fisher. Phoebe found blood spurting from an artery severed by the jagged bone. She quickly stopped the bleeding with pressure from her finger. But when a surgeon arrived, he told her the rupture was too deep inside to be repaired.

Phoebe sat still, her finger in place. At last she forced herself to tell the soldier why.

"How long can I live?" he asked.

"Only as long as I keep my finger on this artery."

For a while, he thought in silence. Then he said, "You can let go."

"But I could not," she wrote. "Not if my own life had trembled in the balance. Hot tears rushed to my eyes, a surging sound to my ears, and a deathly coldness to my lips. . . . For the first and last time during the trials that surrounded me for four years, I fainted away."[21]

Phoebe's patients strained her compassion, and their families strained her patience. Despite her efforts to wipe out the rats that teemed beneath the wards, the pests were so bold that they ate away bloody bandages from sleeping patients, and sometimes the proud flesh from infected wounds. She cared for a wave of improperly vaccinated soldiers, some with smallpox sores so deep that their arms had to be amputated.

But the most maddening tests of Phoebe's mettle came from her coworkers. At first, some harassed her merely for being a woman; after other matrons and female assistants arrived, these men still resisted her efforts to do her job as regulations prescribed. More than anything, they wrangled over the barrel of whiskey issued monthly to each division.

In 1860s medical practice, two- to four-ounce doses of spirits were prescribed for almost any condition. North and South, in hospitals and in the field, bibulous doctors and hangers-on sneaked away uncounted gallons intended for patients. When Phoebe challenged those in her division, they defied her and appealed unsuccessfully to chief surgeon McCaw and even to Secretary of War Randolph. But because she locked the barrel away and kept the key, she still had showdowns with patients and staff who were determined to get a drink, and at least once had to scare them off by clicking the hammer of the little pistol she carried in her skirt.[22]

Soon after Phoebe turned 40 that summer, she heard that there was gossip in Richmond about her life as an unmarried woman among so many men. Asking her sister for advice, she affirmed that her life was morally irreproachable, though necessarily "a little peculiar." Being independent, "perhaps younger and more attractive than the very old and very unattractive women who fill these positions," she said, "the world might put any construction upon the matter they pleased." Rules prevented her from keeping a hospital ambulance out after 8:00 p.m., so without that transportation she had to forgo dinner invitations downtown. To break her loneliness, she decided to move in with one family, then another in the city.

Her earlier generous assessment of Virginians was adjusted that fall when she took a room with the family of Colonel Frederick Skinner of the First Virginia Regiment. The colonel was pleasant and cultivated, she wrote, but the family is "Virginia all over (which means that they would drive you crazy) kind hearted, generous, though very lazy, untidy people, who never have anything in its place or a place for anything, and who if they got hold of your dress by accident would just as likely put it on, always imploring you to do the same."[23]

Though she roomed on Church Hill for months, Phoebe Pember left no record of meeting the best-known strong-willed unmarried woman of the neighborhood. If she and Elizabeth Van Lew had met, perceptive as they were, each must have recognized something of herself in the other.

* * *

Sometime in late 1863, a woman wearing a sunbonnet and carrying a basket on her arm—a rural type that Richmonders called a "chinquapin woman"—rang at the Van Lews' door, bringing a letter addressed to "Miss Van Lew." A wary Elizabeth read it. It was "from the Federal army, asking me to send information at once of the provender & stores, and where the sick from hospitals were being sent &c."

The Van Lews had never seen this countrywoman before. Elizabeth was suspicious. Her bold delivery of books and delicacies to Yankee prisoners despite every bureaucratic roadblock kept her under constant surveillance. More than once, she had looked around to find detectives trailing her in the street. Strange faces had appeared at her windows. Detectives had interrogated boarders at the Van Lew house for evidence of her disloyalty. Now, fearing entrapment, she at first "expressed horror and surprise" at such a letter. But then, for some reason trusting this visitor, she told her she risked danger in bringing it.

The woman was indignant: "I'd like to see anybody put their hands in my pocket!"

That visit may have marked Elizabeth's conversion from defiant Union loyalist and comforter of Yankee prisoners to the most successful Federal spy of the Civil War.

In November, Benjamin Butler, the hard-handed pacifier of Baltimore and New Orleans, had taken command of the Federal Department of Virginia and North Carolina, headquartered at Fortress Monroe. Within days he got a letter and bouquet from Van Lew, offering her services. Its bearer said Elizabeth was "a true Union woman as true as steel." Butler told a colleague that "I could pay large rewards, but from what I hear of her I should prefer not to do it, as I think she would be actuated to do what she does by patriotic motives only."[24]

The general began communicating with her via flag-of-truce boat, calling her "Dear Aunt" and signing himself "James Ap. Jones." Beneath their innocuous chitchat he sent instructions in secret ink, which she made visible with heat and acid. In his first message he said, "I cannot refrain from saying to you, although personally unknown, how much I am rejoiced to hear of the strong feeling for the Union which exists in your own breast and among some of the ladies of Richmond."[25]

Soon afterward Van Lew appeared at General Winder's new office at Tenth and Broad streets, above Capitol Square. Her brother John was with her. This time Elizabeth was carrying in her bosom a letter from Butler to Captain Philip Cashmyer, described as Winder's "head detective," a 38-year-old German-speaking Marylander and prewar master cooper.

Van Lew wrote later that Cashmyer had been one of the rioters who attacked Massachusetts troops marching through Baltimore at the beginning of the war. In Richmond he had arrested the Unionist John Minor Botts and the Yankee spy Timothy Webster. He made himself popular with newspapermen by supplying them with Northern journals. When Winder got rid of the "Baltimore plugs," the imported detectives who had earned such resentment in Richmond, he had retained Cashmyer as his chief aide. On the surface, then, this captain did not seem a likely addressee for a confidential letter from Butler.

As Cashmyer read the message he turned "deadly pale" and seemed near fainting. According to Van Lew, it asked him to come through the lines to communicate with Butler, and promised him safe passage and perhaps tangible reward.* Controlling himself, Cashmyer stepped outside with the Van Lews.

Please, he whispered, "be prudent and never come here again." Then he added, "I will come to see you instead."

Van Lew had taken as much risk in delivering the letter as the detective had by reading it there in Winder's office. "I knew Cashmyer might betray me," she wrote—though their conversations had suggested to her that the captain's "trials and tribulations" in Richmond had "strengthened his loyalty." By that she always meant loyalty to the Union.[27]

Cashmyer's role is not elaborated further in Van Lew's writings or in official records of Union intelligence. But immediately after the war, his aid to Federal investigators made clear where his allegiance came to rest. And within weeks after that letter from Butler was delivered, Van Lew had a hand in a series of underground affairs that could only have profited from a secret friend inside Winder's headquarters.

* * *

Civil War history demolishes any quaint impression that women in Victorian times were too delicate for sometimes hard, always dangerous intelligence work. The sophisticated Rose O'Neal Greenhow, for example, who had informed the Confederates about the Federal army's advance

---

*Apparently inadvertently, Butler as "James Ap. Jones" addressed later letters to "My dear Niece" rather than to "My dear Aunt," a slip that could have caused trouble if detected by Confederate officials. On March 22, 1864, the general enclosed a secret-ink message for Cashmyer from Burnham Wardwell, the Maine-born Richmond ice dealer and Unionist who had been arrested at least twice by Winder's men. Wardwell urged Cashmyer to meet him at New Kent Court House "on business of life-long importance to you and your family." Butler instructed Van Lew to copy and deliver the message.[26]

in 1861, was arrested in Washington and held for ten months, then released and sent south. Feted in Richmond in the summer of 1862, she helped tend the casualties of the Seven Days campaign between tributes to her daring and her charms. President Davis told her, "But for you, there would have been no battle of Manassas."[28]

Navy secretary Mallory understood what made Greenhow such a success: "She started, early in life, into the great world, and found in it many wild beasts; but only one to which she devoted special pursuit, and thereafter she hunted man with . . . resistless zeal and unfailing instinct. . . . She was equally at home with ministers of state or their door-keepers . . . [she] had a shaft in her quiver for every defence. . . . If she had displayed the fruits of her bow and her spear . . . what scalps she might have shown. . . ."[29]

Davis sent Greenhow abroad as a Confederate agent, and by late 1863 she was busy charming officials and financiers in London and Paris.*

The celebrated Belle Boyd, who had crisscrossed the lines as a teenage spy for Stonewall Jackson in the Shenandoah Valley, was arrested twice by the Yankees but released, making her way to England in 1863. After a sojourn on the stage there, she returned to Richmond and displayed her spunk to an early-morning caller at her quarters at the Spotswood. George Bagby wrote that "an officer, loaded with 'tangle-leg,' attempted to penetrate her chamber between 1 and 2 o'clock a.m. She lammed away thrice at him with a revolver, but good luck and a clean pair of heels saved him."[30]

Though the adventures of Greenhow and Boyd are clearly corroborated by others, spy tales by their nature are often hard to document. Many, like that of the cross-dresser Loreta Janeta Velazquez, are hard to believe. By her own account, after her husband was killed in 1861, Velazquez masqueraded as a man and raised and equipped a Confederate cavalry outfit. She served at and after First Manassas before her disguise was uncovered in Richmond. Sent home to Louisiana, she instead tucked her hair up, donned her uniform again, and was wounded twice while fighting in Kentucky and Tennessee. In New Orleans when the Yankees came, she married a captain who was soon killed in action. After that she allegedly became a Confederate agent in Washington and Canada.[31]

There is no official documentation of the widely accepted and em-

---

*On October 1, 1864, en route from London aboard the blockade runner *Condor*, Greenhow insisted on being rowed ashore near Wilmington, North Carolina, rather than risk capture by a pursuing Union gunboat. The rowboat was swamped by a wave, and Greenhow, weighted down by gold sovereigns sewn into a belt beneath her clothes, was drowned. She was buried with military honors in Wilmington.

bellished story that before the war Elizabeth Van Lew freed a young slave and sent her to school in Philadelphia—and then, during the war, brought her back and successfully installed her as a waitress in Jefferson Davis's household. This agent, Mary Elizabeth Bowser, is said to have "had a photographic mind—everything she saw on the Rebel President's desk she could repeat word for word." She overheard Davis's conversations and passed vital intelligence to Van Lew for forwarding across the lines. One source says these messages were picked up by another spy, Scottish-born Thomas McNiven, who drove a bakery wagon that called regularly at the Davis mansion. Bowser's journal of her wartime service was reportedly destroyed by her family before they realized its historical value.[32]

Some historians, especially Southerners, have scoffed at Van Lew's account of her own adventures as a spy, partly because her manuscript is so vivid yet fragmented and partly because she was a Unionist, and a woman at that. Ellen Glasgow, the Richmond novelist, remembered seeing Van Lew in later years—a "frail, shrunken, white-haired old lady, who looked as if she would never have the heart to hurt a mouse," and "was supposed, mistakenly no doubt, to have been a Northern spy during the War."[33]

Another local writer said that the many claiming after the war to have been spies in Richmond were "in the main a sorry crew of self-dramatizing busybodies and Unionists who sincerely wanted to help without knowing how."[34] In the main, he may be right. But in that crew he mistakenly included Elizabeth Van Lew, whose value to the Union was certified in writing by Generals Benjamin Butler; George Sharpe, head of Union military intelligence; and U. S. Grant himself. Grant wrote to Van Lew: "You have sent me the most valuable information received from Richmond during the war."[35]

Sharpe's testimony was broader. "For a long, long time," he wrote, Elizabeth "represented all that was left of the power of the U.S. Government in the city of Richmond." He described how the Van Lews ran through their fortune to help Federal prisoners and hire lawyers for Unionists on trial. "They sent emissaries to our lines—when no one else could for the moment be found, they sent their own servants." They "had clerks in the rebel war and navy departments in their confidence." Miss Van Lew "steadily conveyed" intelligence, Sharpe said, concluding that hers was "the most meritorious case I have known during the war."[36]

THE BITING FROSTS
OF WINTER

*A*s nights lengthened in late fall of 1863, the wind sweeping down the river cut through the ragged clothes of unsheltered Yankees on Belle Isle. In the darkness a sentry overheard prisoners scheming to break free. We'd better go quickly, they told one another, because the guards are about to bring in cannon overlooking the camp. Before the sun set again, General Winder's men had rolled artillery into position, ready to blast canister along the borders of the prisoners' compound.

The Confederates were understandably nervous. Weeks earlier, Northern newspapers had suggested that some mysterious plot was being drawn to take Richmond from within, perhaps for the city's many prisoners to seize it by a sudden, simultaneous uprising. War clerk Jones suspected that a Union division newly arrived at Newport News was assigned to cooperate with such a coup de main.

Jones, never an optimist, thought that if the government did not do something to relieve inflation, Richmond's citizens might rise up, too. "The croakers say five millions of 'greenbacks' and cargoes of provisions might be more effective in expelling the Confederate Government and restoring that of the United States" than all the Union army, he wrote.[1]

Chronic complainers were not alone in their pessimism as the capital faced its third winter of war. In late summer, after the twin disasters of Gettysburg and Vicksburg, Lee had come to confer with Davis about the fall campaign. Afterward the two rode together through the streets of Richmond, and no one on the sidewalks cheered as they passed.

"The clouds are truly dark over us," Davis wrote to a friend. And in his *Southern Literary Messenger*, George Bagby brooded: "In all parts of the country there is great depression, and in many states positive disaffection. To some extent, this is the inevitable result of so many, and so serious disasters. But the root of the prevalent disaffection lies deeper. It cannot be denied that the people have lost faith in their leaders. . . ." Bagby's grievance of the moment was that Davis, out of misplaced loyalty to his friends, held on to unsuccessful generals beyond the mountains.[2]

After the summer's defeats the roller coaster of Richmond's morale had plunged even lower when Federals occupied Chattanooga, eastern Tennessee and Cumberland Gap, cutting the capital's main rail link to the West. "When will this year's calamities end?" Jones asked his diary.[3]

Davis, who had denied Longstreet's request to take a corps westward before Gettysburg, now sent him with two divisions to bolster General Braxton Bragg's army outside Chattanooga. (Union lieutenant Fortescue, imprisoned at Libby, claimed that he and his comrades had warned Washington in a coded letter that Longstreet was on his way.) Soon after arriving, Longstreet's troops led the charge in a costly Southern success at Chickamauga.[4]

Hearing the news, Jones wrote: "The effects of this great victory will be electrical. The whole South will be filled again with patriotic fervor. . . ." But success at Chickamauga was merely tactical, and celebration brief. In that second bloodiest battle of the war, Bragg had lost more men than the Federals, and had failed to follow through. He and his generals squabbled among themselves as much as they fought the enemy.[5]

Davis hurriedly left Richmond for the Chattanooga front, hoping "to be serviceable in harmonizing some of the difficulties" in Bragg's camp. When he headed back toward the capital he disappointed other generals East and West by leaving Bragg in place, assuring further trouble at Chattanooga. Lincoln added to that assurance by putting U. S. Grant in charge of all Union operations between the Mississippi River and the Appalachians, thus pitting him against Bragg. En route back to Richmond, Davis was bussed by admiring women at every stop. But at the blockaded port of Charleston, he saw Fort Sumter being battered to rubble by Federal guns and was glad to press on to the capital.

He returned after a month away. The previous year, bands had welcomed him back from his first Southern tour; this time the president of the Confederacy might have been just any arriving bureaucrat. In his absence workmen had rallied at City Hall demanding that their legislators support a bill to fix prices. Flour was selling at $125 a barrel.[6]

Along the Rappahannock, Confederate troops' spirits dragged as they faced another winter on short rations. General Lee disputed Secretary of War Seddon's leniency toward condemned deserters. Executions were distressing, he said, but necessary to keep his army together. He complained that Richmond was sending only three pounds of corn a day for his horses—"at this rate, the horses will die. . . ."[7]

But there was little to send; feed was so short that the capital's livery stables were charging $300 a month to board a horse. While the president was traveling, Mrs. Davis put her horses and carriage up for sale through a dealer. They brought $12,000, but when friends heard what had happened they bought and returned the team to her. She appreciated the gesture but was back where she had begun: "How the horses, which of course could not be again sold, were to be fed, could not be foreseen."[8]

Captives from Chickamauga poured into Richmond, bringing the total of Yankees in the city's prisons at mid-November to 11,650—of whom 4,622 were in Libby and four other warehouses, 6,300 on Belle Isle, and 728 in hospitals. All of them had to be fed.[9]

* * *

Prisoners piled up in the capital because by the summer of 1863, North-South disputes over exchanges had slowed movement to only a trickle. Thousands of inmates had already been shipped from Richmond to Danville, Salisbury, and points farther south. But disagreements, particularly over Confederate refusal to treat black Union soldiers as legitimate prisoners of war rather than as recaptured slaves, all but shut down the safety valve of exchanges by flag-of-truce boat on the James. Crowding in Richmond increased, and conditions worsened.[10]

Most of the few prisoners still being swapped were either desperately ill soldiers or surgeons and chaplains who had stayed to care for the wounded on the battlefields of summer. When Union surgeon S. J. Radcliffe at Annapolis examined a shipment of sick Federals newly arrived from Belle Isle, he reported: "Every case wore upon it the visage of hunger, the expression of despair, and exhibited the ravages of some preying disease within, or the wreck of a once athletic frame. . . . Their dangling, long, attenuated arms and legs, sharp, pinched features, ghastly cadaveric countenances, deep supulchral eyes and voices that could hardly be distinguished (some could not articulate) presented a picture which could not be looked upon without its drawing out the strongest emotion of pity." Generations later, photographs of some of these returned medical cases reminded Americans of World War II concentration-camp inmates.

A U.S. Navy surgeon, returning from Richmond, maintained that since the Chickamauga prisoners arrived there, an average of fifty inmates had died each day, most from diarrhea, dysentery, and typhoid—"yet cold weather has hardly commenced, and I am horrified when I picture the wholesale misery and death that will come with the biting frosts of winter."[11]

Union brigadier general Dow, a prisoner at Libby, was allowed to visit Belle Isle to oversee the distribution of clothes and blankets that had been shipped from the North. Through visitors from the U.S. Christian Commission, he passed word to Washington that "soldiers on Belle Isle are suffering beyond endurance." He secretly suggested that Union officials send $100,000 in Confederate bills concealed in cans with shipments of jelly, molasses, or dried milk—cash for prisoners to buy necessities, or perhaps bribe their way free.[12]

In response to Union protests about prison conditions, General Winder ordered Major Isaac H. Carrington to investigate. Carrington reported that Libby was clean, but three nearby warehouses were "crowded somewhat beyond their capacity for health and comfort." His findings at Belle Isle were generally favorable, though "some of the tents were dilapidated," and because of unexpected overcrowding, prisoners' meat rations were short.[13]

Winder forwarded this report to Union exchange officers. But the following week, medical director William A. Carrington was more frank in a report intended for Winder only. His findings were little different from what released prisoners had reported, minus the Yankees' vivid descriptions and insinuations of malice. Beyond hunger, cold and sickness, there was "the depressing moral influence prisoners labor under, especially noticeable since they have been told that there is no hope of exchange. They die from slight diseases, having lost all hope. . . ." He urged that more captives be shipped south.[14]

Neither Major Carrington nor Dr. Carrington dealt with Union assertions that prisoners had overheard guards saying that provisions sent from the North to Yankees held in Richmond were being diverted to feed Lee's lean army.[15]

Confederates pointed out that Richmond civilians were suffering, too; the blockade not only cut food supplies, it made quinine, morphine, and other medicines contraband of war. But none of these truths could ease conditions for Yankee captives in hungry Richmond. Existing Confederate prisons farther south were already packed beyond capacity, so late in the year Winder ordered that a major new compound be organized in Georgia, where the weather was gentler and food more available. Twenty-six acres were marked off outside the town of Andersonville, but the first prisoners did not arrive there until the following spring.[16]

Before that outlet opened, the pressure of too many prisoners in Richmond approached the bursting point.

*   *   *

In late November 1863, Richmonders heard whispers that Davis had wept on getting harsh confirmation of his mistake in leaving Bragg in command at Chattanooga.[17] Grant's army had driven Bragg's Confederates off their strong lines on Lookout Mountain and Missionary Ridge, and was ready to march toward Atlanta.

When the defeated Bragg asked to be relieved, Davis again urged Lee to take command of the Army of Tennessee. Lee, whose troops had spent months grappling with George Meade's Federals between the Rapidan and Bull Run, could not be persuaded to leave Virginia. But rumors that he was headed west swept the city. "What will become of us in Richmond if Lee goes away?" George Bagby pleaded.

The ranting Henry Foote led a merciless congressional attack on Davis, charging him with "gross misconduct" for clinging to friends like Bragg despite their failures. After Lee, the ranking possibilities for replacing Bragg were Johnston and Beauregard, both out of favor with the president. Davis thrashed over every alternative before reluctantly choosing Johnston. Then, still unable to admit his friend Bragg's failings, he brought him to Richmond as military adviser to the president.[18]

The newspapers were belatedly campaigning against corruption in army and government. Before the legislature temporarily shut the city's gambling "hells" by authorizing horsewhipping of their operators, those dens had kept special rooms for quartermasters, commissaries, Treasury officials, and the like. Some in such advantaged positions were seen to lose $40,000 in a night. Bagby cited four quartermasters who had started the war poor and now flaunted great wealth: "These cases are known; what must be the number of unknown pilferers?"[19]

But not every alleged boodler went unpunished. Charges of misfeasance in office had at last ended the bitter reign of Captain Alexander at Castle Thunder. Philip Cashmyer, who had worked closely with him, would write after the war that Alexander had "prostituted his authority to the arrest of all persons, Union or otherwise, whom he or his underlings could entrap into any expression of sentiment against those in authority or evasion of military law. This he made the process of a system of robbery, confiscation, and blackmail that [one] would . . . require strong evidence to believe could have been practiced with such impunity. As a prison commandant he was harsh, inhuman, tyrannical, and dishonest in every possible way he could practice these vices."[20]

Amid the outcry for reform, critics turned again on Davis's old friend, Commissary General Northrop, who "is said to be a lunatic." For twenty years while on leave from the army, he had "busied himself in Charleston with the practice of medicine upon the lower classes, requiring every patient to make the sign of the cross before he would prescribe for him." Once "he raised a great row in church by rising from his seat and calling the minister a liar. The congregation would have torn him to pieces if his friend had not pled lunacy on his behalf. . . ."

The author of that paragraph conceded that such stories might not be true, but Northrop's appointment certainly was "queer," and still Davis kept him in office. (Libel law was not vigorously exercised in the Confederacy; printed offenses were more likely to be answered by a challenge to duel than by a lawsuit. Though Northrop read and heard rising insults for almost four years, he did not respond in either way.)[21]

* * *

After a long, glowing autumn, old folks pointed to the heavy crop of persimmons in the Virginia woods, and to corn shucks thicker than usual—signs that a cold winter was coming. A hard freeze gripped Richmond just before Christmas, throwing over the city a cloak of clean white that camouflaged its wartime shabbiness for at least a morning.

Even in the grayest months of war and winter, the blithe spirits of Richmond partied determinedly on. It was, in part, forced frivolity, organized to cheer soldiers who might be gone tomorrow, and to keep up appearances among ladies for whom the conflict was one long social competition.

The nearness of danger and privation compressed time; the progress of romance was often measured in hours instead of years. "Never did a city of its population contain more beautiful and brilliant women than did Richmond," a soldier then young recalled. Ministers solemnized a steady flow of weddings. Afterward men and women who had lost limbs or loved ones were still able to think of those months as life at its fullest.

While the politer set shunned the theater and bawdier public attractions, it often enlivened private evenings with entertainments too sophisticated for moralists like Bagby. He was offended, or at least pretended to be, by "tableaux vivants where divers beauties, contrary to every principle of good taste and Southern feminine delicacy, display their charms through picture frames or stretch their finely moulded limbs on the floor or on sofas and lounges in the picturesque attitudes of famous pieces of sculpture." Gentlemen testified that "the living statuary is by no means so ravishing as the low-bosomed dresses which are now in vogue. . . . One is not surprised to hear that marriages of very doubtful authenticity have occurred in certain circles."[22]

However Bagby's imagination was fired by those tableaux, they were often merely elaborate efforts to illustrate words in the fashionable party game of charades. Volunteer actresses included the most eligible maids of native and refugee society, like "Hetty" and "Jennie," the Cary sisters of Baltimore; their cousin "Connie" from Alexandria; and "Tudy," "Buck" and "Mamie," the Prestons of Columbia. Sometimes even the widow Phoebe Pember joined them after she had found quarters that allowed her to enjoy evenings away from Chimborazo.

Phoebe stumped her audience the night she appeared in a game of charades dressed in military gray. Sighing aloud, she produced from one pocket a hardtack and from another a hunk of army bacon, and began gnawing them hungrily. Repeating this three times, she waited for someone to guess that she was acting out "ingratiate." No one did.

Usually the actors were young soldiers, bureaucrats, journalists, or spry grandfathers, stage props for the ladies. But on at least one occasion the band struck up "See, the conquering hero comes!," curtains parted, and "Forth strode grand 'Jeb' Stuart, in full uniform, his stainless sword unsheathed, his noble face luminous with inward fire."[23]

Connie Cary told of cavalryman Fitz Lee's "new toy . . . a little negro boy," which "when wound up, danced Ethiopian minstrel fashion" while Lee sang "cornshucking tunes." The boy was "the delight of Richmond salons" that winter.[24]

Everyone laughed at the well-worn story of the dashing young blade who excited the ladies "by swelling around . . . in enormous cavalry boots up to his hips, big loud-jingling brass spurs, and gauntlets that almost swallowed his armpits." Approaching a beauty, he saluted and tried to pull off his huge right glove to shake hands. It refused to come off, and while he struggled with it she said sweetly, "Never mind, sir; never mind, you needn't dismount." After fleeing the city in embarrassment, her victim was said to have " 'jined' the infantry and got himself killed at the first opportunity."[25]

No belle of Richmond was petitioned more eagerly than Sally Buchanan "Buck" Preston. Soldier after soldier fell for her, then fell in battle—"there seemed a spell upon her lovers." Among them were gallants with such names as Ransom Calhoun and Bradfute Warwick.[26] The most determined was John Bell Hood of Kentucky, once commander of the Texas brigade, who was badly wounded while leading a division at Gettysburg, then lost a leg at Chickamauga, but kept on fighting.

A tall, sad-eyed, and socially awkward general with a flowing blond beard, he was called Sam by his friends. Between his campaigns and Buck's flirtation with others, she played him along for months, but at war's end she grieved because her family had vetoed their marriage.[27]

Buck's father, Colonel John Smith Preston, rich from sugar plantations in Louisiana, was now head of the Confederate conscription bureau. On Christmas Day, 1863, the table at the Prestons' was loaded as if there were no war: oyster soup, boiled mutton, ham, boned turkey, wild duck, partridge, plum pudding, sauterne, sherry, Burgundy, and Madeira. Outside the door, a gaggle of schoolboys cheered Hood as he entered. Jeb Stuart's towering Prussian aide, Heros von Borcke, dropped in after dinner but did not entertain as usual; shot through the throat in a cavalry fight, he could not speak.[28]

On the streets, boys popped firecrackers, and there was at least the standard quota of staggering overcelebrators. Shopkeepers brightened their windows with bottles of colored liquid, and one restaurant drew a street crowd with a tethered white owl, rolling its great yellow eyes. Eggnog flowed liberally, though holiday demand had driven milk up to $20 a gallon and rough brandy was six times as expensive. At Chimborazo, Phoebe Pember spread twenty-four gallons of nog, a dozen turkeys, and seven gallons of oysters among the few patients left since the pace of nearby war had slowed.

A visiting bishop preached at St. Paul's and assured his listeners: "He who was a man of sorrows and acquainted with grief, who had not where to lay his head, and was hated without a cause, knew how to sympathize with us, who have not a friend or ally on earth."[29]

Robert E. Lee was not in the bishop's audience. In the days before Christmas the Confederate Congress had passed a resolution thanking him for his service, and he stayed to inspect the city's defenses after conferring with Davis. When a Richmond lady invited him to dinner, he chastised her for her extravagance, saying citizens should be ashamed to indulge themselves when soldiers in the field were living on a quarter pound of bacon a day. Since the armies along the Rappahannock had dug in for the winter, Lee might have spent the holiday with his ailing wife. But while his soldiers were hungry and far from home, he would not take his ease. He returned to his headquarters in the field.[30]

Around Belle Isle, ice formed on the river. John Whitten of the Fifth Iowa told his diary that on Christmas, prisoners there "did not get anything to eat today until eight oclock at night and then nothing but turnips."[31] But there was minor celebration when a shipment arrived from the North two days later. Weston Ferris of Connecticut was delighted to draw an overcoat and blanket, and managed to get a shipping box to make a floor for his tent: "Although it was not very soft, it made quite a comfortable bed, and I suffered less from the rheumatism."[32]

*   *   *

"To-day closes the gloomiest year of our struggle."[33]

That was the *Examiner*'s assessment on New Year's Eve. Each January 1 of the war had been gloomier than the one before, and nothing from any direction suggested that 1864 might be brighter. Davis strained to put a good face on Confederate prospects as he and Varina opened the president's house to honor 66-year-old William "Extra Billy" Smith, who had just made a one-hour inaugural speech as Virginia's new governor. Smith got his nickname in the 1830s, when he ran a mail coach service between Washington and Georgia, winning a reputation for extracting extra payments from the government. Before the war he had served as state legislator, congressman, and for four years as governor. When Governor Letcher offered him a political generalship, Smith was an exception among politicians—he declined, saying he was "wholly ignorant of drill and tactics." But apparently that was no disadvantage to a regimental commander; Smith accepted a colonelship, and after two years of war and a serious wound, was promoted to brigadier. Elected governor again in May 1863, he fought at Gettysburg before returning to Richmond to take office.[34]

Smith's predecessor, the doughty John Letcher, left office "in a blaze of apple toddy and speechifications," Bagby wrote. "Honest John has given very general satisfaction, I think, during his arduous gubernatorial term. . . ."[35]

Among those who squelched the chance of any holiday respite for the president was North Carolina governor Zebulon B. Vance, who had written complaining of "friendly" cavalry's depredations in some of his counties and threatening to call out his state militia to defend against Confederate troops. There is such discontent, wrote Vance, that "I have concluded that it will be perhaps impossible to remove it, except by making some effort at negotiation" with the Union.

Davis must have been framing his reply as he went through the motions of hospitality on New Year's Day. He reminded Vance that Lincoln had said that "we can only expect his gracious pardon by emancipating all our slaves, swearing allegiance and obedience to him and his proclamations, and becoming in point of fact the slaves of our own negroes." "This struggle," Davis wrote, "must continue until the enemy is beaten out of his vain confidence in our subjugation. Then and not until then will it be possible to treat of peace."[36]

The only ripple of anticipation that day was in talk of an approaching

hero, a general from the West, an occasion for the kind of festive welcome that had excited the city so often in the days after Sumter. He was
Brigadier General John Hunt Morgan, leader of spectacular cavalry
raids against the Yankees in Kentucky and Indiana before being captured on a venture into Ohio the previous July. Four months later he escaped by tunneling out of prison in Columbus. Because the Yankees had
jailed his captured horsemen as common criminals, Morgan was coming
to urge the same treatment for an equal number of Union prisoners.

On the snowy morning of January 8, a crowd pressed around the Ballard House hotel, clamoring to see the fabled raider. Mayor Mayo escorted him out as bands played and paraded to City Hall. There the
mayor praised Morgan, adding that his name and fame "have been ren-
dered doubly dear to us by the savage cruelty and indignity with which
he has been treated by our savage foe."[37]

Between greetings and conferences, Morgan visited General Dow in
Libby Prison; Federal officials had said they were holding Morgan's
men as hostages for the safety of Dow and his captured command. The
generals exchanged greetings, and Dow congratulated Morgan on his
escape. Then he introduced him to Colonel Abel Streight, Morgan's
Union counterpart in the West, who had been captured eight months
earlier on a raid into Alabama.

As Morgan exchanged gentlemanly banter with the Federal officers
at Libby, he had no idea what was going on two floors beneath his feet.
His exploits had inspired both friend and enemy.

* * *

On Saturday night, January 30, 1864, a 17-year-old boy sneaked out of
Richmond, headed for Major General Benjamin Butler's headquarters
at Fortress Monroe. Five days later, after slipping across the Chickahominy and into Union lines on the Peninsula, he delivered to Butler
this message, written in cipher:

> It is intended to remove to Georgia very soon all the Federal pris-
> oners; butchers and bakers to go at once. They are already notified
> and selected. Quaker knows this to be true. Are building batteries
> on the Danville road.
>   This from Quaker: Beware of new and rash council! Beware!
> This I send you by direction of all your friends. No attempt
> should be made with less than 30,000 cavalry, from 10,000 to
> 15,000 infantry to support them, amounting in all to 40,000 or
> 45,000 troops. Do not underrate their strength and desperation.
> Forces could probably be called into action in from five to ten
> days; 25,000, mostly artillery. Hoke's and Kemper's brigades gone

to North Carolina; Pickett's in or about Petersburg. Three regiments of cavalry disbanded by General Lee for want of horses.
Morgan is applying for 1,000 choice men for a raid.[38]

Butler questioned the messenger, who said he was sent by "Miss
Lizzie" Van Lew.* The boy said he had stayed with her for a week before
setting out, and "Miss Lizzie said you would take care of me . . . [she]
told me what to tell you." Marking the material "Private and immediate," Butler forwarded it to Secretary of War Stanton, assuring him
that it came "from a lady in Richmond, with whom I am in correspondence."[39]

Much of this information had been fed to Van Lew by "Mr. Palmer"
and "Quaker," two other key operatives in the Union underground. Another, "Mr. Holmes," had given the boy $1,000 in Confederate money to
buy his way across the lines.[40]

Charles Palmer was a shipping agent, a "loud-talking, violent" opponent of secession who had been held briefly on treason charges after trying to intercede for John Minor Botts when martial law was declared in
1862.[41] As for "Quaker," the boy told Butler that "he does not wish any
one to know his name; he does not wish to be known by any other
name." By one account, "Quaker" was Thomas McNiven, a Scottish
baker who reportedly picked up information from Mary Elizabeth
Bowser at the president's house.[42]

Van Lew's dispatch and the boy's report from Palmer, "Quaker," and
Holmes all confirmed that, as the Confederates increasingly suspected,
Union officers were planning some kind of strike at Richmond, either to
capture the city or to free the suffering Yankee prisoners. Van Lew's information that the prisoners would be sent to Georgia "very soon" accelerated the Federal plans.

The boy quoted Palmer as saying "that Richmond could be taken eas-
ier now than at any other time since the war began. He thought it would
take about 10,000 cavalry and 30,000 infantry." "Quaker's" suggestion
was to feint at Petersburg, have Meade keep Lee busy on the Rappahannock, land a few hundred men at White House as a distraction, then
rush 10,000 cavalry into the city. Holmes told the boy to inform Butler
that "Drewry's Bluff is the strongest point; he said you must come
around Richmond on the other side."[43]

Behind the battlements of Fortress Monroe, General Butler made his

*This is the earliest surviving official documentation of Van Lew's intelligence dispatches
to the Union army. In 1866, fearful that ex-Confederates would take revenge if they knew
the extent of her undercover work, Van Lew requested from the U.S. War Department all
records of her wartime activities. Only scattered items remain in the National Archives.

own estimate of what was needed. He believed that Richmond had been stripped of defenders to reinforce operations in North Carolina. "Now, or never, is the time to strike," he told Stanton. "On Sunday [two days later] I shall make a dash with 6,000 men, all I have that can possibly be spared. If we win, it will pay the cost; if we fail, it will at least be in an attempt to do our duty and rescue our friends."[44]

Stanton obviously agreed. On February 5, a column of Yankee cavalry under Brigadier General Isaac J. Wistar set out from New Kent Court House on the Peninsula. It reached Bottom's Bridge on the Chicka-hominy, thirteen miles from Richmond, on the next day. At the same time, Union army elements along the Rappahannock crossed and went through the motions of advancing against Lee. But when Wistar's cav-alry tried to cross at Bottom's Bridge at 3:00 in the morning, heavy fire flashed out of the darkness from waiting infantry; a New York private, accused of murdering his lieutenant, had escaped from his Union guards and deserted to warn the Confederates. This pocket of resistance turned the raiders back to base.[45]

Still, the effort made it clear that Butler—and ranking officials in Washington—took seriously the intelligence sent by Van Lew. She and her colleagues, including a 17-year-old boy, were aware of what the Fed-erals hoped to do. And unlike John Hunt Morgan, she also knew some-thing of what was happening at that moment beneath Libby Prison.

*   *   *

Colonel Thomas E. Rose of the Seventy-Seventh Pennsylvania Volun-teers was captured at Chickamauga on September 20, 1863, and arrived at Libby ten days later. The moment he arrived, he began looking for a way out.[46]

The arrival of the Chickamauga prisoners led to further overcrowd-ing at Libby, where rows of men already had to sleep "spoon fashion" against one another and turn over at the same time in the night. To make room, guards had to allow Yankees to cook in a previously unused basement space, in the corner of a dark, straw-filled room the inmates called "rat hell."[47]

One of the prisoners, Frank E. Moran of the Seventy-third New York, later described Rose's quest in detail. From the windows above, Rose saw workmen descend into a sewer line paralleling the riverside canal. With chisels and broken tools pilfered from the workshop, he and Major A. G. Hamilton of the Twelfth Kentucky Cavalry started to dig through the basement wall toward the sewer. But then the Confederates closed off the basement again, so Rose and his companion probed for other ways out.

After almost being caught several times groping about in the dark, they considered and rejected the idea of a mass breakout by force. Then Hamilton found a way to cut through the back of a kitchen fireplace and drop into the "rat hell" below to tunnel again toward the sewer. At one point Rose almost suffocated when he was caught tight in the hole. By then, word of what the growing work party was doing night after night had spread among the prisoners, so Rose swore to secrecy a group first of seventy, then of many more.

Hacking away in the dark with spoons and broken hand tools, hardly able to breathe in the narrow tunnel, Rose inched toward the sewer. Then foul water began to seep in; the sewer was below canal level. Doing their best to seal up and hide that tunnel, the determined soldiers began digging again toward a smaller connecting sewer. After thirty-nine nights of labor in the stench below the prison, they thought they were about to break out at last when they found that the sewer was made of thick oak impenetrable by their dull tools.

But Rose would not quit. He had estimated the distance from the prison to an enclosed yard across Twenty-first Street, about fifty feet away. After poking into the basement wall several times, he found a spot where he began digging in that direction.[48]

In their desperation the tunnelers were now working in shifts, night and day. Routinely, twice a day, prison clerk Ross had to count the inmates. When five of them were secretly digging away below, colleagues tried to sneak to the end of the line and be counted twice to cover their absence. Ross was so annoyed when his count was off that one day a batch of Yankees played a joke on him by tiptoeing to the end of the line. Ross counted first too many, then too few, and exploded.[49]

The prisoners laughed so hard that Ross finally laughed with them, but the next day a reinforced guard came to call the roll by names and found that two men were missing. One of them sneaked back from the tunnel later, telling the guard that he had fallen asleep and missed the count. The other stayed in the fetid basement with the rats until he arranged to come up to sleep at night and descend each day. Then Colonel Rose halted day work; it had become too dangerous. Exhausted and eager to complete the job, one digger broke the surface in the street but was not seen by guards.

Looking out at that broken spot, Rose plotted the course and distance for a final surge of tunneling. But the Confederates had become suspicious and began checking into hidden corners. Discovery seemed inevitable. Rose himself led the digging for two straight days, chunking with his little chisel, sending dirt back out in a wooden spittoon. Finally, after twenty-four consecutive hours at it, he was cramped and gasping for breath. Almost frantic, he pounded upward—and broke through the loose earth and saw the stars above.[50]

Pulling himself through, he quietly inspected the yard and the way out. Then he descended again, dragging a plank to hide the tunnel opening. Back at Libby, he whispered the news to his colleagues. Some wanted to escape immediately, but by then it was 3:00 a.m., too close to first light. Rose organized two groups to steal out the next night, an hour apart, fifteen men at a time.

At 7:00 p.m. on Tuesday, February 9, fifty-four nights after he began digging his first tunnel, Rose led his group down and out to freedom. But before the second batch started, dozens of others heard what was happening and crowded into the basement and the long-secret tunnel. Despite the clatter, no Confederates intervened. At daylight guards found a plank hung from a window by a rope of blanket strips to mislead them away from the tunnel. At morning count, clerk Ross "was non-plussed." When he called the roll alphabetically, "lo! One-hundred and nine Yanks were non-est." Among them were eleven colonels, seven majors, and thirty-two captains.[51]

General Winder was furious, and gave an old-army tongue-lashing to Libby's commandant, Major Thomas P. Turner. After examining the building's exterior he concluded that the only way the prisoners could have escaped was by bribing their guards. He threw all that night's sentries into Castle Thunder, where they were searched for greenbacks. Dragoons raced in all directions in pursuit of the escaped Yankees. Days later, a recaptured officer told the Confederates about the tunnel; "a youthful contraband was then taken into the cellar and started through the hole and presently exhibited his grinning face over the fence of the warehouse yard."[52]

Only one of the escapees was caught within the city limits. But eventually, after cold nights of flight and days of hiding on the Peninsula, Colonel Rose was recaptured within sight of Union pickets. Frank Moran, who rushed to join the exodus and wrote about it, was caught near Charlottesville. In all, 48 of the 109 Yankees were brought back, but 59 made it to friendly lines, and two were drowned trying.*[53]

* * *

The night Rose and his colleagues broke out, Elizabeth Van Lew had disguised herself in old clothes and sunbonnet, with a basket of cakes on

---

*Pennsylvania-Indiana rivalry surfaced in postwar accounts of the escape by admirers of Colonels Rose of the Seventy-seventh Pennsylvania and Streight of the Fifty-first Indiana. Lieutenant A. C. Roach of Indiana wrote a version that differed little from that recounted by Frank Moran—except that in it Streight played the leading role.[54]

her arm, and walked unrecognized to a farmhouse on the outskirts of Richmond. There her brother John was hiding, waiting to flee through the lines after being ordered to report for conscription into the Confederate army. John was 39 years old and had gotten repeated medical exemptions, but as Southern manpower dwindled, deferments were cut back and Congress had ended the substitute system. John, unwilling to fight for a government that he abhorred, was ready to leave home for the duration.

His sister arrived late that night, expecting to tell him goodbye. She went to bed as the farmer's kindly wife sat by puffing a pipe, but "some strange nervousness or presentiment" kept her awake. In the morning her driver came with supplies for John's trip—and word of "great trouble and excitement . . . great danger."

Elizabeth had been involved for weeks in plans for a major prison break. She had prepared to help, had put up blankets over the windows of one of her parlors, and arranged beds in waiting for escapees. But she could not know exactly when the tunnelers would break free. Now, at the very moment when she would have been of most use to the fleeing prisoners, she was "greatly distressed" at being away from home.

Some of the escapees had knocked at the door of her servants' quarters on Twenty-fourth Street, asking for Colonel Streight, who had also got away. They begged to come in. But others stood watching in the darkness, across the street by St. John's Church. The servants, fearing a ruse by Winder's men to trap the Van Lews, turned them all away.

When John Van Lew heard the news from the driver, he realized that official vigilance would be heightened and gave up his hope of crossing the lines to the North. But his sister refused to give up her efforts to prevent his marching to war against the Union.

By early 1864, Elizabeth had recast herself as a half-crazy old woman, visiting the prisons in smudged black clothing and talking to herself. Inside the prisons she made her true self known. She smuggled messages back and forth, often in the double bottom of an antique plate warmer. After she heard one guard tell another that he was going to check that warmer next time, she filled the bottom with boiling water, and when the guard asked to see it, she slipped off the cover and handed him the hot warmer. With an oath, he dropped it.

Yankees who had escaped—some through bribes, some by feigning sickness or acquiring Confederate uniforms—knew that Van Lew was ready to help them on their way. She had begun hiding fugitives, singly or in small groups, in a secret upstairs room where the roof of the great portico met the wall of her mansion. But while her pose as a harmless, dotty spinster fooled many a prison guard, Winder's detectives were still suspicious.

She wrote of how a disheveled young man had come to her house and said, "I wish to tell you something—something that will interest the government."

"I know of nothing you can tell me that would be of interest to me," she said.

He pressed her, asking to board there; when she said she had no room, he offered to sleep in the library, on the floor, anywhere. Finally Van Lew got rid of him, sure that he had been sent to spy. Soon afterward she saw him marching in a Confederate uniform.[55]

Despite the fact that Van Lew was under constant suspicion, General Winder still treated her with special courtesy. (After the prison break, guards were posted to watch the Van Lew house, but as Phoebe Pember put it, the authorities were "too delicate minded to search the premises.")[56] Van Lew's very defiance, her brashness in approaching Winder, may have thrown him off—or he may have thought that by opening his door to her he could catch her in a mistake. Now, with her brother about to be taken away, she walked through streets where cavalrymen rode three abreast scouring the city for escaped Yankees, and called on Winder for help.

She told him frankly that her brother had been conscripted and had deserted. Winder said, "Bring him to me tomorrow morning and I will do what I can for him." When Elizabeth arrived with John, the general looked him over and promised to ask the army physician to extend his medical exemption. The doctor refused, so Winder next wrote to Major Thomas G. Peyton at Camp Lee, asking him to give John three days' furlough and allow him to choose his regiment. He advised John to pick Company C of the Eighteenth Virginia, because "that is mine, and I can protect you." Peyton grumbled but gave the deserter this privilege.

Still not satisfied, Elizabeth and John sought advice from a lawyer, Powhatan Roberts. But Roberts, a Southern patriot, was against exemptions "when men were risking their carcasses." Elizabeth noted that he was not risking his own carcass, and as he praised the Confederacy she raised her arm and burst out, "It is a damned rotten concern, & I pledge myself to do all I can against it!"

She carried out her pledge, yet Winder kept his word to the Van Lews. John joined the specified company. Elizabeth said he never wore an army uniform, and went on duty only once, as a guard during rumors of attack. She wrote that later, when she offered the general $6,000 in Confederate bills for further favors to John, Winder was insulted. Still, he defended special treatment for Van Lew, because, he said, John's conscription was "a clear case of personal animosity to the family."*

When Elizabeth was not at home on the night of the tunnel escape, Colonel Streight and three of his comrades found a friendly woman to lead them to a small house near Howard's Grove Hospital northeast of the city. There another, sickly woman sheltered them. Six days after the breakout, one of the hiding soldiers asked her to bring Van Lew to see them.

Elizabeth came; these men were heroes to her. Afterward she sat and wrote for Streight her long version of the cause of the war, to complete the conversation they had begun that night. Some to whom Van Lew spoke years later have written that Streight and a few comrades hid in Van Lew's house before slipping out of Richmond, but her own account does not corroborate this. Eventually this group of Federals set out to cross the lines on a bitterly cold night. Though their guide abandoned them, they reached Union lines after a long and painful march.[57]

Whether the great tunnel escape was judged a success or a failure depended on whether the judge was one of the majority who made it to freedom or one of those who were caught and returned to even grimmer conditions than before. Colonel Rose, back in captivity, certainly was not satisfied. Neither was "Beast" Butler, and neither was Abraham Lincoln, who personally involved himself in the next scheme to relieve the suffering Union prisoners.

---

*Later, when Lee's pleas for manpower at the front intensified, even Winder's protection was not enough. John Van Lew deserted again in the summer of 1864. This time he made it to the North and returned to Richmond only after the war had ended.

CHAPTER TWENTY

TO DESTROY THE
HATEFUL CITY

*F*or prisoners, deserters, saboteurs, spies, blockade runners, and increasingly defeatist citizens, the paths of flight from Richmond were at least as imaginative as those for slaves on the prewar Underground Railroad.

While patrols were still tracking down the tunnel escapees, detectives arrested a certain Dr. McClure, an embalmer of the dead, for "aiding and abetting the escape of parties going north." In "going about the country with his coffins," war clerk Jones wrote, McClure "has been detected taking Jews and others through the lines. Several *live men* have been found in his coffins."[1]

George Bagby reported "a well-constructed underground rail road from this city to the Potomac, to Williamsburg, and to Norfolk. Negroes find little or no difficulty in escaping. . . ." Under the circumstances, he wrote, "the escaped Yankee officers will owe their recapture to their own stupidity more than to the vigilance of the Baltimore dignitaries who rule this wretched city."[2]

On the midwinter night when a fire broke out in the basement of the presidential mansion, the blaze was confined to one room because the household was awake and alert—the Davises were entertaining upstairs. The *Examiner* reflected helpfully that if the arsonist had waited a few hours, his or her effort would have been more effective. "Fancy having to be always ready to have your servants set your house on fire—bribed to do it," Mary Chesnut wrote. Robberies and servants running away to the Yankees with household silver did not make a happy home.[3]

New rumors of assassination plots ran through the city. Indeed, just before Christmas a bullet had whizzed past Davis's ear as he took an evening ride. Now guards were assigned to follow him on horseback. He told Congress that "spies are continually coming and going in our midst"—something other Richmonders had been saying since Sumter.

He complained that offenders arrested on accurate information were being released because government testimony did not stand up in court. Northern papers, he said, suggested that General Butler was scheming against Richmond. "If, as is not improbable, his designs should point to servile insurrection in Richmond, incendiarism, and the destruction of public works . . . how can we hope to fathom it and reach the guilty emissaries and contrivers but by incompetent negro testimony?"[4]

The answer, he said, was to suspend the writ of habeas corpus again. On February 17, Congress agreed, then adjourned and went home, grumbling about the president and his prosecution of the war.

Within days after Congress had departed, Davis sprang a surprise that would have shaken the Capitol with outrage if the legislators had been there. Apparently without consulting any advisers—knowing what their advice would be—he named Braxton Bragg commanding general, responsible for "the conduct of military operations in the armies of the Confederacy."

The capital's newspapers railed against the idea of seemingly rewarding a general for failure in battle. By doing so, Davis consciously flouted the opinion of most of the South's generals and politicians. But the contentious Bragg's shortcomings had been in command roles, where he had repeatedly failed to follow up tactical success. Back at headquarters he was a competent staff officer. And his new assignment was not what its title implied; he would not command the generals in the field but function as a chief of staff, advising Davis and taking some of the administrative load off the president and Adjutant General Cooper. Nevertheless, resentment of the Bragg appointment roiled official Richmond for days, until the Yankees demanded attention again.[5]

*　*　*

On or about New Year's Day, newly promoted Union colonel Ulric Dahlgren had called at the White House in Washington to see his father's close friend, the president. There, wrote one of his colleagues, "we had an interview with Mr. Lincoln in regard to the raid on Richmond, for the purpose of liberating the prisoners confined there." Reports of cruelty to Union prisoners had aroused Lincoln and all the North, and the president was "very desirous" of relieving their suffering.[6]

George E. Pond, then a lieutenant of Massachusetts infantry, wrote that Lincoln also hoped to stir disaffection in the South by scattering copies of his December amnesty proclamation behind Confederate lines. That announcement promised to restore citizenship and property—except slaves—to all those in occupied territory who took the oath of loyalty to the Union.[7]

After conferring with Lincoln, Brigadier General Judson Kilpatrick reported to Major General George G. Meade, commanding the Army of the Potomac facing Lee. Kilpatrick brought plans for a massive cavalry raid to liberate the prisoners in Richmond and destroy Confederate communications and supplies. Meade was unenthusiastic but, considering the president's sponsorship of the mission, he was ready to cooperate.

Near the end of raw February, Brigadier General George Armstrong Custer and 1,500 Union horsemen crossed the swollen Rapidan River beyond the west flank of Lee's army to draw Confederate cavalry in that direction. The next night, Yankee scouts surprised and captured Southern pickets at Ely's Ford, east of Lee. Kilpatrick and Dahlgren crossed behind them with some 4,000 troopers and rode unmolested toward Richmond while Meade's infantry demonstrated on Lee's left. With the Confederate cavalry distracted and telegraph lines cut, the Kilpatrick-Dahlgren force rode south for more than twelve hours before the capital heard that Yankees were on the way.[8]

Kilpatrick was familiar with the roads above Richmond; he had led the most damaging column of Stoneman's raiders during the battle of Chancellorsville the previous spring. The Yankee plan now was for him to thrust at the capital from the north while Dahlgren split away with some 500 men to cross the James River above Richmond.

Dahlgren would swing downstream on the south side to free the Yankees at Belle Isle, while Kilpatrick dashed straight in to free those at Libby and other prisons. Then Dahlgren would recross and rejoin Kilpatrick. With thousands of prisoners on the loose, they would torch the city and capture Confederate leaders.[9] What they intended to do with those leaders may have led eventually to one of the great tragedies of American history.

At Libby imprisoned Union officers had been secretly notified that the raid was planned, and formed companies to fight as infantry under whoever liberated them. Then they were told that Major Thomas P. Turner, the prison commandant, had planted kegs of gunpowder in the basement, "enough to blow up the prison and prisoners." When artillery was heard in the outskirts, Turner declared that "I do not expect to live if your cavalry get into the city. I shall stick to my post of duty until Kilpatrick reaches here, then every damned Yankee in this place will be blown to hell."*[10]

The presence of a romantic figure like Dahlgren at the head of a raiding column "must have lent inspiration to the daring undertaking, and must have added a kind of an adventurous charm to the entire spirit of this bold and questioning raid."[12] Ulric was the fair-haired son of Rear Admiral John Adolphus Dahlgren, chief of the U.S. Navy's Ordnance Bureau. After service at Second Bull Run, Fredericksburg, and Chancellorsville, young Dahlgren had lost a leg in the Gettysburg campaign. For his dash and bravery, he was promoted to colonel at the age of 21. Now, newly fitted with an artificial leg, he was back in the saddle on the most audacious ride of his life.

As a guide, Dahlgren had an ex-slave who was said to know the way to a little-used James River ford. Plodding through rain and darkness, his riders passed up a chance to capture a Confederate artillery park but destroyed a stretch of railroad. Early on March 1 they struck the James near Confederate Secretary of War Seddon's Sabot Hill plantation in Goochland County.[13]

Slaves informed the Yankees that the former governor, Henry Wise, was visiting relatives at a neighboring manor house, and Wise barely slipped away ahead of the raiders. Mistakenly thinking that another nearby place was the Seddon property, Dahlgren set fire to outbuildings there. Then as he and his men approached Sabot Hill itself, a servant called Aunt Lou rushed in yelling, "Lawdy, chillun, git up and dress quick as yer can. De whole hillside is blue wid Yankees!"

Dahlgren pounded at the door and was greeted graciously by Mrs. Seddon, who told him that his father had been her beau in Philadelphia years before. At that the polite young colonel doffed his hat and issued orders to halt further burning. He and his staff accepted Mrs. Seddon's invitation to step inside, where they chatted over glasses of twenty-year-old blackberry wine. Later the lady's kinfolk maintained that this inter-

---

*Afterward General Winder said this threat was just a bluff to keep Libby's inmates under control, but a Confederate joint congressional committee in early 1865 confirmed that a mine with "a sufficient quantity of gunpowder" had been planted beneath the prison. The prisoners were notified of this, the report said, and the plan succeeded because they "were awed and kept quiet." A few weeks later, the mine was removed.[11]

lude of calculated hospitality had saved Richmond by allowing Wise time to warn the city's defenders.[14]

Dahlgren thanked Mrs. Seddon and turned back to business, only to discover that the ford had been made impassable by heavy rains. Believing the black guide had deceived him, Dahlgren ordered him hanged by the roadside. There local Confederates left the body swinging for a week to show slaves how the Yankees treated their kind.*[15]

There were only two courses left to Dahlgren: abandon the mission or rush straight downriver into Richmond. With speed and surprise, perhaps he could cross there and reach Belle Isle, whose only bridge was from Manchester on the other side.

Approaching the city, his men heard the sound of cannon from Brook Road, which apparently meant that Kilpatrick had attacked ahead of plan. But then the gunfire faded, suggesting that Kilpatrick had been driven off. Hiding his force in the woods until dark, Dahlgren then charged through Richmond's outer ring of defenses but met heavy, coordinated fire from local troops before he reached the second line.[18]

The capital was fully alert; as fleeing country people arrived telling of hordes of Yankee marauders, the alarm bell had brought defense forces running. Underage boys, overage men, and officers on furlough fell in as volunteer privates. Some outfits—including the Armory, Arsenal, and Tredegar battalions—headed for the outskirts directly from their places of work. The Departmental Battalion, its clerk-reservists scattered around the city, mustered first at Capitol Square.

From there 15-year-old Miles Cary shouldered his Springfield and marched with the clerks out Westham Plank Road. After splashing some four miles through rain and mud, they met troops of the Armory Battalion skedaddling back ahead of Dahlgren's troopers. The Departmentals quickly formed a blocking position across the road at Benjamin Green's farm.

Dahlgren, after breaking through the first defenders, ordered his men to dismount and advance as infantry. They drove right over young Cary in the militia picket line before a salvo from the Departmentals' main body turned them back. As the two sides scuffled in the blackness, Cary

---

*Union officers who helped plan or carry out the raid wrote that the hanged man had been sent as a guide from Washington or from Meade's headquarters. One said he had been the orderly of a captured Confederate signal officer.[16] But William Preston Cabell, who wrote a detailed account of Dahlgren's swath through the Goochland County plantations, said the victim was "a burly negro man from the Stanard place" nearby, and the Richmond *Examiner* reported at the time that he was "the boy Martin, property of David Meems, of Goochland." Others identified the victim as Martin Robinson, a former local slave who had become a free bricklayer.[17]

tried to bayonet Dahlgren, the only Yankee who was still on horseback. Dahlgren slashed and stabbed at the boy with his saber before wheeling away.[19]

Dahlgren thought the stout resistance meant that he had struck regular infantry. His surprise foiled, he was now pressed to escape with his command. Turning northeast, he hoped to skirt the defensive works, then make his way southeast toward Chesapeake Bay. During the night his force split and he rode on with only 100 to 125 troopers.

Kilpatrick, meanwhile, had tried to drive into the city from the north and had been repulsed at the intermediate line of defenses on Brook Road. Bivouacking that night in a stinging snowstorm, his force was surprised and scattered by Confederate cavalry led by Major General Wade Hampton. Joined by the troopers who had strayed away from Dahlgren, Kilpatrick fled down the Peninsula. But Dahlgren had farther to ride.[20]

After crossing the Pamunkey and Mattaponi rivers, Dahlgren trotted into a night ambush near Mantapike, in King and Queen County, set by a motley force including home guards and local cavalrymen on furlough. They shot him down at the head of his column—the only man killed in the quick exchange of fire.[21]

As Dahlgren's body lay in the road, 13-year-old William Littlepage of the King and Queen home guard ran out to search it, hoping to find a watch. Because he didn't look in Dahlgren's overcoat he missed the watch. But in the colonel's inner pockets he found a cigar case, a memorandum book, and some folded papers.

William hid in the woods until morning with Edward W. Halbach, the teacher who had organized the company of schoolboy guards, and a handful of others. At daylight the surrounded Yankees gave themselves up, and the Confederates read the material that had been taken from Dahlgren's body.[22]

The papers included a schedule of when the raiders were to cross each stream and check off each assignment, plus special orders for guides, scouts, pioneers, signalmen, engineers and the entire command, and an address from Dahlgren to his men. That address said:

"You have been selected from brigades and regiments as a picked command to attempt a desperate undertaking—an undertaking which, if successful, will write your names on the hearts of your countrymen that can never be erased. . . ."

Perhaps inspired by Henry V at Agincourt, it warned: "Many of you may fall; but if there is any man here not willing to sacrifice his life in such a great and glorious undertaking, or who does not feel capable of meeting the enemy in such a desperate fight as will follow, let him step out, and he may go hence to the arms of his sweetheart, and read of the braves who swept through the city of Richmond."

But what drew the most attention was this sentence:

"We hope to release the prisoners from Belle Island first, and, having seen them fairly started, we will cross the James river into Richmond, destroying the bridges after us, and exhorting the released prisoners to destroy and burn the hateful city, and do not allow the Rebel leader, Davis, and his traitorous crew to escape."

The language of the special orders was still more pointed:

"The bridges once secured, and the prisoners loose and over the river, the bridges will be secured and the city destroyed. The men must keep together and well in hand, and once in the city it must be destroyed, and Jeff Davis and Cabinet killed."[23]

Halbach reported that he turned the papers over that afternoon to Lieutenant James Pollard of the Ninth Virginia Cavalry, who passed them on to Major General Fitzhugh Lee. Lee delivered them to President Davis, and then to Adjutant General Cooper for safekeeping.[24]

When Davis released the Dahlgren papers to the Richmond press, the city roared demands for reprisal. The *Examiner* predictably blamed what had almost happened on "the milk-and-water spirit in which this war has hither to been conducted." It demanded that the captured raiders be executed as criminals, and that retaliation be ordered against the Union "with the most punctual exactitude."[25]

In a heated cabinet meeting, most of Davis's circle urged that at least some of the raiders be put to death as a warning to the Federals. Davis resisted and was backed up by Robert E. Lee, whose son was still in Yankee hands. As George Bagby put it: "Secretary Seddon was in favor of hanging the whole party, but as his voice was only so much idle wind, it amounted to nothing, and the president's rose-water counsels prevailed."[26]

At Libby Prison the captured raiders were locked below with the first black Union soldiers brought to Richmond, taken in skirmishing near Williamsburg. A sympathetic Yankee upstairs wrote that the smoke and stench in the basement from pine cooking fires and sewers was so stifling that those prisoners sometimes had to lie flat in order to breathe. The recaptured Colonel Rose carved a hole in the flooring above and dropped down playing cards, telling the raiders to turn a king face-up on their table when the guard was not looking. Then he fed cornbread and substitute coffee down to them through a funnel made from a broken bottle.[27]

The Dahlgren papers had personalized the war between Lincoln and

Davis in a way unseen before, and Washington's claim that they were falsified made no impression in the South. True, the written exhortations to kill Davis and his cabinet were so blatant that any prudent officer would hesitate to carry them on such a hazardous mission. But Dahlgren, who had lost a leg to the Rebels, was an impetuous cavalryman not yet 22 years old. When Lee sent photographs of the papers to Meade and asked if they represented official Union policy, Meade, of course, said no. Dahlgren's speech was never delivered to his command, and his orders apparently never issued as written, so those who rode with him insisted that they were false.

Dahlgren's father, the admiral, later asserted that in one place in the papers his family name was misspelled, which proved that the documents were counterfeit. But examination of the original showed that the apparent misspelling was caused by ink soaking through from the opposite side of the sheet. Though debate over the papers' validity would run on into the twentieth century, the weight of evidence suggests that they were indeed genuine.*[28]

* * *

From the outset, many in the South believed that Abraham Lincoln had personally provoked the war, and he was blamed for each escalation of casualties and cruelty. Regardless of who had written the Dahlgren papers' words about killing Davis and his cabinet, those words raised official and popular anger. Already there had been the fire set in Davis's cellar, the rifle shot that sang past his ear, the aborted Wistar raid, and copious rumors of plots. Together with all this, the papers taken from the slain young colonel convinced Davis that Lincoln and Stanton had approved a new level of warfare—including arson, pillage, and assassination.

Well before these threats to his person, Davis and his advisers had approved covert operations to encourage the antiwar underground in the North. In February the Confederate Congress authorized $5 million for

---

*Among the minor clues to this effect is an anonymous "Memoranda of the War" held by the Virginia Historical Society, which quotes Custer himself as denying Federal claims that the Dahlgren papers were forged or altered. Custer allegedly said that the night before he and Dahlgren parted, Dahlgren told him "that he would not take Pres. Davis & his cabinet, but would put them to death, and that he would himself set fire to the first house in Richmond and burn the city. He, Custer, did not think this purpose right."[29]

John C. Babcock, one of Pinkerton and Sharpe's key intelligence operatives in and out of Richmond, was closely involved in planning the raid though he opposed it. In his effects at the Library of Congress is a note saying, "Letters found on Dahlgren's body published in Richmond papers. Authentic report of contents."[30]

the purpose, joining the president's unrealistic hope that the peace movement could swing several northwestern states away from Lincoln in the 1864 election. About the time Davis was debating how to punish Dahlgren's raiders, he heard that a secret society of nearly half a million men was organized and ready to carry out sabotage in seven Union states, if only it had the money. He dispatched agents to Canada with $1 million to seek such opportunities and help escaped Confederate prisoners make their way south.

After the Dahlgren expedition Davis gave serious attention to proposals that he had earlier put aside, for similar raids to rescue Southerners held in Union prisons. And after reading the Dahlgren papers, he listened more carefully to a variety of suggested plots to capture Abraham Lincoln, the man who had sent Dahlgren to Richmond, the man who presumably kept the Union in the war.[31]

*   *   *

Although the government spared the lives of the Yankees who rode with Dahlgren, it vented some of its official anger on the body of Dahlgren himself. On the road where he fell, Confederates had searched his clothing, cut off his left little finger to steal a ring, and taken his finely finished artificial leg to do duty for some maimed Rebel. Then they dumped his body over a fence to protect it from hogs roaming the road. When a rough coffin was completed, they buried him in a shallow grave near the junction since called Dahlgren's Corner.

Ostensibly to identify the body and confirm its connection with the Dahlgren papers, officials ordered it dug up and brought to Richmond. There curious citizens looked on the young colonel's face as the open coffin lay in a boxcar at the York River railroad depot. Then Dahlgren was reburied in an unmarked grave among those of Union prisoners, below Oakwood Cemetery on the northeastern edge of the city. "Where that spot is no one but those concerned in its burial know or care to tell," said the *Examiner.* "It was a dog's burial. . . . Friends and relatives at the North need inquire no further; this is all they will know—he is buried, a burial that befitted the mission upon which he came. . . ."[32]

On behalf of Admiral Dahlgren, General Butler asked that the body be returned to Federal hands by flag-of-truce boat. Colonel Robert Ould, the Confederate commissioner of prisoner exchanges, told the officer who had overseen the secret reburial that the Yankees had promised to ease their exchange policy if the body was returned. After some delay, Davis himself ordered that the officer point out the raider's resting place. But when the grave was opened, the body was gone.[33]

Stirred by insults to their hero Dahlgren, Elizabeth Van Lew and the Unionist underground had vowed to find his grave "and remove his honored dust to friendly care." The man who found it was F. W. E. Lohmann, a 37-year-old Pennsylvania-born restaurant keeper and frequent player in Van Lew's intrigues. He turned up a black cemetery workman who had surreptitiously watched the reburial. With Martin Meredith Lipscomb, a peacetime bricklayer in charge of burying Yankees who died in Richmond—and with a handful of cash—Lohmann persuaded this man to disclose the site.[34]

On the stormy night of April 6, more than a month after Dahlgren's death, Lipscomb, Lohmann, his brother John A. Lohmann, and the unidentified workman dug up the body again. They took it in a mule-drawn wagon to William Rowley's farm not far from Oakwood. There Van Lew and a few other reliable Unionists came to view the body. She remarked on how well preserved it was despite the lapse of time. The following day Lipscomb sent a metal coffin from downtown. Into it the body was transferred and then placed in a wagon, covered by a tightly packed load of young peach trees.

Rowley took the reins and drove the hidden cargo into the city's picket line. He was stopped by guards and endured long minutes of questioning and small talk before being allowed to pass without a search. "If one had run his bayonet into the wagon only a few inches, death would certainly have been the award of this brave man," wrote Van Lew, "—and not only death, but torture to make him reveal those connected with him, his accomplices."[35]

Inside the lines, the two Lohmanns rejoined Rowley and directed him to the farm of Robert Orrick some ten miles northwest of the city. Orrick was an important link in the Union's secret "middle line of communication" that ran intelligence on a weekly schedule that winter, from Richmond north through Fredericks Hall to Meade's army.[36] There in Orrick's orchard, Colonel Ulric Dahlgren was buried yet again, and a peach tree planted in the fresh earth above him. After the war his father would finally retrieve his body and take it home.*[37]

Van Lew made it clear that she realized the danger in the scheme to snatch young Dahlgren's remains out of Confederate hands. At various points she and at least six of her active colleagues were involved, in addition to the cemetery workman and the sympathizers who had come to view the soldier's body. If any of them had been arrested and broken

---

*In November 1865, Dahlgren's artificial leg was recovered in Albemarle County, being worn by N. P. Ballard, a Confederate veteran. One of the detectives who tracked it down was named "Lohman," presumably one of the brothers who moved Dahlgren's remains after the raid. He also recovered the young colonel's missing ring.[38]

down under interrogation, the whole Union network in Richmond might have been rolled up. But Dahlgren's fatal effort to liberate the prisoners, and then the insults to his body, so stirred the Union loyalists that they knowingly risked all to retrieve him. They needed good luck and bad weather to succeed, but that success led them into more strategically important missions during the months ahead.

CHAPTER TWENTY-ONE

RATS, IF FAT, ARE
AS GOOD AS SQUIRRELS

*A*fter failing to liberate prisoners with fire and sword, the Federals decided to bring them home peacefully. Posses were still hunting down stragglers of the Kilpatrick-Dahlgren expedition when flag-of-truce boats began steaming along the James between Richmond and City Point, again exchanging Yankees from Libby and Belle Isle for Confederates from Point Lookout and Fortress Monroe.

On Sunday, March 13, 1864, one of those boats brought back Robert E. Lee's son Rooney, who had been swapped for Union brigadier general Neal Dow. That day at St. Paul's the Lees were among fourteen generals from near and far, kneeling to offer thanks for the hundreds of Southern soldiers returning and to ask help for the tens of thousands who were hungry in the field.[1]

What seemed to be half the town crowded at Rocketts landing to greet the homecoming soldiers. The Armory Band, the City Guard, "all the best ladies of the city with baskets of nice things," were there. As the overpacked truce boats *A. H. Schultz* and *William Allison* approached the wharf, 600 men aboard them sang "Hurrah, hurrah, for Southern rights hurrah!" Waving handkerchiefs and hats, the crowd gave them three cheers, the band played "Dixie," and then the prisoners lifted "three cheers for the ladies of Richmond." For a few hours it was as bright as that spring three years earlier, when many of these weary veterans had marched away as innocent boys.

Shouts of recognition rang from boat to shore and back again. Then when the first boat touched, there was a "hush of intense expectation."

Amid it a child screamed, "Father! I see Father!" As soldiers filed off the boat, the crowd opened a lane for them, watching for familiar faces. Many were disappointed; others fell into embraces long dreamed of.[2]

Jefferson Davis, after welcoming and helping serve refreshments to returnees at Capitol Square, could not make light of the circumstances. He had promised the homecoming soldiers that they would soon be back in service; afterward, as he strolled from the square among friendly admirers, one young woman asked whether those soldiers really wanted to go back to war.

Davis pointed to some adolescents playing around the knees of Thomas Jefferson, George Mason, and Patrick Henry at the base of the Washington Monument. "It may be hard," he said, "but even those boys will have their trial."

When a girl asked how the army could be fed, he said, "I don't see why rats, if fat, are not as good as squirrels. Our men did eat mule meat at Vicksburg; but it would be an expensive luxury now."[3]

He walked on without showing a trace of humor.

* * *

The excited gossip from the truce boats was not all of happy homecoming. News quickly ran through the crowds about "a most astounding affair"—the arrest of General Winder's trusted assistant on suspicion of treason.

He was Philip Cashmyer, the same officer who had blanched when Elizabeth Van Lew slipped him a message from General Butler at Winder's office.

As the *Schultz* took a load of Yankees down the river on March 7, Cashmyer had gone along, as he had often accompanied truce boats. On the way he was seen in close conversation with several Union officers. Then, as the prisoners transferred to the Federal steamer *New York*, Cashmyer passed a package to one of the Yankees, who slipped it into his blouse. The Confederate boat's captain stopped the departing prisoner and told him he could not leave unless he surrendered the package. The Yankee, eager to go home, gave it up without argument, then was held back anyway.

In the package were two documents, one in English and one in German, Cashmyer's family language. On first reading, the papers in English were said to include "all orders from Winder's office recently, calculated to afford the enemy full insight into the military organization of Richmond." The boat captain arrested Cashmyer and sent him to Castle Thunder, where Cashmyer himself had deposited many a suspected traitor to the Confederacy.

Since early in the war, Cashmyer had been at Winder's right hand. His friends in the Richmond press did not want to believe the accusations against him. The *Examiner* noted that in his job, with his wide acquaintance in Maryland and Washington, "he was often called on to vouch for the loyalty of persons coming into the Confederacy," and "at his instigation, suspected persons have been arrested, and upon his intercession others have been released." He had traveled freely all over the Confederacy, carrying dispatches of greatest importance. He had enjoyed the full confidence of Winder and others of high rank, "such was the unlimited faith universally reposed to his integrity to the Southern cause." If the charges were true, the damage would be "incalculable."[4]

It would also be an immense embarrassment to Winder and the establishment figures who had relied on Cashmyer. Now, while the suspect was held in the Castle, the suspicious papers had been placed in Winder's hands for safekeeping. After an "informal investigation"— whether by Winder himself is not clear—the documents were described as merely "odd passports on which Cashmyer had traveled," intended to impress his friends back home in Baltimore. There was a letter from a Yankee held on Belle Isle, who recalled an earlier acquaintance with Cashmyer and asked his help to be paroled. As for the papers in German, they were "simply some information for his family, which might read treason if translated backwards."[5]

The charge against Cashmyer was reduced from treason to "very grave indiscretion." He was released from Castle Thunder to face a court-martial, but that authority refused jurisdiction. Cashmyer insisted on a further inquiry, and after it was cleared and reinstated in his job.[6] Later in the spring Winder was transferred to oversee military prisons south of Richmond, including Andersonville. He took Cashmyer with him.

How much intelligence Cashmyer had passed to Van Lew and Butler is uncertain, but he was perfectly positioned for spying and aiding other spies. Winder obviously protected him; whether he did so only as a personal friend or conceivably knew what Cashmyer was up to remains unclear. So do the reasons for Winder's notable tolerance of Elizabeth Van Lew's provocative behavior. He left no memoir when he collapsed and died of a heart attack in South Carolina two months before the war ended. Cashmyer, who was with him when he died, was easy on Winder when he castigated other Confederate prison officials in a letter to Union investigators after Appomattox.[7]

* * *

With winter waning, the Confederate high command spent much of March in tense conferences, debating how to deploy thinning manpower against the imminent Union offensive.

The day before Rooney Lee returned, his father's commissary officer had sent word that the army was out of meat and had only a day's ration of bread. A month later, things were little better. "I cannot see how we can operate with our present supplies," the commander told Davis. "Any derangement in their arrival, or disaster to the R.R. would render it impossible for me to keep the army together. . . ."[8]

Richmond was awash with rumors that this or that Confederate department, or the whole government, or all nonessential workers, or at least some part of the capital's population, would be sent away into the country because it simply could not be fed. Lee had suggested such a move, because food that might sustain his troops was being waylaid by Richmonders, who were hungry, too.

In April General Bragg urged that passenger trains be cut to one a day so the railroads could give priority to shipping provisions, and that all clerks and bureaucrats who could do their jobs somewhere else be sent away. To relieve the capital of the burden of feeding so many Yankee prisoners and the danger of their breaking free, Winder had sent south as many as 400 a day, so many that he had to retrieve some from Danville prisons to keep the exchange process going. In early April, the total number of prisoners left at Belle Isle was down to a hundred.

Then, as cherry trees blossomed in Richmond, news came that Southern troops and gunboats had recaptured Plymouth, on the North Carolina coast. This seemed to take some of the urgency out of Confederate planning; for the moment, Davis decided to send away only a few hundred employees, mostly the women who signed Confederate Treasury notes.[9]

One new factor dominated the Confederate strategy conferences—the new Federal general in chief, Ulysses S. Grant. He had already declared his priorities by making his headquarters not in Washington but in the field, with the army facing Lee.

Grant's arrival from the West was felt in Richmond before he made his first moves on the Virginia battlefront: In April, he halted all prisoner exchanges. "It is hard on our men held in Southern prisons not to exchange them," he explained later, "but it is humanity to those left in the ranks to fight our battles. Every man we hold, when released on parole or otherwise, becomes an active soldier against us at once either directly or indirectly."[10] As far as he was concerned there would be no more scenes of homecoming at Rocketts, no more lightening of Richmond's prisoner burden, no more additions to Confederate regimental rolls by flag-of-truce boat. The squeeze was on.

Grant could see the war whole; he issued orders for a spring campaign to march one Union army toward Mobile on the Gulf coast, one toward Atlanta, and three others deeper into Virginia. Meade, with Grant at his shoulder, would attack Lee—"Wherever Lee goes, there you will go also," Grant told him. Major General Franz Sigel would move up the Shenandoah Valley. Ben Butler would advance up the south side of the James River. Grant realized that against such a concerted, war-wide offensive, the outnumbered Confederates could not effectively shift divisions from theater to theater the way they had done against uncoordinated Union moves in the past.

In a matter of days, roads would dry and troops would march. Lee brought Longstreet back from the West and consolidated scattered detachments to bolster his strength on the Rapidan. Beauregard was ordered up from Charleston to take over the defenses of Petersburg. Grant ordered the brilliantly aggressive Major General Philip H. Sheridan from the West to command his cavalry corps and rounded up more thousands for the Union armies about to attack, keeping his regional manpower advantage at better than two to one. Both sides understood that this could be the final campaign.

*   *   *

At 1 o'clock on the warm, breezy last day of April, Mrs. Davis left her children playing peacefully in her room and took a basket of lunch to her husband's office in the mansion; the president worked so much and slept so little that he sometimes forgot to eat. Varina had just uncovered the basket when their Irish nurse Catharine came running.

In Varina's absence 4-year-old Joseph had strayed onto the balcony across the back of the house, climbed onto the railing and slipped, falling to the brick walk below. His brother Jeff ran down to him. "Joe wouldn't wake up," he told Catharine. The president and his wife knelt at the boy's side but could do nothing. In a few minutes Joe was dead.

"This child was Mr. Davis's hope, and greatest joy in life," Varina wrote. He had often toddled into his father's office, where Davis was glad to interrupt business while Joe said his prayers at the president's knee.

Distraught at Joe's death, Davis kept repeating, "Not mine, oh, Lord, but thine." When a messenger brought a dispatch, Davis held it, at first unseeing, tried to deal with it, and then could not. "I must have this day with my little child," he said, and handed the paper to someone else. Varina's account did not describe her own hysteria, but Mary Chesnut could hear her screams. Mary and other friends gathered at the mansion that evening. By then the only sounds were the president upstairs pacing, pacing, and the nurse weeping on the floor beside the boy's flower-strewn body.

The next day Joe was buried at Hollywood Cemetery with hundreds of Richmond children clustered about, covering his coffin with boughs and blossoms.[11]

Jefferson Davis's physical ailments and mental compulsions had made official life so painful for him that such a sudden personal blow seemed more than a fragile man could endure. Ten years earlier, in Washington, he had been devastated by the death of his infant son Samuel; Joe had replaced Sam as the father's favorite. Now three children were left: Margaret, 9; Jeff, 7; and William, born in the presidential mansion in December 1861. Some solace would come in summer, when Varina bore another daughter, named for herself.

Davis tried to forget his pain in the crisis building around him. He had to. The day after Joe was buried, the new Congress convened to hear a presidential *tour d'horizon* that offered only the faintest glimmer of optimism. Lawmakers promptly began debating whether to adjourn, because the president had laid out so little for them to do. Reports came of Federal infantry movements beyond the Rapidan, and concentrations building down the Peninsula. Scouts sighted heavy boat traffic in Hampton Roads.

Soon after midnight on the morning of May 4, Grant started Meade's Army of the Potomac across the Rapidan onto the east flank of Lee's Army of Northern Virginia. That same morning, Ben Butler's newly named Army of the James loaded aboard transports to head upriver toward Richmond.

"We have many rumors today, and nothing authentic," wrote war clerk Jones the next day, "except that some of the enemy's transports are in the James River, and landing some troops, a puerile demonstration, perhaps. . . . It may be the armies of the United States are demoralized, and if so, if Grant is beaten, I shall look for a speedy end of the invasion."[12]

*   *   *

In the Spotsylvania Wilderness, where Lee had routed Joe Hooker a year before, the Confederates slammed into Grant's force with the same fury that had won at Chancellorsville. For three days the armies fought with little change of ground before Grant held back. Losses exceeded 25,000, most of them Yankees. If the new Federal commander followed his predecessors' pattern, he would withdraw across the Rappahannock and Rapidan to try again much later.

But Grant was not McDowell, McClellan, Pope, Burnside, or Hooker; instead of withdrawing, he ordered the most foreboding tactical shift of the war for the Confederates. He sideslipped south, trying to beat Lee to the key crossroads of Spotsylvania Court House. Lee's advance guard got there first, but barely. Spasmodically, for nearly two weeks, the two sides struggled in close combat. When it was over, another 27,000 casualties were counted—again, most of them Yankees.

Just as Grant was not like the Union generals before him, the Richmond of 1864 was not like the city that had panicked at the threat of a phantom gunboat in 1861, the capital from which a scared Congress had fled in 1862. When Richmonders gathered downtown to hear the news, "it was not long before it was given out that Grant was whipped out of his boots." One man wanted to know how high the price of gold would jump in New York the next day; another bet that it would be at least $200. "A hundred dollars for Lincoln's best joke on the repulse of Grant," someone offered. "Well, boys," a bystander drawled, "the damned Yankees are whipped and we shall have peace now. The North is played out." This banter went on until the bell rang in the square, but for the moment the alarm was just rehearsal; Grant was still forty miles away.[13]

While Grant was hammering Lee at the Wilderness and Spotsylvania Court House, Ben Butler's force landed on Bermuda Hundred, the neck of land at the junction of the James and Appomattox rivers below Richmond. A division of black troops secured City Point, a black brigade moved up the Peninsula across the Chickahominy, and Federal cavalry struck the vital railroads south of Petersburg. Altogether Butler put more than 38,000 troops into motion against the capital. They were less than half as far away as Grant, and there was no Lee between them and Richmond. Indeed, when those Federals approached, the Confederates facing them were counted in the very few thousands.[14]

In Richmond the time for drills was past. The latest rumors were true: The enemy force coming up the James was much stronger than anticipated. Defenders marched north, east, and south from the city. On the streets, "scarcely a man was to be seen without his musket and cartridge box." The hospitals were ready when hundreds of wounded began arriving from Lee's army.

Fearing another raid to free Union prisoners, officials ordered nearly a thousand enemy officers remaining at the Libby to be shipped to Danville, then on to Georgia. Those Yankees were furious; some refused to answer roll call, while others dumped precious sugar and coffee or cut up blankets and books, determined that their captors would not enjoy the luxuries sent from Washington.[15]

"Unquestionably Richmond is in great DANGER," George Bagby advised his readers farther south, "—greater than it was when McClellan menaced it. . . . Every resource, mental and physical, and all the land and naval forces at the disposal of the enemy are brought to bear upon the Confederate capital; and, to tell the truth, its salvation, if it is to be saved, will be due to God and not to man. . . ." The city's ministers seemed to agree, keeping churches open all day so those who could not bear muskets could come in and pray.[16]

With Grant pressing Lee's right, Butler threatening from the south, and assorted distractions on the Peninsula, suddenly a thirteen-mile-long column of 10,000 Yankee cavalrymen thrust into Richmond's northern outskirts. This time it was led by Phil Sheridan.

Frustrated at the Wilderness, Sheridan had told Grant, "If I am permitted to cut loose from this army I'll draw Stuart after me, and whip him, too."[17]

Jeb Stuart, racing south to head the Yankees off before Richmond, stopped briefly at a house near Beaver Dam Station to kiss his wife, who was visiting there. When an aide suggested that catching Sheridan was impossible, Stuart galloped away, saying, "I would rather die than let him go on." Federal horsemen destroyed rail lines, burned mountains of supplies, then felled trees across roads to slow pursuit, but Stuart got ahead of them at Yellow Tavern, barely six miles out of the capital.[18]

Yankees were reported in every direction. Many Richmond ladies sat up all that night, ready to flee, "dressed in all their best clothes with their jewelry on." With the railroads south cut, anxious congressmen cast about for horses.[19] All over the capital, boys tacked up appeals from Governor Smith:

> The enemy are undoubtedly approaching the city, and may be expected at any hour, with a view to its capture, its pillage and its destruction. The strongest consideration of self and duty to the country, calls every man to arms! A duty which none can refuse without dishonour. All persons, therefore, able to wield a musket, will immediately assemble upon the public square. . . . The government confidently relies that this appeal will not be made in vain.[20]

After being summoned and sent home more than once, this time the underage boys and overage men, the exempt and decrepit, were slow to rally. But eventually, as word passed that this emergency was real, they came. Even the city's newspapermen, mostly printers, formed a company of nearly a hundred muskets. All these last-ditch troops were not

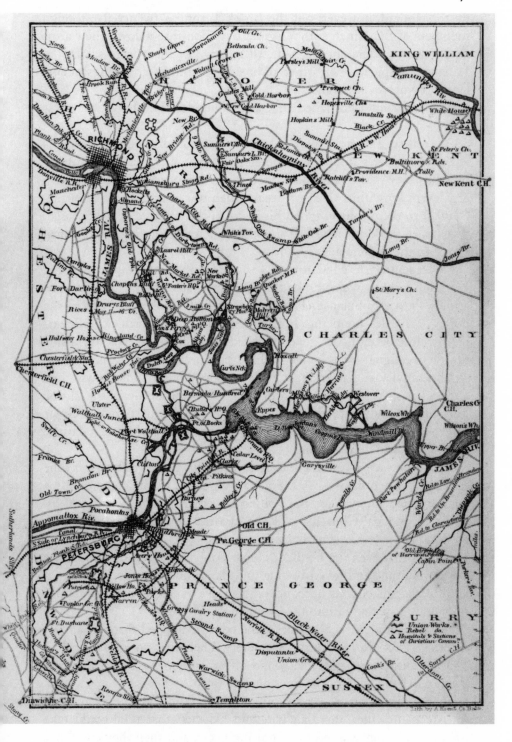

RICHMOND AND PETERSBURG, 1864–65

up to standard, however; out the Brook Turnpike, twenty-five foreign members of the Nineteenth Virginia Battalion threw down their arms as Sheridan's riders approached. All but two of them were said to be Italians, conspicuous on other days selling notions and refreshments along downtown sidewalks.[21]

The reluctant were jailed in Castle Thunder. The brave were less lucky.

At Yellow Tavern, Stuart formed a line of dismounted troopers against Sheridan's advancing Federals, who charged repeatedly, drawing blood as they probed first here, then there. A swarm of Michigan cavalry swept by within yards of Stuart, then was chased back. Shouting "Give it to them!," he emptied his pistol at the Yankees as they passed. The last of those riders fired a single shot before galloping on. It struck Stuart in the abdomen.

Stuart sent Cyrus McCormick, a young Confederate courier, to bring Fitzhugh Lee to take command in his place. Then aides lifted him into a mule-drawn ambulance. The animals at first spooked away from the noise of battle, bouncing him unmercifully. McCormick followed briefly, close behind. The general looked back, shook his head from side to side in resignation, then closed his eyes and folded his arms.[22]

The ambulance had to make wide detours around Yankees who had swerved past Yellow Tavern into the city's defenses along the Brook Turnpike. Finally, late that May 11, it delivered Stuart to the Grace Street home of his brother-in-law, Dr. Charles Brewer. The next day the general realized he was dying.

In pain, he set his affairs in order, willing his horses to his staff officers and his sword to his son. Soon Davis came, kindly staying only a quarter hour. Stuart asked the visiting Reverend Joshua Peterkin of St. James's Episcopal Church for "Rock of Ages" and tried to sing along with him.

At 7:38 that evening, he died. He was only 31 years old. Though he was flamboyant and loved to sing and dance and flirt, he had been a faithful and abstemious husband, who always refused strong drink until surgeons persuaded him to take a sip after his wound.[23]

From the funeral at St. James's, the cortege clopped through almost deserted streets to Hollywood Cemetery. There was no military escort and no music, except for the sound of far cannon, because the honor guard and band were in the lines outside town.

So were Sheridan's riders, groping in the dark for their getaway route via Mechanicsville. Sheridan had told his men that they could take Richmond if they wanted to, but at high cost, and then they could not hold it. But he had "whipped" Stuart, as he had promised Grant.

Though Stuart had blocked his way, now Stuart was gone, and Lee's cavalry would never be the same. Sheridan took his time, just to show that he did not have to hurry, and made his way down the Peninsula to Butler's army on the James.[24]

On this long ride he had begun to earn the reputation that would burn into the nation's memory when he swept the Shenandoah Valley later in the year. Bagby reported that Sheridan's raiders "killed indiscriminately all the animals they could not carry off, even to the hens and chickens. Large families were left without a morsel to eat." Awful distress will follow, he predicted, unless Grant can be driven away—"and of this, to tell the truth, there is small prospect at present. Lee cannot afford to lose the men; he is husbanding them against the next grand assault."[25]

True—but before another assault from Grant, Butler's army pushed along the Petersburg Turnpike into the outer works below Manchester, the first time the Yankees had struck the capital's defenses from south of the James. "Affairs here are critical," Davis advised Lee.[26]

They were more critical than they had to be because defenses in that direction were nominally under Beauregard, whose imperiousness so offended the president. Temporarily ill at Weldon, just below the Carolina line, Beauregard wrote to Davis that if necessary he would serve with pleasure under Lee. Davis shot back, "I did not doubt the readiness of Gen. Beauregard to serve under any general who ranks him. The right of Gen. Lee to command would be derived from his superior rank."[27]

In Beauregard's absence Davis himself rode out from the city several times, effectively serving as commander in the field against Butler. Fortunately for the South, the Union general gave the Confederates time to redeem the situation below Richmond.

Butler had rejected his officers' urging to move promptly on Petersburg, the essential rail center that he might have taken from the few Confederates on hand when he landed. Instead he temporarily cut the main track south of Richmond and turned toward the capital. But he was sluggish; some of his men called the operation a "stationary advance." Before Butler mounted decisive action, Beauregard arrived and pieced together enough reinforcements to take the initiative. Ten days after Butler landed, the Confederates counterattacked at Drewry's Bluff. While they did not destroy the Union force as Beauregard had predicted, they bottled it up on Bermuda Hundred, between the James and the Appomattox.[28]

But never again would success on a single front enable Richmond to relax. When Sheridan departed to the east, there came Butler from the south. When Butler was blocked, there came news of another Union commander, Major General David Hunter, scorching the earth of the Shenandoah Valley to the west. And inexorably there was Grant, now advancing from Spotsylvania to the North Anna River, where Lee's hard-marching troops again awaited him.

For four days the Confederates delayed the Union advance there, until once again Grant swung south, past Lee's right. Their armies skirmished repeatedly at places like Totopotomoy Creek, Haw's Shop, Hanover Court House, and Old Church. By the first of June, they confronted each other at Cold Harbor, only nine miles east-northeast of the Capitol building in Richmond.

Everyone in the city knew that this was not just another hit-and-run Yankee expedition. As Grant approached, war clerk Jones drew a fine line in explaining Richmond's outlook—no "trepidation" or "fear," but some "feverish anxiety." Sarah Lawton, wife of the Confederate quartermaster general, felt momentarily fatalistic as she listened to the rumble of cannon during a stroll on a May afternoon.

"All nature looked her loveliest," she wrote. "This beautiful city is dressed in her fairest robe of leaves and flowers—and amid all the commotion of men, we drew a lesson of peace from gazing awhile on these works of creation. The God of creation is the God of Providence too—and all will be well, however it may end." But then she saw a long line of wounded soldiers, straggling toward the hospital. They looked "so haggard, so emaciated, so suffering, so ragged, so uncared for" that she said to herself, "Can these be the materials of that heroic army, the world's wonder?"

At her husband's urging, Sarah had packed to depart, but she was "very unwilling to leave my 'things' to the mercy of the negroes and the fortunes of a disorganized city."[29]

Everywhere was gossip of a siege, which Mrs. Lawton said "is far more to be dreaded by us than a battle." Jones suspected that Grant meant to take his army south across the James River, "which, if effected, might lose us Richmond, for the city cannot subsist a week with its southern communications cut."

Without knowing it, both were agreeing with Lee, who told Jubal Early: "We must destroy this army of Grant's before he gets to James River. If he gets there, it will become a siege, and then it will be a mere question of time." Already the armies were so close that Lee's wagons bypassed the railroads, coming directly to Broad Street to load supplies from boxcars that had nowhere to go.[30]

Grant brought troops up from Butler's command to strengthen his next attack. Lee sent for reinforcements from as far away as Florida.

When he asked for a division from Beauregard's front and got a typically contentious response, Lee appealed to Davis, saying flatly, "The result of this delay will be disaster." Davis ordered the transfer, and brigades of veterans from Beauregard's force hurried through the city, racing Federal reinforcements to the front.[31]

At Cold Harbor, "Every one felt that this was to be the final struggle," wrote a Federal adjutant, Martin T. McMahon. "No further flanking marches were possible. Richmond was dead in front." The same feeling gripped the city. For days, Jones had told his diary that "the GREAT BATTLE may occur at any hour . . . the GREAT BATTLE is imminent." At last, it was.[32]

On June 1, Lee's men stopped a Union attack that came close to turning the Confederate flank. For another day the armies jostled into position on a line that angled from northwest to southeast between New and Old Cold Harbor. Then, early on June 3, Grant sent his troops head-on against Lee's entrenched and ready divisions, along a front of almost six miles.

"The time of actual advance was not over eight minutes," McMahon said. "In that little period more men fell bleeding as they advanced than in any other like period of time throughout the war." Grant's corps commanders reported that the assault had failed, but he ordered them on. It was useless. Shortly after midday, with thousands of blue-coated soldiers lying dead and wounded between the lines, he suspended the attack.

Years later, Grant said that he had "always regretted" that assault: "Cold Harbor is, I think, the only battle I ever fought that I would not fight over again under the circumstances."[33]

In one month since crossing the Rapidan, his relentless advance had cost the Union nearly 50,000 men. Never again would he try to hammer his way directly into Richmond. Instead, in mid-June he surprised Lee (but apparently not war clerk Jones) by laying pontoon bridges across the James and swinging his army onto the south side.

Until Lee was certain that Grant had moved his main force across, he could not follow, since that would leave open the way to Richmond. The Yankees were running cavalry diversions north and west of Richmond, and Union general Hunter had pushed up the Valley; Lee dispatched newly promoted Lieutenant General Jubal Early to drive Hunter away from Lynchburg into West Virginia.

But Lee had to focus on center stage. Before he concluded that Grant's river crossing was not a feint, the Yankees drove into Petersburg's entrenchments. Beauregard, now conducting a skillful fallback defense with very few troops, pleaded for help. Lee realized what had happened and rushed reinforcements, and Petersburg, for the moment, was saved.

The armies dug in, lengthening and deepening their works outside the town, settling into a way of war that would last for months.

* * *

Amid all the foreboding, there had been bright moments in Richmond, as when one of the latest Yankee prisoners looked around on arrival and said, "Wal! This is a darned sorry lookin' place to fight so much for." His comment circulated and stirred a few rueful chuckles.[34]

In mid-May, at New Market in the Valley, Virginia Military Institute cadets had charged Federal guns and created a proud legend for themselves. While Brigadier General Henry Wise was helping to hold off the invaders before Petersburg, Cadet John Wise, who as a 12-year-old had tried to march to Harpers Ferry, was knocked down by a shell at New Market.

A week later, with matters still dangerously unsettled around the capital, the teenage cadets strutted into Richmond and paraded in the square. Thousands cheered; Davis called the boys "the seed corn of the Confederacy." But the cadets had hardly returned to Lexington when Hunter's Yankees swept through and burned the Institute, as well as the houses of John Letcher and other Southern patriots.[35]

With reprisal in mind, Jubal Early led 10,000 men down the Valley, approaching the Potomac on July 4, crossing into Maryland, and looping into the northern outskirts of Washington. Richmond rumor had a seaborne Confederate force aboard two blockade runners heading from Wilmington, North Carolina, to Point Lookout on the Chesapeake, to free and arm 20,000 Confederates held prisoner there and march them to join Early in Washington. Davis and Lee had indeed planned such an expedition to coordinate with cavalry from Early's command. It would have been the Confederate counterpart of the frustrated Kilpatrick-Dahlgren raid meant to open Richmond's prisons. But because "the object and destination of the expedition have somehow become so generally known," Davis called it off.[36]

Early's thrust into Maryland penetrated Washington's northern suburbs, where he stared across at the works and a tall president in a stovepipe hat stared back. Suddenly it was Grant who had to detach forces to save his capital.

Another Richmond rumor said Washington papers reported that Early had taken Baltimore and citizens there had welcomed him. "Our people are in ecstasies!" wrote war clerk Jones. "This is the realization of the grand conception of a great general, and Lee is immortalized—if only it be true."[37]

But of course it was not true. Early threw a scare into Washington, and his cavalry burned Chambersburg, Pennsylvania, as repayment for what Union general Hunter had done in the Shenandoah Valley. But when Federal reinforcements arrived, the Confederates were overmatched, so they trudged back to Virginia.

Early's diversion had not diverted Grant. Unlike Old Jube, Grant had come equipped to stay. His objective now was to strangle Richmond by taking Petersburg and cutting the railroads that kept the capital alive. There was no mystery about it; even his soldiers saw it. Samuel H. Root of the Twenty-fourth Massachusetts wrote to his wife: "The only thing I expect Grant will endeavor to do will be to take the roads south of Richmond Petersburg & the Danville R Road & then allow them to eat up what stores they may have on hand in Richmond & come to terms or run away if they can."[38]

Union cavalry had already broken each of those railroad links at least once, but out of necessity the Confederates had become experts at repairing them. Grant now intended to take and hold them. Until he did, his raiders had orders to be sure none of the iron rails they left behind were reusable.

The classic siege, long dreaded in Richmond, had begun.

One of its time-honored tactics was tunneling, and within days after the Federals dug their trenches facing Lee at Petersburg, Pennsylvania miners started digging a 500-foot shaft toward the Confederates. Beneath the Rebel works, they planted eight tons of black powder. Grant massed troops behind his line, hoping to pour enough regiments through a sudden opening to fan out and end the whole thing.

At daylight on July 30, the Yankees exploded their mine, blasting a huge crater, throwing men and guns skyward, and wrecking nine companies of Southern infantry. But the Confederates recovered and counterattacked, slaughtering or capturing hundreds of disorganized Federals, including black infantry. Many of these victims were troops who had rushed into the crater and then could not climb out. "A stupendous failure," Grant admitted; "the saddest affair I have witnessed in the war."[39]

The Richmond press was always quick to protest Yankee depredations, including steadily more brutal tactics as the war ground on. When prisoners came in after Cold Harbor, George Bagby described some as "the most hardened, beastly brutes the eye ever beheld—old in years and older in iniquity . . . these devils would have burnt our houses, cut our throats, ravished our women and murdered our babes . . . without a thought of remorse."[40] Politicians had never hesitated to brand Union troops and their leaders as inhuman villains. But Confederate combat soldiers in Virginia, after sharing the universal miseries of the field, had been less malicious toward the men across the lines.

The battle of the Crater changed that.

"It was the first occasion on which any of the Army of Northern Virginia came in contact with Negro troops, & the general feeling of the men toward their employment was very bitter," wrote Porter Alexander.

Since John Brown's raid and the Emancipation Proclamation, many Confederates had believed that the Union's aim was "servile insurrection & massacre" in the South, "& the enlistment of Negro troops was regarded as advertisement of that desire & encouragement of the idea to the Negro." Angered Confederates turned their fury on the black soldiers as well as the white officers who led them. Alexander admitted that "some of the Negro prisoners, who were originally allowed to surrender by some soldiers, were afterward shot by others, & there was, without doubt, a great deal of unnecessary killing of them."[41]

At Chimborazo Hospital, wounded Confederates arrived talking about the Yankee mine as "a mean trick," which is what the Yankees had said two years earlier about Confederate torpedoes sinking ships. But what offended the Southerners most were the thousands of black troops thrown at them to take advantage of that mean trick.

Phoebe Pember said that after earlier battles her Confederate patients had always watched their language around female nurses and had not spoken of enemy troops with personal hatred. But now the wounded Rebels cursed—their "eyes gleamed, and teeth clenched as they showed me the locks of their muskets to which the blood and hair still clung, when after firing, without waiting to re-load, they had clenched the barrels and fought hand to hand."[42]

North and South—in armies and households, in cities and on plantations—relations between blacks and whites were changing, seeming to move in two directions at once.

CHAPTER TWENTY-TWO

A QUESTION OF
FEARFUL MAGNITUDE

After Grant's great offensive subsided into siege, Lawley of the London *Times* wrote from Richmond that "if a man were landed here from a balloon after six months' absence—if he were taken along Grace or Franklin Streets in this city on a summer evening, and told that two enormous armies are lying a few miles off and disputing its possession, he would deem his informant a lunatic." Ladies were laughing, he said; song drifted from open windows. "Richmond trusts and believes in St. Lee as much as Mecca in Mahomet. . . ."[1]

Lawley, always brightening Confederate prospects for his readers beyond the ocean, maintained that Lee had the initiative "now that his hardy antagonist lay foiled, baffled and emasculated before him."[2]

Even some Richmonders who could see the situation plain before them joined in, briefly, to cheer survival as if it were victory. On July 4, the newspapers listed more than 600 slaves who had been recaptured from the Yankees, asking their owners to reclaim them. The city's prisons were bulging with Yankees again. Everyone knew of the horrible losses Grant had suffered on his way south. The pro-Davis *Sentinel* said: "The hundreds of thousands of [Northern] widows and orphans are sending up a wail which cannot fail to reach the unfeeling heart of Lincoln. . . ."[3]

But if there was public relief at not being sacked by Grant's army, the news from farther south gnawed at Jefferson Davis. Pressed by Union Major General William Tecumseh Sherman, Joe Johnston was falling back steadily toward Atlanta. True to form, he refused to tell the president how he meant to prevent Sherman from capturing that crucial rail center.

It was the same kind of balkiness for which Davis might have relieved Johnston two years earlier on the Peninsula had the general not been wounded first. The old feud between the two men had not faded. Now Georgia's governor, Joseph E. Brown, was pleading for help; Judah Benjamin was urging Davis to fire Johnston; and John Bell Hood was bragging about what a fighting general like himself might do there. In mid-July, Davis made Hood a temporary full general and sent him with his one good leg to replace Johnston in command of the Army of Tennessee. That would not stop Sherman.

* * *

Beneath the veneer of laughing ladies and drifting song, nerves stretched taut in Richmond as generals and civilians faced the reality of siege. Frustration and foreboding escalated many a dispute between respectable citizens. Mayor Mayo eased some of these confrontations by placing the parties under peace bond, but occasionally one slipped past him.

Simple odds dictated that John Daniel, who published more provocative commentary than anyone else, would be challenged again and again, and eventually have to pay. In late summer Daniel accused Confederate treasurer E. C. Elmore of being a gambler unfit for such an office of trust. Elmore, a young South Carolinian with a low flash point, invited him to a duel.[4]

Daniel was ill-equipped for combat with any weapon except words. Since his battle wound two years earlier, his right arm had not been fully operative. But no gentleman, certainly none as publicly pugnacious as Daniel was in his *Examiner*, could afford to decline such an invitation.[5]

He liked to say with some smugness that the first person to arrive at his newspaper's office each morning was Davis's body servant, come to fetch a copy for the president. The servant allegedly said that Davis "can't get out of bed or eat his breakfast until his appetite is stimulated by reading every word in the *Examiner*." But if Daniel's diatribes stirred Davis's juices, they hardly settled his stomach, for they were inspired by an enmity "amounting to something like a frenzy." George Bagby, the editor's friend and sometime associate, wrote that "for the sake of power and a competency, he became an outcast from society. At one time he was literally hated or feared by everybody."

By then Daniel had moved from an apartment above his office to a three-story townhouse on Broad Street, where he lived with his books, attended by a cook, a hostler, and the valet who brought his newspapers.

He was harsh with his servants; two of them ran away during the war. He never married. He liked to sit up talking with his few callers far into the night, retiring at 2:00 or 3:00 and breakfasting between 11:00 and noon. He appeared at his office at 8:00 or 9:00 in the evening, packing a little derringer for protection against street thugs and citizens offended by his journalism. He was humorless but quick to appreciate a certain slashing humor in others. His literary model was Jonathan Swift.[6]

When Elmore challenged him, the two appointed seconds who agreed on a time and place: 5:30 a.m. on August 17, 1864, at Dill's farm in Henrico County. There in the misty dawn Daniel lifted his pistol in his left hand, fired, and missed. Elmore's bullet struck the editor in the leg. Everyone's honor was upheld, and the insulted South Carolinian had the satisfaction of knowing that, at least briefly, the injury would keep Daniel off the job.[7]

* * *

Davis must have wished he could get Daniel off his back that simply. But without the *Examiner* there would still be the faultfinding *Whig,* and without any newspapers there would still be complaining politicians, far and near. Governor Brown of Georgia was "first, last and most persistent" in putting his state's rights before national needs—and as the Confederacy's needs grew more desperate, Brown became more contentious. With Sherman bearing down on Atlanta, he tried to dictate strategy; Davis rebuked him with sarcasm.[8]

Complaints from other governors, like North Carolina's Zebulon Vance, were driven more often by the struggle over scarce materials than by ideological extremism. Some states were still holding back uniforms and provisions for their own troops while the Confederacy tried to deal with mortal emergency. But as Grant's strategy brought pressure on all fronts, the most critical shortage was in manpower.

Governors had resisted placing state militia under Confederate control, railed against conscription, and obstructed provost marshals' pursuit of draft dodgers and deserters. Vance and Brown had classified thousands of their citizens as state officials in order to exempt them from the draft. When Davis asked Congress to continue the suspension of habeas corpus beyond August 1 to deal with "deserters and traitors, skulkers and stragglers," Vice President Stephens was not at home in Georgia but in Richmond for a change, presiding over the Senate. After a long speech against the administration, he cast the tie-breaking vote that defeated the president's bill.[9]

Brown and Stephens were the most conspicuous Georgia politicians of the moment, but not all of the state's officeholders were anti-Davis obstructionists. Warren Akin of Cassville, Georgia, had already moved his wife and children away from war once, when he left them behind to come to Richmond that spring as a newly elected Confederate congressman. Three weeks after Akin's arrival, Sherman's invaders burned his abandoned home and law office at Cassville. That summer Akin went back and moved his family ahead of the fighting again, to Elberton.

He had every reason to be bitter toward the Yankees, but in his letters from Richmond he wasted little precious paper on the enemy. He dwelt instead on the loneliness of being away from his family and his boredom as he sat writing while half listening to windy debates on rules and attacks on the Davis administration.[10]

Now and then, something exciting broke the congressional tedium; sometimes it was a close vote like that on martial law, sometimes personal vendetta. There was the day Ben Hill of Georgia emphasized a point in debate with William Yancey of Alabama by throwing an inkstand at him, cutting his cheek and splashing blood and ink on the Senate floor. Another morning, a woman fought her way onto the House floor to horsewhip Representative George G. Vest of Missouri. She was furious that legislators, clamping down on draft evaders, intended to require government clerks to state their ages. Congress promptly moved to exempt women from disclosure.[11]

For hours on end, Davis's old antagonist Henry Foote harangued the House. Foote would fight with almost anyone, even those who agreed with his opinion of the president. Alabama's E. S. Dargan was in midspeech when Foote called him a "damned rascal," at which Dargan went after him with a bowie knife. When Foote made fun of Arkansas's Thomas B. Hanly, Hanly swung at him, and in the melee Foote tore off his shirt.

The *Examiner*'s John Mitchel, a fiery Irish nationalist, could not resist tangling with such a provocative politician. Convicted of treason against British rule at home, Mitchel had been deported to far Tasmania, from which he escaped to America. In a series of U.S. newspapers, he promoted Irish independence, defied the pope, and upheld slavery—Stephens would write that he "did a great deal in bringing on the war." In 1862 he came to Richmond to edit the *Enquirer* after Jennings Wise's death. But eventually he could not abide that paper's pro-Davis line, so in 1864 he switched to Daniel's *Examiner*.

From that editorial pulpit, Mitchel urged the House to expel the disruptive Foote. Beyond that, he challenged the congressman to a duel. When Foote's Tennessee colleague William G. Swan delivered

Mitchel's challenge, Foote insulted him, Swan smote Foote with an umbrella, and Mrs. Foote intervened to beat him away. The mayor headed off the duel with yet another peace bond.[12]

*   *   *

Tension in threatened Richmond raised tempers; politics in Washington raised premature Southern hopes, or fears, of peace. Lincoln faced another election that November, and unlike Davis in 1861, he had serious opposition. War-weary Democrats nominated George McClellan, who maintained that Lincoln had treated him unfairly, to run against him. "The words Armistice and Peace are found in the Northern papers and upon every tongue here," wrote war clerk Jones.[13]

But no encouragement came from the field. In early September Sherman defeated Hood and took Atlanta, and thousands in Richmond went to church to pray for heavenly intervention. Sarah Lawton, worried by Northern invaders close by and at home in Georgia, was unsure of how to react. At daily prayer meetings she heard distinguished leaders ask God that Sherman's communications might be cut, that Atlanta and Petersburg might not fall, that the Weldon railroad might be saved. But she never subscribed to such prayers—"not because I think we may not freely spread our wants and desires before the Mercy-seat—but because I do not know what we want—it may not be what we wish—and so I prefer to say 'Our father, thy kingdom come—thy will be done.' . . ."

Mrs. Lawton, like many in the South, grasped at the hope that bad news might be good: "I often think that the fall of Atlanta, coming just at this time, was designed for one great benefit to us, which is to dissipate those strong hopes of Peace which we feared would have an injurious effect on our country—ungirding the loins of our minds and relaxing our vigilance and courage."[14]

Davis was less sanguine. As autumn began he headed for Georgia, where morale was collapsing and there was renewed talk of a separate peace, to see firsthand what might be done to buck up the Confederates who had lost Atlanta. At about the time the president departed, Jones mused about a revolution, a coup to install Lee as dictator: "It may be a jest to some, but others mean it in earnest."[15]

Outside Petersburg, Lee had brought troops from Jubal Early's army in the Shenandoah Valley to try to keep up with Grant's lengthening siege lines. Phil Sheridan, now commanding Union forces against Early, had him outnumbered about four to one and started driving him back up the Valley. To prevent Lee from returning troops to Early, Grant suddenly struck at the outer line of Richmond's defenses just north of the

James, capturing lightly manned Fort Harrison but being driven away from Fort Gilmer.

Once again the tocsin sounded in Richmond; conscription patrols rounded up men on the streets, penned them in Capitol Square, then marched them off to the front. Two War Department clerks went to the Spotswood to hear the latest news and were grabbed and jailed with 500 others dragooned as last-ditch defenders. As cannon rumbled to the southeast, Postmaster General John H. Reagan and Attorney General George Davis, both under 50 years of age, were arrested and held for an hour before a friend identified them. At the War Office, citizens' appeals against conscription did no good. "Women come there and weep, wring their hands, scold, entreat, beg and almost drive me mad," wrote R. G. H. Kean. "The iron is gone deep into the heart of society."[16]

The concussion of cannon fire shook windows as George Bagby joined a crowd that was trying to see the fighting from a hilltop in the city. Around him he found only four white men, three of them past 50 and the other an invalid; the rest were women, children, and blacks. "In the trenches are all the able-bodied fathers, sons and brothers of Richmond, with this heavy autumn rain pouring down on them," he wrote. "Our fate as a city hangs trembling in the balance."

But soon afterward, Bagby reported that "never before was such a fuss made about nothing": The Confederate artillerymen were firing at what they thought was advancing enemy cavalry. Some swore that the alarm was caused by 150 hogs impressed earlier by the commander of Fort Harrison and now turned loose in the bushes to keep them from the Yankees.[17]

The Federals quickly converted the captured fort into their own strongpoint, and Lee ordered construction of new works inside that stretch of the outer defenses. At the same time, Grant ordered a force under Meade to push farther west at the other extreme of the Richmond–Petersburg lines, aiming to cut the South Side Railroad.

In meeting these thrusts, Lee had to shuttle troops from here to there and back, and never had enough to be confident of holding at any point. In August he had written that the Yankees cut the Weldon Railroad because he could not afford the certain loss of men needed to hold it. In September, after John Hunt Morgan was killed by Union raiders in Tennessee, Morgan's funeral cortege in Richmond was interrupted when its military contingent rushed off to resist Grant at the forts.[18]

* * *

Every report of Federal strength showed it growing. Black Union troops were now conspicuous in the war around the capital. Seeing this, inspecting his own shrinking rolls, Lee on September 2 had written to Davis that blacks should be used wherever possible to free white Southern soldiers for combat. He had not yet officially broached the core question of arming slaves to fight for the Confederacy, but unofficially it had been debated for months throughout the South.

Back in January 1864, Major General Patrick R. Cleburne, an Irish-born star of Johnston's army in Georgia, had circulated a proposal that slaves be enlisted as soldiers and freed as reward for serving. A few of his top officers endorsed it, but Johnston refused to forward it to Richmond. When one of those officers bypassed Johnston's headquarters and sent the proposal on, Davis suppressed it; to discuss even limited abolition would mock the reason for which the South had gone to war.[19]

Yet the subject had indeed been discussed, long before Cleburne brought it up. The Alabama legislature had approved using slave soldiers the previous September. And one of the most thoughtful private reflections on the issue had been set down by the slave-owning Georgia congressman Akin, when he was speaker of his state legislature in late 1862, after Lincoln had announced the Emancipation Proclamation.

"It is a question of fearful magnitude," Akin wrote to his wife. "To call forth the negroes into the army, with the promise of freedom, will it not be giving up the great question involved by doing the very thing Lincoln is now doing?" But if he were sure the alternative was defeat, said Akin, he would not hesitate to enroll slaves—that evil could not possibly be greater than what would follow "subjugation."

The idea of freeing slaves to fight was fiercely opposed by many whites who had cheered their own kin as they marched away in uniform. "Have you ever noticed the strange conduct of our people during this war?" Akin asked. "They give up their sons, husbands, brothers & friends, and often without murmuring, to the army; but let one of their negroes be taken, and what a howl you will hear. The love of money has been the greatest difficulty in our way to independence—it is now our chief obstacle. . . ."[20]

Two years after Akin considered black soldiers as a theory, three seasons after Davis buried Cleburne's proposal, the question was more than theoretical. Hearing the sound of sporadic battle in Richmond's outskirts, ordnance chief Josiah Gorgas doubted that Lee had 30,000 infantry at hand. "The time is coming now when it will be necessary to put our slaves into the field and let them fight *for their freedom*," Gorgas wrote in his diary. The following week he thought that public sentiment was rapidly swinging that way— "the country is prepared to throw Slavery into the purchase of our independence if that be necessary to achieve it. . . ."[21]

Davis came back from Georgia in mid-October after asserting at Macon that Sherman would have to retreat to protect his supply lines—"and when that day comes, the fate that befell the army of the French Empire in its retreat from Moscow will be reenacted. Our cavalry and our people will harass and destroy his army as did the Cossacks of Napoleon, and the Yankee General, like him, will escape with only a bodyguard."[22] Davis named one of his least favorite soldiers, P. G. T. Beauregard, to territorial command to oversee the impetuous Hood there—a selection that plainly demonstrated that the South was running out of generals.

Shortly after returning, the president heard that Sheridan had turned defeat into smashing victory against Early at Cedar Creek. There would be more fighting in the Shenandoah Valley, but now Sheridan had taken control, burning crops and barns, following Grant's orders to turn the Valley into "a barren waste, so that crows flying over it for the balance of this season will have to carry their provender with them." The breadbasket of Virginia would no longer feed Confederate Richmond and Lee's army, and Grant need worry no longer about protecting Washington from a thrust down the Valley. He could concentrate on Petersburg and Richmond without distraction.

Lee, reduced to begging for more troops, for the first time brought up the possibility of losing Richmond. If the entire arms-bearing population cannot be turned out, he wrote, "the result must be calamitous. The discouragement of our people and the great material loss that would follow the fall of Richmond, to say nothing of the encouragement our enemies would derive from it, outweigh, in my judgment, any sacrifice and hardship that would result. . . ."[23]

The day after the Confederate Congress reconvened on November 7, Lincoln was reelected, crushing McClellan and ending the political hopes of peace Democrats in the North. Davis, in a message to Congress, tried to minimize the fall of Atlanta: "There are no vital points on the preservation of which the continued existence of the Confederacy depends," he said—obviously including Richmond.

By then the capital was full of talk that blacks would be put under arms "if worse came to worse." Davis would not concede that things had reached that point. He suggested enlisting 40,000 blacks for labor battalions and freeing them after the war. He held back from arming them as fighting soldiers—but if the alternative became "subjugation," he saw "no reason to doubt what should then be our decision."[24]

Bagby considered that comment "the entering wedge for the use of negro soldiers." The Negro, he maintained, was "happy only as a slave," and under Davis's proposal "is to be punished with freedom, and the example is to be held up for the discontent of all other slaves."[25] The *Dispatch* went to the heart of the matter, saying, "we give up the whole question" by arming and freeing slaves. "Whatever *we* may be fighting for, the Yankees are fighting for 'the nigger'; that is, to abolitionize the South. We are not disposed to gratify them if we can avoid it." But other politicians stepped ahead of Davis; soon afterward, Virginia's Governor Smith urged his legislature to authorize black state troops right away, even if it meant their emancipation.[26]

Congress now openly debated proposals that had once been heresy. In mid-December, Akin sat in the House chamber writing to his wife as a North Carolina congressman argued for appointing commissioners to treat for peace, and against using slaves as soldiers. When the Tar Heel was done, a Mississippian offered a substitute resolution, and the issue was held over for another day, "when we will have much gas and many words expended."[27]

There was much gas and little action in Congress, but there was immense movement in the South's thinking. After three-plus years of war, polite Richmonders at dinner discussed issues the very mention of which could have landed them in Castle Thunder a few months earlier. The cliché of Southern ladies blushing and tittering in false modesty was dead. There was a war-born frankness about relations between men and women, North and South, soldier and civilian, black and white, that would have scandalized antebellum society.

* * *

The slave dealer Silas Omohundro had fallen ill the previous winter, and as his health declined he drank more. On May 13, 1864, he paid $160 for a gallon of whiskey, and eight days later $125 for another gallon. A quart cost him $32 on the twenty-fifth, and another gallon $140 on the twenty-seventh. That was the last entry in his account book; he died soon afterward.[28]

His will was entered at the Richmond courthouse:

> In the first place I do absolutely emancipate and forever set free from all manner of servitude my woman Corinna Omohundro, and her five children, Alice Morton Omohundro, Colon Omohundro, Riley Crosby Omohundro, William Rainey Omohundro, and Geo. Nelson Omohundro, and who are also my children.
>
> I give and devise to the said Corinna Omohundro for and during her natural life and for her sole use and benefit, my entire lot on Seventeenth Street in the city of Richmond, Virginia, with all the buildings thereon and other improvements including the jail. . . .

As Corinna Omohundro has always been a kind, faithful and dutiful woman to me, and an affectionate mother and will continue to be so, and bring up her children in a proper manner, I direct my executor to pay over to her semiannually the interest arising [from investments for the children, etc.].[29]

Corinna, the object of Omohundro's affection for at least sixteen years, had been his slave. Apparently she had passed as white while she lived with him, for no race was specified for her in the 1860 census—neither black nor white nor mulatto.

Silas had bought her luxurious things; she had borne his children and run his household. The origin of their relationship is not clear; a twentieth-century Omohundro-family genealogy says that Silas married Corinna Clark in 1848, but in 1860 the census listed her as Coriner Hinton. She was obviously a woman of character and competence.[*30]

Upon his death, Silas also manumitted another woman and her two children. His will did not state any personal relationship to them. But four other Omohundro slaves were sold by his executor that summer for $15,202 (proving not how far slave values had risen but how far the Confederate dollar had fallen).[31]

Countless times, slave owners had fathered children by their black and mulatto women. Sometimes they treated these women as little more than animals, and at other times they cherished them as secret mistresses; only rarely did they acknowledge them as common-law wives. Yet they often brought up the children of those liaisons as they did their legal offspring. Richmond Judge James Dandridge Halyburton, for example, whose great-aunt was Martha Washington, fathered a son by his mulatto slave in 1849. The judge reared him in his Marshall Street home along with Mrs. Halyburton and the boy's white half siblings until he ran away to the Yankees at the age of 14.[33]

A descendant of Judge Halyburton and that son wrote warmly about the family more than a century later. But the cold business ledgers and court documents that disclose the Omohundro relationship can only suggest the trust and devotion that must have bound Silas and Corinna.

Public laws and political debate pretended that relations between the races were as simple as black and white. That Corinna was one day a

---

*After Silas's death, Corinna married Nathaniel Davidson, a white Richmond coal dealer born in New Hampshire. In 1870 she was running his confectionery on Seventeenth Street. She later moved to Washington. Legal wrangling over Silas Omohundro's estate lasted until 1887. In Pennsylvania, where he had owned property and one or more of his children lived, the state Supreme Court ruled that Corinna had not legally been his wife. But the auditor maintained that she had—not by ceremony but on the basis of "habitation and reputation." The court agreed that she had been Silas's slave.[32]

slave and the next day the free owner of a slave pen proved the contrary. So did the myriad facial complexions of the old South. There was fear in both directions, and there was love—whites often fearing the threat of mass "servile insurrection" while embracing individual slaves as family; some blacks fearing the lash of cruel masters and the law while others nursed and protected white children as their own. But such affection and loyalty existed mainly between whites and house servants, who were a minority among slaves. Thousands of field hands, without those intimate ties to their owners, had fled to Federal lines and now marched in blue uniforms.

Secession, then Lincoln's Emancipation Proclamation, then Federal use of black troops—each step had hardened the official Confederate position that blacks were meant to be slaves, that legally slaves were not persons but property. But as Southern manpower melted away and Northern armies grew despite battle losses, as black soldiers demonstrated that they could fight as well as other men, expediency began to overtake dogma. "Men begin . . . to talk calmly about emancipation," Kean wrote; "some as a cheap price for peace; others as good absolutely because we cannot afford to be under the ban of the world, though right in the abstract."[34]

In Richmond, the Confederacy's very reason for being was crumbling.

CHAPTER TWENTY-THREE

AND NOW THEY WILL REPENT

*P*retending to be undiscouraged, the women of Richmond volunteered to provide a holiday feast for the soldiers in the
trenches. It was a rash promise: With the once-bounteous Shenandoah
Valley devastated by Sheridan, the main north–south railroads cut, track
and rolling stock breaking down, Yankees entrenched on three sides,
and winter closing in, food had become increasingly sparse for ordinary
civilians. Richmond's farm markets were nearly bare, and the Confederate Congress was talking of importing meat from abroad. Meager supplies came from the Piedmont down the James River canal, and from
Carolina by wagon trains that circled west of Union cavalry patrols below Petersburg. But the women knew that the army was suffering more
than they were. They appealed to merchants and farmers for contributions, and pledged delivery to the troops on January 1, 1865.

A Georgia infantryman told of how his squad arose early and expec-
tant on New Year's Day, then waited for the promised feast, and waited,
all day and into the night. Finally, in the darkness before dawn on January 2, a wagon arrived—and each man got a sandwich featuring one
thin slice of ham. Masking his disappointment, a corporal lit his pipe
and said, "God bless our noble women! It was all they could do; it was
all they had." Then every man in the tent broke down and cried.[1]

In the long arc of trenches that reached more than thirty miles from
east of Richmond to southwest of Petersburg, soldiers huddled deeper
into the earth to protect themselves against the harshest winter in memory. Scurvy, pneumonia, typhoid fever, and mounting desertion had

brought Lee's force down to about 57,000 men, including home guards and reservists. They were stretched thinly along those lines, facing Grant's 124,000. In years past the Confederate commander's boldness had offset such numbers, and his soldiers' morale had survived; as long as he could maneuver, he had repeatedly brought more force to bear where it counted. Now his army was pinned to ground, immobile, famishing, and draining away.

Salvos of artillery fire crashed down without warning on the trenches of both sides. Sharpshooters' bullets sang out of nowhere. Men died without ground gained or lost. Nothing seemed to change.

But behind Union lines the Yankees had turned the sleepy steamer station of City Point, now Grant's headquarters, into one of the world's busiest ports. Immense stacks of food and ammunition, acres of cannon and caissons, corrals of cattle and horses, spread inland from the river junction. Before winter set in, Wade Hampton had led a raid that rustled 2,400 head of Yankee cattle for the hungry Confederates at Petersburg, but that surge of protein did not last long. The episode was just a passing embarrassment for the Federals, whose engineers had laid a military railroad that followed the army's extending lines, bringing supplies directly to divisions at the front.

Even all this did not guarantee luxury or high spirits among the Union troops. Occasionally one of them deserted, and occasionally one was shot for trying. Frank McElhanney of the Twenty-fourth Massachusetts was caught, brought out before his comrades, ordered to kneel on his coffin, and executed by a twenty-four-man firing squad. Sam Root, watching, said "he met his death with a careless indifference that indicated a weak mind."

"Since light it rains & still rains & is going to rain," Root wrote later. He asked his wife to imagine him "sitting on the ground with a very small stove in one corner of the tent with large holes in the top to let the heat out. We smile to see ourselves comfortable in a dog kennel. . . ."[2]

In the trenches living conditions were subhuman for all. Canteens of water froze solid beside sleeping soldiers. The Confederates were more miserable because they were hungry, their clothes and blankets were thin, and prospects beyond the cold and mud gave them nothing to smile about. When on quiet days they swapped rumors and newspapers with the Yankees, they learned that after Atlanta, Hood had turned his army back into Tennessee and had been mauled at Franklin and Nashville. Sherman had cut a swath through Georgia and presented the city of Savannah to Lincoln as a Christmas gift. A Union armada was closing in on Fort Fisher, the key to Wilmington, the Confederacy's last operating Atlantic seaport.

On Sunday, December 25, Richmond had tried hard to make the Yuletide bright. In the streets boys fired pistols into the air and there were enough good-natured drunks to set the day apart from the Saturday before and the Monday after.

Davis, whose physical health often seemed a barometer of Confederate fortunes, had been ill while enemies in and out of Congress blamed him for all the catastrophes of autumn. Occasionally rumors that he was dead ran through the city. But by Christmas he was back at his desk in the mansion, immersed in the kind of administrative minutiae that took his mind briefly off the big picture. Varina wrote in retrospect that "every one felt the cataclysm which impended," but while the Davises tried to brighten their children's holiday, no one spoke of that feeling.[3]

Alice West, daughter of a refugee family from near Trevilians Station, scene of a bloody cavalry clash the previous summer, was excited by an invitation to enjoy the Davises' Christmas tree. It was a Virginia holly, decorated with candles and with dolls made of hickory nuts and flannel. Everything was homemade—toy dogs and cats, plus cakes, ginger snaps, coffee, and eggnog. Alice helped Maggie Davis pass out gifts, and the children played hide-and-seek all over the house. Mrs. Davis made her visitors feel special—and then the president came in, "tall and thin and sad, presenting quite a contrast to his wife."[4]

The Davises' cook had hoarded delicacies for days to put together a feast of turkey, beef, mince pie, and plum pudding. Earlier, at services at St. Paul's, the president had seen the tree erected there for city orphans, and in the afternoon he went back there to play Santa Claus, glad to appear before an uncritical audience. That evening he and Varina went to a neighbor's "starvation party," where there was dancing and singing but no refreshments. Each hour of the day—with ersatz, hoarding, orphans, "starvation"—had spoken of the real world beyond.[5]

Warren Akin's cheerless holidays were more typical of that Christmas in Richmond. Alone in his room, he wrote at least nine long letters to his wife in Georgia during the last two weeks of the year. He explained how he was trying to live economically on a congressman's pay in the inflation-ridden city. He was wearing his underwear and nightshirts for two weeks and his socks a week without laundering, and making two shirts last a week. He refused to pay "a dollar a piece for washing socks and handkerchiefs. . . . I can't help it. I do the best I can." He was invited to two eggnog parties but did not accept; his main entertainment outside Congress was going from church to church, reviewing the ministers' performances. "This city is greatly blessed with good preachers," he wrote.[6]

On the morning when Confederate troops in the line were so disappointed by the sparse feast sent by Richmond ladies, J. B. Jones arrived for work at the War Department and found Secretary Seddon before the fireplace with his head drooped onto his knees. "Affairs are gloomy enough," Jones thought. "The question is how Richmond and Virginia shall be saved. Gen. Lee is despondent."[7]

* * *

A muffled blast downriver on January 1 could hardly be heard in the capital. After four and a half months of digging, the Yankees had completed their Dutch Gap canal, meant to bypass a long, dangerous loop in the James. They set off six tons of gunpowder to clear the final bulkhead. The explosion flung up quantities of earth, which fell back into the cut. Federal laborers—mostly black troops—resumed their digging.

After the failure of the Fort Fisher expedition at Christmas, the Dutch Gap fiasco confirmed the military ineptness of Ben Butler. Now that the presidential election was past and Butler's political connections mattered less, Lincoln agreed with Grant's decision to replace him with a professional soldier. But before Butler was fired, the Federal fleet was on its way back to Fort Fisher, and this time the expedition would not fail.

In a farewell message to the men of his Department of Virginia and North Carolina, Butler said that he had "refused to order the useless sacrifice of such soldiers." He was departing, but "the wasted blood of my men does not stain my garments"—an attempted explanation of his failures and a jab at Grant's costly tactics. But for Confederates in Richmond who soon heard of his message, Butler's most provocative words were those addressed "To the Colored Troops of the Army of the James":

"In this army you have been treated not as laborers but as soldiers. You have shown yourselves worthy of the uniform you wear. . . . With the bayonet you have unlocked the iron-barred gates of prejudice, opening new fields of freedom, liberty, and equality of right to yourselves and your race forever."[8]

While Lincoln relieved a political general, he had privately approved a politician's effort to find a cheaper, nonmilitary way to an end that now seemed imminent. With the president's permission, his 73-year-old confidant, Francis Preston Blair, Sr., came to Richmond ostensibly on a private mission, seeking personal papers that raiders had taken from his Maryland home. His arrival started rumors that the city was about to be evacuated.

Blair had known Davis in Washington before the war. To him, he now suggested merging the U.S. and Confederate armies to drive the

French puppet Emperor Maximilian out of Mexico as a way of uniting North and South against a common enemy. That idea as such was preposterous, but Davis said he was willing to negotiate peace between "the two countries" of North and South. Blair took this to Washington and returned to Richmond with Lincoln's assurance that he, too, was ready to talk about peace—in "our one common country." The difference between those phrases seemed unbridgeable, but Blair had opened a conversation that both sides wanted to continue.

Richmonders' feelings toward the well-meaning old emissary were like those toward many a Union loyalist with ties running far back into antebellum times—a combination of personal affection and ideological antagonism. As Blair took the truce boat back toward City Point from one of his missions, a local girl stood aside as he reminisced with her mother. "Poor old Mr. Blair—I could feel almost kindly toward him," the younger woman wrote. "It must be difficult for the old to realize that the possibilities of their youth are now but the dreams of the dotard." Southerners might someday make up with the North as nation to nation, she said, "but never will we be so false to the graves of the dead who during four years have yielded their lives for our independence as [to] submit to [the Union's] base humiliating overtures. . . ."[9]

During Blair's comings and goings Congressman Akin called on Davis and found him not stern and puffed up as reputed but polite, attentive, communicative, "a patriot and a good man." "Were he removed today, we should be *ruined* in a few months," Akin wrote—"and I fear we shall be any way."

"Of course this is intended for *you alone*," the Georgian told his wife. "We are in a deplorable condition—standing on the verge of an abyss, the bottom of which no man can see. When we shall fall into it, or how to be saved from it, is hid from my eyes. . . ."

At night in his lonely room Akin now spent his time darning his worn-out socks, something a servant had always done for him at home.[10] Composing letters in the Capitol, he occasionally stopped when the House went into secret session to debate the question of black soldiers. In mid-January he and his colleagues were subjected to a final fulmination by the tireless Henry Foote.

Foote had been arrested before New Year's Day as he tried to slip north across the Potomac, on what he said was a personal peacemaking mission. After appearing before Judge Halyburton he was released and returned to his seat in the House. Allowed to explain his adventure, he went on so long and so vehemently that the Speaker cut him off. When a motion to expel Foote fell short of a two-thirds vote, another endorsing his arrest was passed. Soon he fled Richmond again, this time reaching the North. Disappointed when the Federals ignored his overtures, he sailed to England and later dispatched an appeal to Tennessee to secede from the Confederacy.[11] From the start, Foote had been an enemy of Davis, seeking every chance to strike at him. But Warren Akin was a Davis loyalist, and less than a month later he too departed, taking leave from Congress to go home and care for his family. He would not return. Hundreds of Confederate soldiers were doing the same thing, without permission. Yet others were holding company and regimental meetings and publishing their determination to fight on.

The First Company, Richmond Howitzers, in camp at Walthall Junction above Petersburg, passed a resolution "spurning all thought of compromise and every hope of peace which has not for its foundation the acknowledgment of our independence and our effectual and eternal separation from the state of the North." It expressed its "unbounded confidence in the invincible arm of the chieftain who has so long and so successfully commanded . . . reverentially acknowledging that he is but the instrument in the hands of Providence."[12]

But after nearly four years of thundering cannon, the very chieftain whom the artillerymen praised in their resolution was desperately thinking of compromise.

*　*　*

Informal, unofficial maneuvering toward peace was made official in late January when each president agreed to name commissioners to explore the possibilities. After balking at suggestions that Vice President Stephens head the Confederate delegation, Davis overcame his reservations and chose Stephens because he had been a friend of Lincoln's in the U.S. Congress. The other commissioners were Senator R. M. T. Hunter, once Speaker of the U.S. House, and Assistant Secretary of War John A. Campbell, former justice of the U.S. Supreme Court.

As they headed down the James expecting to take another boat to Washington, the *Examiner* was pushing for a convention of Southern states to abolish the Confederate constitution and depose Davis. Secretary of War Seddon resigned on February 1; Davis would replace him with Major General John Cabell Breckinridge, former vice president of the United States, who had won respect fighting in the West and the Shenandoah Valley. And at last Davis signed a bill to create a general in chief, voted by Congress as a gesture of no confidence in his own leadership. He named Lee to that post, though the general was reluctant, saying he could hardly manage more than the army outside the besieged capital.

As Sherman's army swept north out of Georgia into South Carolina, talk of peace was everywhere. Despite soldiers' militant resolutions, when Stephens and the Confederate peace commissioners passed the Southern lines, troops in gray cheered. A few minutes later, Union troops cheered louder.

Lincoln sent his secretary of state, William H. Seward, to meet the Confederates at Fortress Monroe rather than in Washington. Three days later Lincoln himself raised the stature of the meeting and the hopes of both capitals by joining the group at Hampton Roads. On February 3, in the salon of the steamboat *River Queen,* the five men had talks that might have ended the suffering without another shot. But their conversation never became negotiation; Lincoln insisted on one nation and the end of slavery, while the Confederates were bound to Davis's bottom line of Southern independence.

Before heading for the conference, Lincoln had advised Grant not to let anything happening there affect his military planning. He was not about to abandon his war aims after spending so much blood to come so far. He knew that if he did not reach those goals aboard the *River Queen,* the Union army would soon win them in the field. The day after Lincoln returned to Washington, Grant sent two corps attacking west at Hatcher's Run below Petersburg. Though they were turned back, they stretched Lee's lines yet thinner.

Substantively, Lincoln had rebuked Davis, but he had also cleared the air for both sides.

Richmond papers published the commissioners' report, asserting that the Union side had demanded complete Southern subjugation. Anger replaced peace talk in the Confederate capital. "New life was visible everywhere," said the *Examiner.* People were saying, "If any man now talks of submission, he should be hung from the nearest lamp post." "Valor alone is relied upon now for our salvation," J. B. Jones wrote. "Every one thinks the Confederacy will at once gather up its military strength and strike such blows as will astonish the world."[13]

Two evenings after the delegates returned, Governor Smith convened a meeting in the African Baptist Church at College and Broad streets to denounce Lincoln's stubbornness and inspire Confederates to soldier on.

Suddenly Davis appeared, unannounced, striding up the aisle. When the governor turned the rostrum over to him, Davis made "the most remarkable speech of his life." That was the judgment of even his devoted critic, Edward Pollard of the *Examiner,* who did "not recall ever to have been so much moved by the power of words spoken for the same space of time."

For more than an hour Davis went on, a strange light seeming to possess his "feeble, stricken face." He asserted that if the South matched Virginia's spirit, it could "teach the insolent enemy who had treated our propositions with contumely that in that conference in which he had so plumed himself with arrogance, he was, indeed, talking to his masters."

When Davis paused, the crowd shouted "Go on! Go on!" He lashed out at Lincoln's approval of the Thirteenth Amendment to end slavery in the Union. Good Confederates should now rush to enlist, he said, and if they did, Lincoln would be suing for peace "before the summer solstice." He ridiculed "the disgrace of surrender" with an army still in the field.[14]

Davis could not concede publicly that the tragic experiment of secession had failed. He refused to admit that willing it to succeed, insisting that it must succeed because it was right, and pledging to defend it unto death could not make it so. In rhetoric, do-or-die absolutism had been a Southern political habit for decades before the war. As crisis developed, it had been intended to bluff the North into letting the Confederacy go in peace. As war began, it was used to inspire soldiers and civilians, and in those early months Davis must have believed it. He and John Moncure Daniel and Henry Wise and the Deep South fire-eaters in Congress had made it treasonous for anyone around them to suggest doubt or to speak of compromise even after the long-dreaded siege began. To do so would mean that the Bottses and Footes and even Lincoln had been right, and that Jefferson Davis had been wrong. That was something Davis would never admit, and now the South went on suffering for it.

His burst of fierce bravado at the African Church was so well received that he helped plan another rally at the church on February 9. The auditorium was overcrowded, with many outside pushing to get in. Moses Hoge invoked the blessing of Providence before Judah Benjamin opened with a splash of cold realism. The South's white soldiers were fought out, said Benjamin; Lee had admitted that without reinforcements he must abandon Richmond—and by reinforcements he meant black soldiers. It must be done, and it must be done now, he said.

"Let us say to every negro who wants to go into the ranks, 'Go and fight, and you are free.' Don't press them, for that will make them run away, and they will be found fighting against us, instead of for us. . . . Let us stop the negro from going over to the enemy by saying, 'If you go over to the Yankees you will get your freedom, but you will perish off the earth, for you cannot live in that cold climate.'" Virginia must lead by sending 20,000 to the trenches within twenty days, and other states must follow, he said. It was the only way.[15]

Vice President Stephens was there, but he did not speak. He listened to Davis assert again that the Confederacy would fight through to victory.

"Demented," Stephens said later.

Davis's rallying cry was at last too much for the vice president. Shortly afterward he told the president he was going home to Georgia. There he went, and stayed. After the war, Stephens wondered whether Davis had based his seemingly demented predictions on the knowledge of some clandestine plot, such as kidnapping Abraham Lincoln.[16]

* * *

For months Confederate operatives in Richmond and Washington had planned to capture Lincoln and hold him hostage for Northern concessions. They hoped to catch him en route to the Soldiers' Home on Washington's northern outskirts, where he spent many nights, then to bring him through southern Maryland to Virginia. This planning could not have gone so far without Davis's approval. It was gathering speed at about the time Davis spoke at the African Church and would have to be carried out before spring, when renewed fighting would make it too late.[17]

Apparently Union agents never detected this plot, although since the previous spring, when Grant settled at City Point, the stream of Federal reports out of Richmond had become a flood.

On January 13, newly breveted Brigadier General George Sharpe, Grant's intelligence chief, wrote that his men had to take a long, circuitous route out of the city because the Confederates had tightened restrictions on travel, seemingly "for the purpose of preventing information going out of the real condition of the city, which is daily becoming worse." Gold was selling at $70 Confederate for $1 U.S.; flour was up to $800 a barrel.

Sharpe confided that one of his agents was an engineer on the vital Danville railroad, which now connected with Greensboro and the lower South. The trainman reported that Lee's army was on half rations, and that beyond Danville the track was cut by flooding, probably for two weeks or more. Another Richmond informant sent Sharpe word saying, "Evacuation is upon everyone's lips . . . not only a matter of talk, but of earnest." Sharpe noted that one of his men, superintendent of a railroad (undoubtedly Samuel Ruth of the R.F.&P.), had attended a gloomy board of directors' meeting. "Our friends quite naturally send us word that the Union sentiment is largely on the gain," Sharpe wrote to General Meade.[18]

Five days later, Sharpe said an informant had heard of "a steamer prepared on the coast of North Carolina, in some creek, to take off the heads of Government. It is to sail for Nassau, and to go this month. . . ." Other agents reported that top Confederates were sending money North, "changing everything they have into gold." Gold by then was up to $107, and flour to $1,200.[19]

"Our news from Richmond is partly verbal, partly written, and partly in cipher," Sharpe told Meade. From Elizabeth Van Lew it came in all three forms.

Inside the back of her watch case, Van Lew kept the cipher Butler had provided for her. After she wrote a dispatch, she secreted it beneath a small couchant lion atop an iron pilaster decorating her library fireplace. Without speaking she left her message there to be picked up by an old black servant, Robert Oliver, who inserted it between the soles of his shoe, then plodded innocently down the road to the Van Lews' farm at Chaffin's Bluff below the city. Sometimes a seamstress working for Van Lew carried information to the farm in the hem of clothing. From there it was quickly relayed down the river into Yankee hands. Inquiries from Butler and later from Sharpe often came back inside a hollow shell hidden in a basket of farm-fresh eggs.[20]

Van Lew wrote that though she was able to contact Butler, "there was too much danger in the system and persons" during his command. Once Grant established headquarters at City Point, she was "more fortunate" in communicating via Sharpe. At times flowers she had picked in her garden were delivered in time to grace Grant's breakfast table the next morning.

She was stubbornly defiant of Confederate authority; when authorities scoured Richmond streets and stables taking civilian horses for army duty, she hid her last remaining steed in her smokehouse until she decided this was unsafe. Then she stabled it in the study of her mansion, where a thick layer of straw on the floor muffled its restlessness.[21]

After many months, Richmond grew accustomed to Van Lew's seeming eccentricity, but she was not ignored. The exact date of one of the most chilling threats to her is not recorded. Slipped beneath her door, crudely scrawled and decorated with a skull and crossbones, it was addressed to "Mrs Van Lough." "Look out for your fig bushes," it said. "There ain't much left of them now. White caps are around town. They are coming at night. Look out! Look out! Look out! Your house is going at last. FIRE. White Caps. Please give me some of your blood to write letters with."[22]

Earlier, Van Lew might have suspected that such harassment was the work of the provost marshal's heavy-handed detectives, someone like old "Anti-Christ" Caphart. But Caphart had departed, and in retrospect even he drew a few lines of sympathy from her. She wrote that he had

become shaky and dropsical, that he had trouble supporting his exten-
sive family on his skimpy pay, and got along only with the help of his
fellow detectives—yet he "still loved to see others suffer & their pains
were his pleasure."

On a raw night that winter, Caphart was waked by a child's wail and
told that he was a grandfather. He raised himself on his bed and said,
"Oh well, I must go up street in the morning and get him a pair of
boots." Then he fell back and closed his eyes forever.[23]

Van Lew persisted in her work, but not without fear. This seemed justified in late January, when detectives at Fredericksburg arrested two of
Samuel Ruth's accomplices, who had helped smuggle conscripts and deserters across the Potomac. In Richmond they brought in two more
Union operatives, F. W. E. Lohmann and John Hancock—along with
Rocketts tavern keeper James Duke, three of his sons, and more than
half a dozen men preparing to flee. Hancock was said to be carrying papers pinpointing defensive obstructions in the James River, reporting
movements of Confederate troops, and other military intelligence.[24]

Detectives then arrested Ruth himself at his R.F.&P. office at Eighth
and Broad streets and clapped him into Castle Thunder, charged with
regularly carrying information to the enemy. Some of those who had
slipped away north with the help of his network had talked freely about
it on the other side, and word had filtered back into Virginia.

Unlike Van Lew, Ruth was discreet in his opinions, so many Richmonders were skeptical of the charges against him. "His friends are slow
to believe him guilty, not only because of his previous good character,
but because of his peculiar and remarkable caution and reticence, and a
most marked disposition to mind only his own business," said the *Sentinel*, unintentionally describing the ideal undercover agent.[25]

Richmond newspapers were asked to delay disclosing these arrests
until more suspects were brought in. The *Examiner*, as so often, ignored
the request, and other papers followed suit. They said the case against
Ruth and his associates relied on the testimony of a "Mrs. Dade" of
King George County. But after she appeared at Ruth's hearing the case
fell apart, "there not appearing against him the first particle of evidence," said the *Sentinel*. "This is exactly what we expected." The *Whig*
called it "outrageous that a respectable citizen should be seized and
thrown into that abominable hole, Castle Thunder, upon no better
ground than a malicious whisper. The charge against Ruth was trumped
up by some of the creatures along the line of the Fredericksburg road,
whose title to free transportation he would never recognize."

Ruth was freed after nine days in the Castle, and researchers have
wondered since whether threats against the key witness or bribes to of-

ficials may have won his release while Lohmann and Hancock stayed in jail.[26]

With his innocence thus certified, Ruth resumed work with inspired vengeance. In February, a Confederate quartermaster captain notified him that he wanted to send 200 tons of tobacco from Richmond to Hamilton's Crossing, the wartime terminus of the R.F.&P., to be swapped across the Potomac for bacon. Ruth immediately passed this on to Charles E. Carter, a courier for General Sharpe. That set in motion a perfectly timed, large-scale raid by Grant's army to break up the exchange of Confederate tobacco for Federal bacon, a trade that had been unofficially tolerated by both governments. The Yankees captured ninety-five tons of leaf, destroyed the Fredericksburg depot, trains, bridges, and miles of track, and took 400 prisoners.*[27]

* * *

Spies were underfoot, food was scarce, prices beyond reach, Grant closing in, Sherman rampaging through South Carolina—yet "meanwhile, the winter was passing in Richmond in most singular gayety."

That is how T. C. DeLeon recalled it, for he traveled among young officers and women determined to dance through the darkness, for whom shortages merely meant a new style of party. They "chatted and laughed as if there were no tomorrow, with its certain skirmish, and its possible blanket for winding-sheet."[29]

At least a few girls felt guilty about it; a committee of them asked General Lee whether he thought they should be dancing at such a time. "Why of course, my child," he said. "My boys need to be heartened up when they get their furloughs. Go on, look your prettiest, and be just as nice to them as ever you can be!"[30]

Soldiers often rode straight from ballroom to battle; many stopped at church to be married on the way. "There seems to be a perfect mania on the subject of matrimony," said Judith McGuire.[31]

At St. Paul's, dashing young Brigadier General John Pegram took Hetty Cary of the Baltimore Carys as his bride—"one of the handsomest and most lovable men I ever knew wed to the handsomest woman in the Southland," wrote Henry Kyd Douglas. President and Mrs. Davis lent their carriage and horses to take the couple to church; on the way the horses balked, threatening to tip the carriage, then

---

*After the war Ruth, Lohmann, and Carter sought compensation from the U.S. government by submitting an itemized account of their wartime services. The list of their supporting witnesses and other petitioners is a useful though incomplete roster of the Unionist underground in Richmond.[28]

Hetty's dress was torn going into church, and her veil almost ripped away as she neared the altar where Dr. Minnigerode waited. Superstitious attendants thought these mishaps foreboding, but otherwise all was happiness.

The couple honeymooned in a cottage near Pegram's command on the Petersburg front. When his division passed in review, Hetty took the honors while Lee stood by with other ranking officers. "A rare light illumined her eyes and her soul was on fire with the triumph of the moment, the horrors of war forgotten," wrote Douglas.

Four days after that parade and three weeks after his wedding, Pegram was shot near the heart in the heavy fighting at Hatcher's Run. He died almost immediately. His bride, now his widow, rode back to Richmond sitting beside his body in a boxcar, then stood in black beside his casket to hear Minnigerode's obsequies at St. Paul's. The band wailed its dirges on the way to Hollywood, in the last such ceremonial procession of the war.[32]

* * *

In mid-February steady sleet made footing treacherous on Richmond's muddy streets. Ice on the river and canal creaked as it began to break up after a record cold spell. Business, in the courts and music halls and skimpily stocked shops, proceeded almost as usual.

Mayor Mayo set bail for a batch of soldiers "arrested in their cups for violating the picayune laws of the city," ordering them "to keep the peace towards everybody except the Yankees." At the Richmond Theater fans of the finer things could enjoy "The Brigand," with "new and beautiful mountain scenery, picturesque and characteristic costumes, a grand corps de ballet and a full and complete chorus." At Budd & McDowell's Opera House, formerly the Varieties, those of less refined taste could catch "laughable burlesques, new songs, jokes &c" from Billy Lewis, Harry Budd, and Miss Alice Ringo; a free brass band concert preceded each performance.

Soldiers and citizens bought newspaper ads to seek properties stolen or strayed:

"$1000 REWARD—Stolen from camp of McGregor's battery, near Belfield, Va, on the night of 28th January, a bay horse, about 15 1/2 hands high, in fine order, right hind foot white, a small white, round spot on the left side, slightly saddle marked on the right side and slightly stringhalted to right hind foot. It is thought the horse has been or will be sold on the route from this camp to Floyd county, Va."

"$1,000 REWARD—Left my house on the night of the 11th instant, two servants—Mary and Cynthia. Mary is a bright mulatto, about 25 or

26 years of age, and about five feet high. Cynthia is a ginger cake color, about five feet, five or six inches high, slender figure and delicate appearance. Left in company with one or two negro men, and supposed to be making their way to the Yankees. I will give the above reward for the two, or five hundred dollars for either of said negroes."[33]

* * *

That Wednesday Robert E. Lee, nominally in command of Confederate armies everywhere since February 6, came up to Richmond from his headquarters outside Petersburg. He strode in and out of the Capitol "as if some great event was imminent." He looked red-faced, cheerful, and vigorous in the mid-February cold, though his beard seemed whiter every day.[34]

But the clerk who thought Lee looked so positive could not see what was going on in the general's mind. The previous week, Lee had written that his troops in snow and sleet had not had a mouthful of meat for three days; they were becoming so weak that they could not march and fight. When new secretary of war Breckinridge opened Lee's message, Commissary General Northrop was there. "Yes," sniffed Northrop, "it is just what I predicted long ago."

Breckinridge passed the letter to Davis, who ordered that meat and whiskey be dispatched to the lines before the commissary department slept. Northrop disdained the order. "Sensational," he said. Breckinridge was amazed and infuriated, and at last Lucius B. Northrop was sacked, to be replaced on February 16 by Brigadier General Isaac M. St. John, who had successfully run the mining and niter bureau. By moving supplies directly from farmers to the railroads to the army, bypassing commissary depots, St. John promptly though temporarily boosted rations in the winter lines.[35]

In the Capitol the Senate was still debating ways to cut the ridiculous number of exemptions from the draft. The House was in secret session again, still debating the use of black troops. Lee had just thanked Henry Wise's Virginia brigade for adopting a resolution of willingness to accept gradual emancipation of slaves if that would bring independence and peace. Lee's public thanks hinted at his assessment of the situation—one bureaucrat said it was "a strong indication (confirmatory) that Gen. Lee is an emancipationist." Privately, the general went beyond hints.[36]

At the family's townhouse on Franklin Street he paced the room as he talked to his son, Custis, who sat by the fireplace with a cigar and the newspapers:

"Well, Mr. Custis, I have been up to see the Congress and they do not seem to be able to do anything except to eat peanuts and chew tobacco, while my army is starving. . . .

"When this war began I was opposed to it, bitterly opposed to it, and I told these people that unless every man should do his whole duty, they would repent it—and now, they will repent."[37]

How long Lee had seen what lay ahead is uncertain: perhaps since the moment Grant began stretching his siege lines about Richmond and Petersburg; perhaps since the day Lincoln was reelected. Perhaps Lee had known since he considered the rolls of the Army of Northern Virginia as winter began and wrote to Davis that without some reasonable approximation of the enemy's numbers, "I fear a great calamity will befall us." Perhaps, indeed, he had known from the beginning.

By now, deep in winter, the situation was so clear to him that he violated a rule he had nearly always kept, stepping across the line that divides soldiers from politicians. Because R. M. T. Hunter was an old personal friend, Lee called on him and said that if Hunter thought there was any way to reach peace without surrender, he should propose it now.

Hunter would not, because he had said the same thing to Davis earlier and the president had refused, apparently telling others that Hunter had become a defeatist. Lee urged Hunter to reconsider, adding that if he himself proposed such a thing it would amount to surrender. True, said Hunter, but if the general thought all hope was gone, he should tell Davis so.

Lee did not respond directly; he spoke of a recent victory after which his troops pleaded for shoes and food. "These and other circumstances betraying the utmost destitution he repeated with a melancholy air and tone which I shall never forget," wrote Hunter.[38]

*　　*　　*

Two days later, the sleet turned to cold rain. At 7:30 that evening, at the First Baptist Church on Broad Street, two blocks from the president's house, the Presbyterian minister Joseph C. Stiles took the pulpit.

For the last four of Dr. Stiles's 70-plus years, around regimental campfires, in brush-arbor chapels and muddy fields, he had preached to troops of the Army of Northern Virginia, promising that they would win if they walked with the Lord. As a chaplain he had stoked the great revivals that swept through the army in the two middle winters of the war. Now, in from the front, he stood in the Greek-temple church to evangelize those who made decisions at the faintly beating heart of the Confederacy.

For two hours he talked, comparing Richmond to other desperately besieged cities of history. He told of the sixteenth-century battle for the

city of Leyden, attacked by the Spanish during "the *80 years* war that re-
sulted in the establishment of the Dutch republic."

Stiles recalled "how famine and pestilence destroyed the population
and the garrison; how corpses putrified in the houses and streets because
men were too few and too feeble to inter them; how the soldiers were reduced to a small band of skeletons; how, when the besiegers taunted
them as rat-eaters and dog-eaters, they replied, 'We are rat-eaters and
dog-eaters; and as long as you can hear a dog bark or a cat meow, know
that we will not surrender! And when the dogs and cats and rats are all
consumed, every man will cook the flesh off his left arm that he live
longer to fight you with his right arm! And when we can do no more, we
will not surrender; we'll *fire the city,* and with our women and children,
perish in the flames!' "

The preacher's eyes shone beneath his thick brows. His gray curls
shook as he spoke. He reached back further, 1,800 years, to tell of the
Roman sentinel posted at the gate of Pompeii when Vesuvius erupted:

"The earth beneath him heaved and rocked, but he kept his post! The
air was whirling madly around him, but he kept his post! Before him the
mountain was belching forth its bowels of fire—but he kept his post!
Behind him the terrified people were fleeing in dismay, and he kept his
post!

"My countrymen!" Stiles roared. "That old sentinel is the model man
for you!"

He wished he could bring all the South's "submissionists and recon-
structionists" to stand before him. "They are four-years men!" he said
with contempt. If he had them there he would "play schoolmaster, put
slate and pencil in the hands of every one of them, and make him work
out this problem: How many of you would it take to make one Dutch-
man? How many four-years men to make one eighty-years man?"

Today's struggle is "a war between despotism and liberty," he said, and
"liberty is strongest because its foundations are God and nature."
Despotism must succumb, he declared, "because it rests upon Sin and
the devil."

"If our armies were reduced to one man: if the enemy's army were
augmented till it included every other man on the globe, that would not
shake my confidence, if we put our trust in God. For before the enemy's
host could succeed, it must go right through the truth, the justice and
the power of Jehovah!"

Thomas Thweatt Tredway, a Virginia legislator from Prince Edward
County, followed the preacher through every minute of his mighty sermon. It echoed inside him overnight, and the next morning as the sun
broke through and a southern breeze freshened the city. Sitting to begin

a letter to his daughter back home at the plantation called Prospect, Tredway tried to reproduce every word of the preacher's challenge.

Stiles had made a "sublime . . . soul-inspiring" talk, "a grand argument and a grander appeal," he wrote. "I wish all of you at home & all the men & women in the Confederate States could have heard it. . . ."[39]

That February morning, Tredway seemed to believe that if every loyal Southerner had been at First Baptist Church, had heard the legends of Leyden and Pompeii the way Joseph Stiles told them, somehow it would have made a difference.

CHAPTER TWENTY-FOUR

WHO WILL ANSWER
FOR THE SLAIN?

*T*he flare of defiance that lit Richmond after Lincoln refused to deal at Hampton Roads was but "a short fever of the public mind," which quickly abated.

"People are almost in a state of desperation," wrote ordnance chief Josiah Gorgas. "Lee is about all we have and what confidence is left rallies around him, and he it seems to me fights without much heart in the cause. . . . The President has alas! lost almost every vestige of the public confidence."[1]

Despite the gloom, despite the fact that departmental officials were boxing their archives for flight, people were still coming to Richmond. How they saw the city in that dark March depended much on where they had come from.

"Sherman's army can't expect to over-run the whole earth," wrote one refugee from South Carolina. "We are safe enough in Richmond. . . . The whole South seems to be rallying there."

She was Malvina Black Gist, a 22-year-old widow whose husband had been killed near Chickamauga. At Columbia she had got a job signing Confederate currency when the Treasury moved that function from Richmond on Grant's approach. Now, on Sherman's approach to Columbia, the Treasury clerks had been sent back to the Confederate capital, and Malvina was excited.

"We have taken Richmond, if the Yankees haven't!" she wrote in her diary. "The city is crowded to suffocation, the streets thronged with soldiers in uniform, officers gaily caparisoned, and beautiful women, beautifully dressed. . . . I should say there is no more brilliant capital among all the nations. Are there great and somber tragedies going on around us? Is there a war? I thought so before I reached Richmond!"

Her spell lasted a few days. As a lively young newcomer and the daughter-in-law of South Carolina's former governor, Malvina was caught up in the capital's near-frantic round of parties, hobnobbing with generals, cabinet secretaries, and the president himself. A cavalry review on the outskirts was "the sight of a lifetime; it thrilled and pulsated all through me," she wrote, giddy as other girls had been in the spring of 1861. "Oh! the seduction, the novelty, the fascination of this life in Richmond! If patriotism is its master chord, pleasure is no less its dominant note, and while it is as indescribable as the sparkle of champagne, it is no less intoxicating."[2]

At one of those parties Malvina met Thomas Conolly, just arrived, an Irish member of Parliament who was even more generously feted by social Richmond. He saw the city with different eyes; his first adjective for it was "wretched." Shops were open with nothing to sell, strewn with empty packing boxes and straw. Streets were full of "rowdies . . . in all habiliments . . . dubious—dull—sparkling—moody furious—mad, raving or stupid intoxication—pickets of mud-stained-slough-hatted raw-boned cavalry . . . mud, mud, mud everywhere. . . ." Conolly noted few women "of the better class" abroad, most of them in mourning. In the Spotswood he heard "a babel of chatter & oaths," the word "Yankee, & Yanks" in every conversation.[3]

* * *

During late February and early March, prisoners of both sides had glutted the hungry city again—4,000 or 5,000 Confederates returned by the Federals, billeted at Camp Lee, with another 10,000 Yankees said to be on their way from Wilmington. Davis and Lee urged the paroled Southerners to go straight back into the lines rather than take the usual postrelease furlough at home, from which they might never return.[4]

Looking beyond the siege lines, Southern leaders faced the fact that in two weeks Sherman had taken Columbia and left it in ruins, Charleston had been evacuated, and Wilmington, the Confederacy's last major port, had fallen. Sherman's divisions were rampaging into North Carolina, driving back the Confederate army that Davis had placed again under Joe Johnston's command.

The president and Congress were determined that if Richmond fell, the Yankees would not profit by capturing stored commodities as they had when they took mountains of baled cotton at Savannah in December. Thus in mid-February Lee passed orders to Lieutenant General

Richard S. Ewell, commanding city defenses, to make standby plans for destroying whatever tobacco and cotton could not be taken away.[5]

James Longstreet, in charge of Lee's forces north of the James River, thought he had picked up a hint from Union major general E. O. C. Ord that Grant now held such a strong hand that he might be willing to discuss peace. Lee was skeptical, but on March 2, with Davis's approval, he sent a secret letter to the Federal commander, proposing a meeting to consider "a satisfactory adjustment of the present unhappy difficulties by means of a military convention."

As Lee dispatched the letter across the lines, he wrote to Davis that he did not believe Grant would consider any terms "unless coupled with the condition of our return to the Union"—and "whether this will be acceptable to our people yet awhile I cannot say." Instead of "our people," he might have said "our president."[6]

That same day, Sheridan's Union army was crushing and scattering the remains of Early's Confederate force at Waynesboro in the Shenandoah Valley and was about to march east across the Blue Ridge to join Grant. Had Lee known this, he might not have bothered to write. With Sheridan coming from the Valley and Sherman from the south, the Union commander had little incentive to talk terms. Lincoln understood this; he directed Grant not to communicate with Lee unless it was to arrange Confederate capitulation, and meantime to press his military advantages "to the utmost."

On March 4, Grant rejected Lee's proposal to talk. That noon Lincoln stood at the east front of the Capitol in Washington to deliver his second inaugural address. With the actor John Wilkes Booth close by among the spectators, the president of the United States hoped and prayed "that this mighty scourge of war may speedily pass away." In words later likened to a sacred poem, he spoke "with malice toward none; with charity for all."

But Richmond paid more attention to what Lincoln said between those remembered phrases: "If God wills that [war] continue, until all the wealth piled by the bond-man's two hundred and fifty years of unrequited toil shall be sunk, and until every drop of blood drawn with the lash shall be paid by another drawn with the sword, as was said three thousand years ago, so still it must be said, 'the judgments of the Lord are true and righteous altogether.'"[7]

In the besieged Confederate capital where preachers and politicians had long assured the public that the Lord would see them through, Lincoln's promise that the lash would be repaid by the sword angered many. "Since both presidents resort to religious justification, it may be feared the war is about to assume a more sanguinary aspect and a more cruel nature than ever before," Jones wrote. Others noted quietly that Lincoln's promise, or threat, applied only if war went on.[8]

* * *

Late the night before Lincoln spoke, Lee had sat in his headquarters near Petersburg, reading and rereading the latest strength reports from his army. Their meaning was inescapable, but he wanted someone else's judgment. He sent for Major General John B. Gordon of Georgia, now a corps commander. After 2:00 a.m., Gordon arrived and Lee told him to go over the reports.

"The revelation was startling," Gordon recalled. Some officers had gone beyond numerical accounting to tell of "depleted strength, emaciation and decreased power of endurance among those who appeared on the rolls as fit for duty." Morale and even discipline were collapsing.

Lee reckoned in thousands of troops: Only 35 of his 50 were fit for duty. Grant had about 150, Sheridan was bringing 20 from the Valley, and another 30 were coming from Tennessee. Approaching from the south, Sherman had perhaps 80 against Johnston's 13 to 15. Altogether, Lee figured, Grant would soon have roughly 280 in the east. To deal with them, the Confederates had about 65.

Lee asked Gordon what he would do.

Gordon was one of Lee's most aggressive generals. Unabashed at being asked rather than told, he said that he would seek peace terms, "the best we can get." If that is impossible, leave Richmond and Petersburg, retreat south, join Johnston and strike Sherman. If neither of those, fight here immediately, before it is too late.

Hesitantly, Gordon asked Lee what he thought.

"I agree with you fully," said the commander.

Lee did not tell Gordon that he had already written to Grant, for that was kept secret between him and Davis. He said he thought that a soldier had no business giving political advice, but at Gordon's urging he promised to talk with Davis again.[9]

If Lee brought up negotiations when he met the president the next day in Richmond, he did not get far. Grant's reply arrived that day, and hardened Davis's stand against even mentioning any terms short of Southern independence. Davis and Lee then focused on plans for pulling out of the capital—not whether to do it, but when and how.

For many weeks evacuation had been more than a matter of nervous rumor. As long ago as January, according to Senator Benjamin Hill, Lee had secretly told congressional questioners that leaving Richmond would not necessarily end the struggle. Hill said Lee told them that militarily, evacuation would in fact make him stronger than before. From "a moral and political" viewpoint, Richmond's fall would be "a serious calamity," Lee reportedly conceded, but once it happened, he could prolong the war for two more years on Virginia soil. Since the war began, he had been forced to let the enemy make strategic plans for him, because he had to defend the capital, but "when Richmond falls I shall be able to make them for myself."[10]

Now, after two more months of mounting catastrophes, Davis asked Lee, If withdrawal is inevitable, why not move immediately? Lee said the army's horses were too weak to pull wagons and cannon through the March mud. In two or three weeks, the roads would be passable.

As soon as he could move, Lee would attack to cut Grant's lines below the Appomattox River, forcing the Federal commander to shorten his position. That would allow Lee to hold him back with fewer men, freeing picked troops to hurry south, join Johnston, and strike Sherman before he came near. If Lee's offensive against Grant's lines failed, he would then abandon Richmond-Petersburg and move to join Johnston with his entire remaining army, hoping to defeat Sherman and then fight Grant in a war of maneuver.

Conferring with Gordon, Lee decided to surprise Grant with a sudden assault on Fort Stedman, a Federal strongpoint just east of Petersburg.[11]

* * *

While eating peanuts and chewing tobacco, Confederate lawmakers in closed session had debated using black troops almost constantly since late 1864. Senator Wigfall spoke for many when he declared that he "wanted to live in no country in which the man who blacked his boots and curried his horse was his equal."[12] But "the idea of employing negroes to help in the defence of their homes has greatly ripened in the publick mind," John Daniel's *Examiner* said after the editor had stormed against it for months. Now Daniel was ill, and the Irishman John Mitchel was substituting for him. In part, the paper blamed "the atrocious ultimatum of the enemy at Hampton Roads" for this evolution in its opinion. But the real reason was that Lee's call for black soldiers had become known, and "the country will not venture to deny to General Lee, in the present condition of affairs, *anything* he may ask for."[13]

In February the surgeon in charge of Richmond's Jackson Hospital asked hired male slaves there whether they would "be willing to take up arms to protect their masters' families, homes and their own from an attacking foe." Sixty of the seventy-two said yes—which, under the circumstances, was less remarkable than the fact that the remaining dozen did not. Throughout the army, officers put the question to their soldiers,

and thousands of white Southerners initially infuriated by the Yankees'
use of blacks were ready to accept help of any color.[14]

But even Lee's influence, even while his army dwindled away, did not
clinch the decision. R. M. T. Hunter, former speaker of the U.S. House,
U.S. senator, Confederate secretary of state, and still a wealthy slave
owner, was the key senator blocking congressional approval. The Virginia legislature demanded that he change his vote or resign. Thus ordered, Hunter finally relented, but not without protest.

His speech to the Senate was a dirge for the peculiar institution.

The South had left the Union thinking it had gotten rid of "slavery
agitation" forever, Hunter said. But to his surprise he had found that
"this Government assumes the power to arm the slaves, which involves
also the power of emancipation." He blamed this assumption for "the
gloom which now overspreads our people." It was seen as "a confession
of despair and an abandonment of the ground upon which we had seceded. . . ."

Secessionists had contended "that slavery was the best and happiest
condition of the negro." But if for serving, "we offer slaves their freedom
as a boon, we confess that we were insincere, were hypocritical. . . ."
And if the very basis of secession is abandoned, "who is to answer for
the hundreds of thousands of men who have been slain in the war? Who
is to answer for them before the bar of Heaven? . . .

"Something in the human heart and head" agrees that if slaves are
scarred by fighting, then they should be free, Hunter conceded. But "if
we could make them soldiers, the condition of the soldier being socially
equal to any other in society, we could make them officers"—and where
might that lead?

Hunter argued that not enough blacks could be enrolled without
stripping the South of labor that was essential to produce food. "If we
depend upon their volunteering we can't get them, and those we do get
will desert to the enemy, who can offer them a better price than we can."
The bill was bad in principle and worse as expediency, he said. He
would vote for it only because he was instructed to do so; he hoped it
would not have the "evil effects" that he feared.[15]

Congress argued into the night after Hunter's shift, and chewed on
the bill for another week before finally passing it on March 13. Promptly
afterward, recruiting notices appeared in the Richmond papers alongside offers of rewards for runaway slaves.

Majors J. W. Pegram and Thomas P. Turner opened a "rendezvous" with
"every arrangement [for] the comfort of the new recruits." They aimed
their appeal at owners and employers rather than at blacks themselves:

Will not the people of Virginia, in this hour of peril and danger, promptly respond to the call of the loved General-in-Chief, and the demands of the Confederate and State governments? Will those who have freely given their sons and brothers, their money and their property, to the achievement of the liberties of their country, now hold back from the cause their servants, who can well be spared, and who will gladly aid in bringing this fearful war to a speedy and glorious termination?[16]

Hopes at first were high. Letters poured into the War Department from "men of military skill and character," offering to raise companies, battalions, and regiments of black troops. "If 300,000 efficient soldiers can be made of this material, there is no conjecturing where the next campaign may end," one determined dreamer said.[17]

But what was happening around them hardly convinced slaves and their masters that their service would be honored, and lift the Confederacy to victory. Just as recruiting began, two slaves named Oliver and George were to be hanged for burglarizing Minnigerode's home. Their drastic sentence was part of the city's response to a surge of crime by increasingly defiant blacks. For cohabiting with a white woman as his mistress, another slave named Richard was given three whippings of thirty-nine lashes each, spaced over a week.

The day after the scheduled hanging of Oliver and George, the newspapers reported that Governor Smith had intervened and sentenced the condemned slaves to the army instead of to execution. "Sentimental and slimy benevolism," the *Examiner* called it. Recruiting officers were outraged, declaring that "these slaves have not been and *positively* will not be enlisted in the Confederate service." The damage to recruiting was already done by the governor's implication that armed service was a form of punishment, a fair alternative to death by hanging.[18]

One night after the black-soldier bill was passed, a red light seemed to float on Richmond's western horizon; many were sure that it was a signal from Sheridan to Grant that the city would be attacked at dawn. It turned out to be only a signal from one defensive camp to another, but learning that did not lighten the atmosphere in the city.

Above the Capitol someone raised the Confederate flag to show that Congress was in session—but it was upside down. Only a few remarked on it as the traditional signal of distress rather than an accident. Inside, lawmakers refused Davis's appeal for another suspension of habeas corpus. Amid a final, rancorous exchange of blame for what was happening, they then adjourned and headed home. Women were offering jewelry and silverware to the Treasury to help subsist the army. Red flags flew in front of houses along Clay Street, where owners were auctioning furniture or renting to the highest bidder.[19]

A commercial traveler who had made many Richmond trips said that as soon as he stepped off the train this time, "I knew something was wrong; there seemed a death-like stillness to pervade the city; every one wore a haggard, scared look, as if apprehensive of some great impending calamity." His banker told him to change whatever Confederate paper he held into specie at once—which he did, at $100 to $1.[20]

Conolly, the Irish M.P., spent an evening at the president's house and found Mrs. Davis's amiability departed; she scathed the Yankees with a "bitter malevolent tongue." Perhaps she was more bitter than usual because when no visitors were present, she was arguing with her husband about her own departure.[21]

By then Davis had disclosed and the papers had printed the previously secret exchange of letters between Lee and Grant, in which the Confederate commander had sought terms. "Sad delusion!" Jones commented.[22]

Other secrets, not published, might as well have been.

As March began, one of Union general Sharpe's Richmond agents had reported that "yesterday afternoon at 2 o'clock . . . there was no bulletin on the boards of the daily newspapers, at the War Office, or elsewhere" to confirm a rumored defeat of Sherman. Sharpe's spy had actually ridden with the Confederate officer of the day to visit posts between the city's interior and exterior defenses. He reported that the Tredegar Iron Works was closed and that machinery from Tredegar and unfinished munitions from the Confederate arsenal were being sent by the James River canal toward Lynchburg. Sharpe said that "our friends" reported a meeting at Davis's house, at which the final decision on destroying stored tobacco and cotton in Richmond was left to General Ewell.[23]

But there was no agreement on what to do about other property that might be of use to the enemy. Joseph Anderson, proprietor of the Tredegar, urged Secretary of War Breckinridge not to destroy the works. The Yankees have more iron mills than they need, Anderson said, and they could bring munitions south cheaper than shipping raw materials to Richmond. Ordnance chief Gorgas agreed, but Secretary of the Navy Mallory said, "If we abandon Richmond it will be done, presumably, without hope of recovery," and so the works should be prepared for destruction.[24]

Federal spies seemed to know of every Confederate stratagem sooner than the officers assigned to carry it out—and some suspected operations so secret that their existence has never been confirmed. "A source which has heretofore been well informed" reported talk of a tunnel being built toward Fort Harrison, the redoubt captured by the Yankees the previous fall. This source also said that Sheridan's destruction of the James River canal above the city on his way east was "the most serious blow ever felt in Richmond," cutting supplies so sharply that butter was up to $20 a pound. Because the government was snatching horses off the streets, suburban farmers were refusing to bring food to market, and "people are really in a deplorable state." "May God bless and bring you soon to deliver us," the spy wrote. "We are in an awful situation."

Sharpe's informant could not have realized how accurate some of his news would turn out to be. He—or she—reported on March 23 that "one of our city officials has said that the Confederates intend to leave here in ten days from this time. . . ." The most visible sign of this intention was the steady dispatch of machinery via the Danville railroad, "which is taxed to its utmost day and night carrying away boxes, most of which are marked Salisbury and some Danville."[25]

These agent reports added to Grant's mounting pile of evidence that the Confederates were planning evacuation. Other messages were of specific tactical value, saving Union lives and costing the Confederates. Samuel Ruth claimed after the war that he had learned of Lee's planned attempt against Grant's lines, and passed word on to the Union commander. He could not tell when the attack would come, "but understood that it would be made as soon as the ground was dry enough to move artillery."[26]

On March 20, Grant had invited Lincoln to City Point for a visit. The president arrived on the twenty-fourth, bringing along Mrs. Lincoln and their son, Tad. Aboard a riverboat, Grant told him he feared that if Lee got away to join Johnston, the war might drag on through the summer. Lincoln went to bed expecting to come ashore the next day to review Grant's troops.

But before dawn on March 25, John B. Gordon sent his Confederates storming into Fort Stedman, capturing that Federal strongpoint and starting to envelop positions right and left. Lee's plan seemed about to succeed, then it faltered. Gordon thought there was a second Union line, which confused matters. Reinforcements did not arrive. After the initial surprise, Union artillery blasted Fort Stedman and counterattacking infantry sealed off the penetration. Lee reluctantly ordered Gordon to withdraw before he lost his whole corps.

The commanding general's two sons, cavalrymen Rooney and Rob, met him as he rode back from Gordon's front. Rob Lee remembered his father's sad face for years afterward. Lincoln telegraphed to Washington that his own son Robert, an aide to Grant, "tells me there was a little rumpus up the line this morning, ending about where it began."[27]

What was to him "a little rumpus" was the last offensive effort of Robert E. Lee and the Army of Northern Virginia. It cost some 3,500 Confederate casualties, most of them captured, but it gained not a foot of ground and probably not a minute of time. One realistic Confederate called it "only the meteor's flash that illumines for a moment and leaves the night darker than before."[28]

Lee wrote to Davis: "I fear now it will be impossible to prevent a junction between Grant and Sherman, nor do I deem it prudent that this army should maintain its position until the latter shall approach too near. . . ."[29]

* * *

The day after the Federals repulsed Lee's attack at Fort Stedman, Lincoln watched from the riverboat *Mary Martin* as Sheridan brought his cavalry divisions across a pontoon bridge to the south side of the James.

After dispersing Early's remnants at Waynesboro, Sheridan had marched his cavalry east across the Blue Ridge and the Piedmont, destroying railroads, bridges, and locks on the James River canal. With bridges out, he could not reach Grant by crossing above Richmond, so he swung north of the city. Major General George E. Pickett's Confederate division, held by Longstreet as a mobile reserve at Manchester, hurried through the capital to meet Sheridan, raising fears of a new Yankee thrust from that direction, then marched back to the south side.

Sheridan's divisions veered away to White House on the Pamunkey, rested and refitted, then crossed below Richmond to join Grant as he prepared the opening blow of his spring campaign. On Sheridan's arrival, Grant had a fast-moving strike force to hurl at Lee anywhere along his thinly manned defenses.

In Richmond, accounts of Sheridan's swath across central Virginia played against the background of talk about imminent evacuation. The *Dispatch* printed a table of distances from Richmond to various towns in Carolina. Judith McGuire was sure that whatever Lee and Davis decided would be right, "but it would almost break my heart to see this dear old city, with its hallowed associations, given over to the Federals." Each morning, as she arrived at the commissary department, she looked to see if any of the boxes packed with records had disappeared, and was relieved as long as they were still there.

Before Sheridan reached Grant, Judith heard that his raiders had been allowed "to commit any cruelty on noncombatants that suited their rapacious tempers. . . . Can we feel patient at the idea of such soldiers coming to Richmond, the target at which their whole nation, from their President to the meanest soldier upon their army rolls, has been aiming for four years? Oh, I would that I could see Richmond burned to the ground by its own people . . . before its defenceless inhabitants should be subjected to such degradation!"[30]

Yet few despaired in public.

Only nine days after Congress approved enlisting black soldiers, thousands of citizens jammed Capitol Square to watch the first three companies parade in their new uniforms, keeping time to fife and drum. Two companies were made up of attendants and nurses from Winder and Jackson hospitals, the third from Captain Turner's recruiting station. The hospital companies were not picked men but of "all sizes, from three feet to six foot six, while complexions ranged from black down to ginger-bread and olive." Reviews of their performance varied: The crowd liked it, but Jones called it "a ridiculous affair." Everyone except perhaps children and the new recruits understood that it was too late to matter, yet there it was—something tangible and strutting instead of more rhetoric and faultfinding.[31]

Even the news from Fort Stedman was encouraging at first, because it totally misrepresented the repulse as a Confederate victory. Davis, however, got the hard facts from Lee, and gently but decisively told his wife that it was time for her to go south. Soon his headquarters would be in the field, he said. There a wife and children "would only embarrass and grieve him, instead of comforting him."

Varina resisted, pleading to stay, but he told her that she could only protect the children and help him by leaving. "If I live, you can come to me when the struggle is ended," he said, "but I do not expect to survive the destruction of constitutional liberty."

Davis gave her all his Confederate money and all his gold but one five-dollar piece. Varina thought of asking Richmond friends to take care of her silverware, but Davis feared that that would cause the friends trouble with the Yankees. She sold her household bric-a-brac, and for it got a sizable check that she never cashed. She had stored barrels of flour, but Davis said "anything in the shape of food" could not go; the people of Richmond needed it.

The day before she left, Davis handed her a pistol and showed her how to load, aim, and fire it. He was afraid she would be stopped by the bands of deserters and thieves roaming the countryside. "You can at least, if reduced to the last extremity, force your assailants to kill you," he advised. But he urged her to flee from any approaching enemy, to make her way to Florida and take a boat abroad if necessary.

"With hearts bowed down by despair," Varina and her children left Richmond. Davis almost collapsed in tears as his children begged to stay. Varina said "it was evident he thought he was looking his last upon us."

With only her clothes and luggage, she headed for Charlotte, some 300 miles southwest, escorted by Davis's private secretary, Burton Harrison. As soon as their train was beyond sight of Richmond, the engine halted and they sat there all night, eventually taking twelve hours to cover the first 140 miles to Danville.[32]

Lee's wife did not leave. He had written to her a month earlier, saying, "Should it be necessary to abandon our position to prevent being surrounded, what will you do? You must consider the question, and make up your mind. It is a fearful condition, and we must rely for guidance and protection upon a kind Providence. . . ." But the arthritic Mary Custis Lee had little choice. She stayed where she was, knitting for the soldiers, and as late as March 28, her husband the general in chief was patiently acknowledging receipt of another bag of socks, assuring her that "the count is all right this time."[33]

Grant was conferring aboard the *River Queen* that day with Lincoln and Sherman, who had come up from his army advancing through North Carolina. Admiral David Dixon Porter joined them. Lincoln said that once the Rebels were defeated he intended to welcome them back as U.S. citizens. Sherman proposed to slash north into Virginia, cutting the Richmond & Danville railroad and blocking Lee's line of retreat from Richmond and Petersburg. As Grant laid out his plans, he assured the president that this would be the final campaign.

The next morning, it began.

CHAPTER TWENTY-FIVE

WE MAY NEVER MEET AGAIN

For two months John Moncure Daniel had gradually weakened
in will and body as he lay in a tubercular fever at his Broad Street
home. Richmond's newspapers were reporting little about the
fighting beyond Petersburg, which made sophisticated men suspect the
worst. But enough driblets of news had reached Daniel for him to concede to close friends that the Southern cause was now hopeless and the
best course was "reconstruction on the best terms we could make."

Daniel would not see his fears come true. On the morning of March
30, the doctor found his pulse weak and turned to mix him a stimulant.
When he approached with a toddy of French brandy, Daniel had rolled
onto his back, folded his hands on his chest, closed his eyes, and died.[1]

He was "the pride and ornament of the Southern press," wrote his
successor at the *Examiner*. He departed "in the very crisis and agony of
a grand revolution which he had contributed more to bring about than
any other single individual. . . . If it be decreed that this Confederacy is
to be free and potent and honoured among the nations of the world,
there is no human agency to which we shall owe that result more than
that of John Moncure Daniel."[2] But if that were not to be, at least
Daniel would be spared life in the ruins of his revolution.

U. S. Grant had force-marched three divisions of the Army of the
James from north of that river to strengthen his drive against Lee's right
flank, west of Petersburg. He struck the Confederates around Hatcher's
Run before heavy rain slowed the operation late on March 29. Sheridan's cavalry and two infantry corps thrust west the next day near Din-

widdie Court House, trying to turn Lee's flank or stretch his lines so far that they had to break.

The rain let up on the final day of March, and Sheridan drove on beyond the right end of Lee's line, where some 10,000 Confederates tried to hold off 50,000 Union troops. For a while they did, Pickett's infantry forcing the Yankees back toward Dinwiddie Court House, then setting up around the vital crossroads of Five Forks.

Lee told Pickett the following morning that he and Fitz Lee must "hold Five Forks at all hazards." The battered Rebels dug in, singing "Annie Laurie" and "Dixie" as if they were back at Manassas in the first bloom of the Confederacy. But this time they were overwhelmed, almost half of them captured. This smashing Federal victory at Five Forks opened the way to Lee's rear and the South Side railroad.

In it Grant saw a chance to "end matters right here." Calm amid cheering headquarters officers, he scrawled a message, then stepped out and said, "I have ordered an immediate assault all along the lines." He sent a correspondent to Lincoln with a collection of Confederate battle flags taken by Sheridan. Aboard the *River Queen,* the president shook out the captured colors and shouted, "This means victory! This is victory!"[3]

* * *

With Grant's guns muttering in the background, some Richmonders had tried that Saturday to pretend the war was far away. Boys and girls played April fool's tricks; any seemingly lost purse on the sidewalk might fly away when a passerby leaned to pick it up.

That evening Secretary Breckinridge, Postmaster General Reagan, and other Confederate officials kept watch at the War Department, just as cabinet members had waited for news during the first big battle at Manassas. But at Mrs. John Enders's house, the Irish M.P. Thomas Conolly found "a merry party," with beauteous young women and dancing. They were doing what he called "curious quadrilles unlike anything I ever saw, a sort of country dance"—perhaps he was seeing the Virginia reel for the first time. Miss Mary Enders could play every request by ear, and the gaiety went on until midnight.[4]

The day had begun on a note of tense optimism, the *Sentinel* saying, "We are very hopeful of the campaign which is opening, and trust that we are to reap a large advantage from the operations evidently near at hand." The City Council held a special Saturday meeting; still concerned for the unfortunate, it approved more funds for the Richmond Soup Association and the Male Orphan Society. It resolved to pursue unpaid gas bills, heard a complaint that the keeper of Shockoe Hill bur-

ial ground was not clothing or paying his black gravediggers per con-
tract, and received a quarterly report from the city measurer of wood.[5]

Jefferson Davis, too, turned his head from what he knew was coming.
Burrowing in administration, he wrote to Lee that there was little
progress in enlisting black soldiers. Yet the adjutant general was still
sending recruiters to try, in places like Lynchburg and Halifax. "Work,
work, work," one officer urged; if Virginians knew how General Lee felt
about it they would volunteer their slaves for service. "Their wives and
daughters and the negroes are the only elements left us to recruit from,
and it does seem that our people would rather send the former even to
face death and danger than give up the latter."[6]

For weeks Phoebe Pember at Chimborazo Hospital had been watching government clerks pack to leave, wondering what she should do if
the Confederacy crashed around her. When she sent off requisitions for
drugs, the surgeon general advised her to use herbal remedies. The sick
laughed at these "yarb teas," not realizing why they got them instead of
licensed medicine. Phoebe resolved to stay with her patients, "on the
ground that no general ever deserts his troops." But she was frankly
afraid of what would happen when the Yankees came.[7]

To defend against raiders like Dahlgren and Sheridan, Richmond's
hospital attendants and recovering patients had been assigned to
standby battalions. Stacks of rifles, ammunition, and equipment waited
between wards. At Chimborazo, H. E. Wood, a wounded sergeant of
the Eighteenth Virginia, organized clerks, stewards, and convalescents.
"Scarcely an able-bodied soldier among them," Wood recalled. "I suppose every State in the Southern Confederacy was represented."

That night columns of troops tramped through Richmond and across
Mayo's Bridge as Lee summoned Longstreet with Brigadier General
Charles W. Field's division from north of the river to meet Grant's
offensive beyond Petersburg. That left Major General Joseph B.
Kershaw's shrunken command as the only infantry division in the
lines protecting the capital. General Ewell, commanding Richmond's
defenses, scraped the bottom of his reserve barrel to fill in beside those
veterans.

Sergeant Wood had gone to bed when a major came galloping to
Chimborazo, ordering him to gather his troops and report promptly to
Ewell at Capitol Square. As the major and the convalescent sergeant
talked, exploding shells were "painting hell on the sky" toward Petersburg.

On the green behind the Capitol, Ewell stood on the wooden leg he
had worn since Second Manassas, surrounded by army and civil officers,
pointing this way and that. He had only three hospital battalions to oc-

cupy the trenches being vacated by Field's division. As these units marched past Rocketts and out of the city by the Darbytown Road, what was left of the Virginia Military Institute cadets joined them. After the Yankees burned their school in Lexington, the cadets had been quartered at the former General Hospital No. 1, the building that before the war had been Richmond's almshouse. Now they went into the works alongside Ewell's irregulars.

Sergeant Wood positioned "a soldier here and there in sight of and in calling distance of each other," ordering them to put on "the most warlike and formidable display" to make the Yankees think the lines were as fully manned as ever. Only yards away, the Yankees were trying to make the Rebels think the same about their lines, thinned by earlier departures toward Petersburg.

Near Fort Harrison, bands on both sides filled the darkness with the last of the hundreds of musical exchanges that had drifted back and forth between contending camps in the past four years—"Dixie" vying with "Hail Columbia," and "My Maryland" with "The Star-Spangled Banner." "Very fine," wrote a soldier of the Thirteenth New Hampshire, "but exceedingly deceitful."[8]

Despite the pretense, soldiers on both sides understood late that evening that things were about to change. The red glare of bursting shells in the distance stirred Captain McHenry Howard, assistant inspector general of the capital's defenses, near Chaffin's Bluff. Flash after flash lit his tent until individual explosions blended into a continuous rumble. Howard and friends stepped outside, mounting the earthworks for a better view southwestward.

The night was dark with low clouds, the atmosphere damp and heavy. For half an hour Howard watched, feeling "something particularly awful in these half-suppressed, but deadly, signs of a far-off struggle, when contrasted with the perfect tranquility immediately around us." Concluding that for the moment it was someone else's fight, they turned in to sleep while they could.[9]

Grant's flat statement that he had directed "an immediate assault all along the lines" was not literally true. That night his generals were told to keep their divisions in close contact with the Confederates, probing to detect any withdrawals, ready to attack if given an opening. Meanwhile massed Union cannon fired as if there were no end to their ammunition, pounding Petersburg and the long Confederate line until well after midnight. Hoping to crush Lee before he could get away and try to join Johnston, Grant ordered his all-out attack on the Petersburg front to begin at 4:00 a.m.[10]

Richmond had heard guns before, much nearer than those. Because the Yankees had been turned back so many times, most citizens thought of their capital as "an impregnable Gibraltar," confident that "as long as Lee stood for the defence of Richmond, Richmond was safe." The winter had been hard, but so had every winter of the war. Morale had plunged, but hopes had always risen and Lee had always fought most brilliantly with the coming of Virginia's spring.[11]

* * *

"It seemed to me that a more perfect day could not have dawned on the earth since the creation. . . ."[12]

That is how a New England officer on the works east of Richmond reacted to Sunday morning, April 2. In the city, Secretary of the Navy Mallory thought that "the old city had never, during the war, worn an aspect more serene and quiet." A lady recalled that it was the kind of day "when delicate silks, that look too fine at other times, seem just to suit; when invalids and convalescents venture out into the sunshine."[13]

J. B. Jones was up early, paying more attention to rumor than to weather. He heard on the street that Pickett had met "fearful loss" beyond Petersburg on Saturday. The absence of any official report must mean the worst, he thought, and substituting reserves for veteran troops in the Richmond defenses must mean "an emergency of alarming importance."[14]

But to the uninformed majority, no news from the front was good news. Now, by some trick of the breeze, they could not hear what was happening around Petersburg. Last night's clouds were gone. If shells were bursting somewhere, no flashes could be seen against the soft hazy sky. Past budding trees and daffodils, thousands of Richmonders strolled to church.

Without Varina, Davis sat alone in his pew at St. Paul's. The Irishman Conolly was there, escorting lovely Nannie Thomas. So was the English correspondent Francis Lawley. So were Connie Cary, Sallie Brock, Emmie Crump, assorted generals, ranking bureaucrats, men on crutches, women in mourning—an auditorium more than full, if we believe all the many who claimed afterward to have been there.

It was the first Sunday of the month, communion Sunday. The powerfully eloquent Minnigerode, still speaking with a slight Hessian accent, had completed his regular service. As he remembered it, the congregation was on its knees, about to receive communion. Others recalled that the minister had just read Zechariah 2:20—"The Lord is in his holy temple; let all the earth keep silence before him"—when he paused and looked up. From the rear of the church the pompous sexton, William Irving, came down the aisle, touched the president on the shoulder, and handed him a message. Connie Cary, sitting behind Davis, said that a gray pallor came over Davis's face as he read it.[15]

The telegram, sent by Lee to Breckinridge, had arrived at the War Department at 10:40 a.m. It reported that Grant's troops had broken through the lines around Petersburg and ended, "I advise that all preparation be made for leaving Richmond tonight. I will advise you later, according to circumstances."[16]

Davis rose "with singular gravity and determination" and left quietly, hat in hand. Those watching understood that whatever this meant, it was serious; soon the sexton returned to summon another high official, then another and another. Minnigerode urged his audience to stay and be calm. Some said he managed to preside over collection of the weekly offering before the congregation rose to depart. By then "he might just as well have tried to turn back the waters of Niagara Falls."

His parishioners swarmed out into the sunshine, wondering what had happened. The first thing some saw was piles of documents burning outside government offices across the way.[17]

The crushing news interrupted services in churches all over Richmond. At Second Presbyterian, Moses Hoge was in mid-sermon when a messenger came up the aisle and gave him a note. Hoge glanced at it, then bowed his head on the lectern for a long moment before speaking. "Brethren," he said, looking up. "Trying times are before us. General Lee has been defeated; but remember that God is with us in the storm as well as in the calm. We may never meet again. Go quietly to your homes, and whatever may be in store for us, let us not forget that we are Christian men and women, and may the protection and blessing of the Father, the Son and Holy Ghost be with you all."

His congregation, almost entirely women and children, exited in hushed tears to hear the news that was sweeping Richmond.[18] At the African church well-dressed black worshippers emerged smiling, some looking eagerly down the street as if they expected the Yankees at any moment.[19]

Davis walked from St. Paul's around the corner of Capitol Square to his office in the Custom House. There he got the latest report from Lee, declaring it "absolutely necessary that we should abandon our position tonight," and heard the news that A. P. Hill had been killed. Then he sent runners to bring in his cabinet, Governor Smith, former governor Letcher, and Mayor Mayo. He explained the situation to them and told them to pack their archives to leave.

He also sent a message to Lee outside Petersburg, protesting that evacuating so quickly would mean the loss of "many valuables." Lee, who had been warning the president since late February that this day was coming, ripped up the president's telegram, saying, "I am sure I gave him sufficient notice."[20]

At the *Examiner* office John Mitchel rushed out a predated April 3 edition. In its last editorial, the once thunderous journal reported: "The decisive battle of the war in Virginia, as far as it concerns the fate of Richmond, is believed to have been fought on yesterday. . . . General Lee's lines were penetrated in several places, and all attempts to recover the lost ground were unsuccessful. This is believed to decide the fate of Richmond. It is not for us to write any particulars as to the future."[21]

People on the streets eyed passing officials for some sign of what to think. Most of those in high places walked glumly on, but at least one put a nonchalant face on the situation. It was Judah Benjamin, strolling to the State Department. Stephen Mallory remembered "his pleasant smile, his mild Havana, and the very twirl of his slender, gold-headed cane contributing to . . . that careless confidence of the last man out-side the ark, who assured Noah of his belief that 'it would not be such a h—— of a shower, after all.' "[22]

Yet even Benjamin could not conceal his inner quaking from those who got a closer look. In early afternoon he sent for the French consul, Alfred Paul, to warn him of what was coming. Paul later reported to Paris that Benjamin's hands and voice shook as he said that though the government was moving to Danville, evacuation was "simply a measure of prudence" and he hoped to return in a few weeks. Paul did not know whether the secretary "was motivated by a persisting illusion or by a lack of sincerity, two things which characterize this statesman."

From Benjamin's office the consul went to General Ewell, who sent him to the provost marshal to secure protection for the French-owned tobacco in Richmond's warehouses. The harried provost scrawled orders for a guard detail in chalk on the side of Paul's carriage.[23]

Journalists and officials knew enough to believe the news. But at first many others refused to. Repeatedly since Pawnee Sunday, bad tidings had arrived during church services and turned out to be false as often as real.

One lady came home from St. Paul's crying, "Oh! . . . have you heard that the city is to be evacuated immediately and the Yankees will be here before morning? . . . What can it all mean? And what is to become of us poor defenceless women, God only knows!"

"Don't be desponding," said a younger friend. "I don't believe they are going to evacuate, for that has been the false report so often, it is noth-ing but another of our Sunday rumors."

But she trembled as she spoke, feeling that this Sunday rumor was true. She was afraid the news would devastate her sick sister, so she went to a neighbor's "to ask for a little brandy . . . to enable her to bear the dreadful communication I had to make." Her neighbor was running from room to room, tearing her hair and wailing over what might happen to her 16-year-old daughter with no father there to defend her—"they say the black wretches are in the very front of Grant's army, and will rush into the city before any decent white men are here to restrain them!"[24]

At midday, beer-hall keeper Gottfried Lange was idling on the corner of Fourth and Broad streets, smoking his pipe, when the one-armed captain of the guard at Davis's mansion came by and told him, "Tonight Richmond will be evacuated."

The words hit Lange "like a thunderbolt." He thought back to his childhood in Germany, when his birthplace was shelled, burned, and plundered. Determined to save something, he rushed home and told his wife to pack the family's valuables and best clothes in a metal chest and sent his children out to hear more news. In his cellar he dug for four hours, sweating, to bury the chest beneath an iron sheet and layers of sand and brick.[25]

Emmie Crump, daughter of the assistant Treasury secretary, set out that afternoon to teach at a black Sunday school as she did every week. Friends on the street turned her back; there would be no class that day. Her father was gone on official business. Her mother gave the family valuables for safekeeping to their erstwhile servant, a trusted old black man now free. Mother and daughter sewed what was left of their gold coins into strong belts to tie beneath their dresses.[26]

Fannie Walker, a copyist at the Bureau of War, saw her chief, R. G. H. Kean, struggling with as much hand luggage as he could manage. She asked if she and her mother, a Treasury clerk, should leave, too. "I cannot advise a lady to follow a fugitive government," Kean said. In tears, he said goodbye.[27]

Crowds had gathered at the Spotswood and at General Ewell's office, a block away at Seventh and Franklin streets, swapping rumors, trying to confirm them. At first those who knew had been evasive; one man with government connections told a friend he was "not at liberty to communicate" what he knew—but there had been terrible fighting near Petersburg.

"Favorable or unfavorable?"

"So far as we have heard, unfavorable." Then, lowering his voice, "I'll tell *you* that I shouldn't be surprised if we are all away from here before twenty-four hours."[28]

In such trickles and then in a flood, reality swept over Richmond. The banks opened their doors at 2:00, notifying customers to come and get their deposits. Officials packed what gold was left into kegs, loaded it on wagons, and carted it across the river.[29]

At 4:00, Mayor Mayo officially announced to the City Council that the Confederate government was departing. Governor Smith came to the special council meeting and promised to leave two militia companies behind to maintain order. Fearing a repetition of what had happened to Columbia six weeks earlier when Union troops got into barrels of whiskey, the council appointed twenty-five men in each of Richmond's three wards to see that all liquor supplies were destroyed. The mayor and a citizens' committee were authorized—"in the event of the evacuation"—to meet the Federal army and arrange the peaceful surrender of the city.[30]

Bureaucrats, remembering Union raider Dahlgren's reported intention to kill high Confederate officials, were unsure how far down into the departments such a Union policy might reach. None looked forward to life in a Yankee prison. There were no clear orders about who was to go, though those who had families were advised to stay. Lower-level government employees made their own decisions, and most opted to leave.

Gradually the streets filled with men waving farewell to families that had taken them in, wagons and carriages bouncing away with trunks and boxes, servants carrying bundles toward the rail stations, horses plodding to roads west. Here and there friends carried a pale sick soldier on a stretcher, unsure where to head, while thousands of helpless casualties lay waiting in the city's hospitals. Columns of refugees set out along the canal towpath toward Lynchburg. Men rich in Confederate dollars offered all they had left for a horse, some even offered $1,000 in gold, but few horses were to be had. Only now was the little remaining bullion in the Treasury, estimated by some at less than $500,000, boxed for shipment. Sent to the Richmond & Danville depot, it sat unguarded until midshipmen of the Confederate naval academy took responsibility.

Rear Admiral Raphael Semmes, who earlier had captured or sunk sixty-nine Union vessels as captain of the high-seas raider *Alabama*, had taken command of the James River Squadron in January. His three iron-clad rams and seven steamers had little to do but stay alert in case the Federals broke past Confederate shore batteries blocking the river below Richmond. The South's makeshift naval academy, whose students included sons of Semmes and Breckinridge, had attended classes aboard the steamer *Patrick Henry*, stationed at Drewry's Bluff. Now Semmes's sailors were about to become a naval brigade for service ashore, and the midshipmen under Lieutenant William H. Parker were assigned as official guardians of the Confederacy's Treasury on wheels.[31]

Jefferson Davis kept working at his office while aides packed his executive papers. At about 5:00 p.m., Breckinridge sent word that a special train had been reserved for the president and ranking officials. Davis should be at the Danville depot by 7:00, to depart by the only remaining railroad to the south.

The president walked calmly across the square toward home, stopping to answer civilians who asked whether all they had heard was true. Women seemed especially understanding; if he told them the success of the cause demanded evacuation, they accepted it, at least in conversation with him. "The affection and confidence of this noble people in the hour of disaster were more distressing to me than complacent and unjust censure would have been," Davis recalled.[32]

At the mansion he gathered a few personal belongings, toilet gear, a pair of pistols, photographs of Varina and of Lee. He made a last tour of the house in which he had celebrated the triumphs and suffered the tragedies of the Confederacy. There two of his children had been born, his cherished son had died, and his wife had wept as she departed. Near 7:00 a carriage arrived, and he headed for the station with a newly lit cigar between his teeth.[33]

Moses Hoge had tried to carry through his Sunday routine, attending a late-afternoon prayer meeting at the Reverend Charles H. Read's Central Presbyterian Church. But he slipped out early, and at home Susan persuaded him that he should leave Richmond with the government. He had, after all, been accused of acting as a Confederate agent. Reluctantly, Hoge made his way to the station and the presidential train. There he found others who believed their public life had made them likely targets for Yankee vengeance. Among them was the journalist George Bagby, whose wife had told him, "You must follow the Confederate fortunes as long as there is any Confederacy."[34]

For hours the quartermaster had been putting together trains to take officials, archives, and treasure off along the battered rails of the Richmond & Danville. At the other end of the line, the clicking telegraph key first told the puzzled trainmaster at Danville to hold all cars, then to send all possible rolling stock to Richmond, and finally "Too late"—the capital was being evacuated.[35] Because the five lines that once served Richmond ran on different grades to different depots, assembling cars and locomotives at the R. & D. yard was a "most serious and perplexing" puzzle. A prearranged signal from a shift engine's whistle summoned trainmen, including a number who had spent the war hoping and secretly working for this day.

The English correspondent Francis Lawley and some of his foreign friends would get away northward by Samuel Ruth's Fredericksburg railroad. But increasingly anxious hundreds jammed the R. & D. depot, where Home Guard soldiers had orders to hold back anyone without a pass from Breckinridge. A few smooth talkers cajoled their way through, explaining how important they were to the cause, and others slipped aboard in the wake of some documented traveler. Women had less trouble passing, some because they were attached to ranking officials, some merely because they looked like ladies—for "crinoline in the South is not circumscribed by man's arbitrary rules." But most of those who came pleaded and stormed in vain.

Among them was the slave dealer Robert Lumpkin, desperate to save his final inventory—a coffle of some fifty blacks chained together. He begged to be allowed to take them aboard but was turned away. So ended the slave trade in Richmond.[36]

One train went off carrying Treasury employees, another with the quartermaster, and another with telegraph operators and crewmen. Davis was scheduled to leave at 8:30 p.m., and he and his department heads were there ahead of time. But he insisted on waiting, sitting in the railroad president's office with Breckinridge, hoping to hear better news from Lee.

It did not come. At 11:00, Davis boarded his car, leaving Breckinridge to follow later. Benjamin, Mallory, Reagan, and Attorney General George Davis were already aboard. Secretary of the Treasury George A. Trenholm of South Carolina, perhaps the richest man in the South, had arrived in an ambulance. Ailing with neuralgia, using morphine for his pains, he also brought a hamper of "supplies for the inner man," peach brandy that he shared with his fellow travelers. Benjamin still put on a brave front, reminding them of "other great national causes which had been redeemed from far gloomier reverses than ours."[37]

Conversation quieted as the presidential train jerked and then clacked slowly across the James. On the Manchester side the track curved close to the stream, overlooking Belle Isle, now dark and empty of all but the dead. Light from bonfires of documents danced against buildings in Richmond and reflected on the surface of the broad river. As the train headed southwestward, those aboard looked back at Thomas Jefferson's columned temple on Shockoe Hill, so long the parliament and symbol of Virginia and the Confederacy. Now legislature and governor, Congress and president were gone, and it was capitol of nothing.

CHAPTER TWENTY-SIX

THE EARTH SEEMED
TO WRITHE IN AGONY

*F*or four years Richmond had endured martial law, conscription, impressment of servants and property, bureaucratic arrogance, enemy raids, overcrowding, underfeeding, and horrendous casualties. Now those who had sacrificed and served unselfishly were left adrift with profiteers and shirkers to fend for themselves. That night few thought of any organization or cause beyond family and survival.

Soon after dark the VMI cadets so recently stretched along the lines between Forts Gilmer and Harrison regrouped to march back into the city. At Capitol Square, Governor Smith thanked and dismissed them. They were free to go, he said, to go home or with the army, whichever they chose. Smith himself was heading up the canal towpath, hoping to reach Lynchburg and organize further resistance in the mountains of Virginia.[1]

The Confederate government was gone and the army was going. Gradually the thousands fleeing and the thousands staying realized that law and order had departed, too. To the rabble, this was opportunity.

The City Council's resolution to destroy all liquor in case of evacuation backfired; as militia knocked in the heads of barrels, threw bottles crashing into the streets, and poured kegs into the gutters, the reek of whiskey drew thirsty roughnecks from all directions. Male and female, civilians and army stragglers, "the vilest of the vile," they rampaged ahead of the official ax wielders, grabbing casks and cases. Others came behind them, dipping up spilled spirits in hats and boots, some even lapping from the gutter like animals.

Rather than leave remaining food supplies to the Yankees, officials threw commissary warehouses open. The crowd pushed in, furious at seeing how much flour and bacon had been locked away during the city's long deprivation. Some sober citizens, hesitant at first, joined this sanctioned plunder. The growing crowd turned to private shops and warehouses, taking shoes, candy, anything. Because city gas lines had been cut off, some looters lit paper torches to see what they were stealing, then tossed the burning paper aside.[2]

Here and there proprietors made a brief futile stand, offering to shoot down anyone who broke into their stores. Andrew Antoni saved his confectionery on Main Street at Eleventh by giving the mob all the candy inside. "It's every man for himself, and the devil for us all tonight," a citizen with a load of hats told a soldier who held back only briefly before joining the looting.[3]

* * *

The skeleton force of Confederate troops left in the works outside Richmond knew little of what was happening in the city. With orders to pull out quietly, they sat still until after nightfall. Then they sang longer and louder at their usual Sunday-evening prayer meetings, poked their picket fires to burn high, and otherwise pretended to be staying. During all this, soldiers muscled any equipment they could carry to wagons drawn by miserably scrawny teams, out of sight behind the lines. Dozens of cannon, hundreds of tents, and piles of baggage had to be abandoned. The enemy heard this busyness and stood alert.

Soon after midnight most of Kershaw's veteran division and Custis Lee's patchwork command of artillerymen and home guards started moving across the James by the Confederate pontoon bridge near Drewry's Bluff, and hurried west to join R. E. Lee. They left behind only pickets and a thin screen of cavalry under Brigadier General Martin W. Gary.[4]

Ewell was still in command of the forces in and around Richmond, but he was now a general without an army. All the city's prison guards had marched off, escorting the Yankees from Libby and Castle Thunder. The Local Brigade, made up of clerks, technicians, and what Ewell called foreigners, had dwindled to a handful of men.

To control the streets he had only a detail of convalescents in the square. He ordered them to stop the plundering, but their commander soon admitted that they could not. Hoping to intimidate the looters with a show of force, Ewell ordered his staff and couriers to mount up and scour the streets, and sent word to Kershaw to rush his leading regiment into town.

Dick Ewell was in the most delicate situation of his sometimes brilliant, often controversial career. Responsible for protecting the erstwhile capital against pillage and Yankees, he also had standing orders to destroy the cotton, tobacco, and other valuable commodities in Richmond's warehouses to keep them out of enemy hands. In fact, little was there except tobacco, and it was as overvalued in Virginia minds as cotton had been to those in the Deep South.

Meeting earlier with the City Council, Ewell had urged that a volunteer force be raised to keep order if the city was evacuated, but this request got nowhere. He had inspected the warehouses and ordered most of the leaf moved into buildings that he concluded could burn without endangering the city. Two of these were on Cary Street; another was near the Petersburg depot at Eighth and Byrd streets. Ewell charged the provost marshal, Major Isaac H. Carrington, with carrying out the order. On the night of April 2, Carrington assigned officers to these warehouses and asked the fire department to have crews ready to keep the planned blazes from spreading.[5]

*   *   *

Elizabeth Van Lew sat waiting, with a giant U.S. flag neatly pressed and ready to greet Grant's conquering army. Someone came to warn that Confederate soldiers had been overheard saying that her house would be burned before they left. She borrowed a wheelbarrow and loaded her silver plate, gold, and family papers for hiding. At about midnight, her doorbell rang.

She opened it—not to Confederates with torches but to two fugitives from the emptied Castle Thunder, who had slipped away as the prisoners trooped through the dark streets to be sent south. She took them in and hid them. Later a woman accused of spying arrived, having escaped from her guards after marching miles into the country.[6]

Philip Whitlock, quartermaster clerk, had been called in to pack departmental records for shipment south. After working into the night, he started to go home but was blocked by guards ordered to form employees into a company to join Lee's retreat. Whitlock, long convinced that the cause was hopeless, said, "This did not suit me . . . I knew that there would be no use." He broke out through a barred basement door. Hurrying home, he detoured around "the rabbel pilliging the stores in Main St."[7]

Finding his wife with an apron full of Confederate money she had gotten for plug tobacco and cigars, he realized that his remaining tobacco was worth more than any amount of Confederate cash. He was "afraid that the rabbel [would] break in and robb me." So he shouldered one 125-pound box at a time up three flights of stairs into hiding, and wondered later where he had found such strength.[8]

Amid this confusion some loyal Confederates were pushing their way across the river into the city instead of fleeing.

During a lull in the desperate fighting beyond Petersburg that afternoon, Lee's adjutant, Colonel Walter Taylor, had made one of the least likely requests ever heard by the commanding general: Could he have permission to run up to Richmond and get married? His fiancée was there alone and he wanted to take her along on whatever path the army took. He would hurry right back. Lee, confident of his faithful aide, said yes.

Taylor rode into Petersburg and commandeered a railroad engine to chase down the last ambulance train taking the wounded to Richmond. Catching and boarding the train three-fourths of the way along, he reached the capital just before midnight. He rushed to Lewis D. Crenshaw's mansion on West Main Street, where his beloved Elizabeth Saunders waited. The groom wrote that his were the only dry eyes in the parlor as Dr. Minnigerode formalized their marriage by candlelight. Before dawn, Taylor was on horseback, crossing the river on his way to rejoin Lee, who had started his retreat westward at about 11:30 p.m.[9]

Even later than Taylor's wedding, a teamster from Petersburg halted at the Manchester end of Mayo's Bridge, waiting for a chance to cross against the tide of refugees. He drove an ambulance wagon; in it was the body of Lieutenant General A. P. Hill, a fighter whose death on any other day would have sent the South into mourning. This time there were no dirges, no cortege, no honors at all. Hill's nephew had come ahead from the battlefield to ask a cousin to take charge of the body and bury it in Hollywood Cemetery if possible.

When at last the driver made his way into the city, these two young men went in search of a coffin. They found one at Belvin's furniture store, which had been broken open in both front and rear. Taking the body to a vacant office, they washed the general's face and slipped off his gauntlets. A Yankee bullet had cut off Hill's left thumb and passed straight through his heart.

Seeing that in this chaos they could not bury the general at Hollywood, the cousins squeezed his body into the coffin, put it back aboard the ambulance, and joined the stream of those departing. Recrossing to Manchester, they took it to the Chesterfield County farm where Hill's parents were refugees from Culpeper. There they buried it until it was moved to Hollywood, and later to the Hill monument on Richmond's Hermitage Road.[10]

* * *

In the Union divisions facing Richmond, soldiers cheered telegrams announcing Grant's smashing Sunday offensive at Petersburg. After getting marching rations that evening, many sat silent and sleepless, wondering whether they would survive their own expected assault against the deep Confederate defenses they had watched for so long. At about 2:00 a.m., Lieutenant J. Livingston de Peyster of the Thirteenth New York Artillery, an aide to Major General Godfrey Weitzel, heard a deep rumble northward. He climbed the seventy-foot wooden signal tower at Weitzel's Twenty-fifth Corps headquarters and saw fires burning in the city. Weitzel sent a company out to capture a Rebel picket for questioning; at about 3:00, it brought in a soldier from the Thirty-seventh Virginia Artillery, who said he did not know where his general or his battalion had gone.

Brigadier General George F. Shepley, Weitzel's chief of staff, was sure that this meant the city was being evacuated. In a few minutes a deserter ran in saying just that. Then a black man came racketing past the pickets in a buggy, standing up as he drove full speed, yelling, "Dey am runnin' from Richmond! Glory! Glory!"[11]

Farther along the Federal front two deserters from the Tenth Virginia Battalion crossed into Brigadier General Charles Devens's division and said the Confederates were pulling out. Devens sent a staff officer to alert his brigades. Word passed up and down the Union works, and troops roused themselves to peer into the still darkness, trying to catch some clue to confirm the good news. Some who believed it let themselves go: "Oh my Lord what a morning!"[12]

At about 4:30 a.m., "a huge volume of smoke like an illuminated balloon shot high into the air, followed by an explosion that shook the earth under our feet." This was the CSS *Virginia*, Admiral Semmes's flagship, named after the former *Merrimack* that had battled the *Monitor* three years earlier. Semmes set his ironclads afire as he and their crews retreated upstream in wooden gunboats. One by one, the warships' magazines exploded, sending shells arcing to burst in the sky.[13]

In the city the blast shook awake the few who had managed to sleep that hectic night. Virginia Dade had closed her eyes to nightmare visions "of black-faced, blue-coated ruffians, with savage yells and gleaming sabres." What seemed only moments later, there came "the most awful and terrific sound that had ever sent the life-blood curdling to my heart," like "the wreck of matter and the crush of worlds." After a brief, terrified silence, her sister spoke up in the darkness: "The death-knell of the Southern Confederacy! and all the bloodshed and suffering of our poor soldiers gone for naught!"[14]

For the tense Yankees, that explosion was the starting gun of a race to be first into Richmond. "The concussion was terrific," wrote Lieutenant Royal B. Prescott of the Thirteenth New Hampshire in Devens's division of the Twenty-fourth Corps. "The earth shook where we were, and there flashed out a glare of light as of noonday, while the fragments of the vessel, pieces of timber and other stuff, fell among my pickets. . . ."

A colonel came galloping, his horse spooked by the explosion, and ordered Prescott to head into the city. As the New Hampshiremen felt their way past three lines of defensive brushworks, they barely made out a belt of bright-colored tags on little sticks across the front of the Confederate fortifications. The Rebels, in their hushed haste to leave, had not taken time to pull the flags that marked their shallowly buried torpedoes. Thus the Yankees lost only one man as they filed along narrow paths through minefields that might have cost hundreds of casualties.[15]

Cheering, they surged into the Rebel earthworks, soldiers laughing in triumph as they straddled abandoned artillery pieces. Officers reformed them to march in column north along the Osborne Turnpike. Near where the turnpike met the New Market Road, they were joined by a few troops of the Fifth Maryland. Halting at Tree Hill, the site of Unionist Franklin Stearns's plantation, they looked out on "a city in flames."[16]

General Weitzel dispatched two aides, Majors Atherton H. Stevens, Jr., and Emmons E. Graves, with forty troopers of the Fourth Massachusetts Cavalry to scout ahead and contact whoever still held authority in Richmond. This detachment trotted past hordes of soldiers that if turned loose might have become a destructive mob.

The race to be first had turned into "a wild rush" along roads and across fields. When infantry crowded the way, artillerymen broke out shovels to fill in ditches and cut a path through the Confederate works for their horses and cannon, then hurrahed off cross-country. "Never did schoolboys show more enthusiasm; never did the wildest of fanatics make a more vigorous rush for the goal."[17]

Brigadier General Edward A. Wild resented the way his neighbor in the lines, Brigadier General Alonzo G. Draper, had "started his whole brigade for Richmond without any baggage whatever . . . in haste to be there first, he did not break camp. . . . He ran his Staff through the midst of my advance guard to break them up and get the 36th there first. . . ."[18]

If "there" was the Capitol in Richmond, the Thirty-sixth U.S.C.T.

did not get there first. The Thirty-sixth was a regiment of U.S. Colored Troops from Brigadier General August Kautz's division of Weitzel's Twenty-fifth Corps. Neither Wild's nor Draper's black brigades got there first, though for a while the Thirty-sixth led the race. When Kautz's and Devens's commands met at the intersection of the Osborne and New Market roads, Devens claimed the right-of-way by virtue of seniority. Kautz yielded the road on that account, but his men struck out across the fields. Then, along with all the others rushing for the city, both divisions were halted below Gillie's Creek, near the wharves at Rocketts.[19]

Waiting for permission to move in, thousands of Union troops, many of them former Virginia slaves, gaped at a "sight that none will ever forget."[20]

"We began to realize as we had not till then that Richmond had fallen and that this was one of the great days of the Lord," wrote a Connecticut soldier. "Right out there in the open in sight of the flaming city we went wild with excitement . . . we yelled, we cheered, we sang, we prayed, we wept, we hugged each other and threw up our hats and danced and acted like lunatics for about fifteen minutes. . . ."[21]

"The city was wrapped in a cloud of densest smoke, through which great tongues of flame leaped in madness to the skies," one of Devens's aides recalled. "Ten thousand shells bursting every minute in the Confederate arsenals and laboratories were making an uproar such as might arise from the field when the world's artillery joins in battle."[22]

The greatest blast came from the arsenal, said to store three-quarters of a million shells, below the brick City Almshouse that had recently sheltered the VMI cadets. The explosion pulverized the arsenal, splintered the frame Negro almshouse nearby, overturned tombstones in Shockoe Hill Cemetery, and rocked the entire city. "Thousands of windowpanes were blown out; the doors of houses were torn out of their hinges. Chimneys caved in, damage everywhere," wrote Gottfried Lange. John Leyburn said, "It might almost have awakened the dead. The earth seemed to writhe in agony . . . stupendous thunders roared around." Yet in the fields between the city and the creek where the advance units halted, cows grazed as calmly as if there had never been a war.[23]

Majors Stevens and Graves did not have to ride far to meet what was left of authority in Richmond. Out of the city's turmoil a rickety barouche came jostling along the turnpike, flying a white shirttail on a stick and bearing Mayor Joseph Mayo. With the old and rumpled mayor were William H. MacFarland, Loftin Ellett, and Judges John A. Meredith, W. H. Lyons and W. H. Halyburton. As they started out to meet the Yankees, they had passed the last of Gary's Confederate cavalry heading into town to cross the river.

The city officials halted at the road junction, where Stevens and Graves rode up at roughly 6:30 a.m. The mayor offered Stevens a note:

> To the General Commanding the United States
>   Army in front of Richmond:
> The Army of the Confederate Government having abandoned
> the City of Richmond, I respectfully request that you will take
> possession of it with an organized force, to preserve order and
> protect women and children and property.
>   Respectfully,
>   Joseph Mayo, Mayor.[24]

Stevens assured the civilian officials that Union commanders had strict orders to protect the city, and offered to send troopers to destroy whiskey before the army moved in. When Mayo said this was already done, Stevens invited the mayor to ride with him while the other Richmonders followed in carriages.[25]

By then the flames and looting were far beyond control.

*   *   *

Precisely who started which fire when will never be settled, but apparently there were scattered blazes in downtown Richmond hours before Provost Marshal Carrington ordered the stored tobacco destroyed. Some may have been caused by paper torches carelessly thrown aside by looters, some by drifting embers from street fires of official papers and trash, some intentionally set by vandals after stores were ransacked; a burning boat lodged against the short canal bridge at Fourteenth Street was blamed for setting it afire.[26]

Ewell, later captured and imprisoned by the Federals, angrily denied that he was responsible for burning the city. "I had taken every precaution possible, and the people must blame themselves," he wrote. At least two fires were "kindled by the mob" before his troops torched the warehouses. "The arsenal was set on fire and the hose cut by irresponsible persons without authority. In spite of our guard at the bridge it was set on fire by someone evidently with a view to cut off our retreat." Ewell also said that vandals had tried to burn the Tredegar Works but had been turned back by Anderson's armed workers.[27]

Individual soldiers offered wildly varied versions of when the official burning began. H. M. Sturgis, who had been on guard at the Soldiers' Home, said that at about 10:00 on Sunday night he was given the keys to a warehouse with instructions to burn the tobacco inside. "We

knocked in the heads of three hogsheads, pulled out the hands of tobacco, and my comrade shaved up some splinters and I struck the
match. . . . The responsible source of the orders I know not."

W. L. Timberlake, who had done picket duty on the outskirts, said
his unit was brought in on Sunday night and ordered to destroy papers
at the provost marshal's office on Broad Street, and then to burn the
Shockoe Warehouse on Cary Street.

Lieutenant Colonel R. T. W. Duke of the Local Brigade said that
soon after 2:00 a.m. he left two junior officers to carry out Ewell's order
and then collapsed in sleep, to be awakened when the arsenal exploded.
"This woke me up most effectually," he recalled.[28]

But Carrington maintained that the blazes set at Ewell's order did
not start until after Ewell and Breckinridge had departed, shortly before
daybreak.

Carrington's final instructions were to try to maintain order, to stay as
long as he safely could, and then to burn the tobacco before leaving. As
Ewell and Breckinridge said goodbye at Fourteenth and Cary streets,
Ewell told Carrington that "the firing of tobacco could not be longer
delayed." Carrington sent orders to waiting officers, he said, and
Shockoe and Von Groening's warehouses on Cary Street were promptly
set ablaze. The detail standing by at the tobacco warehouse beside the
Petersburg depot, however, sent back word that in the confusion,
wounded Confederates had been moved there, so Carrington withdrew
the orders to burn it.[29]

At first the smoke from the brightly burning warehouses rose straight
into the dawn sky, but soon a southeast breeze came up and whipped
flames into the business district. They quickly flared upward through
the city's tallest structure, the Gallego flour mill at the east end of the
boat basin, just across narrow Twelfth Street from Shockoe warehouse.
Then they spread into shops along Cary Street and uphill into hotels
and offices.

The coming of day drew more looters into the streets—convicts from
the emptied penitentiary, blacks encouraged by the departure of authority, hoodlums and bourgeois alike. As the blaze roared higher, the pil-
laging tapered off, but between those carrying away booty and those
fleeing for safety, between those cowering in their homes and those hurrying under orders to join Lee's retreat, no one was fighting the fire.

"I shuddered," recalled Mary Fontaine—"Richmond burning and no
alarm. . . . I watched those silent, awful fires, I felt that there was no effort to stop them, but all like myself were watching them, paralyzed and
breathless. After a while the sun rose . . . a great red ball veiled in a
mist."[30]

Just as Yankees contested for the honor of being first into Richmond, many Confederate soldiers claimed that they were last to leave. Gary's cavalry brigade was the final army command to cross the river. Captain E. M. Boykin rode through the streets and saw at curtained windows "the sad and tearful faces of the kind Virginia women, who had never failed the soldier in four long years of war and trouble . . . it was a sad thought . . . that we seemed, as a compensation for all that they had done for us, to be leaving them to the mercy of the enemy; but their own General Lee was gone before, and we were but as the last wave of the receding tide."[31]

Rebel troops separated from their comrades were still dragging their way to Mayo's Bridge. Private John L. G. Woods of the Fifty-third Georgia, a bandsman left on picket by Kershaw's division, told how "to our utter astonishment and amazement, we awoke to the realization that the army was all gone." Grabbing blanket, haversack, canteen, and drum, he struggled into town to find citizens and soldiers scooping whiskey from the gutters. As a teetotaler he found this "disgusting." But he was also hungry—when he saw women carrying armloads of greasy bacon and rolling barrels of flour through the streets, he joined those emptying the huge commissary by Mayo's Bridge and was almost trapped inside when the crowd panicked at cries of "Fire!"[32]

Captain D. B. Sanford maintained that Phillips' Georgia Legion, also of Kershaw's command, crossed while the bridge was afire, "and we had to run with all our might and shinney from side to side of the bridge to keep from being burned to death. No other soldiers could have crossed this bridge after we did."[33]

The man in charge of protecting, then destroying the bridge was Captain Clement Sulivane, a staff officer to whom Ewell had given command of the Local Brigade of reserves. "Such a scene probably the world has seldom witnessed," Sulivane wrote. "As the immense magazines of cartridges ignited, the rattle as of thousands of musketry would follow, and then all was still for the moment, except the dull roar and crackle of the fast-spreading fires." Gary led his cavalry with sabers aloft to clear a way through the crowd, and reined up while his rearguard dashed onto the bridge. Then, saluting Sulivane, Gary called, "All over, goodbye; blow her to hell," and trotted across.[34]

Sulivane's brigade, by then barely 200 men under Captain Edward Mayo, quickly followed the cavalry. Among them was W. L. Timberlake, who insisted that after Gary's horsemen crossed, his outfit hurried onto the bridge past men waiting with kindling, tar, and turpentine, and then "the torch was immediately applied. . . . I contend that Company D, 2d Virginia Battalion, were the last. . . . If any crossed after we did, they need have no fear of the other world, because they surely were fire-proof."[35]

With his engineer officer, Sulivane walked away from Richmond, lighting the tinder spaced along the bridge. Reaching the island at mid-river, he looked back and saw blue-coated horsemen clattering up Main Street and down to the end of the flaming bridge. The Yankees fired a few random shots and the last Rebels retreated to Manchester. There they watched the enemy occupy Richmond and "heard the very welkin ring with cheers as the United States forces reached Capitol Square. . . ."[36]

*   *   *

On the sidewalk, Mary Fontaine "did not move, I could not move, but watched [a] blue horseman ride to the City Hall, enter with his sword knocking the ground at every step, and throw the great doors open, and take possession of our beautiful city; watched two blue figures on the Capitol, white men, I saw them unfurl a tiny flag, and I sank on my knees, and the bitter, bitter tears came in a torrent."[37]

Those two blue figures were Majors Stevens and Graves, who led their cavalry squadron through Rocketts at about 7:00 and entered city streets where flaming buildings threatened to collapse from both sides. No one raised a hand against the riders. At the square they found hundreds of rich and poor Richmonders evicted by fire, now homeless, with bedding and household items gathered in haste and piled on the grass.

Without slowing, the officers strode into the Capitol and climbed to the roof. There they ran up the little yellow guidons of Companies E and H of the Fourth Massachusetts Cavalry.[38]

Major Stevens thus won official credit for hoisting the first Yankee flag, but there was predictable competition for having been first to cross into Richmond. Captain William J. Ladd of Devens's staff wrote that he had raced a group on horseback and beaten them to Capitol Square. He maintained that after fending off a drunken Confederate sailor wielding a cutlass, he realized that he was alone and returned to the Union lines before Stevens reached the Capitol. In the years ahead, obituaries in New England newspapers would often tell of old soldiers who had the local reputation of being first.[39]

But the mass of troops was halted at Gillie's Creek until Weitzel ordered Colonel Edward L. Ripley's brigade of Devens's division to lead the way into Richmond. According to Prescott, Weitzel himself rode through and ordered the lieutenant's picket detachment to follow him into town. Prescott said he lost his way in the smoke and confusion but made it to the Capitol at 7:20 a.m., and so his troops had been first. He asserted that on his arrival there was no flag atop the Capitol, but that one went up shortly afterward.*[40]

After Stevens and Graves raised their guidons over the Capitol, Lieutenant de Peyster of the Thirteenth New York Artillery rode in with a big U.S. flag that had formerly flown over occupied New Orleans. Unstrapping it from his saddle, he climbed atop the Capitol with Captain Loomis L. Langdon, Devens's artillery chief, took down the cavalry guidons, and ran up the Stars and Stripes.

The two young officers, aware of how many thousands had died for this moment, stood on the peak of the roof and lifted a toast. Below them, many among the pathetic crowd of recent Rebels sent cheers into the billowing smoke of the city.[41]

Weitzel, an 1855 graduate of West Point, trotted in ahead of the Thirteenth New Hampshire, which marched west on Main Street with colors flying. Across Shockoe Valley and up the hill the Yankees strutted, then turned right on Governor Street to Capitol Square. Ripley had his brigade's three regimental bands out front, playing "Yankee Doodle" and other airs long unheard in Richmond. Hordes of well-wishers, mostly black, greeted the conquerors, offering to carry their packs and weapons, handing them fruit and whiskey. Officers alongside grabbed bottles and smashed them with their swords.

A soldier with the Eleventh Connecticut thought that "Our reception was grander and more exultant than even a Roman emperor, leading back his victorious legions with the spoils of conquest, could ever know. We brought Government, Order and Heaven born Liberty. The slaves seemed to think that the day of jubilee had fully come. How they danced, shouted, waved their rag banners, shook our hands, bowed, scraped, laughed all over, and thanked God, too, for our coming. Many heroes have fought for this day and died without the sight. . . . It is a day never to be forgotten by us, till days shall be no more."[42]

Weitzel said, "When the mob saw my staff and me, they rushed around us, hugged and kissed our legs and horses, shouting hallelujah and glory." Then he came to the terrified women and children huddled on the square—a sight that "would have melted a heart of stone."[43]

At City Hall the 29-year-old Weitzel accepted Richmond's formal surrender and ordered his aide, Captain Horace B. Fitch, to draft a message to Grant. Because the army had outrun its telegraph wire he sent a cavalry courier three miles back to the nearest transmission point—and

*Prescott alleged that "a light colored boy" named Richard G. Forrester, who had formerly run errands for state legislators, had hidden a national flag taken down when Virginia seceded, and hoisted it as the Yankees stacked arms below. Other accounts make no mention of such a person.

since Grant was in the saddle pursuing Lee, newspaper readers as far away as Detroit read Weitzel's historic dispatch before it reached the commanding general:[44]

> We took Richmond at 8:15 this morning. I captured many guns. The enemy left in great haste. The city is on fire in two places. Am making every effort to put it out. The people received us with enthusiastic expressions of joy.[45]

At the Capitol, Weitzel set up office in the old Senate chamber and told the 25-year-old Ripley to take control of the city. "I have no orders further to communicate; except to say that I wish this conflagration stopped, and this city saved, if it is in the bounds of human possibility. You have *carte blanche* to do it in your own way."

Ripley urged Weitzel to keep other commands out of the city, and Weitzel ordered Kautz's black division to occupy the inner line of defenses rather than settling in downtown. According to Ripley, there was still "more or less trouble from the disorder of the colored troops, many of whom stole in and went directly to their old masters and mistresses to enjoy their day of triumph over them."[46]

But not all the eager black regiments were banished to the outskirts. Colonel Charles Francis Adams, Jr., of the Fifth Massachusetts Cavalry, grandson and great-grandson of presidents, asked Weitzel "as a special favor" to let his black troopers share the glory by marching through downtown streets. Weitzel approved, and said "this fine regiment of colored men made a very great impression on those citizens who saw it."

"The cavalry thundered at a furious gallop," said Mary Fontaine. "Then the infantry came playing 'The Girl I Left Behind Me' . . . then the negro troops playing 'Dixie' . . . then our Richmond servants were completely crazed, they danced and shouted, men hugged each other, and women kissed, and such a scene of confusion you have never seen"—all this amid a city burning.[47]

Weitzel ordered his staff to collar every able-bodied man, black or white, to fight the fire. The fierce updraft of the blaze was blowing flaming brands across the city to drop on roofs many blocks away. Moses Hoge's parsonage at Fifth and Main streets caught fire three times, but like many other houses was saved by men and boys on the roof with buckets of water and wet blankets. Captain Lewis Weitzel, the general's brother and aide, heard a servant call from an endangered house on Franklin Street. A young woman there said her mother was bedridden and might need help. The invalid was Mrs. Robert E. Lee. At young Weitzel's request, Ripley sent three men with an ambulance to stand by in case the fire reached her house. Although the United Presbyterian

Church burned half a block away, the house next door caught fire, and embers blew onto her roof, Mrs. Lee remained safe.[48]

When a company of the First New York Volunteer Engineers moved in to help Devens's division fight the blaze, Yankee mechanics got the city's two fire engines to work, but the heat drove them back block by block. Soldiers and civilians joined bucket brigades. The most successful tactic was purely defensive, pulling down threatened buildings to create firebreaks before the flames took over. The firefighters struggled for at least five hours before the breeze shifted and the blaze was contained sometime before 2:00 p.m., though flames still flared up and smoke rose over the gutted blocks for days afterward.

The heart of the city was in charred ruins.

Nine hundred homes and businesses were destroyed. All the banks; the American and Columbian hotels; the *Examiner, Enquirer,* and *Dispatch* offices; the General Court of Virginia and the Henrico County courthouse, with irreplaceable records; the arsenal and laboratory; Gallego and Shockoe mills; the Danville and Petersburg railroad bridges and depots; Mayo's Bridge, the only one that handled foot and horse-drawn traffic; a dozen drugstores, two dozen groceries and even more saloons, shops and warehouses; all or part of at least fifty-four blocks— gone.

Wreckage blocked the streets. Only ghostly brick shells stood between Eighth and Fifteenth, from Main Street to the river, and between Fourth and Tenth from Canal Street to the river. The thick granite structure of the Custom House, used as Jefferson Davis's office and the Confederate State and Treasury departments, had defied the fire and a timely shift of wind had diverted flames from the Spotswood Hotel. But a Richmonder long familiar with downtown said that as he stood in the shambles, he could hardly tell which block had been which.[49]

Weitzel was deeply satisfied by the day's work. "The rebel capitol," he wrote, "fired by men placed in it to defend it, was saved from total destruction by soldiers of the United States, who had taken possession. The bloody victories which opened the gates of Richmond" were fought by others, "but my men won equally as great a one in the city although it was bloodless."[50]

As soon as he arrived, Weitzel had sent details to free the captives in Libby and Castle Thunder; the would-be liberators found the doors swung wide and the prisons empty. Frederick Chesson of Connecticut, who earlier had been "dejected, ragged, hopeless, tired . . . hooted at and jeered at" as a prisoner in Richmond, rode around Libby shaking his fist at its walls. Ripley's men started refilling the prisons with looters and

Confederate army stragglers rounded up off the streets, soon packing Libby "so full they boiled up upon the roof." Federal sentries stood at street corners.[51]

Informed that Davis's mansion was vacant, Weitzel inspected it and found its pantry nearly bare, but everything else in order. Thus, late that Monday, the commander of the occupying force moved with his staff into "elegant quarters" in the White House of the Confederacy. He assigned General Shepley, his chief of staff, who had been military governor of New Orleans, to the same duty in Richmond. Ripley made his headquarters at City Hall, Devens in the governor's mansion, and Lieutenant Colonel Frederick L. Manning, provost marshal of the Army of the James, set up in the House of Delegates chamber of the Capitol.[52]

To some of the women who had been the backbone of Confederate Richmond, the restrained way in which the victors claimed their spoils was nevertheless insulting. Thirteen-year-old Emmie Sublett had not lived long under the old flag; she wrote that "the Yanks came in . . . and first of all placed the *horrible stars and stripes* (which seemed to me to be so many bloody gashes) over our beloved capitol. O the *horrible wretches!* I can't think of a name dreadful enough to call them. . . . " Looking up at that flag, Anna Deane wrote that "my heart sickens with indignation, to think that we should ever have loved it."[53]

At Chimborazo, Phoebe Pember had seen the long columns wind past from Rocketts until "there was hardly a spot in Richmond not occupied by a blue coat." She was impressed by the Yankees' quietness and courtesy, and the fat horses and shiny trappings that contrasted so with the wasted appearance of the departed Confederates. Polite women stayed home behind closed doors, or went abroad with veiled faces and averted eyes, because "they could not bear the presence of invaders, even under the most favorable circumstances."[54]

But on Church Hill, Elizabeth Van Lew was transported with joy. "In an incredibly short space of time by magic every part of our city was under the most kind and respectful of guards," she wrote. "What a moment! . . . Civilization advanced a century. . . . Oh! army of my country, how glorious was your welcome!"[55]

She did not waste time in celebration, for the war was still on. General Grant was concerned for her safety; as soon as the Yankees moved in, he sent an aide with a guard detachment to protect her. But they did not find her at home. She was downtown, poking through papers strewn ankle-deep around what had been the War Department, looking for secrets that might be of use to the Union.

CHAPTER TWENTY-SEVEN

OUR SOUL BOWED
DOWN TO THE DUST

*E*arly on Tuesday afternoon, April 4, an admiral's barge with twelve sailors at the oars angled toward the riverbank not far from Libby Prison. A gang of black laborers stopped work to watch as the unannounced craft pushed in. Suddenly one of the older workmen recognized the barge's tall, silk-hatted passenger and threw down his shovel: "Bress de Lord, dere come de Messiah! Dar is Mass Abram Linkum sure enuff!"[1]

There he was, sure enough, the president of the United States, stepping ashore in conquered Richmond barely a day after the last Confederate defenders had departed. His coming touched off another explosion, this one of celebration by newly freed slaves whose shouts were remembered as minstrel dialect by Yankee memoirists. One of those Yankees was Rear Admiral David Dixon Porter, who arranged Lincoln's bold visit and accompanied him each step of the way.

After congratulating General Grant in Petersburg the previous day, Lincoln had returned to City Point to hear that the capital had fallen. Almost casually, he announced that he would go up to Richmond in the morning. Porter set about organizing a grand presidential entry past rows of Union gunboats with flags flying, and up to a point the demonstration came off as planned. Union vessels swept fifty-one Confederate torpedoes from the river and then stood by the channel, waiting to salute the president.

Lincoln boarded Porter's flagship *Malvern*, which steamed past cheering naval crews, floating debris, and occasional loose mines until it came to a maze of sunken Rebel boats. Here the president transferred to Porter's barge, with a tug towing it on upstream. Then it reached another obstacle; Vice Admiral David G. Farragut, the hero of New Orleans, had hurried into Richmond behind the army and then started down to meet Lincoln aboard the erstwhile Confederate flag-of-truce boat *Allison*. Near a barrier of pilings driven to obstruct the river, the *Allison*'s engine failed and she swung across the narrow passage, almost blocking it.

Porter left the tug behind and the barge slipped through, sailors straining at the oars. As they approached the city, Lincoln and Porter saw no friendly troops along the riverfront, so they continued upstream until the barge caught in the rapids near downtown. The oarsmen jumped overboard and pushed off, and after turning back, the old seadog Porter ordered them to put in at "the only practicable looking landing we saw."[2]

* * *

For hours before Lincoln stepped off the barge, the smoking city had been calm, recovering from the terrible binge of the previous day. After a Monday of fire and looting, cheers and brass bands, victors and defeated had lain quiet in the early darkness. When General Ripley rode through the streets after midnight, "not a human being was encountered" except the guards at street corners; "not a ray of light from a house gave a hint of life within." At Moses Hoge's home, Lelian Cook awoke and thought that she had never known Richmond to be so still.[3]

Few proper Richmonders stirred from their homes until hunger brought them out. General Weitzel had ordered that the poor be fed from captured commissaries and from supplies of the U.S. Sanitary and Christian commissions that moved in with his troops. Close behind them came Yankee sutlers, the horse-drawn grocer-confectioners who had followed the army since First Bull Run.

But Confederate scrip was now worthless: Richmonders who had boxes of bills went from wealth to poverty overnight. Gold and greenbacks were rare. Rather than humble themselves before the recent enemy, many of the once-prosperous who still had black servants dispatched them to cadge food from soldiers. But Mrs. Lee sent breakfast on a tray to the guard posted in front of her home.[4]

Army engineers were linking pontoons to bridge the James at Seventeenth Street. Work parties pulled down tottering walls that fell into the streets, then cleared lanes through the debris. Mechanics hastened to put the railroads into operation. Old, female, and very young civilians ventured out onto porches, still feeling their way into their new relationship with the Yankees. Ripley had been besieged on Monday by women asking for protection, but the peaceful first twenty-four hours of occupation eased this anxiety.[5]

Some well-to-do householders were afraid troops would take over their homes the way Weitzel had moved into Davis's mansion. Emmie Crump told of how her family's free black servant Peter came in to assure her mother, "Don't you be scared, Miss May, I done tell 'em you is a good union woman!" This made young Emmie so indignant that she had to be restrained from hanging out a Confederate flag to disprove the slander. But other Federal officers found Richmond landladies surprisingly hospitable and were pleased to accept invitations to move in—until they realized that their hostesses expected the new boarders to supply the establishment from the Yankee commissary.[6]

General Devens installed himself in the governor's mansion, despite the fact that Smith had left behind his wife and one of their daughters. Mrs. Smith and the daughter had shuddered there through the fire and looting, and when Devens came he let them stay on upstairs. One of the general's staff captains was sitting on the mansion steps when a distant hubbub of voices rose to an uproar, breaking the early-afternoon calm. Miss Smith, worried, looked out a window and called down to the captain, "What's the trouble?"[7]

* * *

The workmen at the landing had come running to the presidential barge, and hundreds of other blacks promptly flocked around, laughing, weeping, shouting "Glory, hallelujah!" and "Thank you, Jesus!" Porter said that no election wire could have carried news of the president's arrival as fast as it circulated throughout Richmond. Some celebrants wanted to shake their savior's hand, some to kiss his coattails, and others kneeled to kiss his boots.

Porter was afraid Lincoln would be crushed by the adoring masses, or that an assassin would slip through with a pistol or dagger. The dozen sailors from the barge tried to clear the way with bayonets, and occasionally the admiral laid about with the flat of his sword. As the growing throng pushed past piles of debris, the president himself looked uneasy. "Bad featured white men" were in among his admirers, and Porter thought he saw more hatred than merriment on faces peering down out of windows. Those faces "were looking at the man they had been taught to believe was a monster in human shape, but who in fact carried the kindest of hearts within him, and whose soul was over flowing with the most generous sentiments toward the Southern people."

The approaching uproar worried Miss Smith at the governor's mansion, but in all the noise there was not a disrespectful word—except from some on the fringes who heard "the president!" and, thinking it was Jeff Davis, cried "Hang him! Hang him!"

When an old black man doffed his hat and bowed, Lincoln paused and silently returned the gesture—"a death-shock to chivalry, and a mortal wound to caste," one Yankee wrote. A young girl rushed forth, kissed Lincoln's hand, and said, "God bless you, only Friend of the South," and later he told of her with emotion. At last, as the crowd surged on, a squad of cavalry came galloping, surrounded the president's party, and escorted it to the Confederate White House.

Porter had imagined a gaudier entry into the city, but later he realized that "that would have looked as if [Lincoln] came as conqueror to exult over a brave but fallen enemy. He came instead as a peacemaker, his hand extended to all who desired to take it. . . . I doubt if there was a person in Richmond who saw the president that day who did not say, 'This cannot be the man who has been represented to us as a monster, we see no horns or hoofs and there is less of the devil about him than there is in Jeff Davis.'"

Some Confederates watching this boisterous procession ruefully remembered the bright morning when Davis had been cheered through the streets on arriving from Montgomery. Now the Federals discovered that the evacuation fire had "produced a strong revulsion in our favor. It added to the feeling generally prevalent of indignation against Jeff . . . [who had] alienated entirely the good will of the people. But Lee is fairly idolized, and his word is law. . . ."[8]

Weitzel had gotten a dispatch with Lincoln's estimated time of arrival at Rocketts wharf, but before reaching there to greet him, he heard that the president was already at the mansion. Rushing back to play host, he found Lincoln sitting at Davis's desk, having a glass of water while the officers around him shared a bottle of whiskey from the cellar. Outside, people were "vociferating for the president," who stepped to the door and bowed to three cheers. After General Shepley dispersed the crowd, Lincoln shook hands with the generals who had taken Richmond, inspected the home that the president of the Confederacy had so recently vacated, and had a light lunch. Then the pleasantries were interrupted by Davis's assistant secretary of war, who had stayed behind when the government fled.[9]

John Archibald Campbell, one of the peace commissioners Davis had sent to meet Lincoln at Hampton Roads during the winter, had come to see Shepley as soon as the Yankees arrived. Learning that Lincoln was at City Point, he asked if he might visit him there. Now Lincoln summoned him, apparently expecting to hear some official peace feeler from the Confederate government. Campbell made it clear that though he had suggested this to Secretary of War Breckinridge before his departure, he brought no such message. Instead, there where Davis had lived, he voiced a plea that would never have been tolerated by the stubborn Southern president—a proposal to take Virginia out of the tottering Confederacy.

"When leniency and cruelty play for the conquest of a kingdom, the gentlest player will be the soonest winner," Campbell said; if Lincoln reached out to such men as former governor Letcher, R. M. T. Hunter, and General Lee himself, they would be eager to help in pacification. Indeed, if the Virginia legislature were allowed to meet, it would be quick to repeal the ordinance of secession and accept the peace terms that Davis had so often rejected.[10]

Considering the military situation, whether Virginia formally accepted Lincoln's conditions would soon be moot. But Lee was not yet defeated. Retreating toward Amelia Court House, forty miles southwest, he hoped to find provisions that he had ordered stockpiled there and then move on to join Johnston near Danville. Neither Lee nor Lincoln could realize how close the end lay—that there were no Confederate supplies at Amelia and that in two days Grant's divisions would cut away nearly half the skeletal Confederate army at Sayler's Creek. To the president's knowledge, the bloodshed might go on for months—but if Virginia made peace, her example might influence the rest of the ravaged South.

As Lincoln met with Campbell, Davis was trying to reassure Confederates from his refugee capital at Danville, declaring that the loss of Richmond merely opened a new phase of struggle:

"I will never consent to abandon one foot of the soil of any one of the States of the Confederacy; that Virginia . . . whose bosom has been bared to receive the main shock of this war; whose sons and daughters have exhibited heroism so sublime as to render her illustrious in all times to come; that Virginia, with the help of her people and by the blessing of Providence, shall be held and defended, and no peace ever be made with the infamous invaders of her homes by the sacrifice of any of her rights or territory. . . ."[11]

But Davis, who had never spoken for all Virginians, now spoke for very few. His arrival at Richmond four springs earlier had been cheered, but in the long run it had meant destruction and despair. If he and the cotton states had gone their way without reluctant Virginia, if they had fought their war where they lived, the suffering would have ended far sooner. Thousands of burned homes would still be standing, and hundreds of thousands of the dead would still be living. Now Richmonders who had not dared to risk prison by expressing their resentment were free to talk without fear of eavesdropping detectives. Even those who had willingly fought or nursed the wounded and endured privation could feel betrayed now by a government that left their city aflame as it abandoned them. If Davis's defiance at Danville had been heard that day in Richmond, it would have stirred as many bitter curses as amens.

* * *

Lincoln seemed impressed by what John Campbell proposed, and invited him to talk again the next day. Then, with Weitzel as his guide, the president went sightseeing in "what was left of Richmond"—this time in a two-horse carriage with a guard of cavalry, an entourage of perhaps 200 in all. They rode out Broad Street to Camp Lee, where U.S. Colored Troops were quartered and a stream of Richmond blacks came looking for long-lost relatives.

The president missed seeing the Twenty-eighth U.S.C.T. march along Broad Street toward camp and halt amid a "vast multitude" that clamored for a speech. In response, the regimental chaplain stood and "proclaimed for the first time in that city freedom to all mankind," then was so overcome that he could not continue.

Later a black woman came to ask if anyone knew a former slave who had been sold as a small boy to Robert Toombs, the Georgian who became a Confederate general and secretary of state. The woman had seen Toombs in Richmond and learned from him that the boy had run away to Ohio. She asked the chaplain, "What is your name?"

"Garland H. White," he said.

"What was your mother's name?"

"Nancy."

"Where were you born?"

"Hanover County, in this state."

"Where were you sold from?"

"From this city."

"What was the name of the man who bought you?"

"Robert Toombs."

She was hard to satisfy; question followed question, until at last she said: "This is your mother, Garland, whom you are now talking to, who has spent twenty years of grief about her son."[12]

Thousands of Richmonders, slaves only two days before, soared in euphoria at greeting black soldiers as liberators. Past such scenes, Lincoln's party swung back to inspect the vandalized Capitol, its square littered with worthless Confederate bonds and government documents.

Gazing up at the towering statue there, the president mused, "Washington is looking at me and pointing to Jeff Davis," off to the southwest. From the square Lincoln could view the smoking ruins in three directions. He visited Libby Prison and Castle Thunder, now full of Confederates, and by one account "gave way to uncontrollable emotions" as he saw how Union captives had lived.[13]

Between leaving the Confederate White House and returning to the river, Weitzel asked the president how the conquered Confederates should be treated. To the general, Lincoln said a few offhand words that deserve to be remembered as much as his most carefully drafted speeches: He did not want to give Weitzel formal orders on the subject, but "If I were in your place, I'd let 'em up easy—let 'em up easy."[14]

But radical politicians in Washington, most of whom had not seen devastated Virginia, had neither Lincoln's heart nor his foresight.

Lincoln thought of spending the night at the still-functioning Spotswood, but Porter urged him to stay aboard the USS *Malvern,* now anchored off downtown Richmond. Porter's concern for the president's safety seemed justified that evening when two suspicious characters tried to board the boat with messages for Lincoln, then disappeared when challenged.

On Wednesday morning Campbell arrived with local lawyer Gustavus A. Myers. The president "spoke with freedom and apparent decision," saying he would consider Campbell's suggestion about the legislature overnight, then send instructions to Weitzel.[15] When Campbell and Myers said they did not think an oath of allegiance should be required from defeated Virginians, Lincoln left that decision to Weitzel, who said it had not been done generally in New Orleans, and "I . . . certainly do not feel disposed to do it here."[16]

Shortly after that meeting, another caller aboard the *Malvern* gave Lincoln reason to wonder whether he should be so accommodating. This was Duff Green, a 73-year-old politician, publisher, and industrialist who in 1860 had gone to see Lincoln at Springfield on President Buchanan's behalf to discuss the Republican's views on secession. Now, though Green arrived carrying a club "big enough to knock a horse down"—of which Porter gently disarmed him—Lincoln assumed that he, too, wanted to talk peace. Instead, Green lashed out:

"Well, sir, I hope you are satisfied. You have burned and destroyed our towns and laid waste our estates. You have caused weeping and wailing throughout the whole South with your hellish acts, and your mercenaries have cut the throats of hundreds of Southern people and their blood cries aloud for vengeance. And now, you come to glut your eyes with the sight of the misery you have created. . . ."

Lincoln turned on him. "No, sir," he said. "You have cut your own throats and you have unfortunately cut many of our throats in so doing. Our interview is ended, sir! I received you as a penitent, but I find you are an insolent beggar."[17]

Porter believed that this exchange shifted Lincoln's thinking on how to answer Campbell's proposal. But the next day, after returning to City Point, the president ordered Weitzel to allow "the gentlemen who have acted as the Legislature of Virginia" to gather in order to withdraw the state from the struggle. When Weitzel told General Shepley to announce this through the newspapers, the shrewd Shepley, a judge in civilian life, was surprised. He asked to read the president's letter and told Weitzel, "General, this is a political mistake. Don't you lose that letter, for if you do, your Major General's commission may not be worth a straw."

Shepley's judgment was correct; within a week, Republican radicals had forced Lincoln to reconsider. The president wrote to Weitzel, insisting that he had not authorized the legislature proper to convene but only those individuals with de facto power to act for Virginia. Besides, by then the whole idea was overtaken by events. "Do not allow them to assemble," Lincoln said, "but if any have come, allow them safe return to their homes."[18]

* * *

As Lincoln departed Richmond, Northern newspapermen, politicians and peddlers, the curious, the ambitious, and the greedy were swarming in. It was the city that had "stood longer, more frequent and more persistent sieges than any in Christendom," wrote young George Alfred Townsend, who had transferred from the New York *Herald* to the *World:*

"This town *is* the Rebellion; it is all that we have directly striven for; quitting it, the Confederate leaders have quitted their sheet-anchor, their roof-tree, their abiding hope. Its history is the epitome of the whole contest, and to us, shivering our thunderbolts against it for more than four years, Richmond is still a mystery."[19]

En route to Fredericksburg, Francis Lawley's journalistic conscience overrode his fears as he realized that he was fleeing "one of the most momentous events in history." After taking the last train north, the London *Times* correspondent got off at a waystop and caught a Federal supply train back to Richmond. There, despite his renowned Confederate bias, he wheedled a pass to the front.[20]

His brass was at least equaled by Thomas Morris Chester of the Philadelphia *Press,* the only regular black correspondent for any major newspaper. Chester began his first dispatch from Richmond: "Seated in the Speaker's chair, so long dedicated to treason. . . ."

He had to fight off an indignant Confederate challenger who interrupted his writing in the House chamber of the Capitol. "Richmond has never before presented such a spectacle of jubilee," Chester reported. "What a wonderful change has come over the spirit of Southern dreams." He wrote that Richmond whites had become exceedingly polite to newly freed blacks, even calling them "Mr. Johnson" or "Mrs. Brown," and shaking hands with a respectful nod. Former masters searched black regiments for their ex-slaves, he said, to ask for "a good character"—a recommendation to the Yankees. Later Chester spoke at a "grand jubilee meeting" in the First African Church, "where Jeff Davis has frequently convened the conspirators to plot and execute treason."[21]

Rumors of a great victory by Lee over Grant, followed by others that Davis had been captured and would be exhibited in Capitol Square, seemed to come from some distant land of the past. Reports of Confederate success were hardly credible when Mary Todd Lincoln, unhappy that her husband had not brought her along to Richmond, and Julia Dent Grant, feeling neglected when her husband set out after Lee, could come sightseeing as if on holiday.

Mrs. Lincoln arrived from City Point without fanfare, accompanied by her son Tad, Senator Charles Sumner, and a "charming party" of ladies that included her seamstress and closest friend, the former slave Elizabeth Keckley.[22]

Mrs. Grant, aboard her husband's dispatch boat, came amid a group of ladies who rode in a carriage through a seemingly deserted capital. Returning to the boat, that evening she sat "looking out and listening to the familiar home-like twitter of the little river frogs and watching the bright stars looking down upon the broad calm river." She thought of the tragic years just past—"How many homes made desolate! How many hearts broken! How much youth sacrificed! How much treasure lost!"—and she wept, "for what, I could not tell. . . ."[23]

But Mrs. Grant's tears were unseen, and the official compassion of Lincoln and Weitzel made but slight impression on some of Richmond's die-hard Confederate women. Young Emma Mordecai was disgusted by what she saw around the Capitol: The square "looked filthy, and was thronged with a motley crowd of native & foreign negroes, where a negro was never before seen. . . . All looked disconsolate, desolate and defiled."

Emma was nettled by what she heard from once-obsequious servants at Rosewood, the Mordecais' suburban home. One of them, Cyrus, said he would live on there but would work no more. All the land belonged to the Yankees now, and they were going to divide it among the colored people, he told her.

"There was no redress, no refutation" to this, Emma wrote, so she walked away, little consoled by another servant, Mary, who said, "I just as leave be slave as not."[24]

Defiance burned hottest among young women, who had learned hatred of Yankees for much of their lives—or perhaps they merely showed it most because, unlike men, they could get away with it. At first many of them went out with their faces thickly veiled, averted their eyes from oncoming Yankees, and crossed the street rather than walk beneath the U.S. flag.[25]

There were predictable run-ins—like that outside the Rutherford house on Twenty-second Street, occupied as headquarters of Edward Wild's black brigade: A "fine looking colored man" posted as guard soon had a dispute with "three ladies, belonging to the elite of the town, [who] came sailing down the sidewalk." The guard followed orders by walking his post close to the fence, but city law had said that blacks must always pass on the curb side. When he would not yield, the women turned back, saying "they would go home and tell their father, and he would see if they could not walk the streets of Richmond without being stopped by a nigger."[26]

When two officers of the Fortieth Massachusetts took an evening ride across the river in Manchester, they heard a piano being played inside a house and reined up to listen. A man invited them in and presented them to his wife and two daughters, who "bowed stiffly but spoke not a word." The younger girl, "a minx of perhaps sixteen, arose and switched out of the room in high dudgeon, volunteering the information as she went that she was a rebel, dyed in the wool, and wouldn't disgrace herself by remaining in the same room with Yankee officers." The wife upbraided her husband for being civil after his coolness toward South Carolina officers a few nights earlier.

"These gentlemen are my friends, while the others were my enemies," he told her. Turning, he introduced himself as Gilbert Mason—"I'm a Baptist minister, and this is the way I've lived since the war commenced."

He was a Union man, he said, a friend of John Minor Botts, and had been thrown into jail three times for telling his congregation that "God would punish them for their accursed support of slavery."

His courtesy toward the officers did not move his wife and daughters. When one of the officers asked 17-year-old Missouri Mason to play something, she refused to do any "Yankee tunes" but gave them "Dixie," "Maryland, My Maryland," and "Farewell to the Star-Spangled Banner." Before they left the girl presented each of them a miniature Confederate flag.[27]

In those lean days there were situations when even the defiant had to bend to Yankee rule, and even the righteous had to conform to worldly orders. Both sides laughed at the oft-told story of the girl who balked upon being informed that she must take the oath before receiving army rations.

"No, indeed, sir," she said. "I never swore in all my life!"

The relief agent said patiently, "But you must take the oath, my good girl, or I cannot give you the rations."

"No, indeed, I can't, sir. My mother always taught me never to swear."

When the agent persisted, the girl was "overcome at last by the dreadful conflict between her hunger and her high sense of moral duty." With eyes downcast, she said, "Well, sir, if you say I must, then . . . Damn the Yankees!"—and held out her hand for the hard-earned rations.[28]

* * *

The wreckage and poverty of Richmond, the hundreds of helpless Confederates in the city's hospitals, and the many thousands in its cemeteries helped veteran Union troops to sympathize with the conquered Rebels. But some civilians from Washington, men who had never experienced the brotherhood of soldiers, were offended by the humanity with which Weitzel and his men treated the recent enemy.

George A. Bruce of Devens's staff wrote that there were probably enough Northern senators and representatives walking Richmond's streets to convene a session of the U.S. Congress. At the Capitol, a military court recessed to welcome Vice President Andrew Johnson; Bruce said that Johnson sat beside him and made it clear that what he feared most was "the tender heart of President Lincoln."

"If I was President," Johnson told him, "I would order Davis, Lee, Longstreet, and all the prominent leaders before a military commission." Slamming his fist on the desk, he added, "when convicted of treason, they should be hung."[29]

Assistant Secretary of War Charles A. Dana, the New York editor sent fact-finding for Secretary Stanton, reported that Richmond's "inhabitants now number about 20,000, about half of them of African descent"—a low estimate, approximately a hundred thousand below the city's wartime peak, and barely half its prewar level. Dana said that "the rich as well as the poor are destitute of food." He wrote that U.S. troops had captured roughly 1,000 Confederate prisoners in the city, as well as about 5,000 wounded in nine hospitals, and at least 500 cannon, 5,000 muskets, 30 locomotives, and 300 railroad cars.[30]

When Dana encountered Johnson at the Spotswood, the future president, who sometimes took a drink, harangued him for twenty minutes against accepting Confederates as citizens without some conditions or punishment. According to Dana, "he insisted that their sins had been enormous" and unless punished "they might be very dangerous in the future."[31]

The irascible Stanton needed no urging to harden treatment of the South. Dana reported to him that while even Richmond's dedicated Rebels were "humbled and silenced," their humility seemed only to cover their deep enmity. He did not consider Federal feeling in Richmond "half as sincere as Weitzel believes," though throngs of civilians were applying for Union rations. (When they succeeded, many of those civilians still went hungry, because a staple of the Union commissary was strong Yankee salt cod, and as Phoebe Pember said, "few gently nurtured could relish such unfamiliar food.")[32]

Stanton repeatedly second-guessed Weitzel. He demanded to know by what authority the general was issuing rations to the population, and after Weitzel solved a problem about church prayers with a reasonable compromise, Stanton said his solution was "not satisfactory."[33]

When Ripley called Richmond ministers in to discuss resuming services, the Episcopalians maintained that they were obliged to continue praying for President Davis until their absent bishop ordered otherwise. "The controversy was warm and amusing," wrote Ripley, "as I sat in the middle of the parlor, a mere boy, with 20 or more reverend gentlemen laying down the ecclesiastical laws to me." To fend off military interference, Dr. Minnigerode wrote a long letter about separation of church and state, based of course on the Federal Constitution. But Ripley declared that services would "be conducted with regard to loyalty to the United States," and reminded Minnigerode that "I have an abundant supply of clergymen to assign to such pulpits as may be needed to conduct loyal services."

When the ministers withdrew, he turned to meet with the city's theater managers, who hardly missed a day before reopening for audiences of Yankee soldiers who paid in welcome U.S. dollars.[34]

That Sunday at St. Paul's, Davis's pew was kept empty. Ruffians had broken in during the evacuation and scrawled profanities in the Bible and hymnal. The correspondent Townsend admired the handsome ladies present: "Poor, proud souls! Last Sunday many of them were heiresses; now many of them could not pay the expenses of their own funerals."[35]

For the opening lesson, Minnigerode thrust to the heart of Richmond's plight by choosing the Forty-fourth Psalm, which concludes:

"Yea, for thy sake we are killed all the day long; we are counted as sheep for the slaughter.

"Awake, why sleepest thou, O Lord! arise, cast us not off for ever.

"Wherefore hidest thou thy face, and forgettest our affliction and our oppression?

"For our soul is bowed down to the dust: our belly cleaveth unto the earth.

"Arise for our help, and redeem us for thy mercies' sake."

In a clear monotone, Minnigerode read on to the Forty-sixth Psalm. Everyone listening understood how "fearfully applicable" the words were:

"There is a river, the streams whereof shall make glad the city of God, the holy place of the tabernacles of the Most High.

"God is in the midst of her; she shall not be moved; God shall help her, and that right early. . . ."

Then the organ soared, and Madame Ruhl, St. Paul's vocal soloist and choir director, outdid herself, "quivering and trilling, like a nightingale wounded, making more tears than the sublimest operatic effort, and the house reeled and trembled. . . ."[36]

When Minnigerode reached the point at which he had prayed by habit for Davis, he prayed instead for "all those in authority." And when word of this reached Washington, an indignant Stanton informed Weitzel that Richmond churches must show "no less respect for the President of the United States than they practiced towards the rebel chief, Jefferson Davis."

Through channels, Weitzel asked Lincoln's permission to disclose their conversation in Richmond, when the president had advised him to "let 'em up easy." Though Lincoln did not recall any mention of prayers, he telegraphed Weitzel: "I have no doubt that you have acted in what appeared to you to be the spirit and temper manifested by me while there."[37]

Thus Lincoln supported Weitzel, at least obliquely, and prayers for "all those in authority" became the temporarily accepted form. But a few days later, Major General E. O. C. Ord replaced Weitzel and ordered him to take his Twenty-fifth Corps south of Petersburg.

Many thought that Weitzel was relieved of occupation command because of the controversies over the legislature and church prayers. Others believed that Ord, who had never liked black troops, simply wanted Weitzel's corps out of the capital. Soon all the blacks in Ord's department were transferred to the Twenty-fifth Corps, and it was shipped off to Texas. Weitzel wrote to General Butler, "You know the niggers had to leave there. The smell was offensive to the F.F.V.'s."[38]

Weitzel was bitter over his treatment. He told of how he received letters abusing him for putting out the fire rather than letting all Richmond burn and was accused by Northern newspapers of being a "flunky." "I was delighted to get out of Richmond and get back to real military duties," he wrote. "Richmond was too near Washington. . . . I do not believe that the unfortunate people of Richmond ever were aware how near they came to being governed to death, after they were rescued from destruction by fire."[39]

In the first days of occupation, Richmond had been at the mercy of a general whose heart was as large as his president's. Ord, too, treated the captured capital leniently. The people of Richmond had been fortunate, in some ways, even in their gravest trauma.

* * *

Late that Palm Sunday, young Virginia Dade sat in a parlor on Franklin Street, gathering her thoughts for evening devotions. City gas lines broken in the fire were still cut off, and store-bought candles had run out. In the parlor the light from a makeshift lamp of cotton string burning in a cup of lard "only served to make darkness visible." Virginia and the women sitting with her were wondering what had happened to loved ones who had fled when suddenly the boom of a cannon broke the quiet. Then came more, and still more, rattling windows across the city.

What could it mean? Lee returning? A riot that only guns could suppress? Some new Yankee triumph?

The parlor door burst open and a Mrs. Brown, an Ohioan who had kept a Confederate clerkship by professing her Southern loyalty for four years, rushed in clapping her hands: "General Lee has surrendered! General Lee has surrendered!"

The women sat stunned and silent. Their anguish was compounded by "disgust at the heartless demonstrations of joy of this deceitful woman over the destruction and despair of her whilom friends."

They did not want to believe the news, but the guns kept up their steady beat, and then guards on the street confirmed it. Neighbors around the former Confederate White House saw lights blazing and heard Weitzel and his officers celebrating. In camps throughout the city, drums beat troops into formation to hear the announcement. Bands played on and on.

The next morning the *Whig,* the first Richmond newspaper to resume publication, told the story: Grant's pursuing divisions had cut ahead of Lee and surrounded the remnants of his Army of Northern

Virginia at Appomattox Court House, eighty-five miles west of Richmond. Lee had no choice but to ask for the terms of surrender. Grant had been generous, paroling Lee and his soldiers on condition that they go home and fight no more.

Davis, still at Danville, had not heard from Lee since leaving Richmond. When he got word, it was brought by 18-year-old Lieutenant John S. Wise, who had been sent to contact Lee from Clover station on the Richmond & Danville railroad. After close escapes from Union cavalry, Wise had ridden into the "flotsam and jetsam" of the once-proud Confederate army after the disaster at Sayler's Creek. There he found his father, who had helped push Virginia and thus Lee into war, who had exhorted Richmonders in 1861 never to turn aside "though your pathway be through fire, or through a red river of blood." The former governor had spent four years of war as a brigadier while some men had advanced from lieutenant to lieutenant general. Now, ragged and muddy, he was urging Lee to face the truth.

"To prolong the struggle is murder, and the blood of every man who is killed from this time forth is on your head," he told the commanding general.

Lee told him not to talk so wildly, and asked what the country would think if he surrendered.

"Country be damned!" said Henry Wise. "There has been no country, General, for a year or more. You are the country to these men."

The next morning young John Wise headed for Danville, and after an exhausting journey reported the army's hopeless situation to Davis and the cabinet. When the president dispatched him back to Lee, the youth heard news of the surrender on the way and returned to find that Davis and his entourage had fled into North Carolina.[40]

At Appomattox, to spare the feelings of the forlorn Confederates, Grant had forbidden his artillerymen to fire salutes in celebration. But Richmond awoke on Monday to what seemed a hundred hundred guns booming from Manchester across the James, from camps in all directions and in Capitol Square itself. On the river every Union boat that had a whistle cut loose in a contest to produce the most noise.

Ex-war clerk J. B. Jones heard it and admitted: "My Diary is surely drawing to a close. . . . All is lost. No head can be made by any other general or army—if indeed any other army remains. If Mr. Davis had been present, he never would have consented to it; and I doubt if he will ever forgive Gen. Lee."[41]

In time, many who understood Lee would wonder that he could ever forgive Davis. According to Charles Dana, Lee told Grant at Appomattox that "he had always been for the Union in his heart, and could find no justification for the politicians who had brought on the war, the origin of which he believed to have been the folly of extremists on both sides."[42] Privately, Lee bared those feelings many times, from before Sumter until his death.

With Lee's force disarmed and paroled, Grant was at liberty to ride triumphantly into the capital that his army had conquered. He returned to City Point, to a gala breakfast aboard his flagship with perhaps fifty generals, where someone assumed aloud that he would head next for Richmond.

"No," said Grant. "I will go at once to Washington."

His wife, surprised, urged him to visit Richmond, as she already had done.

He shushed her. "I would not distress these people," he said. "They are feeling their defeat bitterly, and you would not add to it by witnessing their despair, would you?"[43]

*   *   *

Each previous spring of the war had charged Richmond's spirits, brought stirring news of dangers and triumphs from Fort Sumter, from Seven Pines, Chancellorsville, the Wilderness, and Cold Harbor. This spring, though bursting blossoms and frequent rain promised rebirth, all of Virginia seemed gray.

On Saturday, April 15, a dense drizzle soaked the black ashes of the city. A weary cluster of riders, spattered with mud, slogged onto the Manchester end of the pontoon bridge at Seventeenth Street. One of the three wagons was covered by a sagging patchwork quilt in place of regulation canvas, a field expedient against the weather.

Out front, a gray-bearded officer rode a jaded gray horse. His uniform was soaked through, and rain spilled off his war-stained hat. Beneath it, his face was a portrait of gloom. Yet he sat erect, head up. Although the capital had expected him for days, at first few recognized him. Some of those who did wept at the sight.

As he crossed into Richmond and looked up across the terraced ruins to the Capitol where he had begun his long campaign, word spread that he had come. A few shouts were heard from the sidewalks, bringing more citizens out into the rain. They became a crowd, following him as he wound through the debris. Many of those who now welcomed him were blue-uniformed soldiers of the Union. One of them said, "As I looked into his face, the shadow of Appomattox was upon it."[44]

Slowly and repeatedly, Robert E. Lee lifted his hat to answer those waving and greeting him. Those close by could see how much older he looked than on his arrival in Richmond to take command four Aprils earlier. When he dismounted outside 707 East Franklin Street, men, women, and children reached out to touch and thank him. He found it hard to speak. After shaking a few hands, he bowed politely, backed inside, and closed the door.[45]

THE COMPANY OF KINGS

*A*s tattered Confederate veterans trudged into Richmond from Appomattox, for some Yankees "they took on a different aspect, clothed no longer in rags but with heroism, so that those who had fought against them looked upon them with admiration mingled with their pity." Many a Union soldier reached into his haversack to feed a hungry Rebel.[1]

But that night, a few hours after Lee crossed into the city, a dispatch from Washington swept away this benevolence. Union commanders rushed regiments from the suburbs into the capital, doubling patrols and street guards. Not until morning did the *Whig*, bordered in black, tell the rest of the city that Abraham Lincoln had been assassinated.

To Richmonders this was the last of the momentous Sunday bulletins that had shocked the city so many times since 1861. At first they were unsure what to think.

At Moses Hoge's house, young Lelian Cook saw something significant in the fact that Lincoln had been shot at Ford's Theater on Good Friday, after "the Northern papers had been speaking so extravagantly of his piety. . . . I don't know whether we have cause to rejoice at this or not, but we hope that it is a mysterious Providence and that it will be for our good in the end." But Emmie Sublett, who had called Lincoln's walking tour of Richmond "the monkey show," was wise enough at 13 to be sorry for his death: "I don't know what in the world to do, because I believe the whole South will be punished for it."[2]

Federal soldiers had no doubts about what to think or what to do.

They revered Lincoln. By overwhelming margins they had voted for him the previous fall, though knowing that his reelection would mean the war would go on, and they might never go home. They were sure that there must be some great conspiracy; the shot fired at Ford's Theater in Washington might signal a general uprising. It meant at least that the seemingly innocent Confederate veterans deserved no more pity from the victors. For a while that morning Union troops "pounced with the ferocity of wild beasts upon every rebel soldier they could lay hands upon, beating and driving them from the streets, the poor fellows all the while in ignorance of the cause of their bad treatment."[3]

Grant suspected a wider plot.* From Washington he ordered General Ord to arrest Mayor Mayo, the Richmond City Council, other officials, and paroled Confederate officers in the city. He wanted them locked in Libby Prison: "Extreme rigor will have to be observed whilst assassination remains the order of the day with the rebels."

But Ord, standing up to his general in chief, noted that Lee was among those covered by the order. If he arrested them, he said, "I think the rebellion here would be reopened. I will risk my life that the present paroles will be kept. . . ." He trusted Richmond's citizens, "who, I believe, are ignorant of the assassination, done, I think, by some insane Brutus with but few accomplices."[4]

Ord was right. The assassin and chief conspirator was John Wilkes Booth, the actor who had been the idol of Richmond belles, who had played the part of a Richmond soldier at John Brown's hanging, and had added his histrionics to the clamor for secession. Ever dramatic, he had shouted Virginia's motto, "Sic semper tyrannis!" as he leaped down to the stage after shooting the president. His role in the national tragedy would end when he fled to Virginia and was shot in a burning tobacco barn near Port Royal on the Rappahannock, fifty miles from Richmond.

Grant's fears ebbed a few hours after he issued the arrest order. He changed it to merely a suggestion, telling Ord to use his own judgment about arrests. The outburst of anger from troops and generals was brief. The calculated vengeance of radical politicians would last much longer.

Appropriately, once the conflict was over the soldiers who had fought against the United States were treated more leniently by the government than were the Southern politicians who had brought on the war. Most of the ranking Confederate officials who had fled Richmond, ex-

---

*After declining the honor of parading through conquered Richmond, Grant had also declined the honor of joining the Lincolns at Ford's Theater on Good Friday evening. Not until late that autumn did he make his first postwar visit to Richmond, a low-key stop on a five-day "fact-finding" swing through the South. He barely slowed to shake hands with officials, but he made time to thank Elizabeth Van Lew.

cept those who escaped abroad, spent months in Federal prisons before resuming civilian life. Yet there was no consistent relationship between what men and women had done during the war and what fate and the government did to them afterward.

* * *

Jefferson Davis was captured by Union troops near Irwinville, Georgia, on May 10 and held prisoner for two years at Fortress Monroe. Reports of harsh treatment by his jailers had rekindled sympathy for him in Richmond when he came to the city in 1867 for a treason trial that never took place. Released on bail raised by Horace Greeley and others North and South, he was cheered almost as warmly as he had been on arrival six years earlier, and stayed in the same suite at the Spotswood that had been his first home in Richmond. Then he traveled to Canada and Europe before settling again in Mississippi, where he wrote his self-justifying memoir, *The Rise and Fall of the Confederate Government.* He refused to ask for amnesty and never regained his U.S. citizenship. Four years after his death in New Orleans in 1889, he was reburied in Richmond's Hollywood Cemetery beside his daughter Winnie and his son Joe. There also lie 22 Confederate generals and more than 18,000 other Civil War soldiers.

Varina Davis lived in Savannah and Montreal while she campaigned for her husband's release from prison. After his death she spent her years writing her own intimate memoir of his life. Though sometimes frank about his weaknesses, she was always proud of her marriage to the Confederate president; in her latter days she called herself Varina Jefferson-Davis. She died in 1905 and was buried beside her husband.

Robert E. Lee and Mary Custis Lee's estate at Arlington was appropriated by the Federal government during the war, its grounds turned into a national cemetery. Though Lee was needy in the months after Appomattox, he refused rich offers to capitalize on his fame. Instead, he accepted the presidency of little Washington College in Lexington, which later became Washington and Lee University. There he urged students and defeated soldiers to put aside their bitterness, to rebuild the South, and be good citizens of the United States. He died in Lexington in 1870 and was buried in the college chapel.

Alexander H. Stephens was arrested at his Georgia home on May 11 and imprisoned for five months at Fort Warren in Boston Harbor. Though elected to the U.S. Senate in 1866, he was refused his seat. But after writing his *Constitutional View of the Late War Between the States,* he returned to the House of Representatives in 1873. He held that seat until he was elected governor of Georgia in 1882, and died the following year.

John Letcher, Virginia's governor from 1860 to 1864, returned to Lexington and practiced law. After he and many other wartime officeholders regained their civil rights under the Amnesty Act of 1872, Letcher reentered state politics. He served one term in the House of Delegates, then was defeated after suffering a severe stroke; he died in 1884.

Elizabeth Van Lew had tea with U. S. Grant when the general visited Richmond on his hurried tour of the South in late 1865. In appreciation of what she had done, Grant as president named her postmaster of Richmond in 1869. After eight years in that job and two as a post-office clerk in Washington, Van Lew faced poverty. Shunned by many in Richmond, she was sustained in her last years by the family and friends of the late Major Paul Revere, whom she had aided while he was in prison. After her death in 1900, they sent a massive boulder from Boston's Capitol Hill to be her gravestone in Shockoe Hill Cemetery; later it was defaced in retribution for her role in the war.

John Minor Botts, Union loyalist, after his place of exile in Culpeper County was vandalized by troops of both armies, engaged in Reconstruction politics and published his version of *The Great Rebellion* in 1866. Though a vehement opponent of Jefferson Davis in office, he was one of those who signed the ex-Confederate president's bail bond. Immersed in controversy to the end, he died in 1869 and was buried near Van Lew at Shockoe Hill.

Phoebe Pember wrote *A Southern Woman's Story*, her memoir of service at Chimborazo Hospital, while traveling widely at home and abroad soon after the war. She died in Pittsburgh in 1913 and was buried in Savannah.

Moses Drury Hoge took refuge at Danville, Virginia, and Milton, North Carolina, until he considered it safe to return to Richmond. When his wife, Susan, died in 1868, he wrote: "Now that I have no wife and no country, I have an indescribable feeling of having overlived my time." But he continued as pastor of Second Presbyterian Church for thirty more years. He died in 1899 and was buried in Hollywood Cemetery.

Mary Boykin Chesnut and her husband, James, returned to their ruined South Carolina plantation and spent the rest of their lives deep in debt. For a while as Mary reworked her wartime journal, her only income was from a servant's butter-and-egg business that brought in $12 a month. She died in 1886, and the first version of her acclaimed memoir was not published until 1905.

John B. Jones completed the project he had planned since taking his job as a clerk in the Confederate War Department—his eleventh and only remembered book, *A Rebel War Clerk's Diary*. But he never saw it in print; he died at his prewar home in Burlington, New Jersey, ten months after Appomattox, while the book was on press.

Burton Harrison, the president's private secretary, was captured with Davis and held for nine months, mostly at Fort Delaware. While in prison he began studying law, and after his release he opened an office in New York. In late 1867 he and Constance Cary were married. He prospered in the North before dying in Washington in 1904. Connie, who became a prolific author, died there in 1920, ten years after completing her memoir, *Recollections Grave and Gay*.

Captain George W. Alexander of Castle Thunder notoriety promoted himself, as so many other Confederate veterans did, to the postwar rank of "colonel." After a stay with a street railway company in Memphis, he took control of the *Sunday Gazette* in Washington in 1875. There his conduct provoked one John L. Shaw to charge that he was "a professional blackmailer," among other things less flattering. Alexander died in 1895 in Laurel, Maryland.

Judah P. Benjamin left Jefferson Davis's fleeing party before its capture and escaped from Florida to the West Indies. Making his way to England, he wrote newspaper editorials while qualifying for the bar. After a conspicuously successful British legal career, he died and was buried in Paris in 1884.

Stephen Mallory, captured in Georgia on May 20, was imprisoned for ten months at Fort Lafayette in New York Harbor. He returned to the practice of law in Pensacola and died there in 1873.

Richard S. Ewell was captured at Sayler's Creek during Lee's retreat to Appomattox. Held at Fort Warren for four months, he then returned to his farm in Tennessee. After spending much of his remaining years denying blame for the burning of Richmond, he died in 1872.

George W. Bagby went to New York as a journalist after the war but soon returned to writing and lecturing in Virginia. For a time he was state librarian and co-owner of the *Native Virginian* in Lynchburg. His humorous and nostalgic sketches won a devoted following before he died in Richmond in 1883.

William "Extra Billy" Smith, after taking his refugee state government to Lynchburg and Danville, returned to farming in Fauquier County after the war. In 1877, at the age of 80, the two-time governor returned to politics for a single term in the state legislature. He died in 1887 and was buried at Hollywood.

"Captain Sally" Tompkins, director of Robertson Hospital, immersed herself in postwar work for the Episcopal Church until she reached old age and became one of the first residents in Richmond's Home for Confederate Women. She died in 1916 and was buried with full military honors.

Philip Whitlock, quartermaster clerk, expanded his cigar business, scoring a popular success by introducing "Old Virginia Cheroots." After selling out to the American Tobacco Company in 1891, he became a respected philanthropist and set down his memories of Richmond during the war. He died in 1919.

Henry A. Wise practiced law with his son John after the war. In his 1872 book *Seven Decades of the Union,* he reviewed his fractious career. Until his death in Richmond in 1876, he refused to seek Federal amnesty for himself, but he urged young Virginians to make the best of the postwar situation.

John Sergeant Wise stood up for his father and took his advice. In Baltimore in 1867, he wounded the Richmond journalist-historian Edward A. Pollard in a duel for allegedly insulting the ex-governor. After his father died, John became a Republican, winning a congressional seat in post-Reconstruction Virginia. But because of ill will aroused by his political defection, he left the state to become a corporation lawyer in New York. There he delivered the 1891 Memorial Day oration at Grant's Tomb, praising the late general's "greatness . . . forgiveness and magnanimity." After publishing his memoir, *The End of an Era,* he retired to his native Eastern Shore. He died there in 1913 and was buried with his family at Hollywood.

Matthew Fontaine Maury learned of Lee's surrender while en route from England, where he had been a special agent and secured ships for the Confederacy. He detoured to Mexico, becoming Emperor Maximilian's immigration commissioner and trying to establish a colony of Virginians there. After another sojourn to England he became professor of meteorology at Virginia Military Institute. He died in 1873 and was buried at Hollywood.

Joseph Mayo served his thirteenth and final two-year term as mayor of Richmond after being reelected in 1866 in the first postwar balloting under military government. After leaving office in May 1868, he moved to New Kent County, where he died in 1872. He was buried at Shockoe Hill Cemetery.

John H. Reagan was imprisoned at Fort Warren for seven months, during which he wrote a letter to President Andrew Johnson that helped turn the president toward leniency in the South. Going home to

Texas, Reagan was elected to Congress, where he served for fifteen years before becoming chairman of the Texas Railroad Commission. He died in 1905.

John C. Breckinridge escaped to Cuba, then went to England and Canada before returning to Kentucky in 1869. He was a successful railroad lawyer until his death in Lexington in 1875.

Roger A. Pryor, captured in November 1864 while serving as courier during an informal truce near Petersburg, was released at Lincoln's order just before Appomattox. After the war he pawned his wife's jewelry to finance a move to New York, where he wrote for the *Daily News* and later became a justice of the state supreme court. He died there in 1919 and was buried in Princeton, New Jersey. Sara Rice Pryor published her *Reminiscences of Peace and War* in 1904 and died in 1912.

Edmund Ruffin, his plantations sacked and burned by the Federals, wrote the final entry in his diary ten weeks after Appomattox. He avowed again his "unmitigated hatred to Yankee rule—to all political, social and business connections with Yankees, and the perfidious, malignant and vile Yankee race." Then he put the muzzle of a shotgun to his mouth and used a forked stick to trip the trigger.

* * *

Joseph E. Johnston, after surrendering his army to Union general Sherman near Durham, North Carolina, on April 26, settled in Savannah, where he sold insurance until 1877. Returning to Richmond, he served a term in Congress before moving to Washington and becoming railroad commissioner. Ten months before his death in March of 1891, he came to Richmond to unveil a heroic equestrian figure of his West Point classmate and comrade in arms, Robert E. Lee.

Thousands of citizens, from schoolchildren to bearded and limping veterans, attended the ceremony on a broad boulevard two miles west of the Capitol of Virginia. Among them were more than 200 other surviving Confederate generals. Lee's statue, on its massive stone pedestal, was the first to adorn Monument Avenue, Richmond's pantheon of Confederate nobility. Five of the great men of the Confederacy are memorialized there; four are Virginians—Robert E. Lee, Stonewall Jackson, J. E. B. Stuart, and Matthew Fontaine Maury. The fifth is Jefferson Davis of Mississippi.

Douglas Southall Freeman, Lee's worshipful biographer, is said to have saluted his hero's statue each morning for decades on his way to work as editor of the Richmond *News Leader*. On the seventieth anniversary of McClellan's 1862 campaign against the city, Freeman wrote that "it is not too much to say that whatever is fine and aspiring and unselfish and kindly in the life of Richmond is due to [Lee's] influence more than to that of any other man who ever lived here."

In tribute to those whose history still permeates the city, Freeman wrote that "Every name brings up a picture. Every career has its inspiration. Surely none can walk the old streets they trod, or read their letters or gaze on their relics . . . and not feel grateful that in that high tradition, the humblest son of Richmond can spiritually keep the company of kings."[5]

Most of the old Richmond that Freeman so loved has been overrun by the city's twentieth-century growth as commercial, governmental, medical, and university center. Libby Prison was dismantled and carted away by a Yankee entrepreneur to be rebuilt as an exhibit at the Chicago World's Fair of 1892, and afterward demolished. Elizabeth Van Lew's mansion was used briefly after her death by the Virginia Club, then turned into a tuberculosis sanatorium and finally torn down by the local school board. But the ghosts remain—in the green peace of Hollywood Cemetery, in unmarked brick warehouses whose floors were once soaked with soldiers' blood, in antebellum homes where women waited for sons who did not return, in the public places that deal nostalgia in this most self-consciously historic city.

Lee's sword and Stuart's plumed hat are at the Museum of the Confederacy, and little Joe Davis's artillery officer's uniform is on display at the presidential mansion where he fell to his death. Thomas Jefferson's Capitol and the governor's mansion still function as they did on the October afternoon when 12-year-old John Sergeant Wise ran home to tell of Harpers Ferry. The guard tower that warned of raiding Yankees still stands, and St. Paul's Church is as it was on the April morning when the sexton bustled in with word from Lee that Richmond must be evacuated.

The most intrusive evidence of time's passage may be the wall of office towers in Richmond's financial district, blocking the wartime view from the Capitol, south across the James River into Dixie. But the most conclusive proof may be what happened in 1990 on the portico of that Capitol, where founding fathers of the Republic and defenders of the South's peculiar institution had proclaimed their conceptions of liberty. There, on a January day 125 years after Appomattox, L. Douglas Wilder, the grandson of Richmond slaves, was sworn in as the first elected black governor of any state of the Union.

Notes

1. WHO ARE NOT FOR US ARE AGAINST US

1. John Sergeant Wise, *End of an Era,* p. 80; Samuel Mordecai, *Richmond in By-Gone Days,* p. 166.
2. Wise, p. 63.
3. Ibid., pp. 118–124; *Semi-Weekly Enquirer,* 18 October 1859.
4. *Semi-Weekly Enquirer,* 14 October 1859; Stanley Preston Kimmel, *Mad Booths of Maryland,* pp. 150–153; Charles F. Fuller, Jr., "Edwin and John Wilkes Booth," pp. 481–483.
5. Helen Jones Campbell, "Lincoln Killer Once Popular As Matinee Idol in Richmond," *Times-Dispatch,* 23 April 1950.
6. Edmund Ruffin, quoted in Clement Eaton, *Mind of the Old South,* p. 98.
7. Wise, pp. 89–96.
8. *Semi-Weekly Enquirer,* 25 October 1859.
9. Avery O. Craven, *Edmund Ruffin, Southerner,* pp. 171–173.
10. Elizabeth Van Lew papers, Chap. 1, pp. 1–2. Most of the 500-plus pages in the Van Lew papers are haphazardly numbered and untitled. Part of her writing is an "Occasional Journal," part consists of descriptive narrations and character sketches, and part is her postwar correspondence with Union officials. The New York Public Library has arranged the collection in rough order on microfilm.
11. *Semi-Weekly Enquirer,* 21 November 1859.
12. George W. Libby, "John Brown and Wilkes Booth," p. 138.
13. *Semi-Weekly Enquirer,* 22 November 1859.
14. Ibid., 22, 23 November 1859.
15. J. Gottfried Lange, "New Name, or the Shoemaker in the Old and the New World," p. 132.
16. Craven, pp. 176–177.
17. Philip Whitlock, Ms. autobiography, pp. 85–87.
18. *Semi-Weekly Enquirer,* 3 January 1860; L. A. Wailes, "First Secessionists," p. 145.
19. Craven, p. 176.
20. *Semi-Weekly Enquirer,* 6 December 1859.
21. Ibid., 9 December 1859.

22. *Whig,* 19 January 1860; *Semi-Weekly Enquirer,* 24 January 1860; John Minor Botts, *Great Rebellion,* pp. 178–179.
23. Wise, pp. 61–63.

2.   SAVE VIRGINIA, AND WE SAVE THE UNION

1. F. N. Boney, *John Letcher of Virginia,* pp. 75–77, 84–85.
2. Ibid., pp. 74–90.
3. Clement Eaton, *Mind of the Old South,* p. 92.
4. *Semi-Weekly Enquirer,* 3 January 1860.
5. John Sergeant Wise, *End of an Era,* p. 63.
6. *Semi-Weekly Enquirer,* 3 January 1860.
7. Ibid., 6 January 1860.
8. William Byrd to Perry & Lane, London agents, 1684, quoted in Virginius Dabney, *Richmond: The Story of a City,* p. 9.
9. Alden Hatch, *Byrds of Virginia,* pp. 19–26; Westover Manuscripts, quoted by Samuel Mordecai, *Richmond in By-Gone Days,* pp. 18–19.
10. Vincent Harding, *There Is a River,* pp. 30–38.
11. Dabney, *Richmond,* p. 51.
12. Richard C. Wade, *Slavery in the Cities,* pp. 106–107.
13. Charles Dickens, *American Notes,* pp. 345–348.
14. Frederic Bancroft, *Slave-Trading in the Old South,* p. 88.
15. Cornelius Chase, "Negro Sales or Auctions," Chase family papers; Bancroft, p. 116.
16. William Still, *Underground Rail Road,* p. 391.
17. Ibid., pp. 54–55.
18. Ibid., p. 41.
19. U.S. Census 1860, 3rd Ward Richmond, p. 475.
20. Still, pp. 192–193.
21. *Semi-Weekly Enquirer,* 10 January 1860.
22. *Southern Literary Messenger,* January 1861, pp. 1–4.
23. Daniel W. Crofts, *Reluctant Confederates,* p. 137.
24. Boney, pp. 98–105.
25. George Cary Eggleston, *Rebel's Recollections,* pp. 8–10.
26. Robert O. Gunderson, "Old Gentlemen's Convention," pp. 5–12.
27. Crofts, p. 139.
28. Ralph A. Wooster, *Secession Conventions of the South,* p. 145.
29. Charles C. Osborne, *Jubal,* pp. 40–41.
30. Oscar Penn Fitzgerald, "John M. Daniel and Some of His Contemporaries," p. 13.
31. *Examiner,* 4 March 1861.
32. Robert M. Hughes, "Fighting Editor," p. 9.
33. Virginius Dabney, *Pistols and Poison Pens,* pp. 38–43.
34. George F. Mellen, *Famous Southern Editors,* pp. 389–390.
35. Frederick S. Daniel, *Richmond Examiner During the War,* pp. 7–9; *Examiner,* 3, 12 April 1861.
36. Virginia Convention, *Proceedings,* 1:427–428.
37. Henry A. Wise to Andrew Hunter, 2 April 1861, Massachusetts Historical Society *Proceedings* 44 (Dec. 1912), p. 31.
38. Benjamin P. Thomas, *Abraham Lincoln,* p. 252.
39. John Minor Botts, *Great Rebellion,* pp. 194–196.
40. Mrs. Roger A. Pryor, *Reminiscences of Peace and War,* p. 121.

3.   BLOOD BEFORE NIGHT

1. John B. Jones, *Rebel War Clerk's Diary,* pp. 1–2.
2. *Enquirer,* 13 April 1861.

3. Ibid.
4. Ibid., 15 April 1861.
5. Mrs. Roger Pryor, *Reminiscences of Peace and War,* pp. 122–123.
6. F. N. Boney, *John Letcher of Virginia,* pp. 111–112.
7. Frederick Law Olmsted, *Cotton Kingdom,* p. 33; *Virginia: A Guide to the Old Dominion,* p. 289.
8. *Enquirer,* 15 April 1861.
9. Ibid.
10. John Minor Botts, *Great Rebellion,* p. 206.
11. Jones, p. 4.
12. Boney, p. 112.
13. Virginia Convention, *Proceedings,* 4:122.
14. Ibid., 4:124; Barton Haxall Wise, *Life of Henry A. Wise,* p. 280.
15. Botts, p. 206; Daniel W. Crofts, *Reluctant Confederates,* p. 322.
16. Jones, p. 6.
17. Van Lew papers, Chap. 1.
18. Lewis Dabney Crenshaw, Jr., diary, 16, 19 March 1861; Ben La Bree, *Confederate Soldier in the Civil War,* p. 5.
19. Unknown, Diary of a Richmond girl, 18 April 1861.
20. Sallie B. Putnam, *Richmond During the War,* pp. 20–22.
21. Boney, p. 116.
22. Jones, p. 8.
23. Van Lew papers, Chap. 1, p. 12.
24. Jones, p. 7.
25. Douglas Southall Freeman, *R. E. Lee,* 1:441–443.
26. Freeman, *R. E. Lee,* 1:441–447; Alexandria *Gazette,* 20 April 1861.
27. Putnam, p. 24.
28. George W. Bagby, "Pawnee Sunday," Section 17, Bagby papers.
29. Freeman, *R. E. Lee,* 1:462–465; Freeman, "When War Came to Richmond."
30. Virginia Convention, 4:369–372.
31. Fitzhugh Lee, *General Lee,* p. 95.
32. Freeman, *R. E. Lee,* 1:475–476; J. William Jones, *Life and Letters of Robert E. Lee,* p. 438.
33. Henry Cleveland, *Alexander H. Stephens,* pp. 729–744.
34. Boney, p. 126.
35. *Enquirer,* 25 April 1861.
36. Ibid., 16 April 1861; Thos. A. Fowlkes to Cousin Ed, 16 April 1861, Dickenson & Hill file, Chase family papers.
37. *Enquirer,* 18 April 1861.
38. John S. Wise, *End of an Era,* pp. 165–166; Alfred Hoyt Bill, *Beleaguered City,* p. 47.
39. *Examiner,* 19 April 1861.
40. Louis H. Manarin, ed., *Richmond at War,* pp. 30–31.
41. *Examiner,* 26 April 1861.
42. Freeman, "When War Came to Richmond"; Boney, pp. 122–130.
43. Freeman, "When War Came to Richmond."
44. *Examiner,* 4 June 1861.

4. WE SHALL SMITE THE SMITER

1. William C. Davis, *Jefferson Davis,* p. 338.
2. Heros von Borcke, *Memoirs of the Confederate War for Independence,* 1:15.
3. Thomas Cooper DeLeon, "Inside View of Four Years in the Confederate Capital," pp. 252–253.
4. *Examiner,* 30 May 1861; William C. Davis, p. 338.
5. Unknown, Diary of a Richmond girl, 31 May 1861.

6. W. C. Davis, p. 339.
7. George Alfred Townsend, *Campaigns of a Non-Combatant,* p. 330; Mary Boykin Chesnut, *Mary Chesnut's Civil War,* p. 82; Virginia *Cavalcade* (autumn 1962), p. 16.
8. Thomas Cooper DeLeon, *Four Years in Rebel Capitals,* p. 104.
9. Sallie B. Putnam, *Richmond During the War,* p. 38.
10. *Examiner,* 1 June 1861; Varina Davis, *Jefferson Davis,* 2:202–203.
11. *Examiner,* 4 June 1861.
12. Mrs. D. Giraud Wright, *Southern Girl in '61,* p. 55.
13. New Orleans *Daily Crescent,* 9 July 1861.
14. DeLeon, *Four Years,* p. 95; Diary of a Richmond girl, 5 June 1861.
15. DeLeon, *Four Years,* p. 96.
16. Ibid., p. 96; Putnam, p. 36.
17. George Cary Eggleston, *Rebel's Recollections,* pp. 20, 31–38.
18. *Examiner,* 4 June 1861.
19. Ibid., 1 June 1861.
20. Ibid., 15 June 1861.
21. Chesnut, pp. 247, 285–286, 344, 765–766.
22. Ibid., p. 83.

5. WE HAVE BROKEN THE SPIRIT OF THE NORTH

1. Samuel Mordecai, *Richmond in By-Gone Days,* p. 293.
2. *Examiner,* 26 June 1861.
3. Ibid., 11 July 1861.
4. Ibid., 13, 18 June 1861.
5. Edward Budget, "Family Budget," 14 July 1861.
6. Mary Boykin Chesnut, *Mary Chesnut's Civil War,* p. 84; *Examiner,* 13 June 1861.
7. Peyton Harrison Hoge, *Moses Drury Hoge,* pp. 145–148.
8. J. William Jones, *Christ in the Camp,* p. 264.
9. Richard Maury, *Brief Sketch of the Work of Matthew Fontaine Maury,* pp. 6–8; Patricia Jahns, *Matthew Fontaine Maury & Joseph Henry,* pp. 190–192; Richmond *Times-Dispatch,* 14, 20 February 1904.
10. Richmond *Times-Dispatch,* 14, 20 February 1904.
11. John B. Jones, *Rebel War Clerk's Diary,* p. 29; *Examiner,* 24 June 1861.
12. *Examiner,* 27 June 1861.
13. Ibid., 24 June 1861.
14. Ibid., 25 June 1961.
15. Ibid., 27 June 1861.
16. Daniel von Groening to Rob. Evans, Liverpool, 3 June 1861; to Homer & Sprague, Boston, 27 June 1861; to Messrs. Gildenmeister & Ries, Bremen, 3 July 1861, Von Groening papers.
17. *Examiner,* 7 June, 2, 4 July 1861.
18. Ibid., 4 July 1861.
19. Ibid., 1 July 1861.
20. Ibid., 5 July 1861; Chesnut, p. 90.
21. William C. Davis, *Jefferson Davis,* p. 347.
22. Richmond City Council, minutes, 8 July 1861; *Examiner,* 9, 13 July 1861.
23. Nathan Miller, *Spying for America,* p. 98.
24. Thomas Cooper DeLeon, *Four Years in Rebel Capitals,* p. 120.
25. W. C. Davis, p. 350.
26. DeLeon, pp. 122–124; Mrs. Eugene McLean, "Northern Woman in the Confederacy," p. 443; John B. Jones, p. 34; *Enquirer,* 26 July 1861.
27. Chesnut, pp. 105–106.
28. Sallie B. Putnam, *Richmond During the War,* p. 63; *Examiner,* 23 July 1861.
29. W. C. Davis, pp. 350–353; *Examiner,* 23 July 1861.
30. *Examiner,* 25 July 1861.

31. Chesnut, p. 111.
32. Ibid., p. 107.
33. *Examiner,* 30 July 1861.
34. Ibid., 29 July 1861.

6.   THE PERFECTION OF TRUE WOMANHOOD

 1. G. H. Northam, "Woman's Sphere."
 2. Maria Mason (Tabb) Hubard diary, 11 July, 30 September 1861.
 3. Elizabeth Van Lew papers, Chap. 1, p. 11.
 4. Boston *Sunday Herald,* 11 November 1900; William Gilmore Beymer, "Miss Van Lew." p. 87.
 5. Fredrika Bremer, *Homes of the New World,* 2:510–511.
 6. Van Lew papers, Chap. 1, p. 13/20, 16/28.
 7. Charles B. Dew, *Ironmaker to the Confederacy,* pp. 91, 94.
 8. George W. Bagby to Lieutenant George W. Bagby, 25 June 1861, Folder 1, Section 3, Bagby papers.
 9. W. M. Clark, "Confederate Officer Visits Richmond," p. 91.
10. *Examiner,* 24 July 1861.
11. Katherine Helm, *Mary, Wife of Lincoln,* p. 182.
12. William H. Jeffrey, *Richmond Prisons 1861–62,* pp. 8–9.
13. Van Lew papers, Chap. 1, pp. 10, 14.
14. A. F. Blakey, *General John H. Winder, C.S.A.,* pp. 7–8, 11–12.
15. Van Lew papers, Chap. 1, p. 14.
16. Ibid.
17. Sally Tompkins to her sister Ellen, 22 July 1861.
18. Robert W. Waitt, Jr., *Confederate Military Hospitals in Richmond,* pp. 5–18.
19. Mary Maury Fitzgerald, "Captain Sally Tompkins, C.S.A.," p. 13; Elizabeth Dabney Coleman, "Captain Was a Lady," pp. 35–37; Mary Boykin Chesnut, *Mary Chesnut's Civil War,* pp. 133, 149.
20. Coleman, 35–41; *Confederate Veteran* 16, p. 72; Mrs. Bernard Franklin White, *Mathews Men Who Served in the War Between the States,* p. 51.
21. B. B. Vassall to William H. Jeffrey, quoted in Jeffrey, pp. 89–90.
22. Jeffrey, pp. 14–17, 127.
23. Van Lew papers, p. 67.
24. *History of the 27th New York Regiment,* quoted in Jeffrey, pp. 53–54.
25. Mark Mayo Boatner III, *Civil War Dictionary,* pp. 942–943.
26. Jeffrey, pp. 29–31.
27. Van Lew papers, p. 64.

7.   OUR AFFAIRS IN THE HANDS OF NOODLES

 1. Varina Davis, *Jefferson Davis,* 2:161–163.
 2. Mary Wingfield Scott, *Houses of Old Richmond,* pp. 146–148; Richmond *Dispatch,* 8 March 1891; Varina Davis, 2:198–200.
 3. George Cary Eggleston, *Rebel's Recollections,* pp. 201–203.
 4. William C. Davis, *Jefferson Davis,* pp. 357–360; Varina Davis, 2:152–158.
 5. W. C. Davis, pp. 27–28, 358–360.
 6. Mary Boykin Chesnut, *Mary Chesnut's Civil War,* p. 157.
 7. John B. Jones, *Rebel War Clerk's Diary,* p. 40.
 8. Henry Percy Brewster, quoted in Chesnut, p. 184.
 9. Gerry Van der Heuvel, *Crowns of Thorns and Glory,* p. 112.
10. Charleston *Mercury,* 4 October 1861; George W. Bagby, *Old Virginia Gentleman,* pp. 217, 116; Benjamin Blake Minor, *Southern Literary Messenger,* pp. 208–210.
11. Charleston *Mercury,* 2 October, 30 September 1861.
12. Ibid., 10 October 1861.

13. Semple to Bagby, 31 December 1861, George W. Bagby papers, Folder 2, Section 3.
14. Ibid., 22 January 1862.
15. Charleston *Mercury,* 25 October 1861.
16. William H. Jeffrey, *Richmond Prisons,* pp. 39–42; William Morrison Robinson, Jr., *Confederate Privateers,* pp. 149–150.
17. John B. Jones, p. 55.
18. Thomas Bragg, diary, 6 December 1861.
19. Charleston *Mercury,* 30 September 1861; Bagby, *Old Virginia Gentleman,* pp. 217, 116; Minor, pp. 208–210.

8. THE HORRORS OF A POLITICAL CAPITAL

1. Moses Drury Hoge, prayer at Provisional Confederate Congress, 28 November 1861, Hoge papers.
2. New Orleans *Crescent,* 29 November 1861.
3. *Examiner,* 20 July 1861.
4. Ibid., 7 July 1862.
5. New Orleans *Crescent,* 29 November, 2 December 1861; F. N. Boney, *John Letcher of Virginia,* p. 149.
6. E. Merton Coulter, *Confederate States of America,* p. 141; *Southern Watchman,* Athens, Ga., 14 December 1864.
7. New Orleans *Crescent,* 2 December 1861.
8. Charleston *Mercury,* 11 November, 14 December 1861.
9. *Examiner,* 12 May 1862.
10. Richard B. Harwell, *Confederate Music,* p. 30.
11. Charleston *Mercury,* 13 November 1861.
12. Ibid., 23 December 1861.
13. New Orleans *Crescent,* 27 December 1861.
14. Thomas Bragg, diary, 1 January 1862.
15. Sallie B. Putnam, *Richmond During the War,* p. 91.
16. Harwell, pp. 30–33.
17. New Orleans *Crescent,* 27 December 1861.
18. Harwell, pp. 31–32.
19. New Orleans *Crescent,* 4 January 1862.
20. Francis A. Donaldson to Jacob, 23 January 1862, Donaldson scrapbook.
21. Noyes Rand typescript, January 1904, Donaldson scrapbook.
22. Francis A. Donaldson to Jacob, 20 December 1861, Donaldson scrapbook.
23. Ibid., 23 January 1862; Noyes Rand typescript, Donaldson scrapbook.
24. Noyes Rand typescript.
25. Francis A. Donaldson to Jacob, 23 January 1862, Donaldson scrapbook.
26. Ibid.
27. Unknown, Diary of a Richmond girl, 22, 23 January 1862.
28. Thomas Bragg, diary, 3, 8, 17 January 1862.
29. Ibid., 21 January 1862.
30. Judith W. McGuire, *Diary of a Southern Refugee,* pp. 88–93.
31. Burton N. Harrison to A. J. Quinche, 21 March 1862, Harrison papers.
32. Robert Garlick Hill Kean, *Inside the Confederate Government,* pp. 21–22.
33. Craig M. Simpson, *Good Southerner,* p. 268.
34. John Sergeant Wise, *End of an Era,* pp. 185–90.
35. Maria Mason Hubard, diary, 15, 16 November 1861.
36. Helen G. McCormack, *William James Hubard,* 13; Hubard diary, 11 July 1861.
37. Hubard diary, 13 February 1862.
38. Ibid., 14 February 1862.
39. Ibid., 8 March 1862.

9. YOU'LL HAVE YOUR HANDS FULL

1. Confederate Congress, Proceedings, *SHSP* 44 (1928), pp. 38–39.
2. Ibid., pp. 34–35.
3. Ibid., p. 39.
4. *Enquirer,* Extra edition, 22 February 1862.
5. *Enquirer,* 4 March 1862; John Minor Botts, *Great Rebellion,* p. 270.
6. *Enquirer,* 4 March 1862.
7. William M. Robinson, Jr., *Justice in Grey,* pp. 390–91.
8. *Enquirer,* 4 March 1862; *Examiner,* 4, 6 March 1862.
9. *Enquirer,* 4 March 1862.
10. Ibid.
11. Robinson, pp. 390–391; *Enquirer,* 28 February 1862.
12. *Enquirer,* 28 February 1862.
13. Ibid., 4 March 1862; *Examiner,* 6 March 1862.
14. Charleston *Mercury,* 8 April 1862.
15. *Examiner,* 6 March 1862.
16. Elizabeth Van Lew, "Fast Days," Van Lew papers.
17. *Examiner,* 6 March 1862.
18. William H. Winder to "Dear Charles," 28 September 1862, Winder family papers.
19. "E. J. Allen" (Allan Pinkerton) to Major General George B. McClellan, 10 November 1861, Pinkerton's National Detective Agency papers; Pinkerton, *Spy of the Rebellion,* pp. 314–325.
20. Pinkerton, *Spy,* p. 325. Pinkerton's book is filled with improbable dialogue and coincidences, but he was a diligent record-keeper, and the basics of his narrative are usually supported by official sources. He sent McClellan a closely spaced thirty-five-page report on Webster's mission.
21. Ibid., pp. 395–403.
22. Ibid., pp. 494–538.
23. Charleston *Mercury,* 9 April 1862.
24. E. B. Long, *Civil War Day by Day,* pp. 181–182.
25. *Whig,* 18 March 1862.
26. Thomas Cooper DeLeon, *Four Years in Rebel Capitals,* p. 165.
27. Botts, pp. 281–287.
28. Ibid., 287; *Official Records* II, 2:1547.
29. *Official Records* II, 5:917, 919; *Official Records* II, 3:724.
30. Robinson, *Justice in Grey,* p. 416; *Enquirer,* 21 March, 12 August 1862; *Dispatch,* 19 August 1862.
31. Alan Lawrence Golden, "Castle Thunder," p. 24.
32. *Southern Illustrated News,* 14 March 1863; Harwell, *Confederate Theater,* pp. 69–70.
33. "Old Caphart," Van Lew papers.
34. Botts, pp. 288–290.
35. New York *Herald,* 3 April 1862.
36. Unknown, Diary of a Richmond girl, 9 April 1862.
37. Kate Mason Rowland, diary, 7 April 1862; Constance Cary Harrison, "Richmond Scenes in '62," p. 441.
38. DeLeon, p. 192.
39. Unknown, Diary of a Richmond girl, 13 April 1862.
40. *Examiner,* 6, 13 March 1862.
41. Ibid., 14 March 1862.
42. Harrison A. Trexler, "Davis Administration and the Richmond Press, 1861–1865," pp. 187–188.
43. *Whig,* 15 February, 25, 27 March 1862.
44. *Examiner,* 21 April 1862.
45. Ibid., 30 April 1862.

46. Pinkerton, *Spy*, pp. 548–558.
47. *Examiner*, 30 April 1862.

10.   SHELL AND BE DAMNED!

1. Herbert Aptheker, *Negro in the Civil War*, pp. 81–82.
2. William C. Davis, *Jefferson Davis*, p. 417; Charles F. E. Minnigerode, *Jefferson Davis: a Memorial Address*, pp. 8–11; Varina Davis, *Jefferson Davis*, 2:269.
3. Varina Davis, 2:268–269.
4. Moses Drury Hoge to "Dear Bess," 15 May 1862, Hoge papers; *Examiner*, 13 May 1862.
5. J. Thomas Scharf, *History of the Confederate States Navy*, 2:712.
6. *Examiner*, 22 June 1862; *Enquirer*, 25 July 1862.
7. *Whig*, 22 April 1862.
8. *Examiner*, 3 May 1862.
9. Sallie B. Putnam, *Richmond During the War*, pp. 129–130.
10. Scharf, 2:709.
11. Douglas Southall Freeman, *R. E. Lee*, 2:48.
12. John H. Reagan, *Memoirs with Special References to Secession and the Civil War*, p. 92; *Whig*, 16 May 1862; Putnam, pp. 130–131.
13. Putnam, p. 130.
14. Scharf, 2:717.
15. James Russell Soley, "Navy in Peninsular Campaign," pp. 270–271; Scharf, 2:715.
16. Varina Davis, 2:272–276; W. C. Davis, pp. 422–423.
17. Stephen W. Sears, *To the Gates of Richmond*, p. 104.
18. Gustavus W. Smith, "Relative Strength of the Opposing Forces," p. 219.
19. Constance Cary Harrison, "Richmond Scenes in '62," p. 442.
20. Charleston *Mercury*, 14, 20 May 1862.
21. *Examiner*, 26 May 1862.
22. Varina Davis, 2:279; Van Lew papers.
23. Freeman, *South to Posterity*, pp. 112–113.
24. John B. Jones, *Rebel War Clerk's Diary*, pp. 80–81.
25. Harrison, "Richmond Scenes," pp. 443–444; Putnam, pp. 135–136.
26. George W. Bagby, "Sunday After Seven Pines," Section 17, Bagby papers.
27. Freeman, *R. E. Lee*, 2:74–77.
28. Dabney H. Maury, "Recollections of a Virginian," p. 161; Freeman, *R. E. Lee*, 2:66.
29. John B. Jones, p. 82.
30. Freeman, *R. E. Lee*, 2:81–86, 89.
31. Edward Porter Alexander, *Fighting for the Confederacy*, p. 91.

11.   THE DAZZLE OF IT IN THEIR EYES

1. Horatio Staples, MOLLUS Papers Unpublished, Box 3, Folder 7.
2. Douglas Southall Freeman, *R. E. Lee*, 2:250–254; R. A. Brock, ed., *General Robert Edward Lee . . .* , p. 322.
3. Freeman, *Lee's Lieutenants*, 1:284–302; Mary Newton Stanard, *Richmond: Its People and Its Story*, p. 195; Sallie B. Putnam, *Richmond During the War*, p. 143; John B. Jones, *Rebel War Clerk's Diary*, p. 82.
4. Edmund H. Cummins, "Signal Corps in the Confederate States Army," pp. 93–107; H. V. Cavan, "Confederate Military Intelligence," pp. 42–45; Nathan Miller, *Spying for America*, pp. 128–130.
5. Allan Pinkerton, *Spy of the Rebellion*, pp. 414–428, 456.
6. George Alfred Townsend, *Campaigns of a Non-Combatant*, pp. 119–122.
7. Fannie W. G. Tinsley, Memoir.
8. Joseph Jenkins Cornish III, *Air Arm of the Confederacy*, pp. 34–36; Edward Porter Alexander, *Fighting for the Confederacy*, pp. 115–117.

9. John B. Jones, p. 83.
10. Mrs. D. Giraud Wright, *Southern Girl in '61,* p. 78.
11. *Dispatch,* 26 June 1862.
12. Mrs. Roger A. Pryor, *Reminiscences of Peace and War,* pp. 174–176.
13. Tinsley, Memoir.
14. Stephen W. Sears, *To the Gates of Richmond,* p. 200.
15. *Examiner,* 28 June 1862.
16. "Ten Days in Richmond," *Blackwood's Edinburgh Magazine,* October 1862, pp. 392–402.
17. *Examiner,* 28 June 1862.
18. Constance Cary Harrison, "Richmond Scenes in '62," pp. 447–448; Freeman, *R. E. Lee,* 2:131–132.
19. John B. Jones, pp. 86–87.
20. Elizabeth Van Lew, journal, 21, 26 June 1862.
21. E. B. Long, *Civil War Day by Day,* p. 235.
22. Putnam, p. 151.

12. CAN'T YOU WAIT UNTIL WE'RE DEAD?

1. Mrs. Roger A. Pryor, *Reminiscences of Peace and War,* pp. 178–192; Robert W. Waitt, Jr., *Confederate Military Hospitals in Richmond,* p. 2.
2. "Opposing Forces in the Seven Days Battles," *Battles and Leaders,* 2:317.
3. Joseph P. Cullen, "Chimborazo Hospital," pp. 37–40.
4. Charleston *Mercury,* 23 July 1862.
5. Russell V. Bowers, "Chimborazo Hospital."
6. Jennie E. Harrold, Reminiscences of Richmond.
7. John R. Gildersleeve, "History of Chimborazo Hospital," pp. 149–150; Edgar Erskine Hume, "Chimborazo Hospital, Confederate States Army," pp. 189–191; Cullen, pp. 37–40.
8. *Enquirer,* 8 July 1862.
9. *Examiner,* 10 July 1862; *Enquirer,* 12 July 1862; Louis H. Manarin, *Richmond at War,* pp. 192–193.
10. John B. Jones, *Rebel War Clerk's Diary,* p. 87.
11. *Examiner,* 10 July 1862.
12. *Enquirer,* 15 July 1862.
13. Charleston *Mercury,* 28 July 1862.
14. J. Gottfried Lange, "New Name, or the Shoemaker in the Old and the New World," p. 159; *Enquirer,* 3 July 1862.
15. George B. McClellan, address to Army of Potomac, 4 July 1862, McClellan papers, p. 339.
16. Thomas Cooper DeLeon, *Four Years in Rebel Capitals,* p. 303.
17. Edward Porter Alexander, *Fighting for the Confederacy,* p. 117.
18. Theodore Smith to his father, 20 July 1862.

13. AT WHICH ANGELS MIGHT WEEP

1. Henry Kyd Douglas, *I Rode with Stonewall,* p. 119; Peyton Harrison Hoge, *Moses Drury Hoge,* p. 166.
2. Peyton H. Hoge, pp. 158–164.
3. Peyton H. Hoge, p. 167; Moses Drury Hoge to Susan Hoge, 8 July 1862, Hoge papers.
4. Mary Boykin Chesnut, *Mary Chesnut's Civil War,* p. 429.
5. Ibid.; Edward Porter Alexander, *Fighting for the Confederacy,* pp. 89–90.
6. Alexander, pp. 89–90; Joseph C. Ives to his mother, 6 October 1862, Ives papers.
7. Emory M. Thomas, *Confederate State of Richmond,* pp. 87, 105–106; *Whig,* 30 April 1862; *Dispatch,* 24 May 1862.
8. John B. Jones, *Rebel War Clerk's Diary,* pp. 116, 99, 102, 104–105.

9. *Examiner,* 30, 31 October 1862.
10. Ibid., 3, 6 November 1862.
11. Ibid., 31 October 1862.
12. Ibid., 22 January 1862.
13. Robert M. Hughes, *Editors of the Past,* pp. 24–25; A.N. Wilkinson, "John Moncure Daniel," p. 91; George W. Bagby, *Old Virginia Gentleman,* pp. 175–180.
14. J. Cutler Andrews, *South Reports the Civil War,* pp. 27–29.
15. Edward Alfred Pollard, *Life of Jefferson Davis,* p. 162.
16. William C. Davis, *Jefferson Davis,* pp. 170–172; *Dictionary of American Biography,* 3:500–501.
17. *Dictionary of American Biography,* 9:590–592.
18. Chesnut, p. 198, 433.
19. Louis Pendleton, *Alexander H. Stephens,* p. 387.
20. Rembert W. Patrick, *Jefferson Davis and His Cabinet,* p. 41.
21. *Examiner,* 16 October 1862.
22. Ibid., 26 September 1862.

14.   A SCHEME SO ATROCIOUS

1. Silas Omohundro Business Records, Market and General Account Book 1858–1864.
2. Malvern Hill Omohundro, *Omohundro Genealogical Record,* pp. 461–463; 1860 U.S. Census, Henrico County, 1st Ward Richmond, p. 72.
3. Silas Omohundro, Market and General Account Book.
4. Malvern Hill Omohundro, pp. 471–472.
5. Ibid., pp. 464, 472; 1860 U.S. Census, Henrico County, 1st Ward Richmond, p. 72.
6. Federal Writers Project, *Negro in Virginia,* p. 164; Frederic Bancroft, *Slave-Trading in the Old South,* pp. 101–105.
7. Silas Omohundro, Market and General Account Book; *Examiner,* 25 October 1862; John B. Jones, *Rebel War Clerk's Diary,* p. 107.
8. James H. Brewer, *Confederate Negro,* pp. 6–9.
9. J. Wimbish Young to E. H. Stokes, 21, 23 June 1862; J. H. Burnett to E. H. Stokes, 17 August 1862, Chase family papers.
10. John Robertson to E. H. Stokes, 9 July 1862; Chase family papers.
11. E. Merton Coulter, *Confederate States of America,* pp. 318–320; *Official Records* I, 25, pt. 2:790.
12. Confederate Congress, Proceedings, *SHSP* 47 (1930), p. 29.
13. *Whig,* 22 October 1862; *Examiner,* 29 September, 3 October 1862.
14. William C. Davis, *Jefferson Davis,* pp. 474–484, 489–495; Jefferson Davis, *Jefferson Davis, Constitutionalist,* 5:409.
15. William Stanley Hoole, *Lawley Covers the Confederacy,* pp. 12–15.
16. *Times* (London), 4 November, 1 December 1862.
17. Hoole, *Lawley,* p. 15.
18. Thomas Cooper DeLeon, *Belles, Beaux and Brains of the 60's,* pp. 334–335.
19. *Times* (London), 30 December 1862.

15.   ALL THE PATRIOTISM IS IN THE ARMY

1. Susan Hoge to Moses Drury Hoge, 25 December 1862, Hoge papers.
2. Peyton Harrison Hoge, *Moses Drury Hoge,* pp. 168–171.
3. *Times* (London), 18 February 1863.
4. Peyton Harrison Hoge, p. 173.
5. Ibid., pp. 175–176.
6. *Examiner,* 22 January 1863.
7. John L. Burrows, *New Richmond Theater.*
8. Richard B. Harwell, *Confederate Music,* p. 31.

9. Burrows.
10. *Enquirer*, 1 September 1862.
11. *Southern Illustrated News*, 14 February 1863.
12. George Cary Eggleston, *Rebel's Recollections*, pp. 220–222.
13. John B. Jones, *Rebel War Clerk's Diary*, pp. 159–160.
14. Philip Whitlock, Ms. autobiography, pp. 106–111.
15. Eggleston, p. 210.
16. Whitlock, pp. 111–121.
17. Ibid., 123–125.
18. Burton Harrison, "Paean to My Pipe," 4 December 1862, Harrison papers; Daniel E. Sutherland, *Confederate Carpetbaggers*, pp. 31–38.
19. Mary Boykin Chesnut, *Mary Chesnut's Civil War*, pp. 439–440.
20. *Examiner*, 17, 18 October 1862.
21. E. Merton Coulter, *Confederate States of America*, pp. 235–237.
22. Charles B. Dew, *Ironmaker to the Confederacy*, p. 129.
23. Ibid., p. 108.
24. Ibid., pp. 28–30.
25. John B. Jones, pp. 169–175.
26. David L. Burton, "Friday the 13th," pp. 37–38; Josiah Gorgas, *Civil War Diary of Josiah Gorgas*, p. 29.
27. *Examiner*, 15 March 1863; Burton, pp. 37–39.
28. Burton, p. 41.
29. John B. Jones, p. 175.
30. Gorgas diary, p. 25.
31. Burton, p. 40.
32. *Examiner*, 7 December 1863, 13 October 1864.
33. *Whig*, 25 September 1863.
34. J. Gottfried Lange, "New Name, or the Shoemaker in the Old and the New World," p. 150.
35. Ibid.
36. Rembert W. Patrick, *Jefferson Davis and His Cabinet*, pp. 283–284.
37. *Examiner*, 23 October 1863.
38. Coulter, pp. 158–160; 219–223; *Enquirer*, 3 March 1863.
39. Confederate Congress, Proceedings, *SHSP* 47 (1930), p. 122.
40. *Dispatch*, 6 February 1864.
41. Myron Berman, *Richmond's Jewry*, p. 176; Confederate Congress, *SHSP* 47 (1930), p. 122; *Examiner*, 31 March 1863.
42. Memphis *Daily Appeal*, 12 March 1863; *Whig*, 16 February 1863.
43. *Official Records* I, 25, pt. 2:686–688, 693–694.
44. Ibid., pt. 2:683, 687.
45. John B. Jones, p. 180.
46. Mrs. Roger A. Pryor, *Reminiscences of Peace and War*, pp. 237–239; John B. Jones, p. 183.
47. McGuire, *Diary of a Southern Refugee*, p. 203.
48. John B. Jones, pp. 183–184; Varina Davis, *Jefferson Davis*, 2:375–376; William C. Davis, *Jefferson Davis*, pp. 497–498; F. N. Boney, *John Letcher of Virginia*, pp. 189–191; William J. Kimball, "Bread Riot in Richmond," p. 151.
49. John Bigelow, Jr., *Campaign of Chancellorsville*, p. 121.
50. Hall Tutwiler to his sister Nettie, 3 April 1863, McCorvey papers; Margaret Wight diary, Wight family papers, VHS.
51. *Examiner*, 4 April 1863.
52. Ibid., 4, 5 April 1863.
53. Emma Lyon Bryan, Reminiscences, Early family papers; Gorgas diary, p. 29.
54. John B. Jones, p. 185; *Examiner*, 14 April 1863.

16. THE AWFUL HOUR HAS COME AGAIN

1. *Examiner,* 9, 10, 13 April 1863.
2. *Official Records* II, 5:871–892.
3. Kirby diary, Section 18, Aylett papers.
4. Elias Griswold to Winder, 10 November 1862, "Kirby's case" affidavits, Section 18, Aylett papers; *Official Records* II, 5:890.
5. *Official Records* II, 5:905–907.
6. *Examiner,* 24 April 1863.
7. Ibid., 16 October 1862; Columbus *Sun,* 19 December 1863.
8. *Joint Committee Report,* 38th U.S. Congress, 2nd session, pp. 73–74.
9. Meriwether Stuart, "Samuel Ruth and General R. E. Lee," pp. 37–38, 77–81.
10. Warren W. Hassler, *Commanders of the Army of the Potomac,* p. 134; Darius N. Couch, "Chancellorsville Campaign," p. 155; Noah Brooks, *Washington, D.C.,* pp. 56–58.
11. *Examiner,* 20 April 1863.
12. Ibid., 28 April 1863.
13. *Official Records* I, 25:329.
14. John B. Jones, *Rebel War Clerk's Diary,* p. 197.

17. GOD HAS BROKEN OUR IDOL

1. Mary Boykin Chesnut, *Mary Chesnut's Civil War,* p. 477.
2. Mary Anna Jackson, *Memoirs of Stonewall Jackson by His Widow,* p. 448.
3. Chesnut, pp. 477–478; 453.
4. *Examiner,* 4, 5 May 1863.
5. *Official Records* I, 25, pt. 1:1060–1061.
6. Edward Younger, ed., *Inside the Confederate Government,* pp. 55–56; *Official Records* I, 25, pt. 1:770–781; *Examiner,* 6 May 1863.
7. H. G. Armstrong to Burton Harrison, 27 June 1863, Harrison papers.
8. *Examiner,* 4 May 1863.
9. New York *Evening Post,* 1 July 1863.
10. Unknown scrapbook, Ms. 5:7 Un 3:10, VHS.
11. Sallie B. Putnam, *Richmond During the War,* pp. 222–224; Kate Mason Rowland, diary, vol. 2, 9 May 1865; R. L. Dabney, *Life and Campaigns of Lieut.-Gen. Thomas J. Jackson,* pp. 729–733.
12. James Longstreet, "Lee's Invasion of Pennsylvania," p. 245; John B. Jones, *Rebel War Clerk's Diary,* p. 207.
13. *Official Records* I, 25, pt. 1:790.
14. Robert E. Lee, Jr., *Recollections and Letters of Robert E. Lee,* pp. 97–100.
15. Joseph Mayo, broadside, 27 June 1863.
16. John B. Jones, pp. 230–233.
17. J. Gottfried Lange, "The New Name, or the Shoemaker in the Old and the New World," pp. 167–170.
18. *Sentinel,* Extra edition, 7 July 1863; *Dispatch,* 7 July 1863; Thomas Cooper DeLeon, *Four Years in Rebel Capitals,* p. 256; John B. Jones, p. 238; Varina Davis, *Jefferson Davis,* 2:392.
19. DeLeon, pp. 256–257; Junius Henri Browne, *Four Years in Secessia,* pp. 264–265.
20. DeLeon, pp. 256–257; Josiah Gorgas, *Civil War Diary of General Josiah Gorgas,* p. 55.
21. *Official Records* I, 29, pt. 2:640.
22. Louis M. Starr, *Bohemian Brigade,* pp. 184–185.
23. Browne, pp. 265–274.
24. Louis R. Fortescue, "War Diary," 4:37.
25. William S. Long, memoir, Container 12, Breckinridge Long papers.
26. Browne, pp. 265, 274.
27. Weston Ferris, "Prison Life of Western Ferris, Troop B, 1st Connecticut Cavalry."

28. Aaron E. Bachman, Memoirs, pp. 29–30.
29. *Whig,* 30 April 1863.

18.   THOUSANDS OF BAREFOOTED MEN

1. Peyton Harrison Hoge, *Moses Drury Hoge,* pp. 175–186.
2. Moses Drury Hoge to Susan Hoge, 12 August 1863, Hoge papers.
3. Susan Hoge to Moses Drury Hoge, 19 July 1863, Hoge papers.
4. Sallie B. Putnam, *Richmond During the War,* p. 249.
5. Peyton Harrison Hoge, pp. 191–194.
6. *Official Records* I, 51, pt. 2:1043.
7. John B. Jones, *Rebel War Clerk's Diary,* p. 245.
8. Clifford Dowdey, *Experiment in Rebellion,* pp. 302–303.
9. Douglas Southall Freeman, *R. E. Lee* 3:208–210.
10. Mary Custis Lee to "My dear little child," 7th (no month), Peyton papers.
11. Lee to Mrs. Lee, 26 October 1862, in R. E. Lee, Jr., *Recollections and Letters,* pp. 79–80.
12. Lee to Mrs. Lee, 27 December 1863, in R. E. Lee, Jr., pp. 117–118.
13. Mary Custis Lee to "My dear little child," 7th (no month), Peyton papers; R. E. Lee, Jr., p. 111.
14. Mary Custis Lee to "My dear cousin," 28th (no month), Peyton papers; Mary Boykin Chesnut, *Mary Chesnut's Civil War,* pp. 573–574.
15. M. C. Lee to "My dear little child," 7th (no month), Peyton papers.
16. Mary Elizabeth Massey, *Bonnet Brigades,* pp. 72–75.
17. Phoebe Yates Pember, *A Southern Woman's Story,* p. 3.
18. Phoebe Yates Pember to Eugenia Phillips, 13 September 1863, Phillips papers.
19. Pember, *Southern Woman's Story,* p. 42.
20. Ibid., pp. 65–68.
21. Ibid., pp. 46–47.
22. Ibid., pp. 51–64.
23. Pember to Mrs. Jeremy F. Gilmer, 30 December 1863, quoted in Pember, p. 130.
24. Benjamin F. Butler to Commander Boutelle, U.S. Coast Survey Office, 19 December 1863, *Private and Official Correspondence* 3:228–229.
25. "James Ap. Jones" (Butler) to "My dear aunt" (Van Lew), 18 January 1864, in Butler, *Private and Official Correspondence* 3:319.
26. Butler, *Private and Official Correspondence,* 3:564.
27. "Cashmeyer," Van Lew papers.
28. Rose O'Neal Greenhow to Alexander Robinson Boteler, 20 July 1863, Jefferson Davis papers.
29. Stephen R. Mallory to Virginia Caroline Clay, 28 October 1864, Clay papers.
30. George W. Bagby to *Register,* 19 March 1864.
31. Katharine Jones, *Heroines of Dixie: Winter of Desperation,* pp. 86–87; Loreta Janeta Velazquez, *Woman in Battle.*
32. Richmond *Evening Journal,* 2 May 1908; William Gilmore Beymer, "Miss Van Lew," p. 90; Thomas McNiven, "Recollections."
33. Ellen Glasgow, *A Certain Measure,* pp. 65–66.
34. Dowdey, p. 174.
35. Beymer, "Miss Van Lew," p. 86.
36. George H. Sharpe to General C. B. Comstock, January 1867, Van Lew papers; Beymer, "Miss Van Lew," p. 86.

19.   THE BITING FROSTS OF WINTER

1. John B. Jones, *Rebel War Clerk's Diary,* pp. 303–304.
2. Dunbar Rowland, ed., *Jefferson Davis, Controversialist,* 5:555; *Southern Literary Messenger* 37 (1863), pp. 572–573.

3. Jones, p. 276.
4. Louis R. Fortescue, "War Diary," p. 31.
5. Jones, p. 280.
6. Ibid., pp. 291, 299–301.
7. Ibid., pp. 303, 307.
8. Varina Davis, *Jefferson Davis* 2:529; William C. Davis, *Jefferson Davis*, p. 540.
9. *Official Records* II, 6:544.
10. Merton E. Coulter, *Confederate States of America*, pp. 478–479.
11. *Official Records* II, 6:475–476, 571–572.
12. Ibid., pp. 482–483.
13. Ibid., pp. 544–547.
14. Ibid., pp. 587–588.
15. Ibid., pp. 570–571.
16. Coulter, p. 471.
17. Mobile *Register & Advertiser*, 4 December 1863.
18. W. C. Davis, pp. 527–531.
19. Mobile *Register & Advertiser*, 4 December 1863.
20. *Official Records* II, 6:764–765.
21. Columbus *Sun*, 15 December 1863.
22. Mobile *Register & Advertiser*, 2 December 1863.
23. Thomas Cooper DeLeon, *Belles, Beaux and Brains of the 60's*, pp. 219–223, 229–231.
24. Mary Boykin Chesnut, *Mary Chesnut's Civil War*, p. 590.
25. Columbus *Sun*, 11 December 1863.
26. Chesnut, pp. 430–431.
27. Ibid., pp. 804–805, 825.
28. Ibid., pp. 514–515.
29. Mobile *Register & Advertiser*, 25 December 1863.
30. Douglas Southall Freeman, *R. E. Lee*, 3:215–217; Columbus *Sun*, 22 December 1863.
31. John Whitten, diary.
32. Weston Ferris, "Prison Life of Weston Ferris, Troop B, 1st Connecticut Cavalry," p. 4.
33. *Examiner*, 31 December 1863.
34. *Dictionary of American Biography*, 9:361.
35. Mobile *Register & Advertiser*, 30 December 1863.
36. Jones, 319; E. B. Long, *Civil War Day by Day*, p. 450; Coulter, p. 535.
37. *Enquirer*, 11 January 1863; *Whig*, 18 January 1863.
38. *Official Records* I, 33:520.
39. Ibid., pp. 519–520.
40. Ibid., p. 521.
41. *Examiner*, 6 March 1862.
42. Thomas McNiven, "Recollections"; *Official Records* I, 33:520.
43. *Official Records* I, 33: 520–521.
44. Ibid., p. 519.
45. William Swinton, *Campaigns of the Army of the Potomac*, pp. 398–399.
46. Frank E. Moran, "Colonel Rose's Tunnel at Libby Prison," pp. 770–772.
47. Ibid., pp. 771–772.
48. Ibid., pp. 773–780.
49. Ibid., p. 780.
50. Ibid., p. 783.
51. Fortescue, p. 51.
52. Ibid.
53. Moran, pp. 786–790.
54. A. C. Roach, *Prisoner of War*, pp. 98–117.
55. Elizabeth Van Lew, journal, 21 June 1862, p. 543, Van Lew papers.
56. Pember to Mrs. J. F. Gilmer, 19 February 1864, in Pember, *Southern Woman's Story*, 135.
57. "Colonel Streight and his Companion," pp. 259–265, Van Lew papers.

20. TO DESTROY THE HATEFUL CITY

1. Columbus *Sun*, 13 February 1864; John B. Jones, *Rebel War Clerk's Diary*, p. 336.
2. Mobile *Register & Advertiser*, 10 February 1864.
3. Mary Boykin Chesnut, *Mary Chesnut's Civil War*, p. 547.
4. William C. Davis, *Jefferson Davis*, p. 533; Jones, p. 328; Richardson, *Compilation of the Messages and Papers of the Confederacy*, 1:397–398.
5. W. C. Davis, pp. 541–542.
6. James Rodney Wood, Sr., notes, Container 3, Maud Wood Park papers.
7. George E. Pond, "Kilpatrick's and Dahlgren's Raid to Richmond," pp. 94–95.
8. William Swinton, *Campaigns of the Army of the Potomac*, pp. 398–399; Pond, p. 95.
9. J. William Jones, "Kilpatrick-Dahlgren Raid Against Richmond," pp. 540–541.
10. Louis R. Fortescue, War Diary, pp. 75–77; William B. Hesseltine, *Civil War Prisons*, p. 132; *Official Records* I, 33:168–224.
11. *Official Records* II, 8:343–344.
12. Richard G. Crouch, "Dahlgren Raid," p. 179.
13. Lieutenant R. Bartley, Detroit *Free Press*, 11 March 1882, quoted in J. William Jones, p. 516.
14. William Preston Cabell, "How a Woman Helped to Save Richmond," p. 178.
15. Cabell, p. 178.
16. Bartley, in J. William Jones, p. 518; Wood, Container 3, Maud Wood Park papers.
17. Cabell, p. 178; *Examiner*, 5 March 1864.
18. Bartley, in J. William Jones, p. 516; Crouch, p. 184.
19. Harriette Cary, "Diary of Miss Harriette Cary," pp. 558–559.
20. Wade Hampton report, in J. William Jones, pp. 524–526.
21. J. William Jones, pp. 522–540.
22. Edward W. Halbach, in J. William Jones, pp. 546–548.
23. J. William Jones, pp. 540–544.
24. Halbach and Fitzhugh Lee, in J. William Jones, pp. 549, 552–555.
25. *Examiner*, 5 March 1864.
26. Mobile *Register & Advertiser*, 4 March 1864.
27. Fortescue, p. 81.
28. Pond, p. 96; J. William Jones, pp. 544–545, 558–559.
29. Unknown author, "Memoranda of the War Commenced Too Late 1865."
30. John C. Babcock, papers.
31. William A. Tidwell, *Come Retribution*, pp. 247–251; William C. Davis, pp. 543–544.
32. *Examiner*, 8 March 1864.
33. Meriwether Stuart, "Colonel Ulric Dahlgren and Richmond's Union Underground," pp. 157–159.
34. Van Lew papers, p. 307; Stuart, "Colonel Ulric Dahlgren," pp. 162–173.
35. Van Lew papers, p. 310.
36. Wood, Container 4, Maud Wood Park papers.
37. Van Lew papers, p. 314.
38. Washington *Evening Star*, 27 November 1865.

21. RATS, IF FAT, ARE AS GOOD AS SQUIRRELS

1. Mary Boykin Chesnut, *Mary Chesnut's Civil War*, pp. 585–586.
2. Letters from Aunt E., 7 March, 16 March 1864, Kate Mason Rowland papers, vol. 4; *Examiner*, 16 March 1864.
3. John B. Jones, *Rebel War Clerk's Diary*, p. 352.
4. *Examiner*, 9 March 1864.
5. Ibid., 10 March 1864.
6. Ibid., 12, 15, 19, 28 March 1864.
7. *Official Records* II, 8:764–766.

8. Varina Davis, *Jefferson Davis*, 2:531.

9. John B. Jones, pp. 357–362.

10. *Official Records* II, 7:62–63, 607; E. Merton Coulter, *Confederate States of America*, p. 478.

11. Varina Davis, 2:496–497; Chesnut, p. 601; William C. Davis, *Jefferson Davis*, pp. 551–553.

12. John B. Jones, p. 367.

13. *Examiner*, 8 May 1864.

14. Andrew A. Humphreys, *Virginia Campaign of '64 and '65*, pp. 137–139; Douglas Southall Freeman, *Lee's Lieutenants*, 3:452–460.

15. *Examiner*, 7, 8 May 1864.

16. Columbus *Sun*, 7 May 1864.

17. Ulysses S. Grant, *Personal Memoirs*, 2:152–153; Theo. F. Rodenbough, "Sheridan's Richmond Raid," p. 189.

18. Freeman, *Lee's Lieutenants*, 3:416; Theodore S. Garnett, "Dashing Gen. J. E. B. Stuart," p. 575.

19. Sarah Lawton to her sister Clifford, 12, 13 May 1864, in Marion Alexander Boggs, *The Alexander Letters*, pp. 260–261.

20. *Examiner*, 12 May 1864.

21. Ibid., 12, 13 May 1864; John B. Jones, pp. 370–371.

22. Cyrus McCormick, "How Gallant Stuart Met His Death," pp. 99–100.

23. "Death of Major-General J. E. B. Stuart," *SHSP* 7 (1879), p. 107; Freeman, *Lee's Lieutenants*, 3:426–427.

24. "Death of Major-General J. E. B. Stuart," *SHSP* 7 (1879), p. 109.

25. Columbus *Sun*, 24 May 1864.

26. Dunbar Rowland, *Jefferson Davis, Constitutionalist*, 2:209.

27. John B. Jones, pp. 371–372.

28. A. A. Humphreys, pp. 146–157.

29. John B. Jones, p. 382; Sarah Lawton to her sister Clifford, 15 May 1864; to her sister Louisa, 16 May 1864, in Boggs, pp. 262, 267–268.

30. Sarah Lawton to her sister Clifford, 30 May 1864, in Boggs, 263; John B. Jones, 383–385; Freeman, *R. E. Lee* 3:398.

31. Freeman, *Lee's Lieutenants*, 3:502–504.

32. Martin T. McMahon, "Cold Harbor," p. 215; John B. Jones, pp. 384–385.

33. U. S. Grant, *Personal Memoirs*, 2:276; McMahon, p. 220.

34. George W. Bagby to Atlanta *Register*, 11 June 1864.

35. John Sergeant Wise, *End of an Era*, pp. 299–313.

36. John B. Jones, p. 400; *Official Records* I, 40, pt. 3:761.

37. John B. Jones, p. 402.

38. Samuel H. Root to "My dear wife," 25 June 1864, Root papers.

39. Grant, 2:311–315; *Official Records* I, 40, pt. 1:134.

40. Bagby to Atlanta *Register*, 4 June 1864.

41. Edward Porter Alexander, *Fighting for the Confederacy*, p. 462.

42. Phoebe Yates Pember, *A Southern Woman's Story*, pp. 62–63.

22.   A QUESTION OF FEARFUL MAGNITUDE

1. *Times* (London), 4 August 1864.

2. Ibid., 23 August 1864.

3. *Enquirer*, 4 July 1864; *Sentinel*, 1 July 1864.

4. Virginius Dabney, *Pistols and Poison Pens*, pp. 51–52.

5. George W. Bagby, *Old Virginia Gentleman*, p. 201.

6. Bagby, pp. 182–205.

7. Dabney, pp. 51–52.

8. E. Merton Coulter, *Confederate States of America*, pp. 387–388.

9. Ibid., pp. 394–395.

10. Warren Akin, *Letters*, pp. 8–12.
11. Coulter, p. 141; John B. Jones, p. 456.
12. Coulter, p. 143; Alexander H. Stephens, *Recollections*, pp. 224–225; John B. Jones, p. 451.
13. John B. Jones, p. 414.
14. Sarah Lawton to her sister Clifford, 7 September 1864, in Boggs, *Alexander Letters*, pp. 269–270.
15. John B. Jones, pp. 423–424.
16. Ibid., p. 428; Robert G. H. Kean, *Inside the Confederate Government*, p. 174.
17. Mobile *Advertiser & Register*, 1, 5 October 1864.
18. John B. Jones, pp. 413, 421.
19. William C. Davis, *Jefferson Davis*, p. 541.
20. Warren Akin to Mary V. Akin, 14 November 1862, *Letters*, pp. 32–33.
21. Josiah Gorgas, diary, 25 September, 2 October 1864.
22. Dunbar Rowland, *Jefferson Davis, Constitutionalist*, 4:341–344.
23. *Official Records* I, 42, pt. 3:1134.
24. William E. Dodd, *Jefferson Davis*, p. 344; Thomas M. Preisser, "Virginia Decision to Use Negro Soldiers," p. 99.
25. Columbus *Sun*, 8 November 1864.
26. *Dispatch*, 9 November 1864; John B. Jones, 457; *Official Records* IV, 3:914–916.
27. Akin, *Letters*, p. 40.
28. Silas Omohundro Business Records, Market & General Account Book 1858–1864.
29. Richmond City Circuit Court, Will Book 2, 1861–65, pp. 228–229.
30. 1860 U.S. Census, Henrico County, First Ward Richmond, p. 72; Malvern Hill Omohundro, *Omohundro Genealogical Record*, p. 464.
31. Richmond City Circuit Court, Will Book 2, 1861–65, pp. 228–229; Silas Omohundro Business Records, Miscellaneous Manuscripts, 1848–85.
32. 1870 U.S. Census, Jefferson Ward, Richmond, p. 488; Ended Case 494, Richmond Chancery Court.
33. Shirlee Taylor Haizlip, *Sweeter the Juice*, pp. 42–49.
34. Kean, p. 174.

23. AND NOW THEY WILL REPENT

1. John Coxe, "Last Struggles and Successes of Lee," CV 22, p. 359.
2. Samuel H. Root to "Dear Wife," 10 August, 20 November 1864, Root papers.
3. New York *World*, 13 December 1896.
4. Alice West Allen, *Recollections of War in Virginia*, p. 269.
5. New York *World*, 13 December 1896.
6. Warren Akin, *Letters*, pp. 43–44.
7. John B. Jones, *Rebel War Clerk's Diary*, p. 472.
8. *Official Records* I, 46, pt. 2:71.
9. Kate Mason Rowland, diary, 26 January 1865.
10. Akin to wife, 10, 20 January 1865, in *Letters*, pp. 73–76, 86–87.
11. *Examiner*, 17 January 1865; E. Merton Coulter, *Confederate States of America*, pp. 135–136.
12. *Examiner*, 4 February 1865.
13. Ibid., 7 February 1865; John B. Jones, 493.
14. *Examiner*, 7 February 1865; Edward Alfred Pollard, *Life of Jefferson Davis*, pp. 470–473.
15. William C. Davis, *Jefferson Davis*, p. 594; John B. Jones, pp. 495–496; *Examiner*, 10 February 1865.
16. Alexander H. Stephens, *Recollections*, p. 183; William C. Davis, pp. 594–595.
17. William A. Tidwell, *Come Retribution*, pp. 374–375.
18. *Official Records* I, 46, pt. 2:114–115.
19. Ibid., pt. 2:171.
20. William Gilmore Beymer, "Miss Van Lew," pp. 90, 94.

21. "Conscription of Horses," p. 121, Van Lew papers; Beymer, pp. 90, 94, 98.
22. Hand-lettered notice, Van Lew papers.
23. "Old Caphart," Van Lew papers.
24. *Enquirer,* 23 January 1865; *Examiner,* 25 January 1865.
25. *Sentinel,* 26 January 1865.
26. Ibid., 2 February 1865; *Whig,* 2 February 1865.
27. *Examiner,* 10 March 1865.
28. Letters received, U.S. secretary of war, 976–1873, Record Group 109, National Archives.
29. Thomas Cooper DeLeon, *Four Years in Rebel Capitals,* p. 351.
30. Douglas Southall Freeman, *R. E. Lee,* 3:528; Mrs. Burton N. [Constance Cary] Harrison, *Recollections Grave and Gay,* p. 150.
31. Judith Brockenbrough McGuire, *Diary of a Southern Refugee,* p. 329.
32. Henry Kyd Douglas, *I Rode with Stonewall,* pp. 311–312.
33. *Examiner,* 16 February 1865.
34. John B. Jones, pp. 499–500.
35. Robert G. H. Kean, *Inside the Confederate Government,* p. 200; Freeman, *R. E. Lee,* 3:536.
36. *Examiner,* 17 February 1865; John B. Jones, pp. 500–501.
37. Freeman, *R. E. Lee,* 3:538–539.
38. *Lee's Dispatches,* p. 306; Freeman, *R. E. Lee,* 4:3–4.
39. J. William Jones, *Christ in the Camp,* pp. 524–525; Thomas Thweatt Tredway to "My dear daughter," 18 February 1865, Tredway papers.

24. WHO WILL ANSWER FOR THE SLAIN?

1. Edward A. Pollard, *Life of Jefferson Davis,* p. 473; Josiah Gorgas, diary, p. 172.
2. Mrs. Thomas Taylor, *South Carolina Women in the Confederacy,* pp. 277–281; Katharine M. Jones, *Heroines of Dixie: Winter of Desperation,* p. 170.
3. Thomas Conolly, *Irishman in Dixie,* pp. 37–38.
4. John B. Jones, *Rebel War Clerk's Diary,* pp. 504–508.
5. Richard S. Ewell to Robert E. Lee, Spring Hill, Tenn., 20 December 1865, *Official Records* I, 46, pt. 1:1292.
6. *Official Records* I, 46, pt. 2:824; Douglas Southall Freeman, *R. E. Lee,* 4:6–7.
7. Courtlandt Canby, ed., *Lincoln and the Civil War,* p. 366.
8. John B. Jones, p. 513.
9. John B. Gordon, *Reminiscences of the Civil War,* pp. 385–388; Freeman, *R. E. Lee,* 4:7–8.
10. New Orleans *Democrat,* 5 July 1881, reprint from Philadelphia *Press.*
11. Freeman, *R. E. Lee,* 4:9–13.
12. *Enquirer,* 3 February 1865.
13. *Examiner,* 16 February 1865.
14. *Official Records* IV, 3:1193.
15. Confederate Congress, Proceedings, *SHSP* 52 (1959), p. 453.
16. *Dispatch,* 22 March 1865.
17. John B. Jones, p. 519.
18. *Examiner,* 15, 18, 20 March 1865.
19. John B. Jones, pp. 516–521; John Leyburn, "Fall of Richmond," p. 93.
20. New York *Herald,* 13 March 1895.
21. Conolly, p. 60.
22. John B. Jones, p. 520.
23. *Official Records* I, 46, pt. 2:786–787.
24. Ibid., pt. 2:1287–1289.
25. Ibid., pt. 3:78–79, 101–102.
26. Report No. 792, Committee on War Claims, Forty-third U.S. Congress (1874), p. 2.
27. John B. Gordon, pp. 401–411; Freeman, *R. E. Lee,* 4:14–19; Noah Andre Trudeau, *Last Citadel,* pp. 337–351.

28. Henry A. London, letter, 25 March 1865.
29. Robert E. Lee, *Lee's Dispatches to Jefferson Davis*, pp. 345–346.
30. *Dispatch*, 28 March 1865; Judith W. McGuire, *Diary of a Southern Refugee*, p. 334.
31. *Examiner*, 23 March 1865; John B. Jones, p. 522.
32. Varina Davis, *Jefferson Davis*, 2:575–577.
33. Robert E. Lee to Mary Custis Lee, 22 February, 28 March 1865, in Robert E. Lee, Jr., *Recollections and Letters*, pp. 145–147.

25. WE MAY NEVER MEET AGAIN

1. John B. Jones, *Rebel War Clerk's Diary*, p. 525; George W. Bagby, *Old Virginia Gentleman*, pp. 215–216.
2. *Examiner*, 31 March 1865.
3. Horace Porter, "Five Forks and the Pursuit of Lee," p. 708; Sylvanus Cadwallader, *Three Years with Grant*, pp. 306–307.
4. Thomas Conolly, *Irishman in Dixie*, p. 80.
5. *Sentinel*, 1 April 1865; Louis H. Manarin, ed., *Richmond at War*, pp. 589–591.
6. *Official Records* IV, 3:1194.
7. Phoebe Yates Pember, *Southern Woman's Story*, pp. 91–92.
8. H. S. Wood, "More of the Last Defense of Richmond," p. 397; S. Millett Thompson, *Thirteenth Regiment of the New Hampshire Volunteer Infantry*, p. 551.
9. McHenry Howard, "Closing Scenes of the War About Richmond," p. 129.
10. Horace Porter, "Five Forks and the Pursuit of Lee," pp. 715–716.
11. Dallas Tucker, "Fall of Richmond," p. 153.
12. George A. Bruce, *Capture and Occupation of Richmond*, p. 6.
13. Stephen R. Mallory, "Last Days of the Confederate Government," p. 100; Mary A. Fontaine to Marie Burrows Sayre, 30 April 1865, Fontaine letters.
14. John B. Jones, p. 526.
15. Tucker, p. 155; Constance Cary Harrison, *Recollections Grave and Gay*, p. 207.
16. *Official Records* I, 46, pt. 3:1378.
17. *Times* (London), 25 April 1865; Tucker, p. 156.
18. Virginia E. Dade, "Our Women in the War–No. 19."
19. Mallory, p. 102.
20. Douglas Southall Freeman, *R. E. Lee*, 4:55; William C. Davis, *Jefferson Davis*, pp. 604–605.
21. *Examiner*, 3 April 1865.
22. Mallory, pp. 100–101.
23. Warren F. Spencer, "French View of the Fall of Richmond," pp. 181–182.
24. Virginia E. Dade, "Our Women in the War—No. 19."
25. J. Gottfried Lange, "New Name," pp. 188–189.
26. Emmie Crump Lightfoot, "Papers Relating Personal Experiences," p. 2.
27. Mrs. Fannie Walker Miller, "Fall of Richmond," p. 305.
28. Howard, p. 130; John Leyburn, "Fall of Richmond," p. 93.
29. Lange, p. 192.
30. Richmond City Council, minutes, 2 April 1865.
31. J. Thomas Scharf, *History of the Confederate States Navy*, 2:772–777.
32. Varina Davis, *Jefferson Davis*, 2:583.
33. *Life and Reminiscences of Jefferson Davis*, pp. 42–43; Varina Davis, 2:574.
34. Lelian M. Cook, "Girl Describes Evacuation"; Joseph L. King, *Dr. George William Bagby*, pp. 118–119.
35. J. H. Averill, "Richmond, Virginia: The Evacuation of the City and the Days Preceding It," pp. 268–271.
36. Mallory, p. 102; Leyburn, p. 93.
37. Mallory, p. 104; Anna Holmes Trenholm, diary.

26. THE EARTH SEEMED TO WRITHE IN AGONY

1. J. Cabell Early to Editor, *Times-Dispatch*, n.d.
2. *Daily Dispatch*, 1 April 1883; Benjamin W. Jones, *Under the Stars & Bars*, pp. 250–251; H. H. Sturgis, "About the Burning of Richmond," p. 303; Edward M. Boykin, *Falling Flag*, p. 11.
3. E. T. Watehall, "Fall of Richmond," p. 215; Moses Purnell Handy, "Fall of Richmond in 1865," pp. 2–21.
4. McHenry Howard, "Closing Scenes of the War About Richmond," pp. 132–133; S. Millett Thompson, *Thirteenth Regiment of New Hampshire Volunteer Infantry*, p. 555.
5. *Official Records* I, 46, pt. 1:1292–1293; *Daily Dispatch*, 1 April 1883.
6. Van Lew papers, pp. 730–731.
7. Philip Whitlock, Ms. autobiography, p. 128.
8. Ibid., pp. 128–129.
9. Walter H. Taylor, *General Lee: His Campaigns in Virginia*, pp. 277–278.
10. G. Powell Hill, "First Burial of General Hill's Remains," pp. 183–186.
11. Herbert W. Beecher, *First Light Battery Connecticut Volunteers*, p. 661.
12. Frederick Chesson, memoir.
13. George A. Bruce, *Capture and Occupation of Richmond*, pp. 7–8.
14. Virginia E. Dade, "Our Women in the War—No. 19."
15. Thompson, p. 556.
16. Ibid., p. 557.
17. Beecher, p. 663.
18. Edward A. Wild, correspondence, 3 April 1865, folder 2157.
19. Godfrey Weitzel, *Richmond Occupied*, p. 52; Bruce, p. 14.
20. Bruce, p. 556.
21. Chesson, memoir.
22. Bruce, p. 556.
23. J. Gottfried Lange, "New Name, or the Shoemaker in the Old and the New World," p. 192; John Leyburn, "Fall of Richmond," p. 94.
24. *Evening Whig*, 6 April 1865.
25. John A. Meredith, *Daily Dispatch*, 1 April 1883.
26. J. H. Averill, "Richmond, Virginia: The Evacuation of the City," p. 135.
27. Richard S. Ewell to R. L. Ewell, 18 April, 18 May 1865, Fort Warren, Mass., Ewell papers, Reel 1; *Official Records* I, 46, pt. 1:1295.
28. Sturgis, p. 474; W. L. Timberlake, "Last Days in Front of Richmond," p. 303; *SHSP* 25 (1897), p. 135.
29. *Daily Dispatch*, 1 April 1883.
30. Mary A. Fontaine to Marie Burrows Sayre, 30 April 1865, Fontaine letters.
31. Boykin, pp. 12–13.
32. John L. G. Woods, "Last Scenes of War," pp. 140–141.
33. D. B. Sanford, "Last Confederate Command to Leave Richmond," p. 474.
34. Clement Sulivane, "Fall of Richmond," pp. 725–726.
35. Timberlake, p. 303.
36. Sulivane, p. 726.
37. Mary A. Fontaine to Marie Burrows Sayre, 7 May 1865, Fontaine letters.
38. Loomis L. Langdon, "First Federals to Enter Richmond," pp. 308–309.
39. Thompson, p. 578.
40. Ibid., pp. 557–559.
41. Henry Barton Dawson, *Colors of the United States*, pp. 13–17; Weitzel, p. 63.
42. H. S. DeForest, 3 April 1865, *Connecticut Record*, p. 394.
43. Weitzel, p. 53.
44. Ibid., pp. 53–54.
45. *Official Records* I, 46, 2:509.
46. Edward Hastings Ripley, *Vermont General*, pp. 301–302.
47. Mary A. Fontaine to Marie Burrows Sayre, 7 May 1865, Fontaine letters.

48. Lelian M. Cook, "Girl Describes Evacuation"; Weitzel, p. 62.
49. Edward A. Pollard, *Southern History of the War,* 2:495–496.
50. Weitzel, p. 53.
51. Ripley, p. 106; Frederick Chesson, memoir.
52. Weitzel, pp. 53–54; *Official Records* I, 51, pt. 1:1210–1211; Cook, "Girl Describes Evacuation."
53. Emmie Sublett to Emily Anderson, 29 April 1865, Sublett papers; Anna Deane to "My dear Sallie," 12 April 1865, Mary E. (Fleming) Schoole papers.
54. Phoebe Yates Pember, *Southern Woman's Story,* pp. 95–96.
55. Van Lew papers, p. 733.

27. OUR SOUL BOWED DOWN TO THE DUST

1. David Dixon Porter, Private Journal No. 2, Porter papers.
2. Ibid.; John G. Nicolay and John Hay, *Abraham Lincoln,* 10:216–219.
3. Edward Hastings Ripley, *Vermont General,* p. 304; Lelian M. Cook, "Girl Describes Evacuation."
4. John B. Jones, *Rebel War Clerk's Diary,* p. 531.
5. Ripley, p. 304.
6. Emmie Crump Lightfoot, Personal experiences, p. 6.
7. George A. Bruce, *Capture and Occupation of Richmond,* pp. 23–24.
8. Charles Carleton Coffin, *Four Years of Fighting,* p. 511; Porter, Private Journal No. 2; F. A. Macartney to John A. J. Cresswell, 11 April 1865, Cresswell papers.
9. Porter, Private Journal No. 2. (Weitzel's account says that Joseph R. Anderson of the Tredegar Works also came, but he is not mentioned by Porter.)
10. Campbell, *Recollections of the Evacuation,* pp. 175–176; Godfrey Weitzel, *Richmond Occupied,* p. 56.
11. *Danville Appeal,* 8 April 1865.
12. *Christian Recorder,* Philadelphia, 22 April 1865.
13. Bruce, pp. 34–35; Porter, Private Journal No. 2; Coffin, p. 514. (In a more elaborate memoir, published twenty years later, Porter suggests that Lincoln visited Libby Prison soon after stepping ashore, before joining Weitzel. *Incidents and Anecdotes of the Civil War,* pp. 298–299.)
14. Weitzel, *Richmond Occupied,* p. 56.
15. Campbell, p. 176; Weitzel, p. 56.
16. Myers, *Virginia Historical Magazine* 41, pp. 320–322.
17. Porter, Private Journal No. 2.
18. Lincoln to Weitzel, *Collected Works* 8:406–407.
19. Townsend, *Campaigns,* p. 330.
20. *Times* (London), 25 April 1865.
21. Philadelphia *Press,* 11, 12 April 1865; Chester, p. 288.
22. Jean H. Baker, *Mary Todd Lincoln,* p. 398; Elizabeth Keckley, *Behind the Scenes,* p. 171.
23. Julia Dent Grant, *Personal Memoirs,* pp. 150–151.
24. Emma Mordecai to Edward (Cohen), 5 April 1865, Myers family papers; Emma Mordecai diary.
25. Thompson, *13th New Hampshire,* p. 581.
26. Silas Adams, Folder 9, Box 3, MOLLUS Papers.
27. Charles A. Currier, "Recollections of Service with the Fortieth Massachusetts Infantry Volunteers."
28. Herbert W. Beecher, *First Light Battery Connecticut Volunteers,* p. 682.
29. Bruce, pp. 36–37.
30. *Official Records* I, 46, pt. 3:574.
31. Charles A. Dana, *Recollections of the Civil War,* pp. 269–270.
32. Charles A. Dana to Edwin M. Stanton, 6 April 1865, Stanton papers; Phoebe Yates Pember, *Southern Woman's Story,* p. 96.
33. Weitzel, p. 59.

34. Ripley, p. 308; *Official Records* I, 46, pt. 1:1212–1215.
35. George Alfred Townsend, *Campaigns of a Non-Combatant*, p. 347.
36. Ibid., p. 348.
37. Weitzel, pp. 57–61.
38. Weitzel to Butler, 26 April 1865, Butler papers.
39. Weitzel, pp. 60–62.
40. John Sergeant Wise, *End of an Era*, pp. 418–448.
41. John B. Jones, p. 535.
42. Dana, p. 272.
43. Julia Dent Grant, p. 153.
44. Bruce, p. 38.
45. New York *Herald*, 18 April 1865; Douglas Southall Freeman, *R. E. Lee*, 4:161–164.

EPILOGUE

1. George A. Bruce, *Capture and Occupation of Richmond*, p. 39.
2. Lelian M. Cook, "Girl Describes Evacuation"; Emmie Sublett to Emily Anderson, 29 April 1865, Sublett papers.
3. Charles A. Currier, "Recollections of Service with the Fortieth Massachusetts Infantry Volunteers."
4. *Official Records* I, 46, pt. 3:762.
5. Douglas Southall Freeman, "Confederate Tradition of Richmond," p. 43.

Sources

For their cooperation and courtesy, I wish to thank the staffs of the institutions below. If the diaries, letters, or memoirs of a single writer were collected or edited by another person, I have listed them by author rather than editor. The following abbreviations are used for the publications and collections most frequently cited:

B&L—*Battles and Leaders.*

Duke—Special Collections Department, William R. Perkins Library, Duke University, Durham.

LC—Manuscript Division, Library of Congress.

MC—Eleanor S. Brockenbrough Library, Museum of the Confederacy, Richmond.

MOLLUS—Military Order of the Loyal Legion of the United States.

OR—*War of the Rebellion, Official Records.*

SHC—Southern Historical Collection, Wilson Library, University of North Carolina, Chapel Hill.

SHSP—Southern Historical Society Papers.

USAMHI—U.S. Army Military History Institute, Carlisle Barracks, Pennsylvania

VHS—Virginia Historical Society, Richmond.

VSL—Archives Division, Virginia State Library, Richmond.

American Heritage Center, University of Wyoming,
   Laramie.
Civil War Library and Museum, Philadelphia.
Hancock Historical Society, Hancock, New Hampshire.
Huntington Library, San Marino, California.
Maryland Historical Society, Baltimore.
Massachusetts Historical Society, Boston.
National Archives.
New York Public Library.
Richmond Chancery Court.
Richmond City Council.
Richmond City Court.
Valentine Museum, Richmond.
Earl Gregg Swem Library, College of William and Mary,
   Williamsburg.

MANUSCRIPTS

Adams, Silas. Paper read to MOLLUS, 3 December 1913. MOLLUS papers, USAMHI.
Armstrong, H. G. Letter. Burton N. Harrison papers, LC.
Babcock, John C. Papers. LC.
Bachman, Aaron E. Memoirs. Harrisburg Civil War Round Table Collection, USAMHI.
Bagby family papers. VHS.
Bagby, George William. Letters, unpublished manuscripts, scrapbook, clippings. G. W.
   Bagby papers, VHS.
Betts & Gregory, slave traders. Correspondence. Chase family papers, LC.
Benjamin, Judah P. Diary. Benjamin papers. LC.
Bragg, Thomas. Diary. SHC.
Bryan, Emma Lyon. Reminiscences. Early family papers, VHS.
Budget, Edward. "Family Budget." Ms. Camp Manning newspaper, VSL.
Burrill, John H. Letters. *Civil War Times Illustrated* Collection, USAMHI.
Campbell, John A. Memo on meeting with Lincoln on USS *Malvern,* written 26 April
   1865. Campbell family papers, SHC.
Cary, Constance (Mrs. Burton Harrison). Correspondence. Burton Harrison papers,
   LC.
Catton, Bruce. Papers. American Heritage Center, University of Wyoming.
Chase, Cornelius T. Notebook, "Negro Sales or Auctions." Chase family papers, LC.
Chesson, Frederick, 29th Conn. Memoir. *Civil War Times Illustrated* Collection, USAMHI.
Christian, Ann Webster (Gordon). Diary. VHS.
Confederate States of America, Army, Department of Henrico. Papers, 1861–1864. VHS.
Coupland, John R. Letters. Dorsey-Coupland papers, Earl Gregg Swem Library, William
   and Mary.
Crenshaw, Lewis Dabney, Jr. Diary. MC.
Cresswell, John Angel James. Papers. LC.
Currier, Charles A. "Recollections of Service with the Fortieth Massachusetts Infantry
   Volunteers, by Charles A. Currier, late Captain of H and G Companies." Typescript,
   1886. USAMHI.
Davis, Jefferson. Papers. Duke.
Deane, Anna. Letter. Mary E. (Fleming) Schoole papers, Duke.
Denison, George Stanton. Letters. Denison papers, LC.
Donaldson, Francis A. Scrapbook. Civil War Library and Museum, Philadelphia.
Evans, Thomas. Diary. LC.
Ewell, Richard Stoddert. Letters; report on evacuation of Richmond. Ewell papers, LC.

Ferris, Weston. "Prison Life of Weston Ferris, Troop B, 1st Connecticut Cavalry." Memoir, 6 July 1863–23 January 1865. Northwest Corner Civil War Round Table Collection, USAMHI.

Fontaine, Mary A. Letter. MC.

Fortescue, Louis R. "War Diary," vol. 4. Civil War Library and Museum, Philadelphia.

Fletcher, Lucy Muse (Walton). Diary. *Civil War Times Illustrated* Collection, USAMHI.

French, Benjamin Brown. Papers. LC.

Gorgas, William Crawford. Diary. Gorgas papers, LC.

Habersham, Richard W. Letters. Habersham family papers, LC.

Hall, Thomas W. Papers. Maryland Historical Society.

Harrell, Jennie D. Reminiscences of Richmond from 1861 to 1865. MC.

Harrison, Burton Norvell. Papers. LC.

Hoge, Moses Drury. Papers. VHS.

Hope, James Barrow. Letter. Hope papers, William and Mary.

Hubard, Maria Mason (Tabb). Diary. VHS.

Hunt, Francis. Diary. *Civil War Times Illustrated* Collection, USAMHI.

Ives, Joseph Christmas. Letters. Ives papers, LC.

Kautz, August Valentine. "Reminiscences of the Civil War." Kautz papers, USAMHI.

Johnston, Joseph E. Letters. Louis T. Wigfall papers, LC.

Lange, J. Gottfried. "The New Name or the Shoemaker in the Old and the New World: Thirty Years in Europe and Thirty Years in America." Memoir. Translated by Ida Windmueller, VHS.

Lee, Mary Custis (Mrs. Robert E.). Letters. Peyton family papers, VHS.

Lemmon, Robert. Letters. Lemmon papers, Maryland Historical Society.

Lightfoot, Emmie Crump. "Papers Relating Personal Experiences in and Around Richmond During the Days of the Confederacy," MC.

London, Henry A. Letters. SHC.

Long, William S. Memoir. Breckinridge Long papers, LC.

F. A. Macartney. Letters. John Angel James Cresswell papers, LC.

Mallory, Stephen Russell. Diary. SHC.

Mallory, Stephen Russell. Letters. Clement C. Clay papers, Duke.

Maury, Matthew Fontaine, William A. and Richard L. Letters. M. F. Maury papers, LC.

Mayo, Joseph. Mayor's broadside, 27 June 1863. Valentine Museum.

McClellan, George B. Papers. LC.

McCorvey, T. C. Papers. SHC.

McNiven, Thomas. "Recollections of Thomas McNiven and His Activities in Richmond During the American Civil War," VSL.

Military Order of the Loyal Legion of the United States. Unpublished papers, USAMHI.

Mordecai, Ellen. Letters. Alfred Mordecai papers, LC.

Mordecai, Emma. Letters. Myers family papers, VHS.

Morrell, Charles W. Letters. Morrell papers, LC.

Morrow, Henry A., 24th Mich. Letters. Morrow-Boniface family papers, USAMHI.

National Archives, Record Group 109.

Nevins, Allan. Papers. American Heritage Center, University of Wyoming.

Omohundro, Silas. Business Records. VSL.

Parsons, Byron. Diary. Parsons Collection, LC.

Phillips, Philip. Family papers. LC.

Pinkerton, Allan. Letters. Pinkerton's National Detective Agency papers, LC.

Porter, David Dixon. Papers. LC.

Putnam, George Haven. Letters. George H. Putnam papers, American Heritage Center, University of Wyoming.

Richmond Chancery Court, Ended Case 494.

Richmond City Circuit Court, Will Book 2, 1861–65.

Richmond City Council, minutes, 1859–65.

Root, Samuel H., 24th Massachusetts. Letters and memoir. Civil War Miscellaneous Collection, USAMHI.

Rowland, Kate Mason. Memoirs of the War: Diary and Correspondence, edited by a Virginia Girl. MC.

St. Paul's Church. Vestry Book, 1855–64. VHS.

Smith, Marie McGregor (Campbell). Memoir, "Narrative of my Blockade Running." VHS.

Smith, Theodore, 32nd New York. Letters. Jay Luvaas Collection, USAMHI.

Staples, Horatio. Paper read before MOLLUS, December 1914. MOLLUS papers unpublished, USAMHI.

Stanton, Edwin McMasters. Letters. Stanton papers, LC.

Stokes, E. H., slave trader. Correspondence. Chase family papers, LC.

Stott, John W. "Notes on the War." *Civil War Times Illustrated* Collection, USAMHI.

Sublett, Emmie. Letter telling of the evacuation of Richmond. MC.

Tinsley, Fannie W. (Gaines). "Mrs. S. G. Tinsley's War Experience." Memoir, 1862–65. VHS.

Tompkins, Sally. Letters. Archives Division, VSL.

Trenholm, Anna Holmes. Diary. SHC.

Turner, Thomas Pratt. Letter. VHS.

U.S. Congress. Committee on War Claims, Forty-third Congress (1874), Report No. 792. National Archives.

Unknown. Diary of a Richmond girl. Valentine Museum.

Unknown. "Memoranda of the War Commenced Too Late 1865." VHS.

Van Lew, Elizabeth. Papers. New York Public Library.

Von Groening, Daniel. Letterbook. Von Groening Collection, LC.

Ware, Edwin. Letters. Hancock Historical Society, Hancock, N.H.

Washburn, Charles. Letters. Hancock Historical Society, Hancock, N.H.

Whitlock, Philip. Ms. autobiography in record book. VHS.

Whitten, John. Diary, 1861–65. LC.

Wigfall, Louis Trezevant. Family papers. LC.

Wight, Margaret Brown. Diary. Wight family papers, VHS.

Wild, Edward A. General Wild's correspondence. USAMHI.

William H. Winder, Letters. Winder Family papers, Manuscript Division, Maryland Historical Society.

Wood, James Rodney, Sr. Notes for "Civil War Memoirs." Maud Wood Park papers, LC.

PRINTED DIARIES, LETTERS, MEMOIRS, CONTEMPORARY
ACCOUNTS, AND OFFICIAL RECORDS

Akin, Warren. *Letters of Warren Akin, Confederate Congressman.* Bell Irvin Wiley, ed. University of Georgia Press, 1959.

Alfriend, Edward M. "Social Life in Richmond During the War." *Cosmopolitan* (Dec. 1891), pp. 229–233.

Allen, Alice West. "Recollections of War in Virginia." *CV* 23, pp. 268–269.

Anderson, Archer. "Robert Edward Lee: An Address" at the Monument to General Robert E. Lee, *SHSP* 17 (1889), pp. 322–323.

Arnold, William B. *The Fourth Massachusetts Cavalry in the Closing Scenes of the War for Maintenance of the Union: From Richmond to Appomattox.* Priv. pub., n.d.

Atkinson, John Wilder, and others. "The Evacuation of Richmond, April 3, 1863, and the Disastrous Conflagration Incident Thereon." Letters to Richmond *Dispatch*, 24 November 1895.

Averill, J. H. "Richmond, Virginia: The Evacuation of the City and the Days Preceding It." Reprint from Richmond *Dispatch*, 4 July 1897. *SHSP* 25 (1897), pp. 267–273.

[Bagby, George W.] "A Well-Digested Plan for the Relief of Richmond," by "Jeff. McLory Northop" [pseudonym]. *Southern Literary Messenger* (Nov.–Dec. 1863), pp. 726–732.

Bagby, George W. *The Old Virginia Gentleman and Other Sketches.* Scribner's, 1910.

[Bagby, George W.] "The Union: Its Benefits and Dangers." *Southern Literary Messenger* (Jan. 1861), pp. 1–4.

Barnes, John S. "With Lincoln from Washington to Richmond in 1865." *Appleton's Magazine*, vol. 9, No. 5 (May 1907), pp. 742–751.

Bayne, Thomas Livingston. "Life in Richmond, 1863–1865." *CV* 30, pp. 100–101.

Beach, William H. *The First New York (Lincoln) Cavalry: From April 19, 1861 to July 7, 1865.* Lincoln Cavalry Association, 1902.

Beecher, Herbert W. *First Light Battery Connecticut Volunteers 1861–1865: History and Reminiscences.* Vol. 2. A. T. De La Mare, n.d.

Beers, Mrs. Fannie A. *Memories: A Record of Personal Experience and Adventure During Four Years of War.* Lippincott, 1888.

Blackwood's Edinburgh Magazine. "Ten Days in Richmond." October 1862, pp. 392–402.

Boggs, Marion Alexander, ed. *The Alexander Letters, 1787–1900.* University of Georgia Press, 1980.

Botts, John Minor. *The Great Rebellion: Its Secret History, Rise, Progress and Disastrous Failure.* Harper & Brothers, 1866.

Boykin, Edward M. *The Falling Flag: Evacuation of Richmond, Retreat, and Surrender at Appomattox.* E. Hale & Son, 1874.

Bremer, Fredrika. *Homes of the New World.* 2 vols. Harper & Brothers, 1858.

Brooks, Noah. *Washington, D.C., in Lincoln's Time.* Reprint. Quadrangle, 1971.

Browne, Junius Henri. *Four Years in Secessia: Adventures Within and Beyond the Union Lines.* O. D. Case, 1865.

Bruce, George A. *The Capture and Occupation of Richmond.* Priv. pub., n.d.

Bruce, H. W. "Some Reminiscences of the Second of April, 1865." *SHSP* 9 (1881), pp. 206–211.

Burnet, Mrs. Theodore L. "Reminiscences of the Confederacy." *CV* 15, p. 173.

Burrows, J. L. "Recollections of Libby Prison." *SHSP* 11 (1883), pp. 83–92.

Burrows, John L. *The New Richmond Theatre: A Discourse Delivered on Sunday February 8, 1863 in the First Baptist Church, Richmond, Va.*

Butler, Benjamin Franklin. *Butler's Book: Autobiography and Personal Reminiscences of Major-General Benj. F. Butler.* A. M. Thayer, 1892.

Butler, Benjamin Franklin. *Private and Official Correspondence of Gen. Benjamin F. Butler During the Period of the Civil War.* 5 vols. Plimpton Press, 1917.

Butler, William Allen. "At Richmond." *Southern Literary Messenger* (Oct. 1859), pp. 309–311.

Cabell, William Preston. "How a Woman Helped to Save Richmond." Reprint from Memphis *Commercial Appeal.* *CV* 31, pp. 177–178.

Cadwallader, Sylvanus. *Three Years with Grant.* Benjamin F. Thomas, ed. Alfred A. Knopf, 1955.

Campbell, John A. *Recollections of the Evacuation of Richmond, April 2, 1865.* John Murphy, 1880.

Cary, Harriette. "Diary of Miss Harriette Cary, Kept by Her from May 6, 1862, to July 24, 1862." *Tyler's* No. 9, pp. 104–115, and No. 12, pp. 161–173.

Cary, Miles. "How Richmond Was Defended." *CV* 15, pp. 557–559.

Chambers, William. *Things As They Are in America.* Lippincott, Grambo, 1854.

Chesnut, Mary Boykin. *Mary Chesnut's Civil War.* C. Vann Woodward, ed. Yale University Press, 1981.

Chester, Thomas Morris. *Thomas Morris Chester, Black Civil War Correspondent: His Dispatches from the Virginia Front.* R. J. M. Blackett, ed. Louisiana State University Press, 1989.

Clark, W. M. "A Confederate Officer Visits Richmond." *Tennessee Historic Quarterly*, 11 (1952), pp. 86–91.

Cleveland, Henry. *Alexander H. Stephens, in Public and Private; With Letters and Speeches, Before, During and Since the War.* National Publishing, 1866.

Coffin, Charles Carleton. *Four Years of Fighting: A Volume of Personal Observation with the Army and Navy, from the First Battle of Bull Run to the Fall of Richmond.* Ticknor & Fields, 1866.

Confederate Congress: First Congress, First Session, February 22, 1862: Inaugural Ceremonies. *SHSP* 44 (1928), pp. 37–41.

Confederate Congress: First Congress, Second Session, House, September 22, 1862: The
Rights of Citizens. *SHSP* 46 (1928), pp. 208–209.

Confederate Congress: Second Congress, Second Session, Senate, March 7, 1865: The Negro Soldier Question. *SHSP* 52 (1959), pp. 452–457.

Conolly, Thomas. *An Irishman in Dixie: Thomas Conolly's Diary of the Fall of the Confederacy.* Nelson D. Lankford, ed. University of South Carolina Press, 1988.

Cook, Lelian M. "Girl Describes Evacuation: Kept Diary, While Living in Home of Dr.
Hoge, of Fateful Days." Richmond *News Leader,* April 3, 1935.

Cooke, John Esten. *Surry of Eagle's Nest, or The Memoirs of a Staff-Officer Serving in Virginia.* Reprint. Gregg Press, 1968.

Cooke, John Esten. *The Wearing of the Gray: Being Personal Portraits, Scenes and Adventures
of the War.* S. B. Treat, 1867.

Cooper, Alonzo. *In and Out of Rebel Prisons.* R. J. Oliphant, 1888.

Coxe, John. "Last Struggles and Successes of Lee." *CV* 22, pp. 357–359.

Crook, William H. "Lincoln's Last Day." *Harper's Monthly,* (Sept. 1907), pp. 519–530.

Crouch, Richard G. "The Dahlgren Raid." *SHSP* 34 (1906), pp. 178–190.

Cummins, Edmund H. "The Signal Corps in the Confederate States Army." *SHSP* 16
(1888), pp. 93–107.

Dade, Virginia E. "Our Women in the War—No. 19: The Fall of Richmond." Charleston
Weekly News & Courier, n.d.

Dana, Charles A. *Recollections of the Civil War.* D. Appleton, 1898.

Davis, Jefferson. *The Rise and Fall of the Confederate Government.* 2 vols. Reprint. Garrett
& Massie, 1938.

Davis, Varina. *Jefferson Davis, Ex-President of the Confederate States of America: A Memoir
by His Wife.* 2 vols. Belford, 1890.

[Dawson, Henry Barton.] *The Colors of the United States First Raised Over the Capitol of the
Confederate States.* Morrisania, N.Y.: privately printed, 1866.

DeForest, H. S. Letter from the 11th Connecticut, 3 April 1865. *Connecticut Record,* p. 395.
USAMHI.

DeLeon, Thomas Cooper. "An Inside View of Four Years in the Confederate Capital."
The Cosmopolite, vol. 1, No. 3 (Mar. 1866).

DeLeon, Thomas Cooper. *Belles, Beaux and Brains of the 60's.* G. W. Dillingham, 1907.

DeLeon, Thomas Cooper. *Four Years in Rebel Capitals.* Gossip Printing Company,
1890.

Dickens, Charles. *The Works of Charles Dickens: Pictures from Italy and American Notes.*
Thomas Y. Crowell, n.d.

Douglas, Henry Kyd. *I Rode with Stonewall.* University of North Carolina Press, 1940.

Doyle, J. H. "When Richmond Was Evacuated." *CV* 39, pp. 205–206.

Eggleston, George Cary. *A Rebel's Recollections.* G. P. Putnam's Sons, 1878.

Ellis, Thomas H. "The Richmond 'Home Guard' of 1861." Letter to Colonel Joseph Dare,
War Department. *SHSP* 19 (1891), p. 57.

Ely, Alfred. *Journal of Alfred Ely, a Prisoner of War in Richmond.* Appleton, 1862.

Ewell, Richard S. "Evacuation of Richmond: Report of General R. S. Ewell." Letter from
Ewell to Robert E. Lee, December 20, 1865. *SHSP* 13 (1885), p. 247.

Fremantle, Sir Arthur James Lyon. *The Fremantle Diary.* Walter Lord, ed. Andre Deutsch,
1956.

Garnett, Theodore S. "The Dashing Gen. J. E. B. Stuart." *CV* 19, pp. 575–576.

Gerald, S. A. "Last Soldiers to Leave Richmond." *CV* 18, p. 432.

Girard, Charles. *A Visit to the Confederate States of America in 1863.* Reprint. Confederate
Publishing, 1962.

Glenn, William Wilkins. *Between North and South: A Maryland Journalist Views the Civil
War.* Bayly Ellen Marks and Mark Norton Schatz, ed. Fairleigh Dickinson University Press, 1976.

Gordon, John B. *Reminiscences of the Civil War.* Scribner's, 1904.

Gorgas, Josiah. *The Civil War Diary of General Josiah Gorgas.* Frank Vandiver, ed. University of Alabama Press, 1947.

Grant, Julia Dent. *The Personal Memoirs of Julia Dent Grant (Mrs. Ulysses S. Grant).* John W. Simon, ed. G. P. Putnam's Sons, 1975.

Grant, Ulysses S. *Personal Memoirs of U. S. Grant.* Charles L. Webster, 1886.

Greenhow, Rose O'Neal. *My Imprisonment and the First Year of Abolition Rule at Washington.* R. Bentley, 1863.

Handy, Moses Purnell. "The Fall of Richmond in 1865: A Compelling Eyewitness Narrative of the Confederate Collapse." *American Magazine and Historical Chronicle,* Clements Library, University of Michigan, autumn-winter 1992, pp. 2–21.

Harrison, Mrs. Burton H. (Constance Cary). *Recollections Grave and Gay.* Scribner's, 1912.

Harrison, Constance Cary. "Virginia Scenes in '61." *B&L* 1:160–166; "Richmond Scenes in '62." *B&L* 2:439–448.

Hopley, Catherine Cooper. *Life in the South, from the Commencement of the War, by a Block-aded British Subject.* 2 vols. Chapman & Hall, 1863.

Hill, G. Powell. "First Burial of General Hill's Remains." *SHSP* 19 (1891), pp. 183–186.

Howard, James McH. "Brig. Gen. Walter H. Stevens." *CV* 30, pp. 249–250.

Howard, McHenry. "Closing Scenes of the War About Richmond." Reprint from New Orleans Picayune, October 4–11, 1903. *SHSP* 31 (1903), pp. 129–135.

Hughes, Robert W. *Editors of the Past.* Lecture before Virginia Press Association, 22 June 1897. William Ellis Jones, 1897.

Hunt, Sallie. "Our Women in the War—No. 7: Boys and Girls in the War." Charleston *Weekly News & Courier,* n.d.

Hunter, Andrew. Papers. Massachusetts Historical Society, *Proceedings* 44 (Dec. 1912).

Jackson, Mary Anna. *Memoirs of Stonewall Jackson by His Widow.* Prentice Press, 1895.

Jeffrey, William H. *Richmond Prisons 1861–1862, Compiled from the Original Records Kept by the Confederate Government.* Republican Press, 1893.

Jones, Benjamin Washington. *Under the Stars and Bars: A History of the Surry Light Artillery.* E. Waddey, 1909.

Jones, J. William. *Christ in the Camp, or Religion in the Confederate Army.* Reprint. Sprinkle Publications, 1986.

Jones, J. William. *Life and Letters of Robert E. Lee, Soldier and Man.* Neale Publishing, 1906.

Jones, J. William. "The Kilpatrick-Dahlgren Raid Against Richmond." *SHSP* 13 (1889), pp. 515–560.

Jones, John B. *A Rebel War Clerk's Diary.* Earl Schenck Miers, ed. Sagamore Press, 1958.

Jones, Katharine M., ed. *Heroines of Dixie: Spring of High Hopes* and *Winter of Desperation.* Reprint. Ballantine, 1975.

Jones, Katharine M., ed. *Ladies of Richmond.* Bobbs-Merrill, 1962.

Kean, Robert Garlick Hill. *Inside the Confederate Government: The Diary of Robert Garlick Hill Kean.* Edward Younger, ed. Oxford University Press, 1957.

Keckley, Elizabeth. *Behind the Scenes: Thirty Years a Slave, and Four Years in the White House.* G. W. Carleton, 1868.

La Bree, Ben, ed. *The Confederate Soldier in the Civil War.* Courier-Journal, 1895.

Langdon, Loomis L. "First Federals to Enter Richmond," *SHSP* 30 (1902), pp. 308–309.

Lee, Fitzhugh. *General Lee.* Appleton, 1894.

Lee, G. W. C. "Evacuation of Richmond: Report of General G. W. C. Lee, from the 2d to the 6th of April, 1865." *SHSP* 13 (1885), pp. 255–257.

Lee, Robert E. *Lee's Dispatches to Jefferson Davis.* Douglas Southall Freeman and Grady McWhiney, eds. Louisiana State University Press, 1994.

Lee, Robert E. "Secession Is Nothing But Revolution: A Letter of R. E. Lee to His Son 'Rooney.'" Robert E. Bachal, ed. *VMHB* 69 (Jan. 1961), pp. 3–6.

Lee, Robert E., Jr. *Recollections and Letters of Robert E. Lee.* Garden City Publishing, 1903.

Leyburn, John. "The Fall of Richmond." *Harper's New Monthly Magazine* 33 (1866), pp. 92–96.

Libby, George W. "John Brown and John Wilkes Booth." *CV* 38, pp. 138–139.

Longstreet, James. "Lee's Invasion of Pennsylvania." B&L 3:244–251.

Mallory, Stephen. "Last Days of the Confederate Government." *McClure's* (Dec. 1900), pp. 99–107.

Manarin, Louis H., ed. *Richmond at War: The Minutes of the City Council 1861–1865.* University of North Carolina Press, 1966.

M'Anerny, John. "Dahlgren's Raid on Richmond." *CV* 29, pp. 20–21.

Maury, Dabney H. *Recollections of a Virginian in the Mexican, Indian, and Civil Wars.* Scribner's, 1894.

McCormick, Cyrus. "How Gallant Stuart Met His Death." Reprint from *Clarke Courier,* May 15, 1901. *CV* 39, pp. 98–100.

McCrady, Edward, Jr. "Address at Reunion of Virginia Division, A. N. V. Association." *SHSP* 14 (1886), pp. 185–196.

McDade, J. C. "Personal Bravery of President Davis." *CV* 22, pp. 555–559.

McGuire, Judith W. *Diary of a Southern Refugee During the War, by a Lady of Virginia.* E. J. Hale and Son, 1867.

McLean, Mrs. Eugene. "A Northern Woman in the Confederacy." *Harper's Monthly* 128 (Jan. 1914), pp. 440–451.

McLean, Mrs. Eugene. "When the States Seceded." *Harper's Monthly* 128 (Feb. 1914), pp. 282–288.

McMahon, Martin T. "Cold Harbor." *B&L* 4:213–220.

Mell, P. H. "Dr. W. LeRoy Broun." *CV* 10, pp. 225.

Michaux, Jacob. "Youth's Impressions of War Between States." Richmond *Times-Dispatch,* n.d. 1915

Miller, Mrs. Fannie Walker. "The Fall of Richmond." *CV* 13, p. 305.

Minnigerode, Charles F. E. *Jefferson Davis: A Memorial Address, Delivered in St. Paul's Church, Richmond, Virginia, December 11, 1889.* Baughman Brothers, 1890.

Moore, Frank, ed. *The Rebellion Record: A Diary of American Events.* G. P. Putnam's Sons, 1861–65.

Moran, Frank E. "Colonel Rose's Tunnel at Libby Prison." *Century Magazine,* March 1888, 770–790.

Mordecai, Samuel. *Richmond in By-Gone Days.* 2nd ed. Reprint. Dietz Press, 1946.

Myers, Gustavus A. "Abraham Lincoln in Richmond." *Virginia Historical Magazine* 41 (Oct. 1933), pp. 318–322.

Northam, G. H. "Woman's Sphere." *Religious Herald,* Richmond, 30 May 1861.

Olmsted, Frederick Law. *The Cotton Kingdom: A Traveller's Observations on Cotton and Slavery in the American Slave States.* Alfred A. Knopf, 1953.

Paca, Edward Tilghman, Jr. " 'Tim's Black Book': The Civil War Diary of Edward Tilghman Paca, Jr., CSA." Edmund C. Paca, ed. *Maryland Historical Magazine* 89 (winter 1994), pp. 453–466.

Paul, Alfred. "A French View of the Fall of Richmond: Alfred Paul's Report to Drouyn de Lhuys, April 11, 1865." Warren F. Spencer, ed. *VMHB* 73 (Apr. 1865), pp. 178–198.

Pember, Phoebe Yates. *A Southern Woman's Story.* Bell Irvin Wiley, ed. Reprint. Mockingbird Books, 1974.

[Pember, Phoebe Yates.] "Reminiscences of a Southern Hospital, by Its Matron." *The Cosmopolite,* Baltimore, January–April 1866.

Pinkerton, Allan. *The Spy of the Rebellion, Being a True History of the Spy System of the United States Army During the Late Rebellion.* M. A. Winter & Hatch, 1883.

Pollard, Edward Alfred. *A Southern History of the War.* Charles B. Richardson, 1866.

Pollard, Edward Alfred. *Lee and His Lieutenants.* E. B. Treat, 1867.

Pollard, Edward Alfred. *Life of Jefferson Davis, with a Secret History of the Southern Confederacy, Gathered Behind the Scenes in Richmond.* National Publishing, 1869.

Pond, George E. "Kilpatrick's and Dahlgren's Raid to Richmond." *B&L* 4, 94–95.

Porter, Horace. "Five Forks and the Pursuit of Lee." *B&L* 4:708–722.

Porter, Horace. *Campaigning with Grant.* Century, 1897.

Pryor, Mrs. Roger A. *Reminiscences of Peace and War.* Grosset & Dunlap, 1905.

Putnam, Sallie B. *Richmond During the War: Four Years of Observation by a Richmond Lady.* G. W. Carleton, 1867.

Reagan, John H. *Memoirs with Special References to Secession and the Civil War.* Neale Publishing, 1906.

Richardson, James D., ed. *A Compilation of the Messages and Papers of the Confederacy Including the Diplomatic Correspondence, 1861–1865.* 2 vols. United States Printing, 1905.

Richmond *Dispatch.* "Burning of Richmond: Incidents of the City's Evacuation Described." April 25, 1897.

Ripley, Edward Hastings. *Vermont General: the Unusual War Experiences of Edward Hastings Ripley 1862–1865.* Otto Eisenschiml, ed. Devin-Adair, 1960.

Roach, A. C. *The Prisoner of War, and How Treated; Containing a History of Colonel Streight's Expedition to the Rear of Bragg's Army, in the Spring of 1863, and a Correct Account of the Treatment and Condition of the Union Prisoners of War in the Rebel Prisons of the South in 1863–4.* A. D. Streight, 1865.

Rodenbough, Theo. F. "Sheridan's Richmond Raid." *B&L* 4:188–193.

Ross, Fitzgerald. *Cities and Camps of the Confederate States.* Richard B. Harwell, ed. University of Illinois Press, 1958.

Rowland, Dunbar, ed. *Jefferson Davis, Constitutionalist: His Letters, Papers and Speeches.* 10 vols. Mississippi Department of Archives and History, 1923.

Sanford, D. B. "Last Confederate Command to Leave Richmond." *CV* 17, p. 474.

Scheibert, Justus. *Seven Months in the Rebel States During the North American War, 1863.* Confederate Publishing, 1958.

Semmes, Raphael. "Civil War Song Sheets: One of the Collections of the Maryland Historical Society." *Maryland Historical Magazine* 30 (1941), p. 210.

Smith, Gustavus W. "Relative Strength of the Opposing Forces." *B&L* 2:219

Soley, James Russell. "The Navy in the Peninsular campaign." *B&L* 2:270–271

Southall, John R. "Recollections of the Evacuation of Richmond." *CV* 37, pp. 458–459.

Stephens, Alexander H. *A Constitutional View of the Late War Between the States.* 2 vols. National Publishing, 1870.

Stephens, Alexander H. *Recollections of Alexander H. Stephens: His Diary.* Myrta L. Avary, ed. Doubleday & Page, 1910.

Steuart, Richard D. "How Johnny Got His Gun." *CV* 32, pp. 166–169.

Stevens, Fred. S. "The First Federal to Enter Richmond." Reprint from Richmond *Dispatch,* February 10, 1893. *SHSP* 30 (1902), pp. 152–153.

Stiles, John C. "Shock Officers." *CV* 33, p. 77.

Stiles, Robert. "It Was Obedience Even Unto Death: Grave in Hollywood Recalls a Story of Devotion to Duty." Reprint from Richmond *Times,* October 29, 1899. *SHSP* 27 (1899), pp. 17–25.

Still, William. *The Underground Rail Road.* Reprint. Johnson Publishing, 1970.

Stone, John H. "The 'Diary' of John H. Stone, First Lieutenant, Company B, 2nd Maryland Infantry, CSA." Thomas G. Clemens, ed. *Maryland Historical Magazine* 85 (1990), pp. 115.

Sturgis, H. H. "About the Burning of Richmond." *CV* 17, p. 474.

Sulivane, Clement. "The Fall of Richmond: No. 1—The Evacuation," *B&L* 4:725–726.

Swinton, William. *Campaigns of the Army of the Potomac.* Scribner's, 1882.

Taylor, Walter H. *General Lee: His Campaigns in Virginia 1861–1865, with Personal Reminiscences.* Reprint. Morningside, 1975.

Thompson, S. Millett. *Thirteenth Regiment of New Hampshire Volunteer Infantry in the War of Rebellion 1861–1865.* Houghton Mifflin, 1888.

Timberlake, W. L. "The Last Days in Front of Richmond." *CV* 22, p. 303.

Timberlake, W. L. "In the Siege of Richmond and After." *CV* 29, pp. 412–414.

Townsend, George Alfred. *Campaigns of a Non-Combatant, and His Romaunt Abroad During the War.* Blelock, 1866.

Tucker, Dallas. "The Fall of Richmond: Graphic Description of Events of Evacuation-Day." Richmond *Dispatch,* 3 February 1902.

United Daughters of the Confederacy, South Carolina Division. *South Carolina Women in the Confederacy.* 2 vols. The State Company, 1903–07.

U.S. War Department. *The War of the Rebellion: A Compilation of the Official Records of the Union and Confederate Armies.* Prepared under the direction of the secretary of war by Robert N. Scott. Government Printing Office, 1880–1900.

Unknown. Scrapbook of clippings. Ms. 5:7 Un 3:10, VHS.

Unknown. "The Death of Major-General J. E. B. Stuart." Includes reprint from Richmond *Examiner. SHSP* 7 (1879), pp. 107–110.

"V & C." *The City Intelligencer, or Stranger's Guide.* Macfarlane & Fergusson, 1862.

Velazquez, Loreta Janeta. *The Woman in Battle: A Narrative of the Exploits, Adventures and Travels of Madame Loreta Janeta Velazquez, Otherwise Known As Lieutenant Harry T. Buford, Confederate States Army.* C. J. Worthington, ed. Belknap, 1876.

Virginia Convention, 1861. *Proceedings of the Virginia State Convention of 1861, February 13–May 1.* George H. Reese, ed. 4 vols. Virginia State Library, 1965.

Von Borcke, Heros. *Memoirs of the Confederate War for Independence.* Reprint. Morningside House, 1985.

Wailes, Dr. L.A. "The First Secessionists." *CV* 30, p. 184–185.

Ware, William H. *My Last Four Months of the Confederacy.* Priv. pub., n.d. USAMHI.

Watehall, E. T. "Fall of Richmond, April 2, 1865." *CV* 17, p. 214.

Weir, Sally Royce. "Trip to Richmond in 1863." *CV* 16, pp. 623–624.

Weitzel, Godfrey. *Richmond Occupied.* Louis H. Manarin, ed. Civil War Centennial Committee, 1965.

Wise, John Sergeant. *The End of an Era.* Curtis Carroll Davis, ed. Thomas Yoseloff, 1965.

Wood, H. E. "More of the Last Defense of Richmond." Reprint from Richmond *Times-Dispatch. CV* 16, p. 397.

Woods, John L. G. "Last Scenes of War—How I Got Home." *CV* 27, pp. 140–143.

Wright, Mrs. D. Giraud. *A Southern Girl in '61.* Doubleday, 1895.

CONTEMPORARY NEWSPAPERS AND PERIODICALS

Alexandria *Gazette*
Athens *Southern Watchman*
Atlanta *Register*
Blackwood's Edinburgh Magazine
Charleston *Mercury*
Columbus *Sun*
Danville *Appeal*
Danville *Register*
Frank Leslie's Illustrated Newspaper
Georgia *Dispatch*
Harper's Weekly
Harper's Monthly Magazine
Illustrated London News
Knoxville *Register*
London *Times*
Memphis *Appeal*
Memphis *Inquirer*
Mobile *Register & Advertiser*
Montgomery *Daily Mail*
Nashville *Union & American*
New Orleans *Daily Crescent*
New Orleans *Democrat*
New York *Evening Post*
New York *Herald*
New York *Tribune*
Philadelphia *Christian Recorder*

Philadelphia *Press*
Religious Herald
Richmond *Daily Dispatch*
Richmond *Enquirer*
Richmond *Examiner*
Richmond *Sentinel*
Richmond *Whig*
Southern Illustrated News
Southern Literary Messenger
Southern Punch
Washington *Evening Star*

SECONDARY SOURCES

Anderson, Joseph R., Jr. "Anderson's Brigade in Battles Around Richmond." *CV* 31, pp. 448–451.

Andrews, J. Cutler. *The South Reports the Civil War.* University of Pittsburgh Press, 1985.

Aptheker, Herbert. *Negro Slave Revolts in the United States, 1526–1860.* International Publishers, 1939.

Aptheker, Herbert. *The Negro in the Civil War.* International Publishers, 1938.

Baker, Jean H. *Mary Todd Lincoln.* New York: Norton, 1987.

Bancroft, Frederic. *Slave-Trading in the Old South.* Reprint. Ungar, 1959.

Beach, William H. *The First New York (Lincoln) Cavalry: From April 19, 1861 to July 7, 1865.* Lincoln Cavalry Association, 1902.

Berman, Myron. *Richmond's Jewry, 1769–1976: Shabbat in Shockoe.* University Press of Virginia, 1979.

Beymer, William Gilmore. "Miss Van Lew." *Harper's Monthly Magazine* (June 1911), pp. 86–99.

Beymer, William Gilmore. *On Hazardous Service: Scouts and Spies of the North and South.* Harper & Bros., 1912.

Bill, Alfred Hoyt. *The Beleaguered City.* Alfred A. Knopf, 1946.

Blakey, A. F. *General John H. Winder, C.S.A.* University of Florida Press, 1990.

Boatner, Mark Mayo III. *The Civil War Dictionary.* David McKay, 1959.

Bowers, Russell V. "Chimborazo Hospital (1862–1865)." *The Scarab,* Medical College of Virginia alumni magazine. Reprinted by Virginia Civil War Centennial Committee. n.d.

Brewer, James H. *The Confederate Negro: Virginia's Craftsmen and Military Laborers, 1861–1865.* Duke University Press, 1969.

Brock, R. A., ed. *General Robert Edward Lee: Soldier, Citizen and Christian Patriot.* Richmond: B. F. Johnson, 1897.

Broun, William Le Roy. "Confederate Ordnance During the War." *CV* 12, p. 20; reprint from *Journal of the United States Artillery.*

Burton, David L. "Friday the 13th: Richmond's Great Home Front Disaster." *Civil War Times Illustrated* 21, No. 6 (Oct. 1982), pp. 36–41.

Canan, H. V. "Confederate Military Intelligence." *Maryland Historical Magazine* 59 (Mar. 1964), pp. 34–51.

Canby, Courtlandt, ed. *Lincoln and the Civil War: A Profile and a History.* George Braziller, 1960.

Chesson, Michael B. *Richmond After the War, 1865–1890.* Virginia State Library, 1981.

Coleman, Elizabeth Dabney. "The Captain Was a Lady." *Virginia Cavalcade,* vol. 6 (summer 1956–spring 1957), pp. 35–41.

Comer, Jane Wood. "Moses D. Hoge: A Minister for the Confederacy." *UDC Magazine* (Apr. 1990), pp. 32–34.

Cornish, James Jenkins III. *The Air Arm of the Confederacy.* Richmond Civil War Centennial Committee, 1963.

Coski, John. *Capital Navy.* Savas Woodbury, 1996.

Coulter, E. Merton. *The Confederate States of America 1861–1865*. Louisiana State University Press, 1950.

Craven, Avery O. *Edmund Ruffin, Southerner: A Study in Secession*. Louisiana State University Press, 1966.

Cresap, Bernarr. *Appomattox Commander: The Story of General E. O. C. Ord*. A. S. Barnes, 1981.

Crofts, Daniel W. *Reluctant Confederates: Upper South Unionists in the Secession Crisis*. University of North Carolina Press, 1989.

Cullen, Joseph P. "Chimborazo Hospital, That Charnel House of Living Sufferers." *Civil War Times Illustrated*, vol. 19, No. 9 (Jan. 1981), pp. 36–41.

Cunningham, H. H. *Doctors in Gray: The Confederate Medical Service*. Louisiana State University Press, 1958.

Dabney, Robert Lewis. *Life and Campaigns of Lieut.-Gen. Thomas J. Jackson*. Blelock, 1866.

Dabney, Virginius. *Pistols and Pointed Pens: The Dueling Editors of Old Virginia*. Algonquin Books, 1987.

Dabney, Virginius. *Richmond: The Story of a City*. Doubleday, 1976.

Dabney, Virginius. *Virginia: The New Dominion*. Doubleday, 1971.

Daniel, Frederick S. *The Richmond Examiner During the War, or the Writings of John M. Daniel*. For the author, 1868.

Davis, Burke. *Jeb Stuart: The Last Cavalier*. Reprint. Fairfax Press, 1988.

Davis, Burke. *To Appomattox: Nine April Days, 1865*. Rinehart, 1959.

Davis, William C. *Jefferson Davis: The Man and His Hour*. HarperCollins, 1991.

Dean, Eric T., Jr. "'We Live Under a Government of Men and Morning Newspapers': Image, Expectation, and the Peninsula Campaign of 1862." *VMHB* 103 (Jan. 1995), pp. 5–28.

Dew, Charles B. *Ironmaker to the Confederacy*. Yale University Press, 1966.

Dowd, Willis Bruce. *Three Measures of Meal*. Riverdale Press, 1910.

Dowdey, Clifford. *Experiment in Rebellion*. Doubleday, 1947.

Dowdey, Clifford. "General Lee's Unsolved Problem." *American Heritage* 6, vol. 3 (1955), pp. 34–39.

Dufour, Charles L. *Nine Men in Gray*. Doubleday, 1963.

Duke, Maurice, and Daniel P. Jordan, eds. *A Richmond Reader, 1733–1983*. University of North Carolina Press, 1983.

Duling, Ennis. "The Duke of Richmond." *Civil War Times Illustrated* 23, No. 9 (Jan. 1985), pp. 40–47.

Earp, Charles A. "The Amazing Colonel Zarvona." *Maryland Historical Magazine* 34 (1939), pp. 336–343.

Eaton, Clement. *A History of the Southern Confederacy*. Macmillan, 1954.

Eaton, Clement. *The Mind of the Old South*. Louisiana State University Press, 1967.

Edwards, William B. "One-Man Armory: Colonel J. H. Burton." *Virginia Cavalcade*, vol. 12, no. 2 (autumn 1962), pp. 28–33.

Evans, Eli N. *Judah P. Benjamin, the Jewish Confederate*. Free Press, 1988.

Fahrner, Alvin A. "William 'Extra Billy' Smith, Governor of Virginia 1864–1865." *VMHB* 74 (Jan. 1966), pp. 68–87.

Felt, Jeremy P. "Lucius B. Northrop and the Confederacy's Subsistence Department." *VMHB* 69 (Apr. 1961), pp. 181–195.

Fitzgerald, Mary Maury. "Captain Sally Tompkins, C.S.A." *Richmond Magazine* (May 1931), pp. 13–18.

Fitzgerald, Oscar Penn. "John M. Daniel and Some of His Contemporaries." *South Atlantic Quarterly*, Durham, vol. 4, 1905, pp. 13–17.

Flood, Charles Bracelen. *Lee: The Last Years*. Houghton Mifflin, 1981.

Freehling, William W. *The Road to Disunion: Secessionists at Bay, 1776–1854*. Oxford University Press, 1990.

Freeman, Anne Hobson. "A Cool Head in a Warm Climate" (Joseph R. Anderson). *Virginia Cavalcade*, vol. 12, No. 3, winter 1962–63.

Freeman, Douglas Southall. *Lee's Lieutenants*. 3 vols. Scribner's, 1943.

Freeman, Douglas Southall. *R. E. Lee*. 4 vols. Scribner's, 1934–35.

Freeman, Douglas Southall. "The Confederate Tradition of Richmond." *Richmond Magazine*, June 1932, p. 42.

Freeman, Douglas Southall. *The South to Posterity: An Introduction to the Writing of Confederate History.* Scribner's, 1951.

Freeman, Douglas Southall. "When War Came to Richmond," Bicentennial Issue, Richmond *News Leader*, 8 September 1937.

Fuller, Charles F., Jr. "Edwin and John Wilkes Booth: Actors at the Old Marshall Theater in Richmond." *VMHB* 79 (Oct. 1971), pp. 477–483.

Fuller, J. F. C. *Grant and Lee: A Study in Personality.* Indiana University Press, 1957.

Gaddy, David Winfred. "William Norris and the Confederate Signal and Secret Service." *Maryland Historical Magazine* 71 (Summer 1975), pp. 166–188.

Gildersleeve, John R. "History of Chimborazo Hospital, Richmond, Va., and Its Medical Officers During 1861–1865." *Virginia Medical Semi-Monthly*, July 8, 1904, pp. 148–154.

Godwin, Parke. A *Biography of William Cullen Bryant, with Extracts from His Private Correspondence.* Russell & Russell, 1883.

Golden, Alan Lawrence. "Castle Thunder: The Confederate Provost Marshal's Prison 1862–1865." MA thesis, University of Richmond, 1980.

Gunderson, Robert G. "The Old Gentlemen's Convention." *Civil War History*, vol. 7, No. 1, pp. 5–12.

Haizlip, Shirlee Taylor. *The Sweeter the Juice.* Simon & Schuster, 1994.

Harding, Vincent. *There Is a River: The Black Struggle for Freedom in America.* Harcourt, Brace & Jovanovich, 1981.

Harwell, Richard Barksdale. "Brief Candle: The Confederate Theater." *Proceedings of the American Antiquarian Society*, 81 (1972), p. 41.

Harwell, Richard B. *Confederate Music.* University of North Carolina Press, 1950.

Hassler, William. "Wildman Wigfall." *Civil War Times Illustrated* 23, No. 2 (Apr. 1984), pp. 24–37.

Hassler, William W. "'Willie' Pegram, General Lee's Brilliant Young Virginia Artillerist." *Virginia Cavalcade* (autumn 1973), pp. 13–19.

Hatch, Alden. *The Byrds of Virginia.* New York: Holt, Rinehart and Winston, 1969.

Hatcher, William E. *Life of J. B. Jeter D. D.* H. M. Wharton, 1887.

Helm, Katherine. *Mary Wife of Lincoln: By Her Niece.* University of Illinois Press, 1983.

Hemphill, W. Edwin. "Bibles Through the Blockade." *The Commonwealth*, vol. XVI (Aug. 1940), pp. 9–12, 30–32.

Hesseltine, William B. *Civil War Prisons: A Study in War Psychology.* F. Ungar, 1964.

Hoge, Peyton Harrison. *Moses Drury Hoge: Life and Letters.* Presbyterian Committee of Publication, 1899.

Hoole, William Stanley. *Lawley Covers the Confederacy.* Confederate Publishing, 1964.

Hoole, William Stanley. *Vizetelly Covers the Confederacy.* Confederate Publishing, 1957.

Horan, James D. *Desperate Women.* G. P. Putnam's Sons, 1952.

Hubbell, Jay B. *The South in American Literature, 1607–1900.* Duke University Press, 1954.

Hughes, Robert M. "The Fighting Editor." Address before the Virginia Press Association, January 15, 1926. *William and Mary College Quarterly Historical Magazine*, vol. VII, No. 1 (Jan. 1927), pp. 1–16.

Hume, Edgar Erskine. "Chimborazo Hospital, Confederate States Army, America's Largest Military Hospital." *Virginia Medical Monthly* (July 1934), pp. 189–195.

Humphreys, Andrew A. *The Virginia Campaign of '64 and '65.* Scribner's, 1883.

Johns, Frank S., and Anne Page Johns. "Chimborazo Hospital and J. B. McCaw, Surgeon-in-Chief." *VMHB*, 62, No. 2 (Apr.), 1954, pp. 190–200.

Johnson, Ludwell H. "Trading with the Union: The Evolution of Confederate Policy." *VMHB* 78, No. 3 (July 1970) pp. 308–325.

Johnson, Robert U., and Clarence C. Buel, eds. *Battles and Leaders of the Civil War.* 4 vols. Century, 1887.

Johnston, Angus J., II. "Disloyalty on Confederate Railroads in Virginia." *VMHB* 63 (Nov. 1955), pp. 410–426.

Johnston, Angus J., II. "Lee's Last Lifeline: The Richmond & Danville." *Civil War History* 7, No. 3 (Sept. 1961), pp. 288–297.

Jones, J. William. *Christ in the Camp, or Religion in the Confederate Army.* Reprint. Sprinkle Publications, 1986.

Jones, J. William. *Life and Letters of Robert E. Lee. Soldier and Man.* Neale Publishing, 1906.

Jones, Virgil Carrington. *Eight Hours Before Richmond.* Henry Holt, 1957.

Jones, Virgil Carrington. *The Civil War at Sea.* Vol. I, *The Blockaders.* Holt, Rinehart and Winston, 1960.

Jordan, Ervin, Jr. *Black Confederates and Afro-Yankees in Civil War Virginia.* University of Virginia Press, 1995.

Kimball, William J. "The Bread Riot in Richmond." *Civil War History* 7 (Sept. 1961), pp. 149–154.

Kimball, William J. "Richmond Begins the Work of War." *Virginia Cavalcade* (spring 1961), pp. 13–18.

Kimball, William J. "Richmond 1865: The Final Three Months." *Virginia Cavalcade* (summer 1969), pp. 38–47.

Kimball, William J. "War-Time Richmond." *Virginia Cavalcade* (spring 1962), pp. 33–40.

Kimmel, Stanley Preston. *The Mad Booths of Maryland.* Dover, 1970.

King, Joseph L. *Dr. George William Bagby.* Columbia University Press, 1927.

Klutz, Theo F., Jr. "The Boy Who Saved Richmond." *CV* 6, pp. 213–214.

Life and Reminiscences of Jefferson Davis by Distinguished Men of His Time. R. H. Woodward, 1890.

Litwack, Leon F. *Been in the Storm So Long: The Aftermath of Slavery.* Alfred A. Knopf, 1979.

Manarin, Louis H., and Clifford Dowdey. *The History of Henrico County.* University Press of Virginia, 1984.

Mapp, Alf J., Jr. *Frock Coats and Epaulets.* Reprint. Madison Books, 1987.

Massey, Mary Elizabeth. *Bonnet Brigades.* Alfred A. Knopf, 1966.

Massey, Mary Elizabeth. *Ersatz in the Confederacy.* University of South Carolina Press, 1952.

Maury, Richard L. *A Brief Sketch of the Work of Matthew Fontaine Maury During the War 1861–1865.* Whittet & Shepperson, 1915.

McCormack, Helen G. *William James Hubard, 1807–1862.* Richmond: Valentine Museum and Virginia Museum of Fine Arts, 1948.

McPherson, James M. *Battle Cry of Freedom: The Civil War Era.* Oxford University Press, 1988.

McPherson, James M. *The Negro's Civil War: How American Blacks Felt and Acted During the War for the Union.* Ballantine, 1991.

Mellen, George F. "Famous Southern Editors: John Moncure Daniel." *Methodist Review,* Nashville (July–Aug. 1897), pp. 378–395.

A Memorial of Paul Joseph Revere and Edward H. R. Revere. Coulter Press, 1913.

Miller, Nathan. *Spying for America.* Paragon House, 1989.

Miller, Randall M., and John David Smith, eds. *Dictionary of Afro-American Slavery.* Greenwood Press, 1988.

Minor, Benjamin Blake. *The Southern Literary Messenger, 1834–1864.* Neale Publishing, 1905.

Mogelever, Jacob. *Death to Traitors.* Doubleday, 1960.

Moore, Josiah S. *Annals of Henrico Parish.* Williams Printing, 1904.

Nicolay, John G., and John Hay. *Abraham Lincoln: A History.* 10 vols. Century, 1890.

O'Brien, John T. "Factory, Church and Community: Blacks in Antebellum Richmond." *Journal of Southern History* 44 (1978), 509–536.

Omohundro, Malvern Hill. *The Omohundro Genealogical Record: The Omohundros and Allied Families in America.* McClure Printing, 1950–51.

Osborne, Charles C. *Jubal: The Life and Times of General Jubal A. Early, CSA, Defender of the Lost Cause.* Algonquin, 1992.

Patrick, Rembert W. *Jefferson Davis and His Cabinet.* Louisiana State University Press, 1944.

Pendleton, Louis. *Alexander H. Stephens.* G. W. Jacobs, 1908.

Preisser, Thomas M. "The Virginia Decision to Use Negro Soldiers in the Civil War, 1864–1865." *VMHB* 83 (Jan. 1975), pp. 98–111.

Quarles, Benjamin. *The Negro in the Civil War.* Little, Brown, 1953.

Rachleff, Peter J. *Black Labor in the South, 1865–1890.* Temple University Press, 1984.

Ramage, James A. *Rebel Raider: The Life of General John Hunt Morgan.* University of Kentucky Press, 1986.

Richardson, Albert D. *The Secret Service: The Field, the Dungeon, and the Escape.* Reprint. B. Blom, 1971.

Ripley, Edward Hastings. *Vermont General: The Unusual War Experiences of Edward Hastings Ripley 1862–1865.* Otto Eisenschiml, ed. Devin-Adair, 1960.

Robinson, William M., Jr. "Drewry's Bluff: Naval Defense of Richmond, 1862." *Civil War History* 7, No. 2 (June 1961), pp. 167–175.

Robinson, William M., Jr. *Justice in Grey: A History of the Judicial System of the Confederate States of America.* Harvard University Press, 1941.

Robinson, William Morrison, Jr. *The Confederate Privateers.* Yale University Press, 1928.

Rosen, Robert. *Confederate Charleston: An Illustrated History of the City and Its People During the Civil War.* University of South Carolina Press, 1994.

Rosenberger, Francis Coleman. *The Virginia Reader: A Treasury of Writings from the First Voyages to the Present.* Dutton, 1948.

Ross, Ishbel. *First Lady of the South.* Harper & Bros., 1958.

Rubin, Louis D., Jr., ed. *The History of Southern Literature.* Louisiana State University Press, 1985.

Saint Paul's Church. *Rev. Charles F. E. Minnigerode, D.D., Presbyter of the Diocese of Virginia.* James Pott, 1895.

Sale, Marian Marsh. "Disaster at the Spotswood." *Virginia Cavalcade,* vol. 12, No. 2 (autumn 1962), pp. 13–20.

Scharf, J. Thomas. *History of the Confederate States Navy from Its Organization to the Surrender of Its Last Vessel.* 2 vols. Rogers & Sherwood, 1887.

Scott, Mary Wingfield. *Houses of Old Richmond.* Valentine Museum, 1941.

Scott, Mary Wingfield. *Old Richmond Neighborhoods.* Whittet & Shepperson, 1950.

Scribner, Robert L. "Belle Isle." *Virginia Cavalcade* (winter 1955), pp. 8–13.

Scribner, Robert L. "Slave Gangs on the March." *Virginia Cavalcade* (autumn 1953), pp. 10–13

Scribner, Robert L. "Submission, Coercion or Secession?" *Virginia Cavalcade* (autumn 1953), pp. 43–47.

Scribner, Robert L. "The Code Duello in Virginia." *Virginia Cavalcade* (autumn 1953), pp. 28–31.

Seager, Robert, II. *And Tyler Too: A Biography of John and Julia Gardiner Tyler.* McGraw-Hill, 1963.

Sears, Stephen W. *To the Gates of Richmond.* Ticknor & Fields, 1992.

Shaw, John L. "Facts Concerning 'Colonel' George W. Alexander, Publisher of the *Sunday Gazette,* Washington, D.C." Priv. pub., 1876.

Simpson, Craig M. *A Good Southerner: The Life of Henry A. Wise of Virginia.* University of North Carolina Press, 1985.

Southern Historical Society Papers. "The Richmond Ambulance Corps." *SHSP* 25 (1897), pp. 113–115.

Stanard, Mary Newton. *Richmond: Its People and Its Story.* Lippincott, 1923.

Starr, Louis M. *Bohemian Brigade: Civil War Newsmen in Action.* Alfred A. Knopf, 1954.

Stern, Philip Van Doren. *An End to Valor.* Houghton Mifflin, 1958.

Stern, Philip Van Doren. *Secret Missions of the Civil War: First-Hand Accounts by Men and Women Who Risked Their Lives in Underground Activities for the North and the South.* Rand McNally, 1959.

Strode, Hudson. *Jefferson Davis.* 3 vols. Harcourt, Brace, 1955–1964.

Stuart, J. Meriwether. "Of Spies and Borrowed Names." *VMHB* 89 (Oct. 1981), pp. 308–327.

Stuart, Meriwether. "Colonel Ulric Dahlgren and Richmond's Union Underground, April 1864." *VMHB* 72 (Apr. 1964), pp. 152–204.

Stuart, Meriwether. "Dr. Lugo: An Austro-Venetian Adventurer in Union Espionage." *VMHB* 90 (July 1982), pp. 339–358.

Stuart, Meriwether. "Operation Sanders, Wherein Old Friends and Ardent Pro-Southerners Prove to Be Union Secret Agents." *VMHB* 81 (Apr. 1973), pp. 157–199.

Stuart, Meriwether. "Samuel Ruth and General R. E. Lee: Disloyalty and the Line of Supply to Fredericksburg, 1862–1863." *VMHB* 71 (Jan. 1963), pp. 75–109.

Suhr, Robert Collins. "Torpedoes, the Confederacy's Dreaded 'Infernal Machines,' Made Many a Union Sea Captain Uneasy." *America's Civil War* 4, No. 4, pp. 59–62.

Sutherland, Daniel E. *The Confederate Carpetbaggers.* Louisiana State University Press, 1988.

Thomas, Benjamin P. *Abraham Lincoln: A Biography.* Alfred A. Knopf, 1952.

Thomas, Emory M. *The Confederate Nation: 1861–1865.* Harper & Row, 1979.

Thomas, Emory M. *The Confederate State of Richmond.* University of Texas Press, 1971.

Tidwell, William A. *April '65: Confederate Covert Action in the Civil War.* Kent State University Press, 1995.

Tidwell, William A., with James O. Hall and David Winfred Gaddy. *Come Retribution: The Confederate Secret Service and the Assassination of Lincoln.* University of Mississippi Press, 1988.

Trexler, Harrison A. "The Davis Administration and the Richmond Press, 1861–1865." *Journal of Southern History* 16 (May 1950), pp. 176–195.

Tyler, Moses Coit. *Patrick Henry.* Houghton Mifflin, 1888.

Tyler-McGraw, Marie, and Gregg D. Kimball. *In Bondage and Freedom: Antebellum Black Life in Richmond, Virginia.* Valentine Museum, 1988.

Valentine Museum. *Richmond Portraits in an Exhibition of Makers of Richmond 1737–1860.* The Museum, 1949.

Van der Heuvel, Gerry. *Crowns of Thorns and Glory: Mary Todd Lincoln and Varina Howell Davis: The Two First Ladies of the Civil War.* Dutton, 1988.

Wade, Richard C. *Slavery in the Cities: The South 1820–1860.* Oxford University Press, 1964.

Waitt, Robert W., Jr. *Confederate Military Hospitals in Richmond.* Richmond Civil War Centennial Committee, 1964.

Wallace, Lee A., Jr. *A Guide to Virginia Military Organizations 1861–1865.* Virginia Civil War Commission, 1964.

Webb, Alexander S. *The Peninsula.* New York: Scribner's, 1881.

West, George Benjamin. *When the Yankees Came: Civil War and Reconstruction on the Virginia Peninsula.* Parke Rouse, Jr., ed. Dietz Press, 1977.

White, Mrs. Bernard Franklin. *Mathews Men Who Served in the War Between the States.* Teagle & Little, 1961.

Wiley, Bell Irwin. *Southern Negroes, 1861–1865.* Louisiana State University Press, 1974.

Wise, Barton Haxall. *The Life of Henry A. Wise of Virginia, 1806–1876.* Macmillan, 1899.

Wooster, Ralph A. *Secession Conventions of the South.* Princeton University Press, 1962.

Wright, R. Lewis. *Artists in Virginia Before 1900: An Annotated Checklist.* University of Virginia Press, 1983.

Writer's Program, Work Projects Administration, Virginia. *The Negro in Virginia.* Hastings House, 1940.

Writer's Program, Work Projects Administration, Virginia. *Virginia: A Guide to the Old Dominion.* Oxford University Press, 1940–41.

Yearns, Wilfred Buck. *The Confederate Congress.* University of Georgia Press, 1960.

Index

A NOTE ABOUT THE AUTHOR

Ernest B. "Pat" Furgurson, author of the widely praised Chancellorsville 1863, *is a native of Virginia and descendant of Confederate soldiers (one of his wounded great-grandfathers was captured in Jackson Hospital when Richmond fell in 1865). He was on the staff of the* Richmond News Leader *before beginning a long career as Washington and foreign correspondent for the* Baltimore Sun. *His other books include biographies of two controversial Southerners, General William C. Westmoreland and Senator Jesse Helms. He and his wife live in Washington, D.C., and Delaplane, Virginia.*

A NOTE ON THE TYPE

This book was set in a modern adaptation of a type designed by the first William Caslon (1692–1766). The Caslon face, an artistic, easily read type, has enjoyed over two centuries of popularity in our own country. It is of interest to note that the first copies of the Declaration of Independence and the first paper currency distributed to the citizens of the newborn nation were printed in this typeface.

Composed by NK Graphics, Keene, New Hampshire
Designed by Anthea Lingeman